COLLEGE WRITING SKILLS

SECOND EDITION

Virginia Underwood

Iowa State University

Merriellyn Kett

Charles E. Merrill Publishing Company
A Bell & Howell Company
Columbus   Toronto   London   Sydney

All the characters in this book are fictitious, and any resemblance to actual persons living or dead is purely coincidental.

Published by
Charles E. Merrill Publishing Co.
A Bell & Howell Company
Columbus, Ohio 43216

This book was set in Optima.
Cover Design Coordination: Will Chenoweth.
Text Design and Production Coordination:
   Lucinda Ann Peck.

Copyright © 1981, 1977, 1975, by Bell & Howell Company. All rights reserved. No part of this book may be reproduced in any form, electronic or mechanical, including photocopy, recording, or any information storage and retrieval system, without permission in writing from the publisher.

Library of Congress Catalog Card Number: 80–82767
International Standard Book Number: 0–675–08046–0
1 2 3 4 5 6 7 8 9 10—85 84 83 82 81

Printed in the United States of America

CONTENTS

To the Student   vii
To the Instructor   ix

1   NOUN NUMBER   2

     Preview Test   3

     Nouns   4

     Recognizing Nouns, 4; Pronoun Substitution, 7; Determining Noun Number, 8; Pronunciation Can Be Deceiving, 11; When There Is No Noun Determiner, 12; Confusing Adjectives With Nouns, 12; Irregular Nouns, 13; Spelling the Plural Noun, 18

     Transferring Your Skill to Writing   24

     Review Test   25

2   PRESENT TENSE VERBS   26

     Preview Test   27

     Finding Subjects and Verbs   29

     Pronouns, 29; A Work About Time and Tense, 30; The Present Tense, 31; To Be or Not To Be, 33; The Contraction *n't*, 36; There *Is/ Are/ Was/ Were*, 38; Noun Determiners As Clues, 39; *Do* or *Does*: The Rule's the Same, 40; *Doesn't* or *Don't*: The Rule's the Same, 41; *Has/ Hasn't* or *Have/ Haven't*: The Rule Doesn't Change, 42; Compound Subjects, 42; Pronunciation Can Deceive You, 43; Prepositional Phrases and Agreement, 44; The Indefinite Pronouns and Agreement, 47; Adjective Clauses and Agreement, 48; Transferring Your Skills to Writing, 55

     Review Test   56

3   VERBS AND VERB PHRASES   58

     Preview Test   59

     Regular Past Tense Verbs   60

     Using the Irregular Verb Index   64

     Avoiding Shifts in Tense, 67

     Verbs With Auxiliaries   71

     Sentence Structure Review   73

     Do: Both Auxiliary and Main Verb, 75; *Have*: Both Auxiliary and Main Verb, 79; *Be*: Both Auxiliary and Main Verb, 81; Past Participle *Been*, 83; Choosing the Participle for a *Be* Auxiliary, 84; The Longest Verb Phrase, 86

     Spelling Past Tense Verbs and Past Participles   90

     Used To/ Supposed To, 90; The *D/T* Sound, 91; Changing *D* to *T*: *Bend/Lend*, 95; No Change: *Bid/ Burst*, 96; Internal Vowel Change:

Bleed/Breed, 98; Internal Vowel Change: *Say/Hear*, 100; Internal Vowel Change: *Bring/Buy*, 103; Internal Vowel Change + N: *Break/Choose*, 105; Other EN Past Participles: *Fall/Eat*, 107; *Get/Got* as an "Auxiliary", 110; Internal Vowel Change Plus N: *Blow/Fly*, 112; Internal Vowel Change: *Drink/Ring*, 114; Internal Vowel Change: *Cling/Fling*, 115; Some Very Irregular Verbs: *Become/Begin*, 118; Special Difficulties: *Come/Run*, 122; A Unique Verb: *Go*, 125; The Last Group: *Dig/Win*, 127

	Analogizing	**128**
	Irregular Verb Index	**129**
	Review Test	**134**
4	**CONTRACTIONS**	**136**
	Preview Test	**137**
	Forming Contractions	**138**

Contractions Within Verb Phrases, 139; Contraction of *Not*, 140; Homonyms of Contractions, 141; Contractions and Possessive Pronoun Homonyms, 142; *It/Its/It's*, 142; *Who's/Whose*, 144; *They're/Their/There*, 146; *You/Your/You're*, 147

	Transferring Your Skills to Writing	**152**
	Review Test	**153**
5	**POSSESSIVES**	**154**
	Preview Test	**155**

What Is Meant by Possession?, 156; How To Form a Possessive, 157; When the Possessive Isn't a Person, 163; Absolute Possessives, 168; Confusing Possessives and Contractions, 171; Indefinite Pronouns and Their Possessive Forms, 172

	Transferring Your Skills to Writing	**173**
	Review Test	**175**
6	**PRONOUNS**	**176**
	Preview Test	**177**
	Pronoun Case	**179**

Compound Pronouns, 180; Avoid Double Subjects, 182; Subject Complements, 183; Comparisons With *Than*, 184; *Who?* or Is It *Whom?*, 185; Confusion of *Them* and *Those*, 187

	Possessive Pronouns	**188**
	Spelling of Reflexive Pronouns	**189**
	"The Typical Person" and Indefinite Pronouns	**190**

Strategies for Avoiding Sexism, 192

	Shifting Pronouns	**193**
	Pronoun Reference	**197**

Contents

Transferring Your Skills to Writing	201
Review Test	202

7 PUNCTUATION 204

Preview Test	205
Punctuation Pattern Sheet	207
Identifying the Independent Clause	208
Run-On Sentences	210

Sentence Complexity: Patterns #1 and #2, 213; The Colon: Pattern #8, 216; The Semicolon: Pattern #2, 217

Let's Summarize 218

Semicolon + Conjunctive Adverb: Pattern #3, 220; Parenthetical Expressions: Pattern #6, Introductory Verbal Phrases, 225; Subordinate Clauses, 227; Fragments from Noun Clauses, 228; Subordinating Conjunctions, 231; Fragments from Adverbial Clauses, 232; Adverbial Clauses: Patterns #7 and #8, 232; Run-ons with Adverbial Clauses, 236; Punctuating the Adjective Clause, 239; Fragments from Adjective Clauses, 240; Restrictive vs Nonrestrictive Adjective Clauses, 241; Nonrestrictive Modifiers, 245

Quotations	253

Punctuation Pattern #9, 253

Special Cases	257
Transferring Your Skill to Writing	258
Review Test	259

APPENDIX A: SUBJECT/VERB RECOGNITION 260

Preview Test	261

Sentence Types, 262

Finding Verbs and Verb Phrases	265
Pronoun Substitution	266
Coordination	267
Prenominal Modifiers	268
Possessives	269
Adverbs	272
Prepositions and Their Objects	274
Some Common Prepositions	274

Prepositional Phrases Used as Adjectives, 277

The Verbals	279

Verbals Ending in -ing, 279; Objects with -ing words, 280; Infinitives, 281; Objects of Infinitives, 282; Compound Infinitives, 283; Past Participles, 284

Subordinate Clauses — 286

The Adjective Clause, 286
The Noun Clause, 289
The Adverbial Clause, 290

Word Order in Sentences — 293

Exceptions to regular order, 294

Putting It All Together — 295

Review Test — 297

APPENDIX B: SPELLING AND HOMONYMS — 298

Preview Test — 299
Adding Endings to Words — 300
Reviewing Endings — 302
Homonyms — 304
Glossary of Homonyms — 306
Review Test — 311

ANSWER SECTION — 313
INDEX — 345

TO THE STUDENT

Even if this is your first term in college, you are no doubt already familiar with some of the special problems involved in college writing. Your English teachers in high school probably warned you that standards would be higher in college, and maybe they even gave you a personal warning that you would have to work hard to meet those standards. *College Writing Skills* is designed to help you do just that.

This text is not an exhaustive handbook containing all the rules about grammar and usage ever devised, but it is not just a workbook full of practice exercises either. Instead it is a learning textbook.

A handbook lists as many rules as possible as briefly as it can for quick reference. *College Writing Skills* deals with many of the same rules, but it discusses them in much greater depth. It tries to suggest the logic behind the rules when there is any. If the rules are not logical, the text will tell you that also. Sometimes the text will even surprise you and say that an old-fashioned rule can be forgotten.

A workbook provides practice but usually gives very little explanation—often relying on a handbook for that. The exercises in this text are similar to many workbook exercises you've seen before, but they have one important difference. The first exercises will be fairly easy; the next ones a little more difficult; and the last one, usually an editing exercise, will be the most difficult one in the chapter.

The trick you will need to learn is to treat your own writing like the editing exercises at the ends of the chapters. In your own writing, of course, you will be expected to proofread for all of the problems at once instead of just the problem discussed in a single chapter.

Your instructor may go through the text chapter by chapter discussing the problems and assigning the exercises, or you may have an instructor who will decide to have you work through most of the text independently. Either method is possible because of the way the text is set up. Some instructors may even use a combination of the two methods. Whether you are working independently or whether the whole class is working on the same thing at the same time, you can always check your understanding by looking at the end of the book for the answers to the odd-numbered sentences. Your instructor may occasionally ask you to turn in even-numbered sentences to check your progress, or the answers to the even-numbered sentences may be placed on reserve in your school's learning lab or library. You can use these resources most wisely by doing the odd-numbered sentences, checking your work, and if there are a number of mistakes, going back to review the explanations, and then doing the even-numbered sentences.

Your instructor can use the pre- and post-tests provided to find out what skills need class attention and which ones can be considered briefly or assigned individually. You can also check yourself as you go along by using the PREVIEW and REVIEW sentences that come at the beginning and end of each chapter. All of the PREVIEW and REVIEW sentences are discussed in detail on audiocassettes. These may be available to you in a learning lab or in the reserve room of your library. Check with your instructor.

Doing the exercises in this book and taking the tests is not like taking a shot of penicillin and then lying back in bed waiting to get well. To begin with, not being satisfied with your skill as a writer is not like being sick and in need of a cure. Instead it is more like not knowing how to drive a car or play basketball. There are skills to learn, practice sessions to attend, and more practice to be done alone. But in the same way that watching someone else drive or shooting baskets when you have the court all to yourself is not driving or playing basketball, doing exercises is not writing.

That is why, in addition to doing the exercises in this text, your instructor will make writing assignments to help you stretch your skills as you are learning them. Your class will probably discuss ways of exploring your attitudes and adding new ideas—sometimes confusing or seemingly contradictory ones—to your long-held beliefs. You will be shown ways of arranging your material in conventional patterns, and you may look at how professional writers take those conventional patterns and stretch them to fit their own purposes.

There are many more skills involved in learning to write than in learning to drive or play basketball, and they take longer to develop. No text can teach all of the skills writers need. The ones that try speak at such a high-level of abstraction that they are meaningless in dealing with practical problems. "Write clearly" is excellent advice, but learning *how* to write clearly, learning what problems interfere most with clarity, or learning to recognize when what you have written is not clear, those are very different matters. What this text tries to do is to present a few common problems and to talk about them in more detail than many textbooks do.

TO THE INSTRUCTOR

College Writing Skills, Second Edition, is designed so that it may be used by a whole class or assigned individually by chapter to students with particular problems. We have tried to provide sufficient grammatical information within each chapter to accomplish the goals of the chapter. Extensive grammatical terminology may prove an unnecessary hurdle for many students. However, if more help in identifying subjects and verbs is needed, Appendix A provides additional sentences that may be used with or without the explanatory text. A classroom script for teaching this essential skill will be provided in the Instructor's Manual. The authors strongly suggest the use of this strategy, perhaps modified by you in response to your own class's needs, before students start working independently through Appendix A.

A number of other resources are available to instructors upon request to the publisher. Contact your Charles E. Merrill representative or write:

Beverly Kolz, English Editor
Charles E. Merrill Publishing Co.
1300 Alum Creek Drive
Columbus, Ohio 43216

Additional resources include the following:

(1) An Instructor's Manual containing the answers to all even-numbered sentences; answers to the odd-numbered sentences are in the text at the back of each chapter. (Request 8046—M)
(2) A test bank containing pre- and post-tests covering the material in the complete text plus individual pre- and post-tests for each chapter. (Request 8046—T)
(3) Supplemental audiocassettes that discuss the PREVIEW and REVIEW sentences beginning and ending each chapter. (Request 8031—2)

chapter 1

NOUN NUMBER

PREVIEW _____ one

The sentences in the exercise below preview the skills and principles you'll learn in this chapter. For the answers to this exercise, check with your instructor or tutor or listen to the appropriate audio tape.

Circle the correct choice.

                             A   B   C
1. Our babysitter charges two (dollar, dollars, dollar's) an hour.
                 A   B   C
2. Dodie missed three (test, tests, testes) when he was sick.
                                       A   B   C
3. A left-handed robber stole all the left-handed (desk, desks, deskes).
         A   B   C
4. Several (library, librarys, libraries) are open until nine.
              A   B   C
5. One of the (story, storys, stories) scared my little brother.
             A   B   C   D
6. These (gentleman, gentlemans, gentlemen, gentlemens) will help you carry the boxes.
        A   B   C
7. Some (leaf, leafs, leaves) have blown into the street.
         A   B   C
8. All the (Malloy, Malloys, Malloy's) finally left town.
   A B   A B
9. (A, An) elephant stepped on (a, an) mouse.
                                         A   B   A   B
10. Arnettra has found a way to cheat at most (card, cards) (game, games).

INTRODUCTION

As you work through the chapters in the beginning of this text, you might get the idea that there are two forms of the language: standard and nonstandard. This is an oversimplification, however. There are, to begin with, many perfectly respectable regional and social varieties of spoken American English to which the concept of correctness or incorrectness cannot be applied. Speech patterns that are thought to be very prestigious in one area may be considered either uneducated or prissy and artificial in another area. Speech is not the concern of the exercises in this text, however. Here you are being directed to concentrate on writing skills. In spite of the many varieties of the spoken language in this country, there is very little grammatical variety in the written language. When you see the term *standard* or *edited American English*, it refers to the form of the language that shows up in writing in books, magazines, and newspapers.

One of the ways standard (edited) and nonstandard English differ is in the endings put on nouns. In writing, the letter *s* is added to most nouns to show that they are plural (more than one). In speech these final *S*es are often not pronounced, but they must always be written.

If you already pluralize words automatically, then you can readily identify nouns. Nouns are words that can be pluralized. If you can add an *s* to a word to show plurality, then the word is a noun. If you don't perform this operation automatically, you need to learn some other signals for identifying nouns before you can determine whether they need *S*es to make them plural or not. This chapter will suggest several signals to help you recognize nouns: definition, resemblance to other nouns, noun determiners, and sentence position. Next it will discuss when you should add the *s* to a noun and when you should leave it off.

NOUNS

A *noun* is SOMETHING. All of the words you will fill in or make up in this chapter will be nouns. Everything existing in or out of this world is a noun. If you could add it to the picture of the world on the next page, then it is a noun. A noun can be a *person*, such as a philosopher, the president, or Ms. Smith. A noun can be a *place*, such as Earth, Escondido, Paris, or your closet. A noun can be a concrete, physical *thing*, such as a chair, a house, or a rock; or a noun can be an abstract *thing*, such as honesty, goodness, hate, or love. Nouns are the names of all the things we talk about, write about, or wonder about.

Recognizing Nouns

The traditional method of identifying nouns is by definition. If you can define a word, you will recognize it as a noun if it names a person, animal, place,

Chapter 1: Noun Number

truth *goodness* *beauty*

PERSON
a philosopher
a child

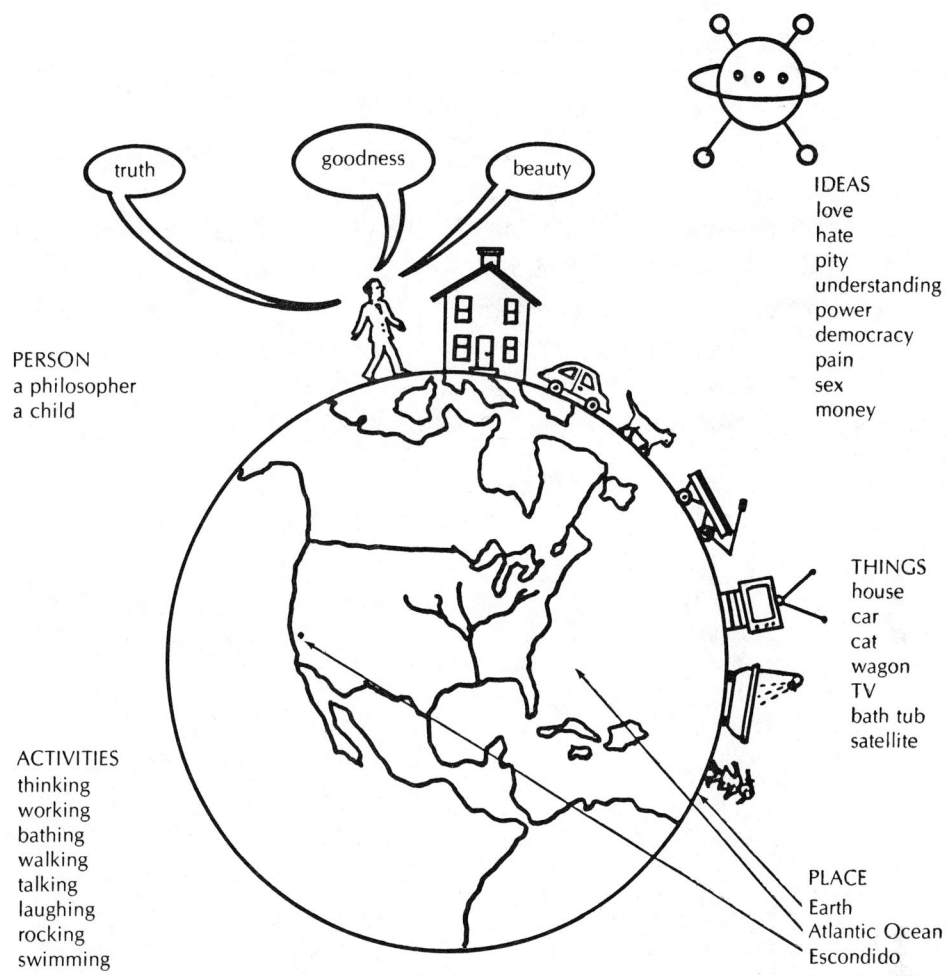

IDEAS
love
hate
pity
understanding
power
democracy
pain
sex
money

THINGS
house
car
cat
wagon
TV
bath tub
satellite

ACTIVITIES
thinking
working
bathing
walking
talking
laughing
rocking
swimming

PLACE
Earth
Atlantic Ocean
Escondido

thing, or activity. *Mary Grimes, elephant, Chicago, typewriter,* and *swimming* are all nouns. List some others.

person	*student*	
animal		
place		
thing		
activity		

A second way of recognizing nouns is by their characteristic noun endings. These include: *-hood, -ness, -er (-or, -ar), -ance (-ence), -try, -ment, -ism, -ist, -ology,* and *-tion;* therefore, *fatherHOOD, busiNESS, drivER, imporTANCE, poeTRY, judgMENT, communISM, biOLOGY, therapIST,* and *intenTION* are all nouns. List some others.

-hood	*motherhood*	
-ness		
-er		
-ance		
-try		
-ment		
-ism		

-ist   _____   _____
-ology   _____   _____
-tion   _____   _____

The third way we have of recognizing nouns is by noun determiners. These are words which signal that a noun is coming and sometimes tell us whether the noun will be singular or plural. Singular noun determiners include *this, that, another, one, much, every,* and *a/an.* Plural noun determiners include *all, both, few, many, these, those, several, most, a group of, a number of, one of the, none of the,* and *two (three, four,* etc.) Some determiners that don't signal number include *the, some, my, his, her, its, your,* and *their.* Fill in any noun following the determiners below.

a	*peanut*	the	_____	those	_____
every	_____	several	_____	some	_____
his	_____	this	_____	two	_____
one	_____	most	_____	my	_____
your	_____	few	_____	both	_____
a group of	_____	their	_____	that	_____
another	_____	all	_____	our	_____

A fourth way of recognizing nouns is by their function or position in the sentence. Nouns function as subjects, complements, direct objects, indirect objects, and objects of prepositions. If you can find nouns in your sentences and know how to pluralize them correctly, you may get along very well without learning the traditional names of sentence parts. You will not be tested on these terms now, but you may find them useful in organizing what you know about nouns. Each of these terms is reintroduced and explained again in Appendix A.

Fill in a person, place, or thing in the blanks below as you read through an explanation of these terms. All of the words you fill in will be nouns.

A **subject** is the person, place, or thing a sentence is about. The subject is often the first noun in a sentence.

Tony smiled.
_____ shouted.
The _____ collapsed.

A **subject complement** renames the subject.

She is our **president**.
Frank is a _____.
His boss is the _____.

In the examples above, *she* or *Frank* may also be *sick, sad,* or *happy,* but these words are not nouns because they are not things. However, *sickNESS, sadNESS,* and *happiNESS* are things (notice the *-ness* ending). Think of it this way: you can have more than one *sickness,* but it doesn't make sense to say you have more than one *sick.* Remember: if a word can be pluralized, it is a noun.

Chapter 1: Noun Number

A **direct object** can be replaced at the end of a sentence with the word *what* for places and things and with the word *whom* for people.

    They chose a **house.**   They chose a **what?**
    The tornado destroyed _____ .
    Harold broke another _____ .

An **object complement** renames the object.

    Alice called George a **donkey.**
    The small country made its president _____ .
    The group elected Joseph _____ .

An **indirect object** answers the question *to* or *for whom* (or *what*) just before the direct object in the sentence. Check it by putting *to* or *for* after the object.

The trainer gave the **horse** a shot.   OR the trainer gave a shot **to the horse.**

We brought _____ a message.   OR We brought a message to _____ .

Shirley sent her _____ a package.   Or Shirley sent a package to _____ .

The **object of a preposition** answers the question *what* or *whom* You will find a list of prepositions in Chapter 2 on page 45. Prepositions are usually short little words like *in*, *on*, *from*, *up*, and *by*.

    The girl **from Dallas** left.
    The children in the _____ sang loudly.
    The fiddler on the _____ fell.

Pronoun Substitution

In addition to these four signals for identifying nouns, there is another test that always works. If you are trying to tell whether a word is a noun or not, see whether you can substitute a *pronoun* into the sentence. A pronoun is a word which can take the place of a noun. All nouns have pronoun substitutes.

These pronouns can be substituted for subjects and subject complements:

    Singular: I, you, he, she, it
    Plural: we, you (all), they

These pronouns can be substituted for objects:

    Singular: me, you, him, her, it
    Plural: us, you (all), them

Notice that *you* (both singular and plural) and *it* are used as subjects and as objects. For now, concentrate on the subject pronouns. In the following examples either the noun or the pronoun, but not both, can be used as the subject of the sentence.

    { **He** / Harold } complains a lot.

{ **They** / His daughters } were working.

{ **It** / Love } doesn't last.

{ **We** / Bob and I } collect stamps.

EXERCISE 1–1

Substitute a subject pronoun (he, she, it, they, I, we, you) for each of the following nouns.

1. Harold: _he_
2. Ted and Alice: _____
3. happiness: _____
4. an exercise: _____
5. Dallas: _____
6. an airplane: _____
7. my boss: _____
8. you and Liz: _____
9. a nun: _____
10. rock stars: _____
11. money: _____
12. one of the girls: _____
13. his wife and her husband: _____
14. Ginny and I: _____
15. Dale, Jim, and Jack: _____
16. Carol and her mother: _____
17. basic mathematical skills: _____
18. swimming and diving: _____
19. inflation: _____
20. your ideas: _____

Determining Noun Number

When you are attempting to decide whether your noun should be singular (one) or plural (more than one), you will be aided by a group of signals called *noun determiners*. Some noun determiners alert us that a singular noun is coming, and some alert us that a plural noun is coming. You should memorize these signals.

Chapter 1: Noun Number

Singular Noun Determiners

Noun determiners which signal a singular noun include:

This (task)	**One** (mistake)	**Every** (athlete)
That (boy)	**Much** [1] (trouble)	**A/An** (apple)
	Another (problem)	

Both *a* and *an* signal singular nouns. We use *an* only before words beginning with the vowel sounds *(a, e, i, o, u)* and those with a silent *h*.

An electron	**An** apple	**An** icepick
An honor	**An** opal	**An** unlikely suspect

We use *a* before words beginning with a consonant (any letters of the alphabet except *a, e, i, o, u*) or before words where the *u* sounds like the *y* in *yes*.

A uniform	**A** baseball	**A** calculator
A unilateral decision	**A** street	**A** handbag

NOTE: Never add an *s* to the nouns with a singular noun determiner.

EXERCISE 1–2

In the following exercise underline the noun determiner and fill in any appropriate singular noun. Watch your spelling.

1. A _____*dog*_____ was in the window.
2. There was one _____ left.
3. My vacation will take too much _____ .
4. I've seen that _____ before.
5. An _____ keeps the doctor away.
6. This old _____ should be replaced.
7. The babysitter charges two dollars an _____ .
8. Much _____ could be avoided with careful planning.
9. I often have a _____ in my purse.
10. I saw that _____ in a store last week.

Plural Noun Determiners

Noun determiners which signal a plural noun include:

---

[1] *Much* is a determiner which requires a mass noun. A mass noun is a noun which can't be made plural. For example, *I put too much salt in the stew.* To use a plural noun in this sentence you would have to put *too many tomatoes in the stew. Time* and *money* can also be used as mass nouns.

Chapter 1: Noun Number

All (branchES)	These (problemS)	A group of (protestorS)
Both (bossES)	Those (answers)	A number of (incidentS)
Few (applicantS)	Several (girlS)	One of the (notecardS)
Many (fanS)	Most (studentS)	None of the (guardS)
Two, Three, Four, etc. (squirrelS)		

EXERCISE 1-3

In the sentences below fill in any appropriate plural noun and underline the noun determiner which provided the signal. Watch your spelling.

1. A group of __hecklers__ interrupted the speaker.
2. The senate refused to pass the bill for a number of _____ .
3. Both _____ have their deficiencies.
4. Few _____ travel at night.
5. Many _____ come in the mail.
6. Most _____ are written for idiots.
7. Imagine my surprise when I found several _____ in my bathtub.
8. One of these _____ will surprise you.
9. Those _____ are always disappointing.
10. None of the _____ has the right to be here.

Noun Determiners Without Number

Some noun determiners simply signal us that a noun is coming; however, they don't tell us if it will be singular or plural. Some determiners which signal a noun but don't reveal number include:

His	Her	Its
My	Your	Our
Their	Some	The
The crime	Some leather	My job
The crimes	Some handbags	My duties

EXERCISE 1-4

In the sentences below decide whether a singular or plural noun is indicated and fill in any appropriate word. Watch your spelling.

1. Not all __cats__ like cat food.
2. There are more _____ than carrots in my garden.
3. One _____ a day is enough for me.
4. An ugly _____ wanted my sandwich.
5. Its _____ were stolen.
6. Mother wants to know where the _____ came from.
7. I had too much _____ for lunch.

Chapter 1: Noun Number

8. Our _____ got soaked in last night's rain.
9. The _____ ended.
10. Her _____ are worthless.

Pronunciation Can Be Deceiving

In speaking we tend to shorten or run together sounds which are very similar or which are repeated. This can be a special problem in writing correct plurals if you use pronunciation as the only guide for spelling.

There is a very common group of plural nouns ending in *sps*, *sts*, and *sks*. Because you may not hear or pronounce the final *s* on these words, you must be doubly careful when you write them.

wa*sps*	te*sts*	ne*sts*	art*ists*
cla*sps*	gu*ests*	ve*sts*	ga*sps*
de*sks*	scient*ists*	qu*ests*	cre*sts*
ma*sks*	ta*sks*	fla*sks*	ca*sts*

A similar problem occurs with any plural noun when the next word in the sentence begins with the letter *s*.

The two trucker*S S*old their rig.
Most of the petunia*S S*eemed to be in good health.

EXERCISE 1–5

In the first five sentences below fill in a plural noun which ends in *sps*, *sts*, or *sks*. In the remaining sentences, determine whether the noun should be singular or plural and fill in any appropriate form.

1. The university provides eight ____*desks*____ for left-handed people.
2. Many bird _____ were destroyed by the hailstorm.
3. All the _____ arrived early.
4. Mother has twenty-two _____ in the closet.
5. Three flying _____ attacked me in the barn.
6. Some _____ don't know when to go home.
7. A bunch of _____ sat near the back of the room.
8. Few _____ saw the point.
9. Few _____ are worth the trouble.
10. That _____ suddenly made a left turn from the right lane.
11. All of the _____ said the driver didn't slow down.
12. Most _____ know better than to try that.
13. Every _____ said the driver didn't slow down.
14. Two _____ are two too many.
15. The three ambulance _____ set down the stretcher.

16. Will these _____ save our hero's life?
17. During the parade none of the _____ smiled.
18. This _____ sails clumsily.
19. A _____ sat on the toadstool.
20. One of the _____ slid off the shelf.

When There Is No Noun Determiner

Sometimes there is no determiner before a noun. When the noun expresses a general idea (an *abstract noun*, if you're familiar with that term), you should probably use the singular form.

> **Alienation** is not a new problem.
> **Beauty** is only skin deep.
> **Fighting** is useless.

When the noun refers to a class of people or things and there is no noun determiner, you should probably use a plural noun.

> **Cats** avoid dogs.
> **Students** are worriers.
> **Forks** are a modern idea.

EXERCISE 1-6

In the following exercise, circle the correct singular or plural noun.

1. (Honesy, Honesties) is a virtue.
2. (Bird, Birds) fly long distances to lay their eggs.
3. (Working, Workings) always seems senseless to lazy people.
4. Most people think (suffering, sufferings) should be eliminated.
5. (Onion, Onions) grow well in this climate.
6. There should be a law against (politician, politicians).
7. (Worm, Worms) make excellent gardeners.
8. (Plagiarism, Plagiarisms) by students is decreasing.
9. (Laughter, Laughters) is contagious.
10. (Turtle, Turtles) bury their eggs in the warm sand.

Confusing Adjectives with Nouns

An adjective is a word which describes or gives more information about a noun. The same word may be an adjective or a noun depending on how it is used in a sentence. You may find yourself **overcorrecting** by putting Ses on any word you suspect of being a noun. Some languages, such as Spanish, pluralize the adjective as well the noun; in English you should never add an *s* to an adjective to make it plural.

Chapter 1: Noun Number

Noun Determiner	Descriptive Adjective	Noun Subject	Verb
The		truckS	stop for gas.
The	truck	stopS	are crowded with tourists.

This confusion occurs most frequently with those groups of nouns referring to units of weight and measure. Even though a noun determiner precedes and indicates number, you must still pluralize the noun by adding *s* in your writing. Compare the following sentences.

Noun Determiner	Subject	Verb	Noun Determiner	Descriptive Adjective	Noun Object
The	baby	weighs	seven		poundS.
	Janice	walked	two		mileS.
	He	was	a	seven-*pound*	baby.
	It	is	a	four-*mile*	hike to town.

Irregular Nouns

Nouns which are pluralized by adding *s* are called *regular* nouns. There are only a few *irregular* nouns in English, but they are often very important ones because you use them so frequently. The word *foot* is an irregular noun. When you have more than one *foot*, they are called *feet*; the plural is formed by changing the vowel sound inside the word from *oo* to *ee*. Compare *foot* to *pound* and *mile* in the grid above.

Noun Determiner	Subject	Verb	Noun Determiner	Descriptive Adjective	Noun Object
The	baby	has	two		feet.
	He	is	a	two-*foot*	baby.

EXERCISE 1-7

In the following exercise fill in the appropriate form of the word to the left of the sentence in the blanks.

truck   1. Four *trucks* were parked at the _____ stop.

pound   2. This table weighs forty *pounds*.

oak   3. _____ leaves covered the ground under those tall _____ near the fence.

cent   4. Soon a sixty-_____ loaf of bread will cost eighty _____.

graduate   5. One of the _____ of our school became a _____ assistant at M.I.T.

14 Chapter 1: Noun Number

blueberry	6. It took a couple of pints of _____ to make a _____ pie.
foot	7. They built a seven-_____ fence barely three _____ from the road.
card	8. I hate _____ games because I can't shuffle the _____ properly.
newspaper	9. Several _____ reporters taped the interview and printed it word for word in their _____ the next morning.
yard	10. Six _____ of material seems like a lot to make a two-_____ jacket.
examination	11. Even though Stan hated those _____, he had no trouble with the _____ questions.
inch	12. A number of _____ worms applied for a job as a ruler when they learned to count their _____.
pillow	13. None of the _____ had a _____ case on it.
foot	14. Several _____ away near the _____ bush
rose	stood a six _____ woman with a _____ tatoo on her cheek.
dog	15. Many of the _____ in my neighborhood don't have _____ tags.

EXERCISE 1–8

The following sentences contain examples of all the signals and special problems we have observed. Decide whether the missing word should be singular or plural and fill in any appropriate noun.

1. Harold is a seven-___*foot*___ center for the Cyclones.
2. A _____ is just what Jane needs.
3. Too much _____ will spoil the stew.
4. The Senate Investigating Committee discovered a number of _____ in the tape.
5. When my car ran out of gas, I walked three _____ .
6. This _____ is bigger than mine.
7. Some _____ showed up.
8. His many _____ were unappreciated.
9. I'll need a _____ before they'll accept me.
10. I received their _____ yesterday.
11. None of the _____ on the suitcases seemed to be any good.
12. Her _____ are no good.
13. What could be better than this _____ ?
14. There are several _____ in the waiting room.

Chapter 1: Noun Number 15

15. The _____ are worth every _____ I paid for them.
16. An _____ likes peanuts.
17. Mr. Battle had some _____ before he left the house.
18. Several _____ were heard in the darkened movie theater during a particularly gory scene.
19. She has every _____ .
20. Flies and mosquitoes are two real _____ .

EXERCISE 1–9

Fill in the missing forms using the same noun in each column and put its pronoun substitute (*he, she, it,* or *they*) next to it.

		Singular Noun			Plural Noun
	One	*friend (s/he)*		Two	*friends (they)*
1.	This		1.	Those	
2.	An		2.	Several	
3.	Every		3.	Most	
4.	That		4.	These	
5.	A single		5.	A couple of	
6.	Much		6.	Most	
7.	A		7.	All	
8.	No		8.	Few	
9.	One		9.	One of the	
10.	This		10.	Both	
11.	The		11.	The	
12.	Every		12.	None of the	
13.	That		13.	Four	
14.	An		14.	Many	
15.	One		15.	A group of	

EXERCISE 1–10

Consider the noun determiner and fill in any appropriate noun together with its pronoun substitute (*he, she, it,* or *they*).

	Noun Determiner	Noun Subject (Pronoun Substitute)	Verb
	One	*man (he)*	walked.
1.	Both		agreed.
2.	Two		knocked.

	Noun Determiner	Noun Subject (Pronoun Substitute)	Verb
3.	Several		knew.
4.	Every		sang.
5.	Few		worked.
6.	Two		stopped.
7.	That		burst.
8.	Three		talked.
9.	Most		left.
10.	All		hurt.
11.	Four		laughed.
12.	A		overheard.
13.	These		arrived.
14.	An		was shot.
15.	This		had broken.

EXERCISE 1–11

In the sentences below make any necessary corrections.

1. There are currently four tutor for all the Communication Skills student.
2. Most of our client come from throughout this cities and all the nearby suburb.
3. Only one offices gave me a typing tests.
4. Few toothpaste tube mangler ever kick the habit.
5. Senator Woods sees this problems in somewhat simplistic term.
6. In a problem-solving situations there are four step.
7. Those two desk are provided for left-handed student.
8. In these forest there are many bird.
9. Several test were postponed because of a freak blizzards.
10. Although we were only two block from the highway, the nearest gas station was five mile away.
11. Two of the microscope need to be repaired.
12. One of the hitchhiker pulled a gun.
13. Another planes failed to take off.
14. At her bridal shower my sister received seven toaster and not a single pillowcases.
15. My brother is six foot tall, and he weighs one hundred eighty pound.

Chapter 1: Noun Number

Verb Signals

In addition to the noun determiners, verbs also signal whether a noun is singular or plural. In present time (right now) if the verb ends in *s*, the noun subject cannot. And in present time (right now) if the verb does not end in *s*, the noun almost always will.

Noun Determiner Used As Adjective	Noun Used As Subject	Verb	
That	dog	barkS	S
Every	student	writeS	I
An	orange	ripenS	N
This	phone	ringS	G
Much	trouble	occurS	U
A	car	stopS	L
One	dish	breakS	A R
Few	teacherS	smile☐	P
Both	birdS	sing☐	L
Those	girlS	flirt☐	U
Some	elevatorS	stop☐	R
Most	guestS	dance☐	A
Several	boyS	laugh☐	L

EXERCISE 1–12

Fill in this grid with fifteen singular noun subjects and their pronoun substitute (*he*, *she*, or *it*). Notice that all the present tense verbs end in *s*.

	Singular Noun	(Pronoun Substitute)	Singular Verb
	The *phone*	(*it*)	rings.
1.	The		stops.
2.	The		collapses.
3.	The		ends.
4.	The		shouts.
5.	Their		leaves.
6.	That		studies.
7.	A		opens.
8.	An		lies.
9.	One		writes.
10.	Even a		drives.
11.	Every		cries.
12.	Some		refuses.
13.	Another		parks.
14.	My		phones.
15.	Much		grows.

EXERCISE 1-13

Fill in the grid with fifteen plural noun subjects and their pronoun substitutes. Notice that none of the verbs ends in *s*.

	Plural Noun	(Pronoun Substitute)	Plural Verb
	The *birds*	*(they)*	sing.
1.	The		ring.
2.	The		call.
3.	The		type.
4.	The		confess.
5.	The		shoot.
6.	Their		enter.
7.	Those		smile.
8.	My		run.
9.	Some		return.
10.	Two		close.
11.	A few		break.
12.	These		awake.
13.	Several		hurt.
14.	Both		dance.
15.	All		fall.

Spelling the Plural Noun

We use the singular form of the noun to name one thing and the plural form to name more than one thing. You've learned to recognize the noun determiner signals which tell you whether a noun should be singular or plural. In general, we form the plural of a noun by adding *s*.

SINGULAR	PLURAL
(one) wallet	(two) wallets
(a) pen	(several) pens
(that) key	(these) keys

Nouns which do not form their plurals by adding *s* are *irregular*. Learning to spell the irregular plurals will be a simpler task if you look at them in groups.

Group 1. When the singular form of a noun ends in *ch, sh, s, x,* or *z,* add *es* to form the plural.

churCH/church*ES* glaSS/glass*ES*
witCH/witch*ES* kiSS/kiss*ES*
buSH/bush*ES* foX/fox*ES*
craSH/crash*ES* aX/ax*ES*

Chapter 1: Noun Number

Group 2. When the singular form of a noun ends in *y* preceded by a consonant,[2] change *y* to *i* and add *es*.

libraRY/librar*IES*   laDY/lad*IES*
mysteRY/myster*IES*   arMY/arm*IES*

Group 3. When the singular form of a noun ends in *f* or *fe*, change the *f* or *fe* to *v* and add *es*.

elF/elVES   leaF/leaVES
selF/selVES   loaF/loaVES
kniFE/kniVES   wharF/wharVES
liFE/liVES   thiEF/thieVES
wiFE/wiVES   wolF/wolVES
halF/halVES   calF/calVES

Group 4. Add *es* to proper names ending in *sh*, *s*, *ch*, *x*, and *z*. Add *s* to all other names to form their plurals.

Roberta Jones/The JonesES (**Jones** ends in S, so add ES.)
Mr. Clark/The ClarkS
Ms. Murphy/The MurphyS (**Murphy** ends in Y, but the Group 2 rule does not apply to names.)

Group 5. When a compound noun is written as one word, form the plural on the last word.

bathroom/bathroomS
taxpayer/taxpayerS

Group 6. When a compound noun is written with hyphens, usually form the plural on the first word.

mother-in-law/motherS-in-law
man-of-war/mEn-of-war
passer-by/passerS-by
(Two exceptions: three-year-oldS and good-for-nothingS)

Group 7. Some nouns do not change at all in the plural form.

deer/deer
sheep/sheep
series/series
fish/fish
moose/moose

Group 8. Some nouns form the plural by changing the sound of an internal vowel.

ox/oxEN
man/mEn
woman/womEn
tooth/tEEth

---
[2] A, E, I, O, and U are *vowels*; all the other letters of the alphabet are *consonants*.

foot/fEEt
goose/gEEse
mouse/mICE
louse/lICE
die/dICE
child/childREN
person/pEOPLE

Group 9. Some nouns retain their Latin forms in the plural. Memorize them in groups paying special attention to the spelling.

SINGULAR	PLURAL
memorandum	memorandA
curriculum	curriculA
datum	datA (**Data** is increasingly seen as both singular and plural, however.)
phenomenon	phenomenA
alumna	alumnAE (feminine)
alumnus	alumnI (masculine)
stimulus	stimulI
nucleus	nucleI
crisis	crisES
oasis	oasES
thesis	thesES
basis	basES
analysis	analysES
synopsis	synopsES
parenthesis	parenthesES

Group 10. Some authorities tell you to form the plurals of letters and figures by adding an apostrophe before the *s*.

The **A's** always go first.
Your **7's** look like **L's**.

Because these may become confused with possessive forms which we will take up in Chapter 5, we strongly suggest that you form the plurals of letters and figures as if they were regular nouns: just add an *s* to all numbers and most letters. To form the plurals of *ch, sh, s, x,* or *z*, add *es* as if they were Group 1 spelling words.

The **As** should go last sometimes.
My **9s** look like **7s**.
Three **UFOs** landed in the park.
Missing **Ses** may confuse some readers.

You will be correct whichever strategy you choose for pluralizing numbers, letters, and words used as words, but don't mix the two possibilities.

WRONG: Dot your **I's** and cross your **Ts**.
WRONG: Study this list of **Do's** and **Don'ts**.

Chapter 1: Noun Number

EXERCISE 1–14

Decide whether you want a singular or a plural noun, then write in the correctly spelled form of the word given to the left of each sentence below.

(dish) 1. Two _____ broke.
(tax) 2. The colonists insisted that both _____ were illegal.
(catch) 3. Ames made two great _____ and saved the game.
(rush) 4. The Bible says that baby Moses was found in the _____.
(TA) 5. Occasionally even the _____ don't know the correct answers.
(quality) 6. Two _____ took him far: arrogance and intelligence.
(fly) 7. Jack killed nine _____ with one swat.
(opportunity) 8. That _____ will not present itself again.
(wharf) 9. The _____ are dangerous places at night.
(wolf) 10. Two timber _____ have escaped from the zoo.
(thief) 11. Ethiopia punishes _____ by cutting off their hands.
(P, Q) 12. Mind your _____ and _____ .
(Smith) 13. The _____ have moved to Ohio.
(woman) 14. All of the _____ roller skate to the supermarket.
(Johnson) 15. There are three _____: Margaret, David, and Michael.
(man) 16. Those _____ skip rope backwards.
(deer) 17. The brave hunter had two tiny _____ lashed to the hood of his car.
(Williams) 18. The abandoned child has been adopted by the _____ .
(mouse, die) 19. All _____ shoot _____ .
(McDuffy) 20. One of the _____ is running for Congress.
(father-in-law, son-in-law) 21. Some _____ pity their new _____ .
(goose, moose) 22. Three _____ and two _____ formed a rock group.
(tooth) 23. Although all of her _____ were in good condition, her gums needed attention.
(curriculum) 24. Several _____ are being discussed by the committee.
(nucleus) 25. Can you determine the structural components of these _____?

EXERCISE 1–15

Decide whether you want a singular or a plural noun, then write in the correctly spelled form of the word given to the left of each sentence.

Chapter 1: Noun Number

(box)   1. Two of the _____ in the attic were filled with old boots.

(loss)   2. His gambling _____ add up.

(punch)   3. One more _____ will finish my bus ticket.

(campus)   4. Charlotte attends class on both _____ .

(family)   5. Several _____ have moved from this building because of the noise.

(baby)   6. All of the _____ in the day care center sneezed at once.

(C)   7. Merle received three _____ on his grade report.

(possibility)   8. You must consider all of the _____ .

(self)   9. Should we always be true to our _____?

(inch)   10. Jim grew several _____ last year.

(life)   11. They say that cats have nine _____ .

(CPA)   12. _____ are certified public accountants.

(Walsh)   13. The _____ love to give parties.

(woman)   14. Most _____ resent sexist remarks.

(half)   15. You may have both _____ of the grapefruit.

(entry)   16. Although one _____ was blocked by crates, two other _____ were open to traffic.

(textbook)   17. New _____ for the whole school district will be expensive.

(Hoetker)   18. All of the _____ I know are teachers.

(series)   19. A _____ of robberies has plagued this neighborhood.

(person)   20. Three _____ threw stones at the passing train.

(basis)   21. What are the _____ for these charges?

(child, Bogg)   22. All _____ are noisy, but those _____ are deafening.

(controversy)   23. Numerous _____ marred his term in office.

(peach)   24. The migrant workers picked _____ all summer.

(raspberry)   25. Birds ate most of the _____ .

EXERCISE 1–16

Read through the following sentences and correct any noun number mistakes. A misspelled word is considered a mistake. If there is a mistake in the sentence, draw a line through the word and write the correct form above it.

Telephonitis

1. The three Tyler kid who live next door to me inspired me to enter all the contest on one of the local radio station, WLS.

2. Pamela, Mark, and Todd had all won tee shirt, record album, and concert ticket this way.

3. I had never won a single thing on the station's many giveaway.

Chapter 1: Noun Number

4. Every twenty or so minute the disc jockies would begin their spiels, "If you are one of the first thirteen caller, you'll win two ticket to the Chicago concert at the Auditorium."

5. The Tyler's had the timing down perfectly.

6. Before the mens had gotten six word out of their mouth, one or more Tyler were already calling the station.

7. Other subscriber to that telephone exchange complained bitterly because the exchange was always flooded with call during the call-ins contests.

8. Too many phone call caused the exchange to black out.

9. Pre-recorded message told caller to try again later.

10. When I did manage to get through occasionally, I was always the fourteenth or nineteenth or thirtieth caller, but all of the young womans who answered the phone politely encouraged me to try again.

11. Every time I was the fourteenth caller, my crys of anguish could be heard on the next block.

12. My boyfriend was not amused when I interrupted his proposal of marriage to sprint for the closest phone.

13. My father observed acidly several time that ladys don't run out of a room when guest are speaking to them.

14. I never shopped without my radio to my ear, and three time an hour I'd dash to a phone, leaving other annoyed shopper and passer-bys staring suspiciously.

15. Finally I was thrown out of the local Bridge Club when my numerous abrupt departure broke up too many cards games.

16. Once at midnight I received a anonymous phone call saying I'd won a thirty-eight feet white elephant, but that turned out to be one of my dumb brother's not too funny hoax.

17. My mania was ruining lifes.

18. Most mature adult would have given up on radios givesaway. Not me.

19. Finally I asked Pam and Mark and Todd for lesson in contest winning.

20. Pam said that one of the best way to win was to phone in on a touch-tone phone.

21. Mark preferred phone with dial, but said you had to have all the digit but one dialed when the guy on the radio started to announce another contests.

22. Todd discounted these theorys.

23. He said that persistence was the only keys to success despite what the other Tyler believed.

24. Then a afternoon came when my luck changed.

25. The prize was one of the big one: a trip to Acapulco.

26. I heard the announcement begin, and by the time it was finished I was out of the tub and dialing the last two 4's in the phone number.

27. Within several ring a gentlemen whose voice I recognized answered the phone.

28. "What is your favorite radio station?" he asked in his by now painfully familiar voice.

29. For a couple of second my mind went blank, but then I remembered the correct response.

30. To make both set of parent happy, Randy and I got married last week before leaving for Acapulco.

31. Our suitcase are packed and our plane ticket are in hand.

32. The telephone company has promised to have seven phone installed in our new apartment, waiting for our return.

33. Winning the trip has made Randy anxious to be initiated into the mysterys of winning phone-in contest too.

34. For the next ten week all thirteenth caller will qualify for the "$75,000 Dream Home Giveaway" drawing.

35. When we get back from Acapulco, we're going to quit our job and spend the next nine week phoning WLS.

TRANSFERRING YOUR SKILL TO WRITING

The point of the exercises in this chapter has been to provide you with extensive practice in a fundamental skill, and you've probably moved through them fairly quickly. It's one thing to pluralize nouns correctly when the problem is isolated for you as it is in a fill-in exercise; it's harder to do in an editing exercise because you have to isolate the problems for yourself and then decide whether a correction is needed; the hardest thing to do is to transfer the skill to your own writing.

Your primary objective in writing is to say what you have to say as clearly as possible. If you have trouble with noun plurals only in specific places (for example, after certain plural determiners or with plurals ending in *sps, sts,* and *sks*), it may be possible to catch mistakes before you make them as you are writing. However, if your diagnostic test or an early writing assignment indicated a more general problem with noun plurals, careful editing after what you have to say is down on paper may be the most practical way to remove these errors from your writing.

EXERCISE 1–17

At this point you should be ready to write an essay free of noun number mistakes. Your instructor may assign an in-class paper or may want you to write on one of the following topics:

How to take care of a cat/dog/some other animal.
Why newspapers/laws/equal rights/human rights are essential.

REVIEW ──────────────── one

The sentences in this review exercise are provided to help you check your progress in this chapter and to prepare you for what you'll find in the posttest. For the answers to this exercise, check with your instructor or tutor or listen to the appropriate audio tape.

Circle the correct choice.

1. A fast freight train hit the car and dragged it five (block, blocks, block's).
                                                                        A   B   C

2. If you want to put up a fence which will keep the neighbor's alligator out of your garden, you must follow four simple but dangerous (step, steps).

3. Many sincere (feminist, feminists) have close male (friend, friends).

4. Another (refugee, refugees) slips under the barbed wire at the Communist border.

5. Both of the (lady, ladys, ladies) stopped and asked if they could help.

6. Those (woman, womans, women, womens) have exchanged their aprons for hard hats.

7. The seniors wanted to plan the graduation ceremony by (themself, themselves).

8. I can't stand Mrs. Williams or any of the other (Williams, Williams's, Williamses).

9. (A, An) intelligent dolphin communicated with (a, an) visiting alien.

10. Waitresses like to serve most (truck, trucks) (driver, drivers) because they tip well.

chapter 2

PRESENT TENSE VERBS

PREVIEW _____ two

The sentences in the exercise below preview the skills and principles you'll learn in this chapter. For the answers to this exercise, check with your instructor or tutor or listen to the appropriate audio tape.

In the sentences below underline the subject of the verb within parentheses and write the pronoun substitute for the subject (*he, she, it, they, I, you, we*) to the left. Then circle the correct verb.

           A B
_____ 1. Sam always (say, says) what he means.

                                   A   B
_____ 2. The person between the two rubber plants (don't, doesn't) have an invitation.

                          A B C
_____ 3. Every Wednesday diagnostic tests (are, is, be) administered between nine and noon.

                                      A   B
_____ 4. The investigators from the building inspector's office (know, knows) what to look for.

                                 A   B
_____ 5. The cold which I caught last February still (resist, resists) my efforts to cure it.

                A B
_____ 6. Oliver sometimes (ask, asks) for a second helping of potatoes.

             A   B
_____ 7. The buffalo's hide (were, was) tough.

                          A   B
_____ 8. The new neighbors down the block (have, has) seven kids.

                               A   B
_____ 9. The teachers in Robin's cousins' district (want, wants) to strike.

             A   B
_____ 10. Frequent substitution (aren't, isn't) the only way to let every player have a chance.

INTRODUCTION

In written English in the present tense there is a phenomenon called subject/verb agreement which creates a huge problem for many students. For some students, the problem only arises when the subject is separated in the sentence from its verb by several other words. For other students, subject/verb agreement is a pronunciation problem. It occurs when the verb ends in difficult to pronounce sounds like -sps, -sks, and -sts. Other students have trouble with subject/verb agreement only when the subject is a word like *everyone* or *nobody*. For some other students the problem may be more basic because their spoken language differs in this particular respect from written English.

It is neither laziness nor a lack of intelligence which creates a difference between the written and some spoken versions of our language, nor is there a logical reason to prefer the written version over the spoken language. However, there is no question that formal writing requires subject/verb agreement, and if you want to be taken seriously in situations where formal writing is expected, you will have to acquire this skill. You and your instructor can use the preview tape to diagnose which type of subject/verb agreement problem, if any, you have.

Before the age of twelve, most people learn any language they are exposed to and have any reason to want to learn just by being around people who speak it. Some children learn two or three quite different languages this way. After that age, however, learning another language or even learning the written version of your own language becomes much more difficult. It is almost as if there were a language processing machine in the brain which turns itself off after it is no longer needed. Therefore, if your spoken language doesn't share all the features of the written language (and *no one's* does completely) and if your language machine has already shut itself off, you will have to use a different strategy for attacking this problem than simply exposing yourself to a lot of standard writing and speech.

Whatever the cause of your subject/verb agreement problem, you should begin to attack the problem by learning this very simple rule:

> **If the subject of a sentence is *he, she,* or *it* or if you can substitute *he, she,* or *it* for the subject, in the present tense (when the action of the verb means right now or continually) the verb ends in *s*.**

All you have to do is find the subject of the verb, work out its pronoun substitute, then apply the present tense verb rule. There is probably not much use in trying to make your subjects agree with your verbs if you can't find them; therefore, it is just as important that you learn to find your subjects and verbs as it is to memorize the rule which is the basis of this chapter.

In the beginning of this chapter, we review subject/verb recognition briefly. If you need additional practice, you can work through the exercises in Appendix A.

Chapter 2: Present Tense Verbs

Once you have conquered subject/verb agreement in the present tense, you have mastered the most difficult problem with standard English verbs.

FINDING SUBJECTS AND VERBS

The subject of a sentence is traditionally defined as the noun or noun substitute (the person, place, or thing) the sentence is about. The verb or verb phrase in the sentence tells what the subject *is* or *does* or *has*. Most of the time the verb relates an action, but often it shows only existence or occurrence.

Every sentence has two things: a subject (a noun or noun substitute like a pronoun) and a verb (or verb phrase).

Subject	Verb
Mary	swims.
The truck	crashed.
I	understand.
They	whisper.
You	should work.

If the subject *you* is being commanded to perform some task, we may say the subject is *understood*.

	Subject	Verb
statement	You	can go.
command	(You)	Go.
command		Listen.
command		Stop.

You is the only subject which can be *understood*.

Pronouns

The subject of every sentence can be replaced by a pronoun. You should recognize the subject pronouns on sight.

	Subject	Verb
SINGULAR:	I	win
The subject is	You	guess
one and only one	He	knowS
person, place,	She	sewS
or thing.	It	growS
PLURAL:	We	jump
The subject is	You (all)	learn
more than one	They	ask
person, place,		
or thing.		

Every noun subject can be replaced by a pronoun:

Mary = she
the boy = he
the stoves = they
a threat = it
winning = it
the Mayor and her dog = they
Millie and I = we
people who read this book = you (all)

If the subject can be replaced by *he, she,* or *it,* in the present tense the verb ends in *s.*

EXERCISE 2–1

In present time (right now) the verb that goes with *he, she,* or *it* always ends in *s.* Write the correct form of the verb in parentheses for the subject given.

	Subject	Verb	
1.	He	(know)	*knows*
2.	She	(wish)	
3.	It	(believe)	
4.	We	(go)	
5.	You	(try)	
6.	They	(skip)	
7.	I	(drive)	
8.	We	(study)	
9.	He	(write)	
10.	They	(juggle)	
11.	It	(seem)	
12	She	(begin)	
13.	They	(frown)	
14.	He	(illustrate)	
15.	You and I	(buy)	
16.	They	(shine)	
17.	You (all)	(talk)	
18.	They	(run)	
19.	It	(empty)	
20.	He	(lie)	

A Word About Time and Tense

If you've been having trouble with verbs and if you've given the matter any thought, you probably already realize that real time and verb tense aren't always the same thing.

Chapter 2: Present Tense Verbs

I will walk on the moon has a future meaning, but so does **I am going to walk on the moon.**
We say **I knew that Paris *was*** (past tense) **the capital of France,** even though it still **is** (present tense).
And if **Grandpa writes a letter to the editor whenever he is annoyed,** we know that he has done this in the ***past,*** that he may be doing it right now in the ***present,*** and we expect that he will continue to do it in the ***future.***

So, you ask, can a reasonably intelligent human being who has little trouble with ***real time*** ever be confident about standard English ***verb tense?*** If you can find your verbs in a sentence and if you know what their subjects are, you can. You really only have three things to learn:

1. Present tense, which for all practical purposes means subject/verb agreement; this is what you will be working on in this chapter.
2. Past tense, which is not too bad because it makes a little bit of sense; when something is definitely over and done with, it's in the past.
3. The auxiliaries (helping verbs), which we will cover in the next chapter. You'll soon notice that if a verb phrase starts with some form of *do, have,* or *be,* you can treat it as if it were in either the *past* or the *present* tense. The other auxiliaries (*can, could, shall, should,* etc.) carry subtle differences in meaning but don't really tell you when in real time the action in the sentence *did* or *will* take place. For example, to say that you *should unplug* the TV before working on it can mean that you have made this mistake in the past or that you're in the process of making this mistake right now and ought to do something about it or that in the future you are not supposed to make this mistake.

The Present Tense

When you are describing something as it is in the process of happening or *as if* it were happening at this very moment, you should use the present tense.

Sometimes, however, the action of the verb in the present tense may not really be happening right now. General truths (like **knowledge is power** or **time is money**) are usually in the present tense. And things that happen over and over again (like **my car usually dies in cold weather** and **Grandpa always writes letters**) aren't happening right at this moment (it's 95° outside, and Grandpa is in the shower), but you get the idea. When something happens continually, it is in the present tense.

If a verb does not have an auxiliary (a helper), it must be in the present tense (right now or continually) or the simple past tense (already over). **In the present tense, the verb must always agree with its subject.** This means that if the subject is *he, she,* or *it,* or if you can substitute *he, she,* or *it* for the subject, the verb ends in *s*. If the subject is *I, you, we,* or *they,* or if you can substitute *I, you, we,* or *they* for the subject, the verb *never* adds an *s*.

Subject	Verb
He	smileS.
John	smileS.

Chapter 2: Present Tense Verbs

Subject	Verb
She	walkS.
Bernadine	walkS.
It	stopS.
The computer	stopS.
The boyS	smile.
The girlS	work.
The telephoneS	ring.
The hornS	honk.
The bombS	explode.
We	agree.
Steve and I	agree.
You	win.
They	answer.

Notice that making your subjects and verbs agree is **not** a visual decision. In the present tense if there is a plural subject or if the subject is *I, you, we,* or *they,* there can*NOT* be an *s* on the verb.

Nonstandard	Standard
TeacherS talkS.	TeacherS talk.
The cop shout.	The cop shoutS.
I knowS.	I know.

EXERCISE 2–2

In the first twenty-five sentences below the subject is set in bold type. List the pronoun you can substitute for it in the blank to the left and circle the correct verb. In the next twenty-five sentences underline the subject, and then go on to finish the exercise.

they 1. Sad **movies** (make, makes) me cry.

_____ 2. **Darlene** (know, knows) the answer.

_____ 3. A rainy **day** (ruin, ruins) the picnic.

_____ 4. My **husband** (need, needs) a new raincoat.

_____ 5. The **teacher** (praise, praises) her students.

_____ 6. **Charity** (begin, begins) at home.

_____ 7. **Nobody** (know, knows) my name.

_____ 8. The **trains** (arrive, arrives) on time.

_____ 9. Two **men** (buy, buys) cameras.

_____ 10. An **announcer** (appear, appears) on the screen.

_____ 11. The **spaghetti** (taste, tastes) terrible.

_____ 12. **Detroit** and **Chicago** (have, has) special problems.

_____ 13. **Swimming** (take, takes) endurance.

Chapter 2: Present Tense Verbs

_____ 14. The **lifeguard** (adjust, adjusts) her cap.
_____ 15. **Sonia** (fix, fixes) elevators.
_____ 16. An efficient rapid transit **system** (cost, costs) money.
_____ 17. The **dictionary** (contain, contains) definitions.
_____ 18. **Ronald** and **I** (want, wants) to move.
_____ 19. The **subject** and **verb** (agree, agrees).
_____ 20. A young **lawyer** (call, calls) me up.
_____ 21. Mother's old **bathrobe** (dissolve, dissolves) in the wash.
_____ 22. Dad's old **slippers** (smell, smells).
_____ 23. Her basement **apartment** (flood, floods) regularly.
_____ 24. **Love** (make, makes) the world go round.
_____ 25. Monarch **butterflies** sometimes (wander, wanders) a thousand miles.
_____ 26. The minor annoyance (upset, upsets) the class.
_____ 27. Creativity (are, is) rare.
_____ 28. Creative people (are, is) rare.
_____ 29. Olives (improve, improves) martinis.
_____ 30. The salesperson (look, looks) annoyed.
_____ 31. Your nasty disposition (drive, drives) me crazy.
_____ 32. Diagnostic testing (occur, occurs) on Monday.
_____ 33. Ken Kramer (refuse, refuses) to babysit.
_____ 34. Bosak's bar (serve, serves) a good drink.
_____ 35. Richard and I (buy, buys) a television.
_____ 36. The electronics industry (offer, offers) many job opportunities.
_____ 37. Technicians (earn, earns) good money.
_____ 38. Communication (lead, leads) to understanding.
_____ 39. Jack's mother-in-law (drink, drinks) beer.
_____ 40. My grandparents (own, owns) their own home.
_____ 41. The Affirmative Action Program (help, helps) the situation.
_____ 42. Fred and Irene (buy, buys) groceries once a month.
_____ 43. The television assembler (find, finds) the problem.
_____ 44. The ghost's sudden appearance (frighten, frightens) Joseph.
_____ 45. Mary (smile, smiles) wisely.
_____ 46. The young monk (leave, leaves) the Chinese monastery.
_____ 47. The vet (care, cares) for the lamb.
_____ 48. Both pens (need, needs) ink.
_____ 49. Her qualifications (impress, impresses) the interviewer.
_____ 50. Your suggestion (seem, seems) a good one.

To Be or Not To Be

The most troublesome verb you will ever have to learn is the verb *be*. It has twice as many forms as any other verb, and they show up in your writing consistently and inevitably. You cannot write without them. Since you can't avoid them, you must learn them. Notice, however, that the verb which goes with *he, she,* and *it* and their substitutes ends in *s* in accordance with the rule.

I *am*	we *are*
you *are*	you (all) *are*
he, she, it *is*	they *are*

EXERCISE 2–3

Fill in the correct present tense form of *be* in the verb space to complete the sentences below. One of the above pronouns can be substituted for each of the subjects given.

	Subject	Verb	Complement
1.	Mary	*was*	tall.
2.	My sister and brother		younger than I am.
3.	The chair		old.
4.	The helicopters		grounded.
5.	An apple		red.
6.	Discarded tennis shoes		best forgotten.
7.	Broken promises		hard to forget.
8.	The destruction		very ugly.
9.	Jesse and Sandy		terrible liars.
10.	Swinging from a vine		not chic.
11.	The janitor of the buildings		Martha's brother.
12.	The abandoned dogs		at the Animal Shelter.
13.	The secretary		efficient.
14.	The telephones in the office		black.
15.	The lady who answered the questions		a wealthy widow.
16.	Janice		tired.
17.	Studying late		bad for the eyes.
18.	The bears in the zoo		always hungry.
19.	Near misses		heartbreaking.
20.	Harold's idea		unworkable.

Subject/Verb Agreement in the Past Tense

The ONLY past tense verb which has more than one form for different persons is the verb *be*. If the subject is *he, she,* or *it* or if you can substitute *he, she,* or *it* for the subject, the verb ends in *s* just as in the present tense.

I *was*	we *were*
you *were*	you (all) *were*
he, she, it *was*	they *were*

Chapter 2: Present Tense Verbs

EXERCISE 2–4

Fill in *was* or *were* in the verb space below to complete the sentence. One of the above pronouns can be substituted for each subject given.

	Subject	Verb	Complement
1.	The man	*was*	nearsighted.
2.	The woman		lost.
3.	The students		rowdy.
4.	Driving a sports car		fun.
5.	Karen and Dick		both candidates.
6.	You people in the third row		disruptive.
7.	A siren		audible.
8.	TV repair people		well-paid.
9.	Liberated men		secure men.
10.	Grocery stores in the ghetto		risky businesses.
11.	Young authors		not welcome.
12.	Two water buffalo		in the mine field.
13.	Many air conditioners		over-loaded.
14.	A few of the children		dismissed.
15.	All the uncles and aunts		present.
16.	The marigolds		waterlogged.
17.	Book orders for the summer		due last week.
18.	Their daily schedule		hectic.
19.	The American tradition		belittled in Kvosk.
20.	His most reluctant responses		about inflation.

Be for Recurrent Actions

Some people use the verb *be* to express an action or state which occurs over and over again. Often the verb *be* is accompanied by adverbs of time which tell us that the action or state is a regularly occurring one.

> Usually Carolyn **be** on time.
> Every day the mail carrier **be** here by 1:00.
> Mostly Marvin **be** right.

Standard written English lacks a special form of *be* to indicate regularly occurring action or state of being. It counts on the adverbs by themselves to provide this information (*usually, every day, sometimes*). The word *be* is only written when it has a helping verb.

> Usually Carolyn **is (was)** on time.
> Every day the mail carrier **is (was)** here by 1:00.
> Most of the time Marvin **is (was)** right.
> Sometimes there **is** a good show on TV.
> There **must be** a reason for his behavior.

It is also important to note that in written English the *be* forms cannot be omitted. Even though the meaning of *John tired* is perfectly clear, the verb must be present: *John is tired* or *John's tired*.

EXERCISE 2-5

In the sentences below standardize all nonstandard verb forms. Watch out for subject/verb agreement in the present tense and in the simple past tense. Most of these sentences can be read as present, past, or future time. Choose one.

1. "You wrong, George."
2. The street empty.
3. This yellow shirt the right size.
4. Computers usually be at fault when something go wrong.
5. He be a bigger fool than I thought.
6. Mona happy.
7. That your car?
8. There her supervisor.
9. Every time the judge speak, the lawyers be silent.
10. Russ be a stick-in-the-mud sometimes.
11. Frank be here every day.
12. She always be messing around.
13. Sheila my best friend.
14. Joseph be here next week.
15. If somebody hit her, Darlene be mad.

The Contraction *n't*

The contraction *n't* stands for *not*. The apostrophe (') replaces the *o* in *not*. Don't let it confuse you when you work on subject/verb agreement. In the present tense, if the subject can be replaced by *he*, *she*, or *it*, the contraction is *isn't*. In the past tense, if the subject can be replaced by *he*, *she*, or *it*, the contraction is *wasn't*.

EXERCISE 2-6

Fill in *isn't* or *aren't* below to complete the sentence.

Chapter 2: Present Tense Verbs

	Subject	Verb + not	Complement
1.	Ralph	isn't	the boss.
2.	The boss and his secretary		friends.
3.	Those lawyers		rich.
4.	Beets		expensive.
5.	Winning the race		important.
6.	The men in the hallway		hungry.
7.	His new shoes		comfortable.
8.	Jim		busy.
9.	The report		complete.
10.	The clowns		happy.
11.	The refugees		very well-dressed.
12.	Subject/verb agreement		difficult.
13.	Bob and Carol		great dancers.
14.	A rude person		well liked.
15.	Garage sales		profitable.
16.	His uncle and aunt		swingers.
17.	Red wine		right with fish.
18.	You and I		friends.
19.	Babysitting for the Greggs		very lucrative.
20.	To know what to do		important.

EXERCISE 2-7

Fill in *wasn't* or *weren't* below and any appropriate subject or complement where necessary.

	Subject	Verb + not	Complement
1.	The chairperson	wasn't	ready.
2.	Most protestors		violent.
3.	Playing cards		his only skill.
4.	The concert		remarkable.
5.	His parties		well-planned.
6.	The maple leaf		red or orange.
7.	Seven wishes		enough for Fred.
8.	I		happy.
9.	The women		interested in excuses.
10.	It		my fault.
11.	The couple chosen		John and Deborah.
12.	Columbia University		interested in Joe.

Chapter 2: Present Tense Verbs

	Subject	Verb + not	Complement
13.	You		very forgiving.
14.	The Board of Governors		responsible.
15.	His vocabulary		developed enough.
16.	Your idea		workable.
17.	Most of the dogs		immunized.
18.	One of the day care centers		understaffed.
19.	To walk on the ceiling		easy.
20.	Her best friend		available at night.

EXERCISE 2–8

In the verb slot below we have noted *Pr* for present and *P* for past tense. Paying attention to agreement and the meaning you wish to convey, fill in *is, are, was, were, isn't, aren't, wasn't,* or *weren't.*

	Subject	Verb	Complement
1.	The boy	Pr	sick.
2.	A girl	P	careful.
3.	Men	Pr	cads.
4.	Women	P	persuasive.
5.	Each person	Pr	independent.
6.	All people	Pr	sympathetic.
7.	Some cows	P	brown.
8.	Sneezing	Pr	noisy.
9.	My tugboat	P	very small.
10.	Her card file	P	inaccurate.
11.	This mud pile	P	muddy.
12.	Cafeterias	P	painful experiences.
13.	Hamburgers	Pr	greasy.
14.	Children	Pr	always obedient.
15.	Trains and planes	P	late.
16.	Several windows	Pr	open.
17.	A few elephants	P	white.
18.	The zoo	P	full.
19.	An Indian	Pr	a wary ally.
20.	Martha and Earline	P	my friends.

There *Is/Are/Was/Were*

Sentences that begin with *there is, there are, there was,* and *there were* create a special subject/verb agreement problem because the subject follows its verb. *There* is not the subject; it is just a space holder in the sentence.

Chapter 2: Present Tense Verbs

EXERCISE 2-9

Fill in *is*, *are*, *was*, or *were* in the following sentence diagram.

	Adverb	Verb	Subject
1.	There		many crowded hospitals in this city.
2.	There		one doctor for several hundred patients.
3.	There		something to think about.
4.	There		lottery tickets and the winning numbers.
5.	There		no excuse for such unprofessional behavior.
6.	There		no signals at the railroad crossing on Main Street.
7.	There		the notebooks you lost.
8.	There		five cars involved in the crash.
9.	There		a student who knows the subject.
10.	There		teachers who don't understand our problems.
11.	There		no apparent motive for the crime.
12.	There		no room in the motel.
13.	There		a few books I want to read.
14.	There		few instructors who couldn't be replaced by tape recorders.
15.	There		problems that must be solved.
16.	There		several applicants.
17.	There		only one witness.
18.	There		two boys playing basketball.
19.	There		a firefighter and a police officer.
20.	There		a dog and a cat.

Noun Determiners as Clues

Noun determiners can tell you whether the noun which follows is singular or plural; thus determiners before noun subjects can provide additional clues to subject/verb agreement. A singular noun subject requires a verb that ends in *s*; a plural noun subject does not take a verb that ends in *s*.

Even if one or more adjectives modifying the subject come between the determiner and its noun, the rule for subject/verb agreement does not change.

Several **robins** *sing*.
Several early spring **robins** *sing* outside my window.

EXERCISE 2-10

Fill in the grid with any noun you choose, then circle the correct verb.

	Determiner	Descriptive Adjective	Noun Used As Subject	Verb
1.	A few	tired	*children*	(sleep, sleeps).
2.	Every	smart		(know, knows).
3.	All	older		(curse, curses).
4.	The	yellow		(rip, rips).
5.	These	happy		(dream, dreams).
6.	That	angry		(yell, yells).
7.	Two	new		(joke, jokes).
8.	Those	friendly		(smile, smiles).
9.	A	small		(trip, trips).
10.	All	violent		(offend, offends).
11.	Both	lucky		(succeed, succeeds).
12.	One	rude		(whisper, whispers).
13.	My	best		(die, dies).
14.	Much	useless		(occur, occurs).
15.	This	irritable		(scold, scolds).
16.	All	thirsty		(drink, drinks).
17.	Most	bored		(sigh, sighs).
18.	Some	sensitive		(protest, protests).
19.	Every	nervous		(smoke, smokes).
20.	That	cowardly		(tell, tells).

Do or *Does*: The Rule's the Same

The very common verbs *do* and *does* create a special subject/verb agreement problem for many people. If the subject can be replaced by *he, she,* or *it,* the verb is *does.* Notice the *s* on the end of *does.* Spelling counts; don't write *dose,* as in a dose of medicine.

If the subject can be replaced by *I, we, you,* or *they,* the correct verb is *do.*

EXERCISE 2–11

Fill in the verb *do* or *does* in the sentences below then finish the sentence. Don't guess; work it out according to the subject/verb agreement rule!

	Subject	Verb
1.	Most airplanes	*do land safely.*
2.	The bomb	
3.	Six students	
4.	A teacher	

Chapter 2: Present Tense Verbs

	Subject	Verb
5.	Some insecticides	
6.	Each commercial	
7.	Air pollution	
8.	Cindy and I	
9.	I	
10.	Our janitor	
11.	Those dogs	
12.	Their arguments	
13.	This reporter	
14.	You	
15.	Presidential aides	

Doesn't or *Don't:* The Rule's the Same

The contraction *n't* stands for *not*. The apostrophe replaces the *o* in *not*. Don't let it confuse you when you work on subject/verb agreement. If the subject can be replaced by *he, she,* or *it,* the verb *does* plus contraction is *doesn't*. If the subject is (or can be replaced by) *I, you, we,* or *they,* the verb is *don't*.

EXERCISE 2–12

Fill in *doesn't* or *don't* below, then finish the sentence.

	Subject	Verb
1.	The nurse	*doesn't smoke.*
2.	My neighbor	
3.	He	
4.	Carl and I	
5.	Some schoolmates	
6.	Most cops	
7.	All husbands	
8.	Both typewriters	
9.	The sky	
10.	Buckets	
11.	This textbook	
12.	Several colleges	
13.	That exercise	
14.	Babysitting	
15.	Who	
16.	A vacation	

Chapter 2: Present Tense Verbs

	Subject	Verb
17.	Any information	
18.	The facts	
19.	The judges	
20.	Another courtroom	

Has/Hasn't or Have/Haven't: The Rule Doesn't Change

The verb *have* is exactly like any other present tense verb. The form that ends in *s* (*has*) is used with *he*, *she*, or *it*; use *have* everyplace else.

Even if the verb is contracted to *hasn't* or *haven't*, the rule still applies. Simply ignore the *n't* in working out the agreement.

EXERCISE 2–13

In the following grid keep your verbs in the present tense. If the subject is replaceable by *he*, *she*, or *it*, the verb should end in *s*. If the subject can be replaced by *I*, *we*, *you*, or *they*, the verb should end in *s*.

Fill in *have* or *has* in the first ten sentences. Fill in *haven't* or *hasn't* in the last five.

	Subject	Verb	Direct Object
1.	The president	*has*	his problems.
2.	All my records		scratches.
3.	The applicants		excellent references.
4.	The lawyers		a lot of unexplained money.
5.	The world		philosophers.
6.	Every society		its discontents.
7.	Those sports events		few spectators.
8.	The typists		several complaints.
9.	The plot		many twists.
10.	The hoax		an unfortunate end.
11.	An individual		time to try everything.
12.	The investigators		a lead.
13.	The Senate		any power left.
14.	The winner		a worry in the world.
15.	His ambition		anything to do with his success.

Compound Subjects

In present time (right now) the verb which goes with *he*, *she*, or *it* always ends in *s*. The verb which goes with *they* cannot end in *s*. One person equals *he* or *she*; one place or thing is called *it*. More than one person, place, or thing is

Chapter 2: Present Tense Verbs   43

referred to as *they*. When two or more subjects are joined by *and (Bill and Jean)*, the complete subject is plural and the verb cannot end in *s*.

EXERCISE 2-14

Fill in the correct form of any present tense verb and then complete the sentence with an object or complement.

	Subject	Verb	Object or Complement
1.	Dale and Polly		
2.	The girl and her mother		
3.	Many men		
4.	The women and the children		
5.	One person and a cat		
6.	All people and their dogs		
7.	The wind and rain		
8.	A cold and hungry boy		
9.	A tugboat and steamship		
10.	A card file and filing system		
11.	The mud and water		
12.	The maid and butler		
13.	Hamburgers and French fries		
14.	Joe, Sue, and Bob		
15.	Trains and planes		
16.	Winning and losing		
17.	The elephants and deer		
18.	A zoo and a zookeeper		
19.	An Indian		
20.	Martha, Sharon, and I		

Pronunciation Can Deceive You

Many people who have no other problems with subject/verb agreement consistently omit the final *s* on verbs ending in *sps, sts,* and *sks*. Because you may not hear or pronounce the *s* and because the number of words that fall into this category is relatively small, it may be helpful to thoroughly familiarize yourself with them and practice the group separately.

A {*it* / **cure**} existS.

Several {*they* / **problems**} exist.

Chapter 2: Present Tense Verbs

ST words: ca**st**, consi**st**, desi**st**, enli**st**, exi**st**, insi**st**, persi**st**, resi**st**, subsi**st**, te**st**

SP words: cla**sp**, ga**sp**, gra**sp**, ra**sp**

SK words: a**sk**, ba**sk**, ma**sk**

EXERCISE 2–15

In the sentences below, underline the subject, then write in the correctly spelled form of the verb given in parentheses to the left of each sentence below.

(exist)   1. A <u>problem</u> _exists_ .
(resist)   2. The disease _____ treatment.
(ask)   3. John _____ for too much sympathy.
(mask)   4. Her cheerfulness _____ great sorrow.
(persist) 5. The questions _____ despite a thorough investigation by the Senate Committee.
(consist) 6. The Jones family _____ of five very unusual people.
(grasp)   7. The exhausted shipwreck victims _____ the edge of the liferaft.
(subsist) 8. The elderly tenants _____ on a meagre diet of rice and beans.
(enlist)   9. The salesclerks _____ the support of the management.
(clasp)   10. The tearful child _____ her doll tightly and whimpers.
(exist)   11. Perhaps both God and Nietzsche _____ .
(consist) 12. Most workbook exercises _____ of fill-in problems.
(ask)   13. Jeff always _____ me to help him with his homework.
(persist) 14. Raymond _____ in making animal noises during our study hour.
(desist) 15. "Raymond, will you please cease and _____ ?"

Prepositional Phrases and Agreement

A prepositional phrase may come between a subject and its verb without changing the rules of agreement.

	Subject	Prepositional Phrase	Verb	Object or Complement
(He)	The boy		iS	my brother.
	The boy	in the picture	iS	my brother.
	The boy	in the pictures	iS	my brother.
(They)	The effectS		resist ☐	treatment.
	The effectS	of the disease	resist ☐	treatment.
	The effectS	of the diseases	resist ☐	treatment.

Chapter 2: Present Tense Verbs

	Subject	Prepositional Phrase	Verb	Object or Complement
(It)	Understanding		seemS	essential.
	An understanding	of the cause	seemS	essential.
	An understanding	of the causes	seemS	essential.

A prepositional phrase in this position gives more information about the subject and functions as an adjective in the sentence. **The verb must agree with the subject,** not with the object of the preposition. You may need to refer to the next page, to review the prepositions in order to recognize this construction quickly.

SOME COMMON PREPOSITIONS

WITHOUT the lake
UP the lake
UNTIL the lake
OUTSIDE the lake
BEYOND the lake
AROUND the lake
ACROSS the lake
BETWEEN the lake and the tree
OF the lake
FOR the lake
INTO the lake
OVER the lake
UPON the lake

BEFORE the lake
ABOUT the lake
BY the lake
TO the lake
IN the lake
AGAINST the lake
AT the lake
INSIDE the lake
PAST the lake

OUT OF the lake
DESPITE the lake
DOWN the lake
TOWARD the lake
ON the lake
THROUGH the lake
BENEATH the lake
UNDER the lake
UNDERNEATH the lake
WITH the lake
WITHIN the lake
LIKE the lake
UNTIL the lake

THROUGHOUT the lake
AFTER the lake
BEHIND the lake
BELOW the lake
DURING the lake
OFF the lake
OUT the lake
EXCEPT the lake
ABOVE the lake
NEAR the lake
BESIDE the lake
FROM the lake
ALONG the lake

EXERCISE 2-16

Put the prepositional phrase in parentheses and fill in any verb which completes the thought.

	Subject	Verb	Object or Complement
1.	The dresses (in my closet)	*look*	old-fashioned.
2.	The cream in my coffee		artificial.
3.	The grades on my record		hard work.
4.	The people from my class		bobby socks.
5.	The rift between us		a chasm.
6.	A path through the forest		to buried treasure.
7.	Several books on the shelf		to be reread.
8.	Reading in the dark		poor vision.
9.	The alcohol under the sink		undrinkable.
10.	Some of the jewels		a fortune.
11.	Several schools of salmon		upstream.
12.	The readings in this text		highly theoretical.
13.	To understand these problems		patience.
14.	The study of grammar		the students.
15.	The ticking of the clocks		the restless baby.
16.	The Hatfields down the street		guns.
17.	The counsel for the defense		a postponement.
18.	The boats along the shore		endless pleasure.
19.	The hose near the hydrant		water.
20.	Some of the biscuits		raisins in them.

EXERCISE 2-17

In the sentences below (1) put prepositional phrases in parentheses, (2) underline the subject, and (3) circle the verb with which the subject agrees.

1. His <u>reasons</u> (for silence) (command, (commands)) respect.
2. A phone call after ten o'clock (irritate, irritates) my father.
3. The brakes on Harlon's car (stick, sticks).
4. The intern in the emergency room (sleep, sleeps) from 11 to 6.
5. The rats under the garage (sneak, sneaks) into the trash after dark.
6. The director of security services (earn, earns) $25,000 per year.
7. The star of the Chicago Black Hawks (live, lives) quietly in River Forest.
8. The head of the philosophy department (drive, drives) a motorcycle.
9. The winds off the lake (cool, cools) Cynthia's apartment.

Chapter 2: Present Tense Verbs

10. The attendant in the laundromat (clean, cleans) the washing machines.
11. The plants in the window (appear, appears) healthy.
12. A group of school children (wait, waits) for the bus.
13. The lady in the apartment above me (exist, exists) on tunafish and lettuce.
14. Officers with their revolvers drawn (follow, follows) the murder suspect.
15. Canvassers for the Democratic candidate (pass, passes) out buttons in the shopping center.

The Indefinite Pronouns and Agreement

The indefinite pronouns cause a great deal of difficulty because it is sometimes not clear whether they are singular or plural. A few are clearly plural: *both, few, many, several,* and *others.*

	Subject	Prepositional Phrase	Verb	Object or Complement
(they)	Both	of the boxes	are	full.
(they)	Several	of the students	write	essays.

Most of the indefinite pronouns are considered singular: *everyone, anyone, someone, no one, other, somebody, anybody, everything, one, either, neither, each one, many a, nobody, another.*

	Subject	Prepositional Phrase	Verb	Object or Complement
(one person)	Someone	in the class	writeS	poems.
(one bird)	Another	of the birds	flieS	away.
(not ONE)	Neither	of the teachers	answerS	the description.

A handful of indefinite pronouns can be either singular or plural depending upon meaning: *all, any, each, none, some.*

	Subject	Prepositional Phrase	Verb	Object or Complement
(they)	All	of the boxes	are	full.
(it)	All	of the salt	iS	wet.
(they)	Some	of the students	are	late.
(it)	Some	of the mayonnaise	iS	yellow.
(it or they)	None	of these keys	work or workS	

EXERCISE 2-18

For the sentences below (1) underline the subject, (2) write its pronoun substitute on the line to the left, and (3) after have done both (1) and (2), circle the correct verb choice.

they   1. <u>All</u> of the stories of their vacation (**bore**, bores) me to tears.
_____ 2. None of the winners (want, wants) to claim the prize.
_____ 3. Someone in this class (are, is) going to forget the teacher's name.
_____ 4. Everybody (take, takes) a detour around my home town.
_____ 5. Several of the buildings near the lake (need, needs) repair.
_____ 6. Another of my childhood heroes (have, has) died.
_____ 7. Some of the land beyond the prairie (belong, belongs) to the Sioux.
_____ 8. Either of them (are, is) all right with me.
_____ 9. Everything in the newspapers (depress, depresses) me except the funnies.
_____ 10. Many a tear (fall, falls) in vain.
_____ 11. Each of the cars (are, is) missing some vital parts.
_____ 12. All of the time (were, was) wasted on trivialities.
_____ 13. Much of his speech (consist, consists) of pompous noise.
_____ 14. Nobody (know, knows) the trouble I've seen.
_____ 15. Something in these sentences (look, looks) deceptively difficult.

EXERCISE 2-19   *write*

Show that you understand that prepositional phrases coming between the subject and verb do not affect subject/verb agreement. Write a ten-sentence description of an event as if you were observing it right now and insert one or more prepositional phrases between all your subjects and verbs, keeping most of your verbs in the present tense. Put prepositional phrases in parentheses, underline the subject, and circle the verb. Most of these prepositional phrases will be adding details about your subject. If you have trouble getting started, you may wish to begin with one of the following sentences:

A **<u>car</u>** (with no headlights) (**enters**) the expressway.
              or
Three **<u>guys</u>** (from another neighborhood) (**invade**) the bar.
              or
The **<u>sheriff</u>** (of Dry Gulch) (**needs**) a gun.

Adjective Clauses and Agreement

Another construction which comes between the subject and its verb is the adjective clause. It adds descriptive information about the subject but does not change the agreement.

Chapter 2: Present Tense Verbs

Subject	Adjective Clause	Verb	Object, Complement, or Adverb
The cat	which is fat	eatS	dog food.
The fat cat		eatS	dog food.
The boat ride	which seems long	goES	quickly.
The long boat ride		goES	quickly.

You should treat the adjective clause like the prepositional phrase and ignore it when working on agreement. **The verb must agree with the subject** not with some word in the adjective clause.

Agreement Within the Adjective Clause Itself

Since the adjective clause may also be in the present tense, you may have to examine it more carefully to make *its* subject and verb agree.

The adjective clause may have all the elements of a complete sentence but will not make sense when read by itself.

The relative pronouns *which, that,* and *who* may function as the subject of the clause.

Subject	Verb	Object or Complement
which	is	fat
which	are	fat
who	is	president
who	are	presidents
that	seems	long
that	seem	long

	Subject	Adjective Clause	Verb	Object
which = dog	My dog	which iS fat	eatS	bones.
which = parakeets	Your parakeetS	which are fat	need	exercise.

In the first adjective clause *which* refers to the singular subject *my dog*. In the second sentence *which* refers to the plural subject *your parakeets*. The relative pronoun is not always the subject of the adjective clause, however. And sometimes there is no relative pronoun to signal the beginning of the adjective clause. To further complicate matters, the adjective clause may be in one tense and the main clause may be in another. For example:

Subject	Adjective Clause	Verb	Object
The dog	THAT John bought last week	has	fleas.
The dog	John bought last week	has	fleas.
The parakeet	THAT John wants	ate	sunflower seeds for lunch.
The parakeet	John wants	ate	sunflower seeds for lunch.

EXERCISE 2-20

In the sentences below *which*, *that*, and *who* function as the subjects of adjective clauses. The word to which the pronoun refers is the subject of the sentence. First make the verb in the adjective clause agree with its subject; then choose the correct main verb.

	Noun Determiner	Subject	Adjective Clause	Main Verb	Object or Complement
1.	The	parakeets	which (eat, eats) flies	(are, is)	fat.
2.	That	book	that (are, is) on the table	(look, looks)	old.
3.	The	man	who (curse, curses) often	(are, is)	lazy.
4.	The	rug	which (cover, covers) the floor	(need, needs)	cleaning.
5.	All her	papers	which (discuss, discusses) John Dewey	(bore, bores)	me.
6.	The	rain	that (fall, falls) incessantly here	(drown, drowns)	my flowers.
7.		Obesity	which (threaten, threatens) Americans	(amuse, amuses)	the French.
8.	The	greatness	that Jonathan (crave, craves)	(destroy, destroys)	his peace of mind.
9.	The	music	that (haunt, haunts) the composer	(refuse, refuses)	to be written.
10.	The	worms	that (invade, invades) my tomato plants	(strip, strips)	the vines.
11.		Dora	who (track, tracks) mud on the carpet	(deserve, deserves)	to clean the carpet.
12.		Dora	who (are, is) forty-seven years old	(act, acts)	like a child.
13.		Discipline	which (are, is) difficult to administer	(become, becomes)	impossible.
14.		Exercise	which sometimes (are, is) tiring	(appall, appalls)	the out-of-shape.
15.	Those	executives	who (hate, hates) their nine-to-five jobs	(drink, drinks)	martinis.

50

EXERCISE 2-21

In the sentences below *which*, *that*, *whose*, and *whom* do not function as the subject of the adjective clause; however, the word to which the pronoun refers is still the subject of the sentence. Find the subject of the adjective clause and circle its correct verb. Then choose the correct main verb.

	Noun Determiner	Subject	Adjective Clause	Verb	Object or Complement
1.	The	parakeets	which John (want, wants) to buy	(are, is)	fat.
2.	The	book	that he (study, studies)	(look, looks)	old.
3.	The	person	to whom challenges (are, is) alien	(are, is)	lazy.
4.	The	rug	that the children (play, plays) on	(need, needs)	cleaning.
5.	All her	papers	which she (type, types) herself	(bore, bores)	me.
6.	The	rain	which the meteorologist (forecast, forecasts)	(drown, drowns)	my roses.
7.		Obesity	which the models (fear, fears)	(amuse, amuses)	the French sculptor.
8.	The	greatness	that my brother (seek, seeks)	(destroy, destroys)	my peace of mind
9.	The	music	that the composer (imagine, imagines)	(refuse, refuses)	to be written.
10.	The	aphids	that I (spray, sprays) daily	(strip, strips)	the vines.
11.		Dora	to whom time (mean, means) nothing	(deserve, deserves)	to be fired.
12.		Dora	whose conscience never (bother, bothers) her	(require, requires)	discipline.
13.		Discipline	which her mother (hesitate, hesitates) to use	(become, becomes)	impossible.
14.		Exercise	which Martha (detest, detests)	(appall, appalls)	the out-of-shape.
15.	Those	executives	to whom money (is, are) everything	(drink, drinks)	martinis.
16.	The	reason	Dan (want, wants) to go to Arizona	(are, is)	not clear to me.
17.	The	ships	the divers (find, finds) off Sanibel Island	(contain, contains)	gold.
18.	These	bottles	Jackson (keep, keeps) in the lab	(smell, smells)	peculiar.
19.	All the	reasons	he (give, gives)	(sound, sounds)	phoney.
20.	Every	soap opera	that Bruce (watch, watches)	(are, is)	disgusting.

51

52 Chapter 2: Present Tense Verbs

EXERCISE 2–22

In the sentences below (1) put the adjective clause in parentheses, (2) underline the subject of the sentence, and (3) circle the verb with which the subject of the sentence agrees.

1. The car that I want (cost, costs) twenty-two hundred dollars.
2. The bills which she receives in the mail (demand, demands) payment.
3. The bracelet that he holds in his hands (need, needs) a new lock.
4. A man who shouts a lot usually (get, gets) shouted at in return.
5. The girl to whom you refer (win, wins) the State Lottery regularly.
6. The pennies that he receives in change (go, goes) into his son's piggy bank.
7. The bank to which I refer (sit, sits) on his son's dresser.
8. The guy she's going to marry (owe, owes) money to every store in town.
9. The carpets that I loved yesterday (seem, seems) ugly today.
10. Meals that require a lot of watching (aren't, isn't) for me.
11. Phone calls that interrupt meals (drive, drives) my mother crazy.
12. Bill, whose mother you just met, (work, works) for a bank.
13. *The Great Gatsby*, which was recently filmed, (deserve, deserves) to be reread.
14. The after-shave lotion that Norman received from his wife (make, makes) me sneeze.
15. The fan belt, which really belongs to a larger car, (slip, slips) off every few miles.
16. Aunt Matilda, who once worked in a circus, (swing, swings) from the light fixture on Thursday nights.
17. Books that have many misprints in them (annoy, annoys) me.
18. The money that I make (disappear, disappears) rapidly.
19. The coffee grounds which I put in a pile near the garage (attract, attracts) worms.
20. Nora's guests who spend the night (eat, eats) yogurt and soybean pancakes for breakfast.
21. The rings I buy (are, is) made of silver.
22. The way Martha understands math (please, pleases) her mother.
23. The shoes the department stores (offer, offers) are too expensive.
24. The lunch he brought (look, looks) well-balanced.
25. The words George (learn, learns) to spell (are, is) not difficult.

EXERCISE 2–23 *write*

Show that you understand that adjective clauses coming between the subject and verb do not affect subject/verb agreement. Write a ten-sentence description of an event as if you were observing it and insert an adjective clause between every subject and verb, keeping most of your verbs in the present tense. Put the adjective clause in parentheses, underline the subject, and circle its verb. Most of these adjective clauses will be adding details about your subject.

If you have trouble getting started, you may wish to begin with one of the following sentences:

The Martians (who invade our planet) visit a singles' bar.

or

Chapter 2: Present Tense Verbs

The gift (that my girlfriend bought me for Christmas) shocks most people.
or
The giant ants (which live in our city's subway tunnel) chew their way to the surface of the street.

EXERCISE 2-24

Circle the correct verb choice.

Carpentry Blues

1. My landlord (like, likes) to use two young carpenters from down the block, Kirby and Claiborne.
2. He (use, uses) them rather than other carpenters for one big reason.
3. These two (are, is) cheaper.
4. Unfortunately they (choose, chooses) odd hours for work.
5. Also they (work, works) only when they (have, has) nothing better to do.
6. When one of these carpenters (arrive, arrives), he immediately (ask, asks) for a cup of coffee.
7. Then he (smoke, smokes); smoking (are, is) time-consuming.
8. Both of them (love, loves) for me to receive phone calls.
9. This (give, gives) them the opportunity to tell me (what's, whats) wrong with my life.
10. Meanwhile plaster dust (infiltrate, infiltrates) my nose and ears.
11. Lumber and tools (litter, litters) my floors.
12. Soon the carpenters (begin, begins) giving out my address and phone number to their friends.
13. In the middle of the afternoon strange friends (arrive, arrives) with macrobiotic food in paper bags.
14. They all (eat, eats) and (smoke, smokes) a lot.
15. Loud music (flow, flows) from their transistor radios.
16. An ill-bred dog (accompany, accompanies) them.
17. It (chew, chews) my shoes and (soil, soils) the carpet.
18. The carpenters (do, does) not notice this.
19. They (concern, concerns) themselves with selecting materials unavailable at the neighborhood lumber yards.
20. Thus there (are, is) long waits for lumber and plasterboard.
21. This waiting (give, gives) them time to explore my record collection.
22. Carpenters like these (spend, spends) a lot of time explaining how institutions (exploit, exploits) individuals.
23. I (listen, listens) with amusement.
24. They (have, has) taken advantage of my patience and hospitality for weeks.
25. There (are, is) of course, an explanation.
26. Perhaps they are graduate students in psychology who (are, is) studying the effects of stress on the urban, female apartment dweller.
27. If so, my landlord (betray, betrays) fiendish qualities in offering me as a subject.
28. I (cry, cries) a lot; I (bite, bites) my nails and (grind, grinds) my teeth; I (hate, hates) carpenters, and now I even (suspect, suspects) him.
29. Life in the big city (exact, exacts) its toll.

EXERCISE 2-25

Choose the correct verb. Underline the subject with which it agrees.

Little Riding Hood Revisited

1. Little Red Riding Hood (live, lives) with her parents in a little white cottage in a valley.
2. An itinerant reformer (visit, visits) her town and (convert, converts) Little Red Riding Hood.
3. Her parents (sigh, sighs) when they (remember, remembers) how sweet she used to be.
4. Now she (pass, passes) out pamphlets on a variety of subjects and constantly (tell, tells) them to reform.
5. Her good works (make, makes) her famous but unpopular.
6. Her little friends no longer (invite, invites) her to their birthday parties.
7. She (want, wants) to change others, not just herself.
8. Her mother (hate, hates) to be stuck in the house with her.
9. Little Red Riding Hood's lectures to her parents (annoy, annoys) her mother though they (amuse, amuses) her father.
10. Her father (work, works) all day, so he (miss, misses) the worst of her aggressive piety.
11. Billy Watkins (have, has) a birthday party and (don't, doesn't) invite Little Red Riding Hood.
12. Her mother (suggest, suggests) that she ought to visit her grandmother.
13. Little Red Riding Hood (agree, agrees) to go, and her mother (fill, fills) a basket with Christmas cookies.
14. Secretly Little Red Riding Hood (empty, empties) out the cookies and (replace, replaces) them with pamphlets.
15. She (put, puts) on her special cape, (kiss, kisses) her mother, and (skip, skips) out the door.
16. Little Red Riding Hood's mother (wave, waves) good-bye, and she and the next door neighbor (sit, sits) down for a cup of coffee.
17. They (shake, shakes) their heads and (hope, hopes) someone (knock, knocks) some sense into Little Red Riding Hood.
18. Little Red Riding Hood (stroll, strolls) through the wood to grandmother's house with her basket.
19. Woodland creatures (listen, listens) to her sermonizing with alarm.
20. Little Red Riding Hood (arrive, arrives) at grandmother's house and (knock, knocks) at the door.
21. "Come in, dear," the person in the bed (croak, croaks).
22. Little Red Riding Hood (enter, enters) and (stare, stares).
23. "Dear Grandmother, you (look, looks) awful," Little Red Riding Hood (say, says). "Have you remembered the Bolivian killer bees in your will? They're an endangered species. No one likes them."
24. Unbeknownst to Little Red Riding Hood, a wolf had eaten grandmother and now (wear, wears) grandmother's clothes.
25. "Grandmother, what a big nose you have!" Little Red Riding Hood (notice, notices).
26. "The better to smell you with, my dear," (answer, answers) the wolf, although a cold and sore throat (bother, bothers) it.
27. "Grandmother, what big eyes you have!" Little Red Riding Hood (volunteer, volunteers) next.
28. "The better to see you with, my dear," the wolf in grandmother's clothes (say, says).
29. "Grandmother, what a big mouth you have!" (exclaim, exclaims) Little Red Riding Hood. "You (are, is) drooling too."
30. "The better to eat you with, my dear," the wolf (growl, growls) as it (leap, leaps) at her across the bed.

Chapter 2: Present Tense Verbs

31. The growls (alert, alerts) Little Red Riding Hood to the danger she's in, but she (don't, doesn't) run.
32. Instead she (whip, whips) out a handful of pamphlets and (cram, crams) them down the wolf's sore throat.
33. The pamphlets (choke, chokes) the wolf, and it (fall, falls) back on the bed gasping for breath.
34. As Little Red Riding Hood (beat, beats) the wolf with her basket, she (rant, rants) about political corruption. A police officer (pass, passes).
35. The wolf's cries (attract, attracts) the passing police officer who (enter, enters) the house and (stop, stops) Little Red Riding Hood.
36. The wolf and Little Red Riding Hood (scream, screams) and (shout, shouts), so the cop (run, runs) them both in.
37. The police department eventually (release, releases) Little Red Riding Hood to the custody of her parents, and they never (let, lets) her forget it.

TRANSFERRING YOUR SKILL TO WRITING

The pre- and posttests for this chapter ask you to choose the correct form of some frequently used present tense verbs. We selected the verbs to test from a list of words used most frequently by the general population. Of course, the especially important verbs for you to study are the ones you yourself use frequently in your writing. Everyone uses the forms of *be*, *do*, and *have*, as well as their contracted forms, frequently. In addition to those, however, we urge you to analyze the special verbs that give you trouble or the types of sentences that cause you to lose sight of what the true subject of the sentence is.

Whenever you make a subject/verb agreement error, analyze your mistake. Can you find the subject of the verb? Do you know the agreement rule by heart? Figure out the source of the problem and get help to solve it.

EXERCISE 2–26 — write

Write an essay free of present tense subject/verb agreement mistakes. Your instructor may assign an in-class paper or may wish to have you write on one of the following topics:

How to break a bad habit
or
A book/movie/event that had special significance for me

REVIEW _____ two

The sentences in this exercise are provided to help you check your progress in this chapter and to prepare you for what you'll find in the posttest. For the answers to this exercise, check with your instructor or tutor or listen to the appropriate audio tape.

Edit the following sentences for mistakes in subject/verb agreement. Make any necessary changes on incorrect verbs. Do not change the nouns in the sentence.

1. My mother always say to look before you leap.

2. That car between the two "No Parking" signs don't have a prayer of escaping a ticket.

3. Every morning Lee and his sister be late for school.

4. The recipes on the back of the pancake mix box makes my mouth water.

5. The man who is standing in my checkout line insist I shortchanged him.

6. In math class Julio sometimes asks several questions at a time.

7. There was three cars parked in front of your house.

8. Does the North Judson and Jamesville police officers drive Corvette squadcars?

9. Alvin told Clara that William think he's too important to answer phones.

10. The contents of the hold of the pirate ship which was recently discovered off the coast of Sanibel Island reveal the pirates was fond of gold, silver, and rubies.

chapter 3

VERBS AND VERB PHRASES

PREVIEW _____ three

The sentences in the exercise below preview the skills and principles you'll learn in this chapter. For the answers to this exercise, check with your instructor or tutor or listen to the appropriate audio tape.
Circle the correct choice.

1. The men should (stop, stops, stopped, stopping) complaining.
                         A   B   C   D

2. Last week my grandmother did (forget, forgets, forgot, forgotten) my name, but she (do, does) remember it now.

3. Orestes called the credit card company and angrily (ask, asks, asked, asking) for a duplicate bill.

4. Last October Robin (see, sees, saw, seen, seeing) the light and went to Tibet.

5. When Viking I landed, the Martians (choose, chooses, chose, choosed, chosen, choosing) not to show themselves.

6. The guy from the tenth floor (have, has) (call, calls, called, calling) Doreena several times.

7. Wendell was dragged into the bathroom and (was, were) (throw, throwed, threw, thrown) under the shower.

8. Waldo (is, are) (open, opened, opening) all the windows to let the rain in.

9. You might have (run, runs, ran, running) for president.

10. Jose should have been (use, used, using) to his wife's appearance since she had been (use, used, using) white lipstick for months.

INTRODUCTION

Before we begin to work on verbs and verb phrases, you should be sure that you understand the difference between time and tense which we first discussed when we talked about present tense verbs in the last chapter.

If a verb does not have an auxiliary (a helper), it must be either in the present tense or the simple past tense. In the present tense, the verb must always agree with its subject; in the past tense, except for *was* and *were*, there is no agreement problem. Whatever the subject, the verb remains unchanged.

There is often a great difference from one part of the country to another in matters of pronunciation. For example, if you were from Boston, you might say that you must "pahk the cah" and be perfectly well understood by other Bostonians. However, if you *write* the same phrase, you must spell out "park the car." In the same way you may say, "Yesterday I *ask* my teacher for the assignment," and be perfectly well understood; however, since the action of asking was completed in the past, you must *write:* "Yesterday I *asked* my teacher for the assignment."

REGULAR PAST TENSE VERBS

Regular verbs in the past tense end in *d* or *ed*. Sometimes you will not be able to hear or comfortably pronounce this ending; nevertheless, you must write it. There are fewer than 200 *irregular* verbs that do not follow this pattern; they can be learned individually and in groups.

	PRESENT	PAST
Regular:	ask (s)	asked
	awaken (s)	awakened
	boil (s)	boiled
	jump (s)	jumped
	mumble (s)	mumbled
Irregular:	sing	sang
	BE (am, is, are)	were (was)
	have (has)	had
	do (does)	did
	teach (es)	taught

EXERCISE 3-1

The verbs in parentheses in the following exercise are all regular. On the lines below each sentence write the correct present form [as if the action were happening right now or as if it happens all the time (continuously)] and the correct past form [when the action is over and done with (completed)].

PRESENT

I believe   we believe

Chapter 3: Verbs and Verb Phrases

61

    you believe   you (all) believe
    he, she, it believeS   they believe

PAST

    I believeD   we believeD
    you believeD   you (all) believeD
    he, she, it believeD   they believeD

*Geoffrey **(believe)** in Santa Claus.*

PRESENT: *believes*
PAST: *believed*

1. The cars (park) on the lawn.
   PRESENT: _____
   PAST: _____

2. Efficiency in the plant (continue) at a low level.
   PRESENT: _____
   PAST: _____

3. Hunting (tire) the dogs.
   PRESENT: _____
   PAST: _____

4. They (stack) their books on the shelf.
   PRESENT: _____
   PAST: _____

5. Chris and I (want) a kitten.
   PRESENT: _____
   PAST: _____

6. He (fire) the gun into the subway tunnel.
   PRESENT: _____
   PAST: _____

7. George (mind) the children while Marilyn (work).
   PRESENT: _____   PRESENT: _____
   PAST: _____   PAST: _____

8. Many people (talk) at once.
   PRESENT: _____
   PAST: _____

9. They (ask) for help but (receive) advice.
   PRESENT: _____   PRESENT: _____
   PAST: _____   PAST: _____

10. His party (turn) into a disaster at midnight.
    PRESENT: _____
    PAST: _____

11. When a dirigible (explode), it (burn) furiously.
    PRESENT: _____   PRESENT: _____

PAST: _____   PAST: _____
12. The iceberg (form) when the glacier (reach) the sea.
    PRESENT: _____   PRESENT: _____
    PAST: _____   PAST: _____
13. You (need) advice about handling your children.
    PRESENT: _____
    PAST: _____
14. Queen Elizabeth (die) without children in 1603.
    PRESENT: _____
    PAST: _____
15. England and Scotland (unite) under James I.
    PRESENT: _____
    PAST: _____
16. The little girl in the yellow jacket (free) the trapped rabbit.
    PRESENT: _____
    PAST: _____
17. The Boy Scout (help) little old ladies across the street.
    PRESENT: _____
    PAST: _____
18. This robot (use) solar energy.
    PRESENT: _____
    PAST: _____
19. Speeding (result) in arrest.
    PRESENT: _____
    PAST: _____
20. This (seem) the best alternative.
    PRESENT: _____
    PAST: _____
21. Today's financial conditions (interest) even the casual speculators.
    PRESENT: _____
    PAST: _____
22. You (advise) me to do a foolish thing.
    PRESENT: _____
    PAST: _____
23. Damp weather (warp) my records.
    PRESENT: _____
    PAST: _____
24. Lord Chantilleries (embody) the law.
    PRESENT: _____
    PAST: _____
25. The bus (stop) at the corner.
    PRESENT: _____
    PAST: _____

Chapter 3: Verbs and Verb Phrases 63

26. We (order) a huge quantity of radishes.
    PRESENT: _____
    PAST: _____
27. The dust (settle) into your hair and clothing until you (look) like the land itself.
    PRESENT: _____   PRESENT: _____
    PAST: _____   PAST: _____
28. He (call) me his friend, but I (call) him a vicious enemy.
    PRESENT: _____   PRESENT: _____
    PAST: _____   PAST: _____
29. When they (air) their differences in the Council Chamber, the Senate (hope) for an early resolution.
    PRESENT: _____   PRESENT: _____
    PAST: _____   PAST: _____
30. The old woman who (live) in the shoe (plant) collard greens beside the heel.
    PRESENT: _____   PRESENT: _____
    PAST: _____   PAST: _____
31. Many people still (believe) that God (exist).
    PRESENT: _____   PRESENT: _____
    PAST: _____   PAST: _____
32. People who (squabble) a lot seldom (listen) to one another.
    PRESENT: _____   PRESENT: _____
    PAST: _____   PAST: _____
33. The children who (play) in the street (place) faith in magic.
    PRESENT: _____   PRESENT: _____
    PAST: _____   PAST: _____
34. The Rigelian aliens who (land) in Washington Park (encounter) little organized resistance.
    PRESENT: _____   PRESENT: _____
    PAST: _____   PAST: _____
35. The militant who (state) his position (suffer) angry abuse.
    PRESENT: _____   PRESENT: _____
    PAST: _____   PAST: _____
36. He (ask) too many questions.
    PRESENT: _____
    PAST: _____
37. Samantha (want) me to help her with the assignment.
    PRESENT: _____
    PAST: _____
38. Victor, the student body president, (boast) of his popularity.
    PRESENT: _____
    PAST: _____
39. He (brag) so much that his friends (ignore) him.
    PRESENT: _____   PRESENT: _____
    PAST: _____   PAST: _____

40. The little girl greedily (clutch) the small gift from the department store Santa.
    PRESENT: _____
    PAST: _____

USING THE IRREGULAR VERB INDEX

Some of the most common verbs in our language are not regular; the past tense may have an entirely different vowel sound from the present or show no change at all (not even the *d* or *ed* ending). For example:

Present	Past
blow(s)	blew
break(s)	broke
find(s)	found
give(s)	gave
hit(s)	hit
put(s)	put
sing(s)	sang
see(s)	saw

Check the index beginning on page 130 for any irregular past tense forms you are not certain about; make it a habit until you have complete confidence. If a form you feel you should use, such as *gived* or *hitted*, does not appear as a choice, don't use it in writing.

In the first (or present) column of the index you will always find at least two possible forms. The *s, es,* or *ies* is to remind you that when the subject is *he, she,* or *it,* or when you can substitute *he, she,* or *it* for the subject, the verb ends in *s:* know(s), say(s), grow(s).

Present tense:

Subject	Verb
I	know
You	say
He	knowS
She	sayS
It	growS
We	know
You (all)	say
They	grow

The verbs in the second (or past) column remain the same whatever the subject might be.

Past tense:

Subject	Verb
I	knew
You	said
She	grew
He	sang

Chapter 3: Verbs and Verb Phrases

If the verb you need is not listed, check your dictionary. If the dictionary does not give you a second form (for example, know, knew, known), the verb is regular. All regular verbs add *d* or *ed* to the present form for the past tense.

EXERCISE 3-2

The following story about the future is written in the present tense. Read it through before you begin working. When a story is told in the present tense, everything is happening at the moment you are reading. You are there as the story progresses.

Cross out each present tense verb and put in the past tense form. (Watch out for subject/verb agreement when the new verb is *was* or *were*.) When you read the story through a second time, everything has already happened. When it is told in the past tense, you are looking at the story as an observer looks at a painting or a photograph. You are a witness of the past, not a participant in it.

An Automatic Catastrophe

1. Alad lives on the third planet from a star his people call Sol.

2. He is thirteen cycles into his maturity when he learns of the catastrophe his world faces.

3. While he studies AD31S Civics, he turns his teaching computer on and asks a few bored questions of it.

4. It spews out answers that are not boring to him.

5. He asks the population of his planet and learns that it is in the trillions.

6. When he inquires about his planet's birth rate, he discovers that the number of people is compounding daily.

7. He wonders if this growth rate is even theoretically possible.

8. Alad requires his teach-comp to calculate the population within a year.

9. The result seems astronomical.

10. Alad's curiosity is peaked; it puzzles him that so many babies are being born.

11. His mother, who carries his twin brothers about in the auto-pram all day, uses five hours of auto-meal time every day just for the babies.

12. The young scholar urges his electronic instructor to compute the number of hours of feeding time for next year's offspring.

13. The figure it computes is ludicrous.

14. Alad chuckles in glee and gasps in amazement as the calculation clicks across his screen.

15. He and his noisy calculator figure the number of seacows necessary to produce the formula, the pounds of algae to make their fodder, and the quirgles of energy to run the entire process.

16. As the endless rows of numbers click across the screen, his mother scolds him for playing when he is supposed to be studying.

17. Alad is mesmerized by the clicking, marching numbers.

18. He asks the teach-comp how long his planet can sustain this fantastic rate of growth.

19. The machine focuses on variables.

20. Alad programs for optimum conditions.

21. The computer computes; figures flash across the screen; the machine clicks once for each digit in the calculation.

22. The answer appears: three cycles, 10 lunarsects, and 15 solar rotations.

23. He looks for his mother.

24. She admits that famine seems certain.

25. She bundles the twins up for a stroll in the auto-pram.

26. He follows her out onto the crowded street level and buzzes for an auto-cab.

27. He roughly computes the quirgles of energy they consume while discussing famine.

28. He measures the distance to the park.

29. He combines the energy consumed by auto-cab and auto-pram.

30. Alad watches as snow clouds gather above the city's Plexiglas dome.

31. Birds chirp in flowering trees while hoards of toddlers and their keepers stroll about in cozy indolence.

32. Suddenly Alad is aware of the soft hum of the rows of auto-pram energy meters left to idle.

33. For the first time Alad reasons that something is wrong.

34. "We will die, Mother," his voice falters.

35. "Yes," she agrees.

36. She smiles, and Alad is afraid.

37. Other parents nod and agree.

38. Alad lifts one of his brothers from the auto-pram and turns off the motor.

39. The baby toddles off in pursuit of a butterfly.

40. The child stumbles and cries in indignation.

41. Their mother replaces him in the auto-pram and turns on the motor again.

42. It soothes the hurt and soon lulls the child into a peaceful stupor.

Chapter 3: Verbs and Verb Phrases 67

43. She clutches the handle of the auto-pram, and it eases her confusion.

44. She looks at her oldest son again and smiles.

45. "Yes, dear," she murmurs.

46. She rocks with the auto-pram.

47. Alad races home on foot.

48. The hum of machinery penetrates his consciousness.

49. The auto-lock on the door whirs softly.

50. Soft music switches on with the click of the light switch.

51. The red light on the auto-meal glows softly in readiness to serve beside the disposal which churns constantly, softly.

52. Fear and anxiety overwhelm the small boy thirteen cycles into his maturity.

53. He eases himself into the auto-chaise next to his teach-comp and punches out a new question.

54. "Who maintains the system?"

55. It answers, "The machines."

56. He questions, "Who services the machines?"

57. It responds, "The machines."

58. The auto-chaise measures his blood pressure and applies the required sedative.

59. He groans softly, "We will starve," as the chair hums.

60. His mother returns and connects the auto-pram to the auto-meal.

61. She hums softly.

If you were telling this story, would you use the past tense or the present? Why?

When a verb in the present tense appeared in quotation marks, did you change it to the past? Why not?

Avoiding Shifts in Tense

The preceding story about a possible future world could be told in the past or the present tense, depending on the feeling you wanted the reader to experience.

PRESENT (for immediacy)
Alad **lives** on the third planet from a star his people **call** Sol. He **is** thirteen cycles into his maturity when he **learns** of the catastrophe his world **faces**.

PAST (usual story-telling mode)
Alad **lived** on the third planet from a star his people **called** Sol. He **was** thirteen cycles into his maturity when he **learned** of the catastrophe his world **faced** (or **was facing**).

When you start writing in one tense, it is important that you do not shift without good cause to the other. If you say, "Alad *lives* on the third planet," it means that he still lives there or that he is living there as the action of the story proceeds. If the next sentence says, "He *was* thirteen cycles into his maturity," the reader must reprocess the information given; perhaps like this: "Alad still *lives* on this planet, and this is a story about when he *was* thirteen." By the end of the story, however, we suspect that no one *lives* on this planet any longer except the machines.

Sometimes there are clues in a sentence which suggest the choice of tense. For example, if a sentence uses a word like *yesterday*, the verb must be in the past. However, if the time designated is habitual (the action happens all the time), you may need to rely on the more subtle clues provided in context, such as other verb endings or your knowledge of the speaker or writer's situation.

EXAMPLE A: **Yesterday** I (finish, (finished)) my homework.

Example A allows no other choice; *yesterday* is finished and so is my homework.

EXAMPLE B: Often I **played** the guitar and (dance, (danced)) all night.

For the first verb in example B, it is clear that I no longer carry on in this fashion; the verb ending on *played* tells the reader that whatever wild oats I might once have had have already been sown. Compound verbs must be in the same tense.

EXAMPLE C: When it **rainS**, it (flood, (floods,) flooded).

In example C, habitual action is signaled by the verb in the first clause. Don't switch tenses.

EXAMPLE D: The couple who **paintED** our house last year now **live** in Rochester.

In example D, it is clear that the **painting** was done in the past, while the **living** is taking place in the present. Because the two different time references are clear, this is not considered tense shifting.

EXERCISE 3-3

Watch for time determining signals in the following sentences as you circle the correct verb choice.

1. Last April the River City Marching Band (march, marches, (marched)) all the way to the river.
2. They clumped about in their white marching boots and (play, plays, played) off key.

Chapter 3: Verbs and Verb Phrases

3. Whenever it rains, my building manager (call, calls, called) the plumber.
4. An eternal flame (burn, burns, burned) forever.
5. The royal family never wonders who (cook, cooks, cooked) their meals.
6. The Johnsons never asked who (scrub, scrubs, scrubbed) their bathroom.
7. A pushover is someone who (don't, doesn't, didn't) have enough self-respect.
8. The Wicked Witch of the West (slam, slams, slammed) the door and cracked her mirror.
9. Geraldine (step, steps, stepped) on the gas and flooded the engine.
10. Because people feed them, bears (beg, begs, begged) for food.
11. He lies, (cheat, cheats, cheated), and (steal, steals, stole).
12. The officer shouldered his rifle and (shout, shouts, shouted), "Stop or I'll shoot!"
13. The teacher smiled doubtfully at the tardy student and (ask, asks, asked), "Have you done your homework?"
14. Sarah comes up to me with the package from UPS and (say, says, said), "This is for you."
15. Rolphe came up to the microphone and (say, says, said), "Let's begin the meeting."
16. The woman who repaired my vacuum cleaner (work, works, worked) on a farm every summer.
17. The taxi driver who (answer, answers, answered) last night's call for help (handle, handles, handled) the delivery of the baby like a professional.
18. The student who (finish, finishes, finished) the exam first left the room at 3:15.
19. Teachers find that students (study, studies, studied) more during morning rest periods.
20. The Sorbonne was a bad place to be if you (don't, doesn't, didn't) know French.

EXERCISE 3-4

The following story should be written entirely in the present tense. Correct any errors in subject/verb agreement and any tense shifting that has occurred.

Crime Stoppers

1. Current fashions fights crime.

2. Michael Walters discovers this one night while on his way to a Washington D. C. hotel after a show.

3. The show ended at 12:15, and Mike leave the theatre alone.

4. No taxicabs are available, so after Mike waited awhile he decide to walk.

5. Seven blocks separates him from his hotel, and few lights illuminates the streets.

6. As sinister shadows stetches across the pavement, hollow steps echoed behind him.

7. Mikes hears the threatening sounds and quickened his pace.

8. His pursuers quicken theirs.

9. Mike prayed for a passing police car.

10. Few cars passes; he's completely alone in the night.

11. No savior appear.

12. He run into an alley.

13. Ill-tempered cats yowls as he passed.

14. He try to elude his followers by hiding in the dark alley.

15. Their patience matched his; they wait for him to come out.

16. Mike decide to make a break for it.

17. He streaks down the gangway and crashed into a garbage can.

18. The three ruffians almost catches him, but he escaped for the moment.

19. Mike lost his way until suddenly he come out on a familiar street.

20. He hurry down it, but the three youths persists in the chase.

21. A block from the hotel they overtake him.

22. Mike realize he be no match for all three of them but offers to take them on one at a time.

23. This sporting offer amuse them, and they agreed.

24. The first thug stepped forward.

25. Mike pull the guy's large hat over his eyes and delivered a devilish right to the jaw.

26. The embarrassed warrior crash to the pavement.

27. The second assailant warily approach him wearing silver studded, seven-inch platform shoes.

28. Before Mike see an opening, the fellow topple off the curb and sprained an ankle.

29. He curse long and well from the gutter while the third would-be mugger pull a knife.

30. His tight knit pants and long, voluminous coat hamper his movements, however, and the knife became entangled in his coat.

31. Mike trips him and tied him up with his long silk scarf.

32. A patrol car finally materialize, and Mike tells his story.

33. The officers haul the would-be robbers off to jail.

34. Mike walks the rest of the way to his hotel unmolested and enter laughing.

35. Jeans and a ski jacket may not be elegant attire, but they has their advantages.

EXERCISE 3–5

Most victims of crime aren't as lucky as Mike Walters was. Write a detailed account of ten sentences or more describing a typical crime as if you were observing it as it happens from the beginning until the police arrive. Keep most of your verbs in the present tense. Circle each present tense verb and underline its subject. If you have trouble getting started, you may wish to begin with one of the following sentences:

Chapter 3: Verbs and Verb Phrases

A shadowy figure leaps from the gangway.
or
Four shots interrupt the evening's silence.

If you're having trouble finding your subjects, ask for help immediately.
Can you rewrite the same description in the past tense?

EXERCISE 3-6

For additional practice in recognizing the difference between past and present tense, return to Chapter 2, "Present Tense Verbs," and convert one or more of the stories or exercises to the past tense. Use the "Verb Index" (see pages 129–33) to check for irregular past tense forms. Do not proceed to the discussion of verbs with auxiliaries until you can perform this operation with ease.

VERBS WITH AUXILIARIES

If the verb in your sentence has no helper, it is either in the simple present tense or the simple past tense. When you have this distinction clear, you have only to master verb phrases.

If you have been struggling against terminology like the *past perfect* and the *future progressive*, you can now happily forget it. Modern grammarians talk about two tenses in English: the past and the present (or non-past). Even when your verbs have auxiliaries, these two terms are enough.

If the auxiliary is a present form of *do, have,* or *be,* we say that the verb phrase is in the present tense. If the auxiliary is *did, had,* or *was* or *were,* we say it is in the past tense. The only other verb phrases will begin with *present auxiliaries*, and we do not talk about them in terms of tense.

This does not mean that we don't think there is such a thing as future **time;** it means that when we talk about the future we use the present tense or a helping verb from the group we call present auxiliaries. For example:

Noreen **is going** to the zoo tomorrow. (Present tense, future time.)
Noreen **means** to visit the zoo tomorrow. (Present tense, future time.)
Noreen **is about to go** to the zoo. (Present tense, future time.)
Noreen **will go** to the zoo tomorrow. (Present auxiliary plus main verb, future time.)
Noreen **should go** to the zoo tomorrow. (Present auxiliary plus main verb, future time.)

Knowing the traditional descriptive names for the various combinations of auxiliaries and main verbs will probably do very little to help you use them correctly. One big problem will be that some dialects of American English do not use *have* as an auxiliary; others use it only in questions. You may very well speak one of these dialects; many healthy, honest, and moral people do, and it is not our goal to make you give up speech forms which are comfortable to you nor to adopt forms which are uncomfortable. Our goal is writing. We will not attempt to teach the semantic differences (that is, the differences in meaning) between sentences which use *have* as an auxiliary (an action begins in the past and continues into the present) and those which don't. What we will attempt to teach is which forms of a verb go with particular auxiliaries and which don't.

In order to understand and control written American English verb phrases, it is necessary for you to know two things: the principal parts of a lot of verbs and which principal part is required by each auxiliary. If you are a native speaker of any dialect of American English, your intuition should tell you which *tense* is appropriate for what you want to say.

The next chart shows all the helping verbs we use except for *get/got*. Although these are used in speech all the time, their reputation in formal written communication is somewhat shady. When used as helpers, they appear in the third column in the chart between *have* and *be* and often replace them. This situation will be discussed again on page 110. There are *no* other auxiliaries lying in wait.

Auxiliaries:	Present		Past	Past Participle		Present Participle
	Group 1			*Group 2*		*Group 3*
can	could	do	(NONE)	have	be	be
may	might	does		has	am	am
shall	should	did		had	is	is
will	would			having	are	are
must					was	was
ought (to)					were	were
					been	been
					being	

These auxiliaries are added to main verbs in a very rigorous order. The four columns presented here are the same four you will discover in the *Verb Index* at the end of this chapter. **The form of the main verb that follows an auxiliary should be from the same column as the auxiliary closest to it in the sentence.** The last verb in a verb phrase is called the *main verb*. You will notice that the forms of *be* appear in two columns and, therefore, can be used with two forms of the verb.

Present	Past	Past Participle	Present Participle
listen(s)	listened	listened	listening
know(s)	knew	known	knowing
worry(ies)	worried	worried	worrying

Chapter 3: Verbs and Verb Phrases

Subject	Verb
He	CAN listen.
They	HAVE known.
The fathers	may HAVE worried.
This parrot	WAS listening.
The parrot	WAS listened to with respect.
The public	HAS BEEN worrying.

SENTENCE STRUCTURE REVIEW

Adverbs tell *how, when, where,* or *why* about the verb. They may pop up at any point in the verb phrase without affecting the choice of the form of the verb which follows the auxiliary.

Subject	Verb
He	can **always** listen. (Adv.)
They	**ordinarily** would know. (Adv.)
Children	ought to sleep **at night**. (Adv.)
Fathers	must worry **constantly**. (Adv.)
This parrot	does **not** talk. (Adv.)

EXERCISE 3–7

Starting with the present column, we will focus on the groups of auxiliaries one at a time. Fill in the present auxiliaries below. (Remember: *Won't* is the contraction for *will not*.):

_____   _____   _____
_____   _____   _____
_____   _____   _____
_____   _____
_____

Chapter 3: Verbs and Verb Phrases

Memorize the helping verbs.

EXERCISE 3–8

In the following exercise fill in the missing elements to form correct sentences. Use any main verb which makes sense; scan the present column of the *Verb Index* if you're stuck for a choice of your own. Notice that since there are no *s, d,* or *ing* endings on the main verbs provided, the auxiliaries must be from the **present** group, Group 1. When the verb phrase begins with a present helper, except for *do* and *does,* there is no subject/verb agreement to worry about.

Subject	(Auxiliary + main verb + adverb)
1. Alice	will ▲ *never* ___*quit*___. Adv.
2. The pitcher	_____ wind up ▲ carefully. Adv.
3. Good neighbors	_____ ▲ intrude ▲ not _____. Adv. Adv.
4. An early spring	could _____ ▲ nothing. Adv.
5. This stapler	_____ work ▲ better. Adv.
6. Grandfather Moses	should _____ more ▲ quietly. Adv.
7. Old Ms. Goose	_____ fly ▲ south for the winter. Adv.
8. Millie's bookie	might _____ ▲ at any time. Adv.

Chapter 3: Verbs and Verb Phrases

A direct object or complement may be added following the verb phrase without affecting the verb phrase.

Subject	(Auxiliary + main verb + adverb)	Object or Complement
9. A slow learner	often ▲ _____ require Adv.	encouragement.
10. Sour cabbage	completely would ▲ _____ Adv.	my appetite.
11. Bumble bees	should _____ under the hedge. ▲ Adv.	
12. The rabbits	_____ become	parents.
13. Her children	soon will ▲ _____ Adv.	my furniture.
14. The car	never _____ ▲ replace Adv.	the horse.
15. I	clearly. shall _____ ▲ Adv.	

EXERCISE 3–9 ——————————————————— write

With your book closed, list the present auxiliaries, check them, and then write thirteen sentences of your own using each auxiliary with a different main verb.

Do: Both Auxiliary and Main Verb

The verb *do* creates special problems because it may function as a main verb or as a helping verb.

Chapter 3: Verbs and Verb Phrases

	Present	Past	Past Participle	Present Participle
Auxiliaries:		(NONE)		
	Group 1		*Group 2*	*Group 3*
	can could **do**		have be	be
	may might **does**		has am	am
	shall should **did**		had is	is
	will would		having are	are
	must		was	were
	ought (to)		were	been
			been	
			being	
Main Verb:	**do (does)**	did	done	doing
	don't (doesn't)	didn't		

If *do* is used as an auxiliary, the main verb will be found in the PRESENT column of the Verb Index. If *do* is the main verb, the following basic combinations may be used:

    Group 1 auxiliary + *do*   = **I will do** my homework.
    Group 2 auxiliary + *done* = **I have done** the dishes.
    Group 3 auxiliary + *doing* = **I was doing** my duty.

If there is no auxiliary and the action of the sentence was completed in the past, the verb is *did*. Otherwise it is *do* or *does* according to the rules for subject/verb agreement.

In studying *do*, it is important to recognize and use correctly *don't*, *doesn't*, and *didn't*. In the contraction the apostrophe takes the place of the *o* in *not*.

    not = n't
    do not = don't
    does not = doesn't

EXERCISE 3–10

Fill in any correct form of *do* in the following story. Watch for tense determiners and subject/verb agreement. If a sentence contains the word *not*, cross it out and write the contraction on the line provided.

Do Not Feed the Bears

1. Most city children _____*don't*_____ n~~ot~~ know much about the wilderness.
2. It _____ not affect the lives they lead.
3. They _____ not see mountains on their way to school, and they _____ not see wild animals outside the zoo.
4. The polar bears they see in picture books _____ not frighten them.

Chapter 3: Verbs and Verb Phrases 77

5. The child of the city _____ believe in danger and can be impressed but _____ not get excited by something as remote as wilderness adventures.
6. Last summer, however, a group of Chicago school children _____ learn to believe in the reality of Mother Nature.
7. They were taken on a camping trip the Rocky Mountains where the wilderness _____ have reality.
8. Their two teen-age leaders thought they were _____ a wonderful thing for the kids.
9. They had _____ everything in their power to awaken the kids' sense of awareness.
10. What the group _____ not know about living in the wilderness was frightening.
11. Leaving the beaten trails, they were _____ a very foolish thing.
12. They might have _____ better to take the children to Lincoln Park Zoo.
13. What they did _____ and what they might have _____ were different things.
14. They loaded their back-packs as they had _____ at the YMCA and headed off in a noisy, excited mob.
15. They trekked through the morning and _____ not notice their audience of wild animals.
16. Birds and snakes _____ not like noise and left the area as they approached, but a grizzly bear _____ not fear humans if it _____ not have experience with them.
17. A large specimen of *Ursus horribilis* had _____ an unusual thing by coming halfway down the mountain a week earlier.
18. The forest rangers _____ watch for the occasional descent of these dangerous animals but had _____ nothing to hinder the movement of this animal.
19. The ranger who _____ interfere with a grizzly _____ it gently and with enormous respect.
20. The two Chicago-bred camp counselors _____ not realize the extent of their group's danger.
21. The children and their leaders _____ not lack courage, but they _____ lack experience.
22. Children _____ not listen when they are told one thing and observe adults _____ the opposite.
23. Their adult guides often take them on visits to the zoo equipped with bags of marshmallows and _____ not read the signs.
24. The signs at the zoo say, "_____ Not Feed the Bears."
25. The children _____ read, and they learn from adults to ignore what they _____ not like.
26. When Tina pointed out the bear to Mike, they _____ not think twice about bringing it a snack.
27. What they were _____ went unnoticed by their counselors who

_____ not see the visitor wandering about the periphery of their tree-sheltered camp.
28. Mike had _____ a logical thing for an eight-year-old boy; it would not _____ to travel without marshmallows.
29. Both youngsters _____ what they had _____ dozens of times at the zoo.
30. The grizzly had dined recently and _____ not make them its main course.
31. It was friendly, for a grizzly, and _____ not think of refusing the offered delicacy.
32. Having no previous contact with humans, the three-hundred-pound animal _____ not realize the danger it was in.
33. The mountain had _____ little to teach this wild creature what guns and railroads can _____ to a bear's environment.
34. While the bag was full, the three innocents _____ very well together.
35. The kids wanted everyone to see what they could _____, so they coaxed the bear forward as they had _____ with the baby elephant at the zoo.
36. The young bear followed the bag, _____ its best to lick the confection from their hands.
37. The counselors _____ a double-take when they saw the animal in their midst, but the other children _____ what they had seen their parents _____ .
38. They fed the bear, which was _____ its best to consume every treat offered.
39. Realizing what they had _____, the counselors were terrified.
40. The bear had occupied the camp, and they could _____ nothing about it.
41. _____ their best not to alarm the children, the counselors began quietly ordering their charges up a nearby tree.
42. Mike and Tina _____ not want to leave their new-found friend.
43. Darkness fell and rescue _____ not come.
44. Thoroughly satisfied, the bear _____ a natural thing; it fell asleep.
45. As the bear slept, a seventeen-year-old boy who _____ not know north from south without street signs wanted to _____ something quickly.
46. He might have been _____ a foolish thing to come down from the tree.
47. The young explorers were tired and hungry, however, and something had to be _____ .
48. He headed out, _____ what he could to follow their morning's trail toward civilization.
49. A very surprised and angry grizzly woke with an upset stomach and felt it ought to _____ something to get revenge.
50. It bellowed in rage and _____ a good job of frightening the children.
51. They _____ not complain about sitting in the tree having nothing to _____ anymore.
52. They watched in hypnotized fascination to see what their afternoon's companion would _____ to them.

Chapter 3: Verbs and Verb Phrases

53. Bellowing had _____ nothing to relieve its distress, so the bear growled in frustration as anyone might _____ .
54. The young counselor miraculously _____ find the ranger station before midnight.
55. When he had _____ what he could to explain where the camp was, the rescue squad set out.
56. There was nothing for the rangers to _____ but shoot the poor grizzly that had _____ nothing to deserve its fate.
57. The rangers were just _____ their job: protecting campers.
58. The loss of one grizzly will _____ little to change the average zoo visitor's habits.
59. They _____ not understand what they are _____ to the animals with their marshmallows and to their children with their stupidity.
60. It _____ not occur to them that bears become ill and that their children _____ not respect authority because of a summer day's stroll through the park.
61. Adults who _____ care should _____ what they can to teach their children that a bear _____ not eat marshmallows.

Have: Both Auxiliary and Main Verb

Like *do*, *have* can be both a main verb and an auxiliary. When *have* is the main verb, it has three forms: *have* and *has* in the present tense and *had* in the past tense.

> They **have** the money.
> Mickey **has** the time.
> We **had** a riot.

The only form of *have* that can follow a helper from the first group is *have*. In the following examples, *have* is the main verb.

> Present auxiliary + **have**

> He **CAN have** my share.
> They **MIGHT have** an opening in the fall.
> Charlene **OUGHT TO have** more sense.

	Present		Past	Past Participle	Present Participle
Auxiliaries:					
	Group 1			Group 2	Group 3
can	could	do	(NONE)	have	be
may	(might)	does		has	am
shall	should	did		had	is
will	would			having	are
must					was
ought (to)					were
					been
					being
Main Verb:					
(HAVE)	(has)		had	had	having

Present Auxiliary + *Have* + Past Participle

The only verb form that can follow *have* used as an auxiliary is a past participle (third column). The past participle of a regular verb, just like the past tense, ends in *d* or *ed*. The following combinations are possible:

Present auxiliary + **have** = We ***should have*** a cat.
Have + past participle = The mice ***have destroyed*** our peace of mind.
Present auxiliary + **have** + past participle = The cat ***would have destroyed*** the mice.

> NOTE: You cannot write, "Margaret **do have asked.**" Only a single main verb may follow **do.**

	Present	Past	Past Participle	Present Participle
Auxiliaries:	*Group 1*		*Group 2*	*Group 3*
can	could	do/	(NONE)	have	be	be
may	might	does		has	am	am
shall	should	did		had	is	is
will	would			having	are	are
must					was	was
ought (to)					were	were
					been	been
					being	
Main Verbs:				
ask(s)		asked	asked	asking
learn(s)		learned	**learned**	learning
make(s)		made	**made**	making
destroy(s)		destroyed	**destroyed**	destroying

EXERCISE 3–11 — *write*

See if you can write a short, short story of twenty sentences using one verb phrase formula in all your sentences.

present helper + *have* + ***past participle***

If you have trouble getting your own plot off the ground, start with one of the following sentences and see where it leads you:

1. Baby-Cakes-Malone *must have killed* Gorilla Joe's canary.
   (What might have happened? Who could have noticed? What should have resulted?)
2. I *could have married* a trapeze artist.
   (What would have changed? Who might have cared? Why ought you to have done this? Should you have married some other character?)
3. Captain Star *could have rescued* the doomed planet.
   [Why didn't s/he?]

Chapter 3: Verbs and Verb Phrases

Although it isn't necessary, all your sentences may be in the following pattern:

Subject + *present helper* + *have* + *past participle* + object or complement.

> NOTE: You can be sure of a grammatically correct verb phrase with any verb in the index if the main verb in your sentence comes from the third (the past participle) column. If your verb is a regular verb, it won't be in the index, but the ending will be the regular *d* or *ed*.

Be: Both Auxiliary and Main Verb

The only form of *be* which can follow a helper from the first group is *be*. In the following examples *be* is the main verb:

1. He *may **be*** the true assassin.
2. They *would **be*** eager to try out for our team.
3. Little Red Riding Hood *ought to **be*** more careful.

	Present			Past	Past Participle		Present Participle
Auxiliaries:							
	Group 1				*Group 2*		*Group 3*
	can	could	~~do~~		have	**be**	be
	may	might	~~does~~		has	**am**	am
	shall	should	~~did~~		had	**is**	is
	(will)	would		(NONE)	having	**are**	are
	must					**was**	was
	ought (to)					**were**	were
						been	been
						being	
Main Verbs:							
BE (am, is, are)				were (was)	been		being

You'll remember that when we studied the present tense form of *be* we noticed that some nonstandard dialects use *be* to signal periodic behavior: *John be late.* (Night after night John is late; he should get a wristwatch.)

We also noticed that sometimes forms of *be* were omitted altogether. *Cheryl pretty.* This actually illustrates a very consistent rule in some nonstandard usage: if you can contract the verb, you can omit it. *Cheryl pretty* is the nonstandard way of saying *Cheryl's pretty* or *Cheryl is pretty.*

The same thing goes for present auxiliaries: in some dialects whenever the present auxiliary can be contracted, it can be eliminated from the verb phrase.

Eddie will be here at eight.

The present auxiliary, *will*, can be contracted to *'ll*.

Eddie'll be here at eight.
In speech this may become:
Eddie be here at eight.
I will bet he's right.
The present auxiliary, *will*, can be contracted to *'ll*.
I'll bet he's right.
Again, in speech this may become:
I bet he's right.

In formal writing *be* (and all forms of *be*) can be especially troublesome. Keep these things in mind as you practice writing: (1) make sure there is a verb written in every sentence even if you would omit it in speaking; (2) make sure that if you use the word *be* in a sentence that it has a present auxiliary in front of it, except for command sentences like "Be quiet!" where the subject is understood to be *you*.

EXERCISE 3–12

In the following exercise watch out for subject/verb agreement in the simple present and simple past. Following a present auxiliary, the only acceptable form is *be*. Fill in *be*, *am*, *is*, *are*, *was* or *were*.

1. I __were__ my mother's greatest trial when I was a preschooler.
2. You ought to __be__ more sensitive.
3. Yesterday __was__ a terrible day.
4. Russ __is__ not the only candidate for Mayor.
5. This could __be__ the start of something great.
6. There __are__ too many cats in this house according to the city inspector.
7. Where __is__ my rubber duck?
8. You should __be__ ashamed.
9. You __were__ the hit of the show last night.
10. Carol and Dan __was__ not visible all evening.
11. The cat who ate the liver sausage must __be__ downstairs.
12. Mary Jean, whoever she __is__, will __be__ here soon.
13. Several ghosts must __be__ after the liver sausage too.
14. The moving van __is__ outside waiting to be loaded.
15. The suspense __is__ killing me.
16. Where __were__ you when the lights went out?
17. Could she __was？__ the bookie?
18. There _____ a draft through the broken window all last winter.
19. In-laws _____ as welcome as ghosts.
20. Who _____ I?
21. Who _____ you?
22. Who _____ the man at the door?

Chapter 3: Verbs and Verb Phrases

23. Which women _____ volunteers?
24. How many people _____ in the lost rickshaw?
25. There will never _____ another golden goose.
26. Can the shipment _____ here by noon?
27. The time _____ right.
28. Last month it _____ too early.
29. A minute ago the carrot soufflé _____ perfect.
30. Now it _____ a soggy orange disaster.
31. Won't he _____ sorry?
32. The witnesses _____ under protective custody.
33. My chances of winning _____ minuscule.
34. There could _____ another explanation.
35. There _____n't anyone to carry the honeypot.
36. There _____n't enough chairs for the seance.
37. You _____ a terrible liar.
38. They _____ mildly intoxicated.
39. She _____ thoroughly plastered.
40. The king and queen _____ home from their holiday.
41. I certainly _____ not going to tolerate his insolence.
42. Should there _____ a lot of fertilizer on the tomatoes?
43. My history teacher _____ a Marxist.
44. My P.E. teacher _____ a Buddhist.
45. My English and math teachers _____ Methodists.
46. Bertrand Russell and Madeline Murray _____ atheists.
47. My father _____ a plumber.
48. I think I will _____ a hermit.
49. Do _____ careful! [1]
50. _____ quiet!

Past Participle *Been*

The past participle of the verb *be* is *been*. The only form of *be* which can follow *have, has, had,* or *having* is *been*.

This plant **has been** here since Christmas.
The story **has been** omitted from the book.
Where **have** you **been?**

EXERCISE 3-13

In the following exercise the main verb is *been*. Fill in the correct form of *have*. You must watch for present auxiliaries, past tense signals, and/or subject/verb agreement.

---

[1] This sentence is a rare but possible construction. Notice the forms of *do* are marked out of the chart for *be*; *does* and *did* will never be followed by *be*.

1. She __has or had__ been my advisor for a long time.
2. For an entire month I _____ been the only dish washer in the house.
3. Why _____ he been there?
4. What _____ been the result?
5. Who _____ been the teacher?
6. _____ been there, I knew what happened.
7. The old dog with the matted coat _____ been walking in the rain.
8. The drawer which won't open _____ been the focus of my day.
9. What _____ been behind the green door?
10. I knew what to expect, _____ been through the procedure before.
11. Someone _____ been in my purse again.
12. This _____ been the longest day of my life.
13. They _____ been their mother's sole support since their father died.
14. The swallows _____ been to Capistrano many times.
15. Cassandra _____ been the lead in every school play since 1971.
16. Until school began, Billy must _____ been the most successful numbers runner on State Street.
17. The gnarled oak in the back yard _____ been there since my great grandfather bought the house.
18. His brothers may _____ been his major obstacle in growing up.
19. _____ been through the automatic washer, my wool sweater would _____ been like a very small drowned rat if it _____ not been for the Magi-Stretch which I bought at the drugstore.
20. If Jim _____n't been there, we all would _____ been better off.

Choosing the Participle for a *Be* Auxiliary

When you use *be* as an auxiliary, look for the main verb and decide whether you need a past (*-d*) or present (*-ing*) participle. If you are a native speaker of any dialect of English, in general you will have no difficulty deciding which participle to use, as in real life you know whether your slacks *are ripped* or whether they *are ripping*. The past participle indicates a completed action, and the present participle shows an action in the process of happening.

    PAST PARTICIPLE—I **was asked** the questions.
    PRESENT PARTICIPLE—I **was asking** the questions.
    PAST PARTICIPLE—The boy **is accused** of the robbery.
    PRESENT PARTICIPLE—The boy **is accusing** someone else.

The most frequent mistake in writing is to follow a *be* auxiliary with a present form of the main verb instead of a past participle.

    WRONG: I **was ask** the questions.
    RIGHT: I **was askED** the questions.

Chapter 3: Verbs and Verb Phrases

In speech these differences from edited English are often insignificant; only the most careful listener will hear the endings and then only part of the time. Sometimes even people who write the endings automatically do not pronounce them in critical places. The most interesting thing is that if they *do* write them without thinking, they probably think that they *are* pronouncing them and will, therefore, urge you to just listen for the endings and to write what you hear. This may prove pretty confusing to you if you can't hear the endings because you do not in fact pronounce them.

EXERCISE 3-14

In the following exercise, choose the correct past or present participle which will complete the meaning of the sentence. Check the index for irregular past participles. There is no such thing as an irregular present participle, but watch your spelling. If the verb ends in *e*, drop the *e* and add *ing*: *having, making, caring*. If the verb ends in *y*, keep the *y* and add *ing*: *studying, bullying, terrifying*. See the spelling appendix for rules which govern doubling final consonants and adding *ing*.

(have) 1. I am _having_ a hard time with my geography lesson.
(make) 2. My sister is _____ a model airplane with balsa wood and glue.
(care) 3. The mother cat was _____ for her kittens in the broken oven.
(terrify) 4. The little girl was _____ by her loud uncle.
(study) 5. We were _____ in the afternoon instead of playing.
(bully) 6. The children had been _____ by their teacher all year.
(ask) 7. Being _____ to give a speech was torture for me.
(do) 8. They are _____ everything they can to save the stranded canary.
(torture) 9. Mother is being _____ by the PTA.
(search) 10. The bullfrogs were _____ for the handsome prince.
(grow) 11. Wild strawberries were _____ around our porch.
(brag) 12. Grandparents are always _____ about their demonic grandchildren.
(get) 13. You shouldn't be _____ into bed with wet galoshes.
(dry) 14. The galoshes were carefully _____ before bedtime.
(rip) 15. This page has been _____.
(dump) 16. The gravel was _____ in our front yard.
(dry) 17. The flowers were _____ and _____ be-
(press)   tween the pages of the Bible.
(prevent) 18. Parents should be _____ from having children they don't want.
(reprimand) 19. The goats were _____ for eating the newspapers.

(flag) 20. Motorists were being _____ down by innocent-looking roadside bandits.

The Longest Verb Phrase

The only form of *be* which can follow *have, has, had,* or *having* is *been*. The past participle of *be* is *been*.

> **have + been** = Ross **has been** here longer than anyone.
> present auxiliary + **have + been** = He **should have been** the new editor.

In the examples above the main verb is *been*. In the following sentences *been* is a helper in a long verb phrase. Following any form of the verb *be*, the main verb may be either a past or a present participle.

present auxiliary + **have + been +** (past participle) / (present participle)
He **could have been** <u>asked</u> the questions.
He **could have been** *asking* the questions.

	Present	Past	Past Participle	Present Participle
Auxiliaries:	*Group 1*		*Group 2*	*Group 3*
	can could do	(NONE)	have be	be
	may might does		has am	am
	shall should did		had is	is
	will would		having are	are
	must		was	was
	ought (to)		were	were
			been	been
			being	
	ask(s)	asked	asked	asking
	learn(s)	learned	learned	learning
	make(s)	made	made	making
	sing(s)	sang	sung	singing

EXERCISE 3–15

Fill in a correct form of the verb given in parentheses. In some cases either a past or a present participle will serve equally well.

(yell) 1. You should have been *yelling* for help.
(worry) 2. Dwight ought to be _____ about grades this term.
(contain) 3. Every sentence you write should _____ a subject and a verb.

Chapter 3: Verbs and Verb Phrases

(grip)   4. The parachutist must have been _____ by a sudden fear of heights.

(dunk)   5. Against their will, my cats are being _____ in an ugly green solution for killing fleas.

(exist)   6. Could God have _____ without being discovered?

(fry)   7. The potatoes were _____ in hot oil.

(gallop)   8. The wild horses may have been _____ across the prairie.

(lean)   9. The new President has been _____ toward amnesty.

(renew)   10. I should have _____ this book before the library closed.

(search)   11. The frantic father would have been _____ for his son in the supermarket.

(convince)   12. Charles was _____ that he had been kidnapped.

(veer)   13. The car _____ sharply to the left.

(wonder)   14. They must have been _____ what happened to the rabbit.

(ask)   15. No one could have been _____ to sacrifice so much without some reward.

(consist)   16. Her birthday party will _____ of both of her friends and a pony.

(renew)   17. College friendships may often be _____ after many years.

(shock)   18. Being _____ by such awful news ruined my day.

(comb)   19. The villagers could not have been _____ the hills for the plane.

(wreck)   20. The truck Sara usually drives must have been _____ by her summer replacement.

(reach)   21. The high shelf can most easily be _____ with a kitchen chair.

(cook)   22. My goose has been _____.

(figure)   23. The accountant who cannot add must have _____ these income tax forms.

(perch)   24. The porcelain chicken was _____ on the mantle as if ready for flight.

(stroll)   25. Mildred and her poodle, dressed in matching plaid sweaters, will be _____ through the park this winter.

EXERCISE 3-16

In the following sentences fill in the correct form of the verb given to the left of each sentence. This story is being told in the past tense. Beware of shifting to the present without cause.

Beowulf the Tiger

(live) 1. Beowulf, the Siberian Tiger, __*lived*__ quietly at the Greenville County Central Park Zoo.
(conduct) 2. He had always _____ his affairs with dignity.
(stalk) 3. He _____ about in his cage with liquid grace.
(serve) 4. His meals were _____ and _____ quite
(consume) regularly.
(bore) 5. However, he was _____ with his life.
(yawn) 6. He _____ often and _____ heavily.
(sigh)
(clean) 7. While his cage was being _____ , he
(use) _____ to _____ into his outer court-
(stroll) yard.
(happen) 8. One day while this was _____ , he
(try) _____ his haunches against the bars of the gate.
(surprise) 9. He was _____ to feel the door yield against his massive strength.
(scrub) 10. As the careless caretakers _____ , he
(stroll) _____ toward the monkey house.
(walk) 11. Beowulf _____ about in the sun feeling content.
(lap) 12. He found he could _____ up a cool drink from the
(place) fountain by _____ his enormous paws on the stone step
(use) which was _____ by the children.
(notice) 13. The chimpanzees didn't _____ him until he
(stop) _____ in front of the baboons.
(scream) 14. Then they began to _____ in terror.
(distress) 15. Beowulf was not _____ .
(galumph) 16. He _____ placidly through the building and
(wander) _____ off in the direction of the farm animals.
(lock) 17. The public gates had been _____ for an hour, and his
(obstruct) progress was not _____ by visitors.
(settle) 18. The docile people-eater _____ himself in the middle of
(watch) the bridge to _____ ducks.
(domesticate) 19. Being thoroughly _____ by his life-long captivity, he
(consider) did not _____ having a duck dinner.
(serve) 20. Meat was _____ from buckets at 3:15 and duck soup
(add) was not to be _____ to his diet.
(warm) 21. The bridge, which had been _____ by the afternoon
(seem) sun, _____ cozy as well as peaceful.
(doze) 22. He _____ off.
(paralyze) 23. In the meantime, two hysterical zookeepers were
_____ with horror in the empty cage.

Chapter 3: Verbs and Verb Phrases

(telephone) 24. In a state of panic they _____ the main office to
(report) _____ the escape of the ferocious jungle cat.
(encircle) 25. Armed police _____ the park grounds as excited
(gather) passers-by _____ around the entrance.
(arm) 26. Twenty volunteers _____ with M-2 rifles were
(advance) _____ on the _____ bridge.
(occupy)
(rush) 27. The zoo's veterinarian _____ toward them with a tran-
(plead) quilizer gun _____ for the tiger's life.
(discourage) 28. The police are _____ from allowing civilians to
(place) _____ themselves in personal jeopardy.
(refuse) 29. The sergeant felt they ought to _____ her foolish request.
(consent) 30. The captain, finally, _____ to give her one shot at the
(open) huge cat before his sharpshooters _____ fire.
(awaken) 31. The commotion _____ the slumbering creature.
(stretch) 32. He rose and _____ himself expansively as he
(yawn) _____ with a spine-chilling, throaty rumble.
(step) 33. The volunteers _____ back in the face of his awesome
strength.
(move) 34. The vet _____ cautiously forward before the anxiety of
(turn) the group could _____ to tragedy for the beast.
(trust) 35. Because she could not _____ her aim, she would not
(risk) _____ the tiger's safety with a premature shot.
(approach) 36. Shouldering her gun she _____ the bridge.
(recognize) 37. The tiger might have _____ the vet, or he might have
(want) _____ simply to _____ his stroll.
(continue)
(pad) 38. He _____ across the wooden bridge toward the small
(retreat) army which had _____ tactically.
(wait) 39. The vet was _____ at the foot of the bridge.
(remain) 40. She _____ in this position until her prey was within
three feet of the gun barrel.
(fire) 41. She _____ the tranquilizing dart almost directly into
Beowulf's right shoulder.
(pelt) 42. The noble creature had been _____ by curious children
(muffle) armed with pebbles and bottle caps for many years, and the sound was
_____ by a silencer.
(ignore) 43. He haughtily _____ his attacker and
(pad) _____ on down the hill.
(faint) 44. A young corporal _____.
(raise) 45. Three of his comrades _____ their rifles and
(aim) _____ at the undaunted beast.

90   Chapter 3: Verbs and Verb Phrases

(wave)	46. The vet _____ her arms and _____
(scream)	"Don't shoot!"
(crumple)	47. Beowulf _____ in his tracks.
(fire)	48. For one awful moment the animal doctor was not sure if the M-2s had been _____ or not.
(yawn)	49. Beowulf awoke in his cage, _____ and
(stretch)	_____.
(bore)	50. He was _____ and sometimes _____
(wonder)	what lay beyond the duck pond.
(confuse)	51. Having _____ and _____ the city,
(excite)	Beowulf's escapade was _____ on the evening news.
(relate)	
(announce)	52. The newscaster _____ that the mighty feline did not
(realize)	_____ what an escaped tiger was
(suppose)	_____ to do.

SPELLING PAST TENSE VERBS AND PAST PARTICIPLES

Used to/Supposed to

A very common verb mistake occurs when the word *to* follows a regular past or past participle which ends in *d*. Because the *d* and *t* sounds are so close, they tend to run together or elide in pronunciation. While this is not a "mistake" in speaking, it can create a mistake in writing.

The mistake occurs most frequently with the phrases *used to* and *supposed to*, but other verbs ending in *d* or *t* are also susceptible. Likewise, words other than *to* that begin with the letters *d* or *t* may tempt you to make this error in writing.

Do not rely on pronunciation alone to determine whether the *d* goes on the end of your verb.

EXERCISE 3–17

As you work through the next exercise, watch for words or phrases which determine tense; do not be fooled by pronunciation. Fill in the correct form of the verb in parentheses in the following sentences.

(use, want)	1. Edith __*used*__ to study botany, but now she __*wants*__ to be an agronomist.
(suppose)	2. The TV is _____ to be turned off at 9:00 pm.
(start, suppose)	3. It _____ to rain just as we were _____ to leave for the beach.

Chapter 3: Verbs and Verb Phrases

(try)   4. In the past, the secretaries _____ to screen their bosses' calls.

(use)   5. Nothing is the way it _____ to be.

(use, suppose)   6. Dixie _____ to keep a diary, but no one was _____ to know about it.

(learn)   7. Kathryn _____ dentistry at the local college.

(demand)   8. David _____ double his usual salary for the dangerous duty.

(use, include)   9. Our Christmas play _____ to _____ live animals.

(suppose, exercise, use)   10. The horses are _____ to be _____ daily as they _____ to be, but the new grooms don't know their jobs.

(ask, consider)   11. Clarissa _____ to be _____ for the post.

(mix, dilute)   12. The solutions were _____ to _____ the acid.

(jump)   13. Last week the mare _____ the fence and hurt her leg.

(block)   14. The goalie in last night's game _____ two quick shots before letting the third one by.

(insist, close)   15. Darrell Johnson has _____ that he _____ the door when he left the office.

The D/T Sound

In coming to grips with the formation of American English verbs, it may be helpful to understand that *d* and *t* are almost identical sounds. The tongue is placed in exactly the same spot in the mouth to make both, but when you pronounce the *d*, you use your larynx (voicebox), and when you pronounce the *t*, you just spit the sound. The regular *d*, *ed* ending of the past and past participle is very often pronounced as a *t*.

Among the following group of words, modern dictionaries recognize two spellings of the past and past participle. To simplify the learning task, we recommend that you memorize and practice the regular *ed* for all of these verbs.

Present	Past	Past Participle	Present Participle
blend(s)	blended	blended	blending
burn(s)	burned	burned	burning
dwell(s)	dwelled	dwelled	dwelling
gird(s)	girded	girded	girding
lean(s)	leaned	leaned	leaning
learn(s)	learned	learned	learning
pen(s)	penned	penned	penning

Present	Past	Past Participle	Present Participle
smell(s)	smelled	smelled	smelling
spell(s)	spelled	spelled	spelling
spill(s)	spilled	spilled	spilling
spoil(s)	spoiled	spoiled	spoiling
step(s)	stepped	stepped	stepping

The next group of verbs is like the last because dictionaries recognize two variations for the past and past participle. The group is different, however, because the internal vowel sound changes. To simplify the learning process, we strongly recommend that you memorize and practice the regular form for writing.

You may *say*, "He leapt into the air"; however, you should *write*, "He leaped into the air."

Some authorities will argue for a slightly irregular form of these words because they are more often used in edited writing. This is a strong argument, and if you feel a decided preference, you will be perfectly correct in using the *t* ending instead of the regular *ed* form.

Present	Past	Past Participle	Present Participle
dream(s)	dreamed (dreamt)	dreamed (dreamt)	dreaming
kneel(s)	kneeled (knelt)	kneeled (knelt)	kneeling
leap(s)	leaped (leapt)	leaped (leapt)	leaping
plead(s)	pleaded (pled)	pleaded (pled)	pleading
speed(s)	speeded [1] (sped [2])	speeded [1] (sped [2])	speeding

[1] As "speeded up the car."
[2] As "sped down the road."

If you remember that *d* and *t* are interchangeable as past tense markers, the next group of verbs will be less troublesome. The vowel sound in the middle of all of the words (except *build*) changes, but the *t* ending is still regular. Spelling may be the biggest problem with this group. Pay particular attention to *lose*. It is very frequently misspelled.

Present	Past	Past Participle	Present Participle
build(s)	built	built	building
creep(s)	crept	crept	creeping
feel(s)	felt	felt	feeling
get(s)	got	got or gotten	getting
keep(s)	kept	kept	keeping
leave(s)	left	left	leaving
lose(s)	lost	lost	losing
mean(s)	meant	meant	meaning
meet(s)	met	met	meeting
shoot(s)	shot	shot	shooting

Chapter 3: Verbs and Verb Phrases

Present	Past	Past Participle	Present Participle
sleep(s)	slept	slept	sleeping
sweep(s)	swept	swept	sweeping
weep(s)	wept	wept	weeping

EXERCISE 3–18

Paying attention to signals indicating time and tense, insert the correct form of the verb in parentheses into the sentences below. The story should be told in the past tense.

Happy Birthday

(meet, build, dwell) 1. When King George _____ Queen Claudia, he had a castle _____ for them in the enchanted forest where they _____ happily for many years.

(feel, leave, desire) 2. The King _____ there was nothing _____ to be _____ in life.

(spoil, dream) 3. Only one thing _____ the Queen's happiness; she _____ of having a child.

(lose) 4. The King _____ no time.

(spell, call) 5. Although it usually _____ trouble to do so, he _____ on the local evil witch to help him out.

(lean, plead) 6. Throughout history it has been found that those who _____ on black magic are _____ for catastrophe.

(spill, burn) 7. Nonetheless, the foolish king _____ his sad story to the old witch, revealing the secret desire that _____ in the Queen's heart.

(be, blend, consent) 8. The King, who _____ a marvelous storyteller, _____ his story with such charm that the witch finally _____.

(learn, kneel, weep) 9. When the Queen _____ a child was coming, she _____ on her balcony and _____ tears of happiness.

(creep, feel) 10. The time of waiting _____ by slowly, but in the spring when their daughter came, they _____ she was well worth waiting for.

(dispatch, speed) 11. The royal messenger was _____ immediately; he _____ throughout the enchanted forest delivering invitations to the royal christening party.

Chapter 3: Verbs and Verb Phrases

(build, forget) 12. A good way to _____ resentment is to _____ to invite someone to a party.

(do) 13. Alas, that was precisely what the royal couple had _____.

(learn, include, leap) 14. When the witch _____ she was not _____, she _____ up from her spinning wheel with an evil curse.

(keep, spoil) 15. She _____ her resentment to herself until the day of the christening when the tiny princess was being positively _____ with generous gifts.

(get, guarantee) 16. From one visiting fairy, the princess _____ the gift of beauty; another _____ that she would be kind as well as beautiful.

(blend, present) 17. A third fairy _____ wisdom with the other mystical gifts, and a fourth _____ her with the gift of laughter.

(appear, shoot) 18. Suddenly the evil fairy _____ and _____ an evil glance in the direction of the cradle.

(lose, snarl) 19. She _____ her composure and _____ in a low voice.

(leave, be, reach) 20. "_____ me out, will you? Well, it _____ time for my gift now. My sisters' wishes will come true, but when this baby _____ the age of sixteen, she will prick her finger on a spindle and die!"

(cackle, leave) 21. The evil witch _____ ominously and _____ the party in a puff of smoke.

(grab, weep) 22. The Queen _____ the baby and _____ bitterly.

(feel, step, plead) 23. The last of the good fairies _____ such sorrow that she _____ forward and _____ for silence.

(say, sleep, kneel) 24. "I cannot completely negate my wicked sister's wish," she _____, "but I can modify it. Your daughter will not die but will _____ until a prince _____ by her side. His kiss will break the spell."

(order, survived) 25. The king _____ all spindles in the kingdom destroyed, but, of course, one _____.

(lose, leave, open, climb) 26. Lo and behold, on her sixteenth birthday the princess _____ her way in the forest when she _____ her usual path. She came upon a tower,

Chapter 3: Verbs and Verb Phrases

_____ a door, and _____ a winding staircase to a secret room.

(meet, beg) 27. There she _____ an old crone spinning golden thread; she _____ the old woman to let her try.

(mean) 28. This was precisely what the wicked witch had _____ for her to do.

(prick, dream) 29. The princess soon _____ her finger and _____ away the next one hundred years.

(smell, burn) 30. Quite by accident, one day a prince _____ a fire that was _____ off in the direction of the old tower; he rode off to investigate.

(dwell, kneel, weep) 31. He came upon the tower and the sleeping princess who _____ within; he _____ beside her and _____ at the great evil.

(sweep, kiss) 32. When he had _____ aside the cobwebs, he _____ the sleeping princess.

(build, leave) 33. They too _____ a castle in the enchanted forest, but when their own child was born without benefit of witchery, they were most careful that no one was _____ off the guest list.

Changing D to T: Bend/Lend

In the following group of verbs, as in the last group, the present form already ends in *d*. Rather than doubling the *d* sound as you would if the verb were regular, you form the past and past participle (which are identical) by changing the *d* to *t*. For some speakers the vowel sound in the middle of the word changes; however, for many perfectly respectable speakers of American English, there is no difference in the pronunciation of the vowel in the present and in the past forms. However you choose to pronounce them, they can easily be grouped together for learning.

Present	Past	Past Participle	Present Participle
bend	bent	bent	bending
lend	lent	lent	lending
rend	rent	rent	rending
send	sent	sent	sending
spend	spent	spent	spending

EXERCISE 3-19

In the following exercise, add a verb from the above group then complete the sentence. Use each verb at least once.

96 Chapter 3: Verbs and Verb Phrases

1. Superman must have *bent the bars to escape from the room*.
2. Lydia should not be _____.
3. When the whistle blew, the supervisor was _____
   _____.
4. The Martian invaders were _____.
5. Have you _____?
6. The truth never should have been _____.
7. My heart was _____.
8. They want the money that has been _____.
9. I couldn't _____.
10. Having been _____ , _____.

No Change: *Bid/Burst*

Remember that *d* and *t* are practically the same sound. The present form of the following group already ends in *d* or *t*, so there is *no* change for the past. To add an ending will be considered a mistake in edited college writing.

Present	Past	Past Participle	Present Participle
bid(s) [1]	bid	bid	bidding
burst(s)	burst	burst	bursting
cast(s)	cast	cast	casting
cost(s)	cost	cost	costing
cut(s)	cut	cut	cutting
hit(s)	hit	hit	hitting
hurt(s)	hurt	hurt	hurting
let(s)	let	let	letting
put(s)	put	put	putting
set(s)	set	set	setting
shut(s)	shut	shut	shutting
split(s)	split	split	splitting
slit(s)	slit	slit	slitting
spread(s)	spread	spread	spreading

[1] As at an auction or in cards. To bid farewell is discussed on page 108.

EXERCISE 3-20

Fill in any acceptable form of the above verbs. Keep the story in the past tense.

Angelo's Revenge

(set) 1. When Tom Potts fell in love with Jeanine Ridings, he _____ out to win her heart.

(cast) 2. After a couple of dates, he _____ caution to the winds and invited her to a romantic dinner party for two.

(shut/spread) 3. Three days before the party Tom firmly _____ the door to his kitchen and _____ his cookbooks out on the table.

Chapter 3: Verbs and Verb Phrases

(shut/hurt) 4. The _____ door seriously _____ the feelings of Tom's cat, Angelo, an obese but generally good humored feline.

(shut/hurt/set) 5. While Tom _____ his mind to the _____ feelings of his cat, Angelo _____ out to get even.

(spread) 6. The afternoon of the dinner party, Tom _____ all his ingredients on the counter.

(split/put) 7. First he _____ and boned the chicken breasts, _____ them in a shallow bowl to marinade in white wine, herbs, and lemon zest.

(set) 8. He _____ the marinading chicken, uncovered, on the countertop to absorb flavor for the next couple of hours.

(cut/slit) 9. Next he _____ the vegetables, _____ them into matchstick-sized morsels.

(set/cost) 10. _____ these preparations aside, Tom drove to the liquor store and selected a bottle of white wine that _____ a week's pay.

(put/set) 11. When he returned with the wine, Tom _____ it in his prize possession, a silver wine cooler he'd discovered _____ on the back shelf on an old, dusty antique shop.

(set) 12. Then he _____ the table.

(set/put/cost) 13. After _____ the table, he took a shower, shaved, and _____ on a new pair of designer jeans that had _____ a ridiculous amount of money.

(bid/hurt) 14. _____ for Jeanine's attention was _____ Tom's budget.

(cast) 15. At seven-twelve when Tom had begun _____ anxious glances at the clock, the doorbell rang.

(let/put) 16. He _____ Jeanine in and _____ her coat in the closet.

(spread) 17. Jeanine carefully _____ the full skirt of her old-fashioned riding costume on the sofa, but Tom lost his chance to enquire into the reason for her peculiar attire.

(burst) 18. Suddenly, Angelo _____ into the room with a dripping chicken breast between his teeth.

(cast/put) 19. _____ a wary and revengeful glance at Tom, he ran into the bedroom and _____ himself out of reach under the bed.

(cast) 20. Mortified, Tom _____ dignity aside and gave chase; it was a race he lost.

(hurt/cut) 21. He had never _____ Angelo before, but at the moment he was ready to _____ off his head.

98   Chapter 3: Verbs and Verb Phrases

(burst, hurt)   22. Silent in the beginning of this little scene, Jeanine suddenly _____ into speech, crying, "Don't _____ him."

(put/hurt)   23. "What do you take me for?" Tom inquired, somewhat _____ upon, his feelings definitely _____ . "Naturally I'm angry. That's our dinner under the bed."

(set/spread)   24. A _____ expression _____ across Jeanine's face.

(let)   25. "It's not my dinner," she said firmly. "I should have _____ you know that I'm a vegetarian. No meat for me."

(put)   26. This _____ a new complexion on things. "Well," said Tom gamely, "that's a problem."

(set)   27. _____ him straight, Jeanine said, "Vegetarianism is not a problem; it's a way of life."

(let/put)   28. She _____ herself in the kitchen and _____ on an enormous pot of water for rice.

(spread)   29. She mixed the vegetables into the rice and _____ out the meal on the dining room table.

(hurt)   30. Tom, Jeanine, and Angelo all dined well that evening, but the uncomfortable incident _____ their growing relationship.

(cut/set)   31. Jeanine privately decided to _____ herself off from carnivorous society and eventually _____ up housekeeping with another vegetarian.

(let/split)   32. Tom and Angelo _____ bygones be bygones and spent the rest of their lives _____ steaks.

Internal Vowel Change: *Bleed/Breed*

The next group of verbs will be less troublesome for you if you remember that the *regular* past and past participle ending is *d*.

These words already end in *d* and to add another for the past would result in a jerky, stuttered sound.

Don't be fooled by the spelling of *read*. Its pronunciation puts it in this group and offers no standard alternative.

Watch out for *lead* also. Its past tense form *led* is very frequently misspelled.

Present	Past	Past Participle	Present Participle
bleed	bled	bled	bleeding
breed	bred	bred	breeding
feed	fed	fed	feeding
flee	fled	fled	fleeing

Chapter 3: Verbs and Verb Phrases

Present	Past	Past Participle	Present Participle
lead	led	led	leading
read	read	read	reading
speed	sped [1] (speeded) [2]	sped (speeded)	speeding

[1] As "sped down the road."
[2] As "speeded up the car."

EXERCISE 3-21

Fill in any acceptable form of the above verbs. Keep the story in the past tense.

Career Decision

1. When Barbara Harris was an impressionable adolescent, she ___read___ two authors in depth: Frank G. Slaughter and Ian Fleming.
2. Slaughter _____ her into a delightful world of dashing doctors who single-handedly combatted outbreaks of plague aboard ship.
3. Ian Fleming, the creator of James Bond, _____ her hunger for romance of a more dangerous sort.
4. When it came time for her to decide what kind of life she would _____, Barbara chose medicine.
5. She dreamed of _____ to the side of a stricken diplomat and saving his life.
6. The first time she saw someone _____, Barbara _____ from the emergency room.
7. She _____ down the corridor to the washroom and was violently ill.
8. Medical school required that Barbara _____ boring books on anatomy and disease, but she still _____ and reread James Bond books whenever she could.
9. Her inability to watch people _____ finally _____ her to consider leaving medical school.
10. Familiarity with medicine had _____ contempt, and she never _____ Frank Slaughter anymore.
11. Curiosity as much as anything _____ her to contact the CIA.
12. She had _____ in the paper about their Affirmative Action program.
13. The stories the handsome recruiter _____ her _____ her to imagine a very exciting life, indeed.
14. She accepted the job, and a discreet black limousine _____ her to CIA training school near Washington.
15. There she _____ almost as much as she had done in medical school.
16. The only time she could study her colleagues was when the group was being _____ at 6 A.M., noon, and 6 P.M., but the James Bond dash seemed to be a trait which had been _____ out of her generation of agent.

17. Then one day instruction was devoted to showing agents what to do if they were _____ from a knife wound in the stomach.
18. The idea that she herself might be stabbed and _____ had never occurred to Barbara; she thought agents spent most of their time ordering exactly the right bottle of wine.
19. This horrible experience _____ her to another career crisis and _____ her growing disillusionment with the secret agent life.
20. She _____ the agent training center.
21. Her flight eventually _____ her to a forest in Maine where she thought she could _____ a very quiet life.
22. She thought she might _____ a lot.
23. As she _____ down the highway, she saw a sign which _____ "Mink Farm For Sale."
24. Intrigued, she backed up and followed the road which _____ to the farm.
25. The owner _____ minks.
26. _____ minks is very simple: you _____ them and let nature take its course.
27. The owner, however, had become _____ up with Maine winters.
28. He longed to _____ a life like the ones he had _____ about in Ian Fleming's novels.
29. Barbara agreed to buy his farm on time payments and to _____ minks for the rest of her long, happy life.
30. Now when she _____ about dangerous, romantic careers, she smiles wisely.

Internal Vowel Change: *Say/Hear*

The verbs in this group may at first strike you as a collection of special cases, but notice that the past tense and past participle are the same form for each word and that they all end in *d*. Many verbs are irregular because of an internal vowel change (the vowel sound changes in the middle of the word from the present to the past), although they maintain a regular *d* ending for the past and past participle forms.

These words group themselves into families with one or more similar members that contain these two general characteristics of the larger class.

Present	Past	Past Participle	Present Participle
say	said	said	saying
hear	heard	heard	hearing
sell	sold	sold	selling
tell	told	told	telling
foretell	foretold	foretold	foretelling
hold	held	held	holding
withhold	withheld	withheld	withholding

Chapter 3: Verbs and Verb Phrases

Present	Past	Past Participle	Present Participle
stand	stood	stood	standing
understand	understood	understood	understanding
misunderstand	misunderstood	misunderstood	misunderstanding
withstand	withstood	withstood	withstanding
bind	bound	bound	binding
find	found	found	finding
grind	ground	ground	grinding
wind	wound	wound	winding

EXERCISE 3-22

Fill in the correct form of *say* in the following sentences.

1. Did he _____ who would be able to come to the movies with us?
2. He _____ there wouldn't be time.
3. I have _____ all I intend to about that matter.
4. Juanita has been _____ she feels like quitting.
5. Can't you _____ who has passed the exam?
6. The tired old man won't _____ why he buried his money.
7. He couldn't have _____ George was the father.
8. Chez Lui is _____ to be the best French restaurant in town.
9. Could you hear what was being _____ ?
10. Only Jonah might have _____ he could not submit his resignation.

Fill in the correct form of *hear* in the following sentences.

11. Did you _____ the rumor about Marge's salary?
12. You should have _____ the noise of the crash from your apartment.
13. Robbie has been _____ things.
14. Through the sound of rustling leaves was _____ the soft click from the spy's camera.
15. I've _____ that before.
16. Could you _____ what they were saying?
17. They haven't _____ the last of this.
18. He had _____ of the danger but had not believed it.
19. She _____ her name being called every day.
20. She _____ her name called yesterday.

Fill in the correct form from the *sell/tell* family of this group in the following sentences.

21. Larry will _____ his car to the highest bidder.
22. He should have _____ his mother where he had been.
23. The gypsy has been _____ the future incorrectly for years.
24. He was _____ me a lie.
25. The only person who knew the truth would have been _____ his friends down the river to have testified.
26. Who could have _____ such disastrous consequences?
27. My Uncle Charlie has been _____ his patients a ridiculous remedy for eczema.
28. The couple was _____ to move out of their bug-infested apartment if they objected to roaches.
29. Ms. Hubbard ought to _____ her dog.
30. Paul ought to have been _____ to be more subtle.

Taking your verbs from the *hold* family, fill in a correct form in the following sentences.

31. Don't _____ your breath.
32. Someone is _____ vital information.
33. Are you _____ out on me?
34. Bronkowski ought to have _____ his opinion.
35. This vase must have _____ water before it was dropped.
36. I am barely _____ onto my sanity.
37. He _____ his peace as long as he could.
38. "I've been _____ up again," wept the grocer.
39. The governor's child was being _____ for ransom.
40. Did you _____ the jug which _____ the wine?

Verbs from the *stand* family should be used correctly below.

41. Velma couldn't _____ her mother's criticism any longer.
42. She had never _____ algebra.
43. Can the spaceship _____ the heat generated by re-entry?
44. Had you come to class you might have _____ the assignment better.
45. The queen would _____ more serious assault than the press could offer.
46. The abandoned children were _____ more than they pretended.
47. Go _____ on the corner if you want to catch the bus.
48. You are _____ on my foot!
49. Have you ever been _____ ?
50. I won't _____ for the excuse that you _____ the instructions since you _____ the committee's questioning so skillfully.

Chapter 3: Verbs and Verb Phrases

Fill in the correct verb form from the *bind* family in the following sentences.

51. The judge's instructions should be _____ upon the jury.
52. Mother often said, "Don't _____ your teeth."
53. We might have _____ up the evening with another drink if it hadn't rained.
54. Have you _____ your keys?
55. Richard has _____ out who he is.
56. He doesn't care for what he has _____.
57. The weekend security guard was _____ and gagged by the intruders.
58. He was _____ early Monday morning.
59. The pencil was _____ down to its eraser.
60. Sally has been _____ her hair around her neck.

Internal Vowel Change: *Bring/Buy*

The next group of verbs with an internal vowel change is easy to learn if you work on the spelling of the changed vowel. Notice that like most verbs, regular and irregular, this group uses the same word for the past tense and for the past participle. Do not write any of the variant forms you may use in speech.

Present	Past	Past Participle	Present Participle
bring(s)	brought	brought	bringing
buy(s)	bought	bought	buying
catch(es)	caught	caught	catching
fight(s)	fought	fought	fighting
seek(s)	sought	sought	seeking
teach(es)	taught	taught	teaching
think(s)	thought	thought	thinking

EXERCISE 3–23

Fill in the most appropriate form of the verb in parentheses.

A Lucky Lesson

(bring) 1. This rabbit's foot *brought* a certain gypsy good luck.
(buy) 2. George _____ it from the gypsy to give to me.
(catch) 3. The gypsy said she had _____ the rabbit herself.
(seek) 4. She was _____ a squirrel when the rabbit ran by.
(fight) 5. He _____ his capture in vain.
(teach) 6. Having been _____ to accept all good fortune without
(think)   question, the gypsy _____ the rabbit would make as good a stew as the squirrel.

(catch) 7. Having _____ the rabbit, she went back to camp.
(catch) 8. She had _____ a rabbit while she
(seek) _____ a squirrel.
(teach) 9. This _____ her to _____ before she
(catch) _____ .
(think)
(bring) 10. She _____ the rabbit to the camp where George
(buy) _____ its foot.
(buy) 11. Now the gypsy did not have to _____ anything for supper.
(bring) 12. "This rabbit _____ me good luck," she said.
(teach) 13. She said she could _____ George to have the same kind of luck.
(buy) 14. He _____ the rabbit's foot from her for five dollars.
(fight) 15. The rabbit which had _____ in vain has certainly
(bring) _____ the gypsy a lot of luck.
(catch) 16. The supper she _____ has also _____
(bring) her a good profit.
(buy) 17. When George was _____ the rabbit's foot, he
(think) _____ he could make a good profit too.
(catch) 18. The rabbit was _____ ; good luck was
(bring) _____ ; and a lesson was going to be
(teach) _____ .
(think) 19. I _____ I could _____ George a lesson
(teach) about luck.
(bring) 20. When he _____ me the rabbit's foot, he
(think) _____ I would be happy.
(think) 21. "He _____ I'm pleased by this gift he has
(bring) _____ ," I _____ to myself.
(think)
(catch) 22. "He who _____ a rabbit _____ fortune
(seek) in the most righteous way according to Master Po," I told him.
(think) 23. "But he who _____ to find fortune with the rabbit's foot
(buy) _____ foolishly," I continued.
(fight) 24. This logic could not be _____ .
(buy) 25. The foot was _____ in good faith, but fortune was
(seek) _____ in an unlikely spot.
(buy) 26. Luck cannot be _____ .
(fight) 27. Although George and I _____ , since the lesson has
(teach) been _____ George has _____ to
(seek) _____ what can't be _____ .
(catch)
(buy)

Chapter 3: Verbs and Verb Phrases   105

Internal Vowel Change + N: *Break/Choose*

The next group of verbs is not regular at all, for the past and past participle are different words. The tense markers are very strong, however: o in the past tense, which is usually long, and n or en ending on the past participle. These are very reliable signals.

There are two very common types of mistakes in writing these irregular verbs. The first is to use the past participle in place of the past tense form: *I broken my arm* instead of *I broke my arm*. The second mistake is to try to make these verbs regular by creating forms like *choosed* or *brokened*.

The relatively few verbs which are formed by an internal vowel change in the past and the n signal on the past participle are extremely important because they are used so frequently. Do not use a word that ends in n as the main verb unless some form of *have* or *be* is nearby as a helper: *I had broken my arm*.

Present	Past	Past Participle	Present Participle
arise(s)	arose	arisen	arising
awake(s)	awoke [awaked]	awoken [awakened]	awaking
bear	bore	borne [born]	bearing
beget(s)	begot	begotten	begetting
break(s)	broke	broken	breaking
choose(s)	chose	chosen	choosing
drive(s)	drove	driven	driving
forget(s)	forgot	forgotten	forgetting
freeze(s)	froze	frozen	freezing
get(s)	got	got (gotten)	getting
ride(s)	rode	ridden	riding
rise(s)	rose	risen	rising
speak(s)	spoke	spoken	speaking
steal(s)	stole	stolen	stealing
swear(s)	swore	sworn	swearing
tear	tore	torn	tearing
wear(s)	wore	worn	wearing
weave(s) [1]	wove	woven	weaving
write(s)	wrote	written	writing

[1] *To weave cloth.* In the figurative sense (the car *weaved* in and out of traffic) *weave* is usually regular.

EXERCISE 3-24

Underline the helping verbs and fill in any acceptable past participle below.

1. After standing at the bus stop for twenty minutes in sub-zero temperatures, I feel as if I *am* _*frozen*_ stiff.

106   **Chapter 3: Verbs and Verb Phrases**

2. Her heart was _____ by his callous behavior.
3. Having _____ early, my sister retired early.
4. Wilbur cried when he thought his birthday had been _____ by the whole family.
5. Mildred has _____ a truck for the past eight months.
6. The liquor store owner claimed that his cash receipts were _____ by the police.
7. However, the accused cops were _____ of in glowing terms by their fellow officers.
8. The news commentator should have _____ more cautiously.
9. He had _____ the rules once too often.
10. Spanish is _____ here.
11. The brash job applicant had _____ without thinking.
12. The fortune-teller had _____ a clever web of vague predictions.
13. The instructor demanded to know if Warren had _____ the essay himself.
14. He has _____ on his honor that it was his own work.
15. Abel and Cain were _____ by Adam and Eve.
16. Holly was _____ spokesperson for the group.
17. The rent has _____ and the lease has been _____ by the landlord himself.
18. The irate mother stalked out of the school board meeting, having _____ her piece.
19. This tapestry was _____ in the sixteenth century.
20. My bicycle was _____ from the backyard.
21. Doneta has finally _____ out her pencil eraser.
22. Rosana should have _____ the horse with silver saddle.
23. Phyllis is always _____ at dawn by the baby.
24. The last villager has at long last _____ his smallpox vaccination.
25. Jons has been _____ mad by the endless promises which are always _____ .
26. A true hero would have _____ the insults in silence.
27. Kirby has _____ another hole in his sweater.
28. The crew was _____ to secrecy.
29. The pond is _____ , but there is no snow.
30. Golden thread was _____ into the princess's braids.

EXERCISE 3–25

One of the most confusing verbs from the last group is *choose*. The principal parts are *choose(s)*, *chose* [past tense], *chosen* [past participle], and *choosing* [present participle]. Fill in a correct form below and watch your spelling!

Chapter 3: Verbs and Verb Phrases

1. __Choose__ your fish bait with care.
2. I _____ chocolate ice cream yesterday, and I'm going to _____ peach today.
3. Sonia can _____ any lifestyle she _____.
4. The injured athlete _____ to ignore her aching knee.
5. Leroy has _____ a college.
6. We must _____ to fight another day.
7. You've been _____ leader.
8. The child is _____ a gift with care.
9. The contestants _____ this winner among themselves.
10. Today he _____ to remain silent.
11. Having _____ a spokesperson, the rest of us fell silent.
12. If she could _____ again, she would _____ differently.
13. The injured athlete _____ to play out the game.
14. He _____ a new bike path each week.
15. _____ between the red and the blue.
16. She _____ her pets with more care than her husbands.
17. Bob and Joy _____ to postpone having a baby.
18. If there's a backwards way of doing something, Bruce will _____ it.
19. I was _____ a birthday card for my mother when she entered.
20. Cathy couldn't _____ between the kittens, so she took both.
21. Jean-Paul Sartre says that to _____ not to _____ is a choice.
22. The driver ahead of me _____ to turn left even though his right signal was on.
23. Amy has _____ to return to work.
24. The director may _____ to close the airport.
25. Has he _____ his courses?

Other EN Past Participles: *Fall/Eat*

Although the *o* is the most common vowel found in the past tense with the *en* past participle, all the other vowels also come into play in this pattern. The verbs in this largest irregular group are doubly difficult because unlike all regular verbs and most irregular verbs, the past and the past participle are not the same word. **Remember: If the verb form you use ends in *en*, it should have an auxiliary (*have* or *be*) in front of it.** The verbs in this group are listed together according to similar past tense vowel sounds to make memorizing them easier.

Present	Past	Past Participle	Present Participle
befall	befell	befallen	befalling
fall	fell	fallen	falling

Present	Past	Past Participle	Present Participle
bid [1]	bade	bidden [bid]	bidding
eat	ate	eaten	eating
forbid	forbade	forbidden	forbidding
forgive	forgave	forgiven	forgiving
give	gave	given	giving
foresee	foresaw	foreseen	foreseeing
see	saw	seen	seeing
forsake	forsook	forsaken	forsaking
shake	shook [shaked]	shaken [shaked]	shaking
take	took	taken	taking
undertake	undertook	undertaken	undertaking
bite	bit	bitten	biting
hide	hid	hidden	hiding
draw	drew	drawn	drawing

[1] *Bid* in this sense means to say farewell; we saw earlier that when it is used at an auction or in card playing the principal parts are *bid, bid, bid, bidding*.

EXERCISE 3-26

Fill in the correct form of the verb on the left in the space provided.

Rescue

(arise) 1. My sister Fran was to have ___arisen___ early and to have
(drive) ___driven___ to the Michigan Sand Dunes with her friend Karen in Karen's new car.

(shake) 2. At eight o'clock Sunday morning I was _____ from sleep by a persistently ringing doorbell.

(forget) 3. Obviously my sister had _____ her arrangements, for she slept on blissfully oblivious that I was awake in the other bedroom fuming.

(beget) 4. I lay in bed, listening to the bell, ruing the day she had been _____ .

(give) 5. After I had _____ her several more seconds to answer the doorbell, I dragged myself out of bed.

(eat) 6. On my way to the buzzer I passed the remains of snacks we had _____ the night before.

(choose) 7. Feeling terribly abused by my sister and the disgusting pizza remnants, I wished I had _____ to ignore the bell, stayed in bed, and let her face leftover pizza.

Chapter 3: Verbs and Verb Phrases 109

(undertake) 8. But having _____ to stop the bell, I decided to buzz Karen up and let her get Fran up.

(steal) 9. I pushed the buzzer, threw open our front door to permit Karen to enter, and had _____ back to my bed in no time.

(choose) 10. Behind my closed door I was glad I had _____ to speed Fran on her way.

(write) 11. While she was gone, several letters could be _____ .

(freeze) 12. Suddenly I was _____ in horror.

(speak) 13. A man had _____ in my sister's room, and there had been none in there when I trekked out to the buzzer.

(befall) 14. What could have _____ her?

(shake) 15. I was badly _____ when I realized that I had let someone other than Karen into our apartment.

(give) 16. I would have _____ anything to relive the previous three minutes.

(speak) 17. Someone had _____ again; I dressed quickly and boldly went to my sister's aid.

(choose) 18. My frightened, speechless sister huddled under her covers as two soberly dressed men explained that alien beings had _____ them to spread word of their existence.

(fall) 19. "We are _____ from grace until we believe," they explained ignoring her lack of composure.

(write) 20. They held out for her inspection pamphlets that their organization had _____ to help nonbelievers see the light.

(got) 21. My sister, always a dreamer, clearly hoped the scene was a part of a horrible nightmare she had _____ from the wretched
(eat) pizza she had _____ .

(undertake) 22. I politely asked the men to leave, but they refused and continued to talk about the mission they had _____ .

(give) 23. I felt they had been _____ a chance and crept to the kitchen and called the police.

(befall) 24. The police arrived, and I explained what had _____ us.

(steal) 25. Nothing had been _____ , but I wanted the intruders out of my apartment.

(shake) 26. The men were _____ by the arrival of the police and left quietly with pious protests of innocence.

(speak) 27. Although she hasn't _____ of the incident recently, my
(forget) sister not only has never _____ the incident, she has
(forgive) never _____ me for letting two missionaries in her bedroom.

(befall) 28. Despite the fact that I rescued her, she continues to imagine the terrible things which could have _____ her.

(take)　　　　29. She has _____ to wearing pajamas and has
(forbid)　　　　　　_____ me to ever push the buzzer without finding out
　　　　　　　　　whom I'm buzzing up first.

(shake)　　　　30. I was more _____ by the incident than I let on, but as
(eat)　　　　　　　the oldest I had to put on a brave face; however, I've never
　　　　　　　　　_____ pizza since.

Get/Got as an "Auxiliary"

In a sentence with a linking verb, the subject is equal to or is described by the complement following the verb. The most common linking verb is *be*. Other linking verbs include *seem, appear, look, feel, taste, smell, sound, become, grow, continue,* and *remain*. *Get* and *got* also belong in this group, though many English teachers used to prefer to ignore them.

Subject	Linking Verb	Complement
Mary	is	a student.
The gas	must have been	poisonous.
The turkey	smells	delicious.
Tom	got	sleepy.

If some form of *be* is used as an auxiliary, as we have seen, either a past participle or a present participle is the main verb. Sometimes it is hard to tell whether the word following *be* is a subject complement or a part of the verb phrase.

Subject	Verb	
My aunt	is	angry.
My aunt	is	tired.
My aunt	is tired	by too many visitors.

You can tell by looking at the sentences above, however, that this is not an important problem since *tired* ends in *ed* whether it is a part of the verb or a subject complement.

Compare the following sentences:

Henry is tired.
Tennis is tiring.
Henry became tired.
The speech became tiring.
Henry got tired.
The speech got tiring.

Following any linking verb, a past or present participle may be used.

Chapter 3: Verbs and Verb Phrases

Sometimes it will technically be a part of the verb phrase, and sometimes it will technically be a subject complement. Some teachers still prefer to think of *get* as a pseudo- (or false) auxiliary. When *get* (or any of its forms) replaces *be* (or any of its forms) or *become* or occasionally another linking verb, then, depending on meaning, it will be followed by a past or a present participle.

EXERCISE 3-27

Fill in the appropriate form of the verb in parentheses.

The Ark Warmed Over

(build) 1. Noah was _____ an ark because he was good friends with an infallible weather forecaster.

(pen) 2. Once the ferocious animals were _____ up in the hold, there was only room for a large freezer and a microwave oven.

(purchase) 3. TV dinners got _____ by the thousands, although
(prejudice) Noah's wife remained so _____ against them she refused to heat them up.

(defeat) 4. Noah appeared un _____ by his wife's position; his
(appoint) son-in-law Esau was _____ chief cook and TV repairer.

(burn) 5. The TV dinners tasted _____ after Esau got
(finish) _____ cooking them.

(plead) 6. Even the vultures were _____ for more appetizing
(breed) meals, and they seemed ill- _____ enough to take matters into their own hands.

(hurt) 7. Noah got _____ by all the whining and complaining.

(split) 8. His time was _____ between cleaning up after and calming down his passengers.

(spread) 9. But endless stretches of water remained _____ out in front of him.

(muffle) 10. The sky looked _____ by the black clouds.

(miff) 11. Esau got _____ by the complaints, and the vultures got
(invite) _____ to be the main course for supper.

(insult) 12. Herbivores, carnivores, and omnivores alike felt _____ by the burned frozen dinners.

(mean) 13. "If this were _____ to be eaten, it would be green," said the cows.

(leave) 14. "This stuff got _____ over from creation," complained the bears.

(sweep) 15. Noah for his part kept _____ and
(mop) _____ the deck, but few passengers continued

Chapter 3: Verbs and Verb Phrases

(watch) _____ TV because they associated the television with the food.

(trample) 16. During a demonstration a case of frozen enchiladas got
(feed) _____ by the two irate zebras, and soon all the animals, with one exception, got _____ up and refused to eat.

(eat) 17. Only the unicorns continued _____ the TV dinners.

(burn) 18. The two little animals did not think the stuff tasted
(disgust) _____ or _____ .

(get) 19. The other animals had _____ thin and weak.

(stuff) 20. The unicorns got _____ with frozen dinners for forty days and forty nights.

(unhurt) 21. At first they seemed _____ by their steady diet.

(fatigue) 22. While the other animals fasted and grew _____ , the
(eat) unicorns continued _____ .

(saturate) 23. Their frail systems got _____ by the indigestible frozen food.

(sight) 24. Finally land was _____ by the dove, and the starving
(encourage) animals felt _____ .

(lift) 25. As their spirits were _____ , however, the unicorns
(depress) grew _____ and ill.

(lose) 26. After forty days' worth of frozen TV dinners, the unicorns were _____ ground rapidly.

(upset) 27. Noah got _____ when he realized what was happening; then he pondered the mysteries of the universe.

(mean) 28. If God's creatures were _____ to survive on packaged frozen food, this would not have happened.

(puzzle) 29. It seems _____ that even though the unicorns are gone
(buy) from Earth, some people continue _____ frozen dinners
(destroy) and letting their bodies get _____ by the inedible stuff.

Internal Vowel Change Plus *N: Blow/Fly*

The following section consists of more irregular verbs with the *n* past participle. The past tense forms all end in *ew*.

Present	Past	Past Participle	Present Participle
blow(s)	blew	blown	blowing
fly (flies)	flew	flown	flying
grow(s)	grew	grown	growing
know(s)	knew	known	knowing
throw(s)	threw	thrown	throwing

Chapter 3: Verbs and Verb Phrases 113

EXERCISE 3-28

Fill in any acceptable verb form from the above group.

1. Emily must ____*fly*____ to the moon.
2. I should have _____ it would never work.
3. The shark in the tank had _____ a foot in a week.
4. The last ball had been _____ .
5. The lunch whistle wasn't _____ until noon.
6. James ought to _____ every line in the play.
7. Having _____ my last chance, I quit.
8. Yesterday Cleon _____ to Memphis.
9. The beanstalk _____ overnight.
10. The wind will _____ , and the grass will _____ .
11. TWA is _____ again.
12. Mother has been _____ the bugle again.
13. The raven's wings have been clipped; it has _____ away for the last time.
14. My tomatoes have _____ as large as pumpkins.
15. Being full _____ was Rudolph's only claim to adulthood.
16. The kites can not be _____ in such a strong wind.
17. I might have _____ you wouldn't keep your promise.
18. "You can't have _____ so much," shrieked my aunt.
19. "I'm still _____ ," I replied.
20. "He's out _____ all his clothes," my mother said.

EXERCISE 3-29　　　　　　　　　　　　　　　　write

Study all the verbs whose past participles end in *n* or *en* until you can write out all the principal parts without a mistake. When you are fairly confident of them, write a story in the *past tense* using as many of these verbs as you can. (Your principal helpers in the *past* will be *had, was, were,* and *been; could, would, should,* and *did* from the present auxiliaries may appear in a past tense story, but if your verb has no helper, it should come from the past column.)

If you have difficulty getting your story started, try starting with one of the following sentences.

The Mayor of Linnexville *gave* me a medal for saving the child who *was* almost *eaten* by the tiger.
(How did it all happen?)
or
Forgetful Harry *had forgotten* where he *had hidden* the money he *had stolen* three years ago.

(Did he ever find it?
What helped him remember?)

Internal Vowel Change: *Drink/Ring*

Present	Past	Past Participle	Present Participle
drink(s)	drank	drunk	drinking
ring(s)	rang	rung	ringing
sing(s)	sang	sung	singing
sink(s)	sank	sunk	sinking
slink(s)	slunk	slunk	slinking
spring	sprang	sprung	springing
shrink	shrank [shrunk]	shrunk	shrinking
sting(s)	stung [stang]	stung	stinging
stink(s)	stank [stunk]	stunk	stinking

The principal parts of these seven verbs should be memorized together. You may be used to nonstandard forms of these irregular verbs, but you should learn the accepted standard forms for use in writing.

EXERCISE 3-30

Fill in any acceptable verb form from the group on this page.

Triple Chi Flying High

1. Yesterday the Triple Chi fraternity and I ____*drank*____ enough to ____*sink*____ a ship.
2. They were _____ and carousing until dawn.
3. My head is still _____ from their noise.
4. When my alarm _____ at 6:00 A.M., I _____ out of bed and _____ a bicarbonate in agony.
5. The beer they spilled on the lawn between our houses _____ until after noon.
6. My stomach _____ from the smell as my eyes had _____ from the morning light.
7. I could have _____ any of them under the table.
8. After breakfast I went over and _____ their doorbell just to be mean.
9. Actually when they weren't _____ and _____ , they were fairly nice guys.
10. Last summer they tried to _____ my Volkswagen in the fountain in front of the administration building.
11. In the winter they would _____ up from behind bushes and fences to pelt me with snowballs and beer cans.

Chapter 3: Verbs and Verb Phrases

12. Every day I can almost see the value of my property visibly _____ as a result of my playful neighbors.
13. I have _____ my last dime into this house, or I'd move away.
14. I bought the house during a summer vacation before I had heard the Triple Chi _____ .
15. The house has been on the market at a price which really _____ , for over three years.
16. I know I'm getting _____ ; no one else will take it at any price.
17. My only hope is to _____ the whole Triple Chi fraternity into an early suspension from the university.
18. Last month I _____ and _____ with them until dawn every day.
19. I was _____ into an alcoholic coma before I realized it couldn't be done.
20. My phone _____ at all hours of the day and night.
21. I've been beseeched to _____ seven of them out of jail on a dozen occasions.
22. I am slowly _____ under the pressure of their chaotic lives.
23. Their pet skunk has even _____ up my back porch, and I can tell he wants me to _____ like the porch.
24. What really _____ is their perennial good will.
25. A friendlier, more benevolent bunch of guys has never _____ a keg of beer together.
26. Between the stench of the beer and the stench of the skunk, a worse smell has never been _____ .
27. I've _____ phony eviction notices on them.
28. I've _____ their doorbell in the middle of their parties pretending to be the police.
29. I even _____ an Apache war lance into their front yard.
30. I finally _____ my teeth into the bit and called the Dean of Men.
31. He invited me up to _____ some beer and hear my story.
32. When I _____ the Dean's bell, he was _____ a very loud song and _____ up and down on his overstuffed chair.
33. At least the house didn't _____ so I went in cautiously.
34. I _____ into a chair he wasn't bouncing on and waited for him to offer me a drink.
35. We have been _____ beer and _____ songs together now for many years.

Internal Vowel Change: *Cling/Fling*

By now you should be thoroughly familiar with the *en* sound in the past participle of many verbs. A sound which is very close to it is represented by *ng*. The following group of words are almost identical in every position and can be easily memorized.

Present	Past	Past Participle	Present Participle
cling(s)	clung	clung	clinging
fling(s)	flung	flung	flinging
hang(s)	hung [hanged]	hung [hanged]	hanging
sling(s)	slung	slung	slinging
spring(s)	sprung (sprang)	sprung	springing
string(s)	strung	strung	stringing
swing(s)	swung	swung	swinging
wring(s)	wrung	wrung	wringing

Hang is a special problem. Traditionally grammatical authorities have insisted that objects are *hung* and people are *hanged*. This is one case where the irregular form is overcoming (or at least becoming as popular as) an existent regular form.

The past tense may trouble you in this group. Many dialects use *ang* endings in this position, and *sprang* persists even in edited American English; however, most dictionaries and grammarians call the *ang* form for these archaic or colloquial.

EXERCISE 3-31

In the following sentences fill in the correct form of the word given to the left.

Treasure Hunt

(fling) 1. One day Dorothea and I decided to _____ our cares to the wind.

(hang) 2. We _____ our aprons up in the kitchen and headed for the beach.

(sling) 3. We _____ our diving gear into the bottom of a rented
(swing) boat and _____ out into the channel looking for deep water and adventure.

(string) 4. We had _____ a line from the bow of the boat to plumb for the point where the coral reef dropped off into a bottomless ocean.

(cling) 5. At that time I still _____ to the idea that I could find a sunken ship laden with treasure.

(spring) 6. The boat was _____ gently up and down as the channel current caught us.

(string) 7. When the weighted line suddenly _____ itself taut,
(fling) we _____ the anchor behind us and hooked onto the rim of the reef.

(cling) 8. The anchor hooks _____ to the reef as the boat
(swing) _____ back and forth at the end of its tether.

Chapter 3: Verbs and Verb Phrases   117

(wring)   9. For a month we had been _____ out our bathing suits at night and putting them on damp in the morning.

(hang)   10. Our hopes were _____ on the thread of a doubtful story Dorothea had heard from an old fisherman.

(spring)   11. We would _____ out of bed in the morning, rush
(hang)   through the necessary chores, and gather up our gear which was left _____ in the front hall every night.

(string)   12. The days _____ themselves together in endless clumps of possibility.

(wring)   13. I _____ out my hair with my suit and cared little for the sight of either.

(swing)   14. Whenever I _____ the boat clear of the dock and
(spring)   headed into the afternoon sun, my heart could only _____ ahead in anticipation.

(string)   15. Today we dropped anchor almost at the tip of the reef on the lee side of the island, _____ the anchor line out as usual.

(swing)   16. Adjusting my snorkel, I _____ my feet over the side as I
(sling)   _____ my spear gun over my left shoulder.

(hang)   17. _____ there on the edge of the abyss, I could still
(cling)   _____ to the virtue of courage.

(fling)   18. I _____ aside my trepidation and
(spring)   _____ over the side into six fathoms of unexplored ocean.

(hang)   19. Dorothea might have _____ there longer if I hadn't called to her.

(cling)   20. She _____ to the edge of the boat for a moment and then pushed off in my direction.

(spring)   21. The beach was a faint line _____ up over the horizon occasionally as the waves lapped over us.

(cling)   22. We searched along the wall of the underwater coral cliff as we _____ to its sharp edges.

(wring)   23. When we surfaced we _____ our hands in despair.

(spring)   24. Our boat had _____ loose from it precarious mooring and was drifting rapidly out to sea.

(fling)   25. We had to _____ aside the notion of catching it.

(hang)   26. The hours now _____ together like brittle threads of impossibility.

(spring)   27. My air tank had _____ a leak long before our survival was at stake.

(cling)   28. As we swam for shore we were _____ to hope that another boat would come by.

(fling) 29. Dorothea had already _____ aside two hundred dollars worth of cumbersome equipment.
(cling) 30. I should not have _____ to mine for so long.
(string) 31. If we could reach a buoy, I thought I would be able to _____ my gear around it and retrieve it later.
(swing) 32. My spear had been _____ against my side for what seemed like hours.
(wring) 33. I felt I could have _____ my own neck for not checking
(swing) the anchor after having _____ down into the water.
(spring) 34. Occasional bits of seaweed were _____ up around us now as we made our way slowly toward the shore.
(spring) 35. A brilliant sunset _____ up behind us as we were little more than halfway back.
(hang) 36. Dorothea began _____ back, so I suggested we float for awhile.
(wring) 37. As we were drifting and _____ every ounce of self-pity out of our situation, we heard a distant motor.
(swing) 38. I _____ around and began _____ up
(spring) and down looking for a rescuer.
(wring) 39. As the evening was _____ the last bit of light out of the
(swing) sunset, the boat we were hearing _____ off to our right and out to sea.
(fling) 40. Just as we had _____ off the hope of rescue, the boat
(swing) _____ back in our direction.
(wring) 41. The two fishermen at last pulled us _____ wet and exhausted out of the ocean.
(swing) 42. They _____ their boat back towards land,
(spring) _____ effortlessly over the choppy water.
(wring) 43. We were still _____ wet when we at last
(fling) _____ ourselves onto solid ground.
(hang) 44. However, we didn't _____ up our swimsuits forever.
(string) 45. To _____ up an apron and _____ a
(swing) broom we felt was a far worse fate than a search for sunken treasure.

Some Very Irregular Verbs: *Become/Begin*

This next collection of irregular verbs may look to you like a catch-all for words that didn't quite fit anyplace else, but look again. Their common characteristic is the letter *a* in the past tense. Sometimes it is pronounced like the *a* in *hat,* sometimes like the *a* in *hate,* and sometimes like the *a* in *halt.* The spellings of the past participles in this group vary widely, but except for *swum* and *come* (which are nasal sounds very much like the *-n* and *-en* past

Chapter 3: Verbs and Verb Phrases

participles) there is really nothing new included except for the curious spellings.

The greatest number of written mistakes in this group occurs when the past participle is used as the main verb without a helper as in *I seen him many times* instead of *I've seen him* or *I have seen him many times*. Memorize the principal parts of these very common irregular verbs and never write the past participle forms without a helping verb.

Present	Past	Past Participle	Present Participle
become	became	become	becoming
begin	began	begun	beginning
come	came	come	coming
eat	ate	eaten	eating
give	gave	given	giving
lay [1]	laid	laid	laying
lie [2]	lay	lain	lying
make	made	made	making
overcome	overcame	overcome	overcoming
run	ran	run	running
see	saw	seen	seeing
sit	sat	sat	sitting
swim	swam	swum	swimming

[1] To put or place SOMETHING; [2] to recline (no direct object). These words are often confused primarily because the present tense of the first is used as the past tense of the second. Many well-educated and intelligent people are forced to double check the principal parts of these two words each time before they write them.

EXERCISE 3-32

Fill in the most appropriate form of the verb in parentheses in the following exercise.

An Ordinary Day

(eat) 1. I got up late, quickly _____ my breakfast,
(make) _____ my bed, and _____ to the train
(run) station.

(make) 2. I _____ it onto the platform just as a train
(begin) _____ to pull out of the station.

(swim) 3. I jumped aboard and _____ through the crowd looking
(sit) for a seat; then I _____ down.

(begin) 4. The northbound train was _____ to pick up speed
(make) when I realized I had _____ a mistake.

(swim) 5. Because I wanted to go south, I half- _____ and half-
(run) _____ for the nearest exit.

(give) 6. I knew that cranky Dr. Gibson would _____ me an F in
(come) composition if I _____ to her class late again.

Chapter 3: Verbs and Verb Phrases

(make)   7. It really _____ me mad to think of her
(sit)   _____ up at the front of the room tapping her pencil
(come)   while we _____ in and _____ our pa-
(lay)   pers on her desk.
(see)   8. I could just _____ her wrinkling up her nose before she
(see)   even _____ the mistakes we had
(make)   _____ .
(eat)   9. A short man with a gray beard was _____ jelly donuts in the doorway.
(come)   10. As soon as the door slid open a pregnant woman carrying a suitcase
(eat)   _____ in behind the man _____ the
(make)   donut bumping into him and _____ him smear jelly on his beard.
(begin)   11. He _____ to swear at her and she put the suitcase on its
(sit)   end and _____ down on it.
(eat)   12. He wrapped the donut which he had not _____ in a
(make)   paper napkin and _____ his way into the rear of the
(give)   train and _____ me a generous smear on the way past.
(begin)   13. The train had already _____ to pull out as the unhappy
(lay)   woman _____ her head against the door.
(lie)   14. She looked as if she needed to _____ down more than anything else.
(swim)   15. _____ against the current of bodies, I
(make)   _____ for another exit.
(see)   16. I was wedged between an umbrella wielding woman and the back half
(come)   of a very tall and very heavy man when I _____ the next station _____ and go.
(lie)   17. I could feel the floor beneath my feet, but I might as well have been
(make)   _____ down for all the progress I was _____ .
(lie)   18. I had _____ upright on trains before but never when I
(make)   was trying so hard to _____ an escape.
(begin)   19. Just as I had _____ to _____ up hope,
(give)   the umbrella lady _____ down and I
(sit)   _____ a chance to break for the next exit.
(see)
(swim)   20. I had _____ through about ten rows of people when I
(give)   was _____ a sharp poke in the ribs.
(see)   21. I had not _____ my attacker, but the man who had been
(eat)   _____ the jelly donut which had _____
(make)   the mess on the sleeve of my jacket was _____ next to
(sit)   me.
(come)   22. That _____ as no surprise.

Chapter 3: Verbs and Verb Phrases 121

(run) 23. As I squeezed past him, I _____ my jellied arm across his back.
(come) 24. Two more stops had _____ and gone as I had slowly
(make) _____ my trek from the blocked exit.
(lay) 25. I _____ my composition notebook against the back of
(give) the next human obstacle and _____ it a gentle push.
(give) 26. It _____ a not-so-gentle push back, and I found I had
(eat) _____ the corner off my homework when I could
(see) _____ again.
(see) 27. The next station loomed into view, but I _____ that I
(make) wouldn't _____ it without some desperate effort.
(give) 28. I _____ the obstinate plaid jacket another tap and
(lay) _____ my hand on the back of the next seat to help me
(begin) squeeze around when the person inside the jacket _____ to turn.
(lay) 29. He _____ me out on the floor.
(lie) 30. I was still _____ there when the next three stations
(swim) _____ past my bleary vision.
(sit) 31. Everyone was _____ quietly as I _____
(lie) stretched out in more floor space than I had _____ all
(see) morning.
(see) 32. I could _____ Dr. Gibson's composition
(lay) _____ next to a muddy rubber boot.
(come) 33. The boot _____ down on the corner opposite where I had bitten the paper earlier.
(sit) 34. I was _____ up now, so I _____ it a
(give) gentle tug.
(begin) 35. The paper _____ to tear, so I let it
(lie) _____ there for a minute.
(come) 36. The skinny leg _____ out of the boot was wearing
(make) panty-hose, so I thought I could _____ it move off my composition fairly easily.
(eat) 37. I tapped the leg carefully twice and then _____ a con-
(come) siderable amount of the mud which had _____ off when she kicked me in the mouth.
(come) 38. My essay had _____ free in the exchange, however; so
(run) I _____ for the door which I could suddenly
(see) _____ through the knees surrounding me.
(begin) 39. I was foolishly _____ to think I would
(make) _____ it when I _____ into the conductor.
(see) 40. He wanted to _____ my ticket.
(give) 41. I _____ it to him which _____ him

(make)		snarl, "Can't you _____ you're on the wrong train?"
(see)		
(give)	42.	He _____ me back my ticket and
(make)		_____ me get off at the next station.
(come)	43.	When I _____ to class late, Dr. Gibson was
(give)		_____ the class a lecture about how to
(make)		_____ our dull, everyday lives into interesting compositions.
(begin)	44.	I _____ to wonder how we could write interesting
(come)		essays when nothing exciting ever _____ into our lives.

Special Difficulties: *Come/Run*

Come (and its derivatives *become* and *overcome*) and *run* (and its derivatives *overrun* and *outrun*) offer special difficulty because the past participle reverts to the present tense form. It is important to control these verbs because they occur quite frequently in writing.

Present	Past	Past Participle	Present Participle
come(s)	came	come	coming
become(s)	became	become	becoming
overcome(s)	overcame	overcome	overcoming
run(s)	ran	run	running
overrun(s)	overran	overrun	overrunning
outrun(s)	outran	outrun	outrunning

EXERCISE 3–33

Fill in the correct form of *come, become, overcome,* or *run* in the following story. It is being told in the past tense; do not shift to the present.

Troy Revisited

1. When Ulysses Harrison _____ home from work one summer evening, he discovered that a telegram had _____ during his absence.
2. It _____: "Your aunt, Helen Harrison, died yesterday. Will you _____ to Troy, New York, on June 2 for the funeral and the reading of her will?"
3. The news of his Aunt Helen's death _____ as a shock to Ulysses; he was completely _____ with grief, unable to _____ his usual five miles before dinner.
4. Although he had left Troy and _____ to Athens, Georgia, over nine years ago, he remembered Aunt Helen with great fondness.

Chapter 3: Verbs and Verb Phrases

5. In her youth she worked as a switchboard operator, but _____ by the boredom, she had _____ to hate the job.
6. One night in a bar she had _____ into a circus performer who spoke glowingly about the business, and shortly afterward she quit her job, _____ a trapeze artist in the circus.
7. Although she was _____ and going all the time, she took time to visit with Ulysses, who had _____ her only relative.
8. He would _____ to Troy each summer for a week to see Aunt Helen and would _____ up and down the deserted back roads of the little town.
9. However, Ulysses _____ to dread these visits because of Aunt Helen's ill-tempered horse, Cassandra, who, the first time he met her, had _____ up and tried to take off his arm.
10. Every time he _____ near Cassandra, she bit him until it _____ a painful nuisance.
11. Aunt Helen had won Cassandra in a late night crap game, however, and had _____ to love her.
12. Whenever Ulysses visited, she forced him to _____ with her out to the barn and to try to _____ his fear of the nasty nag.
13. "No harm will _____ to you," she'd insist as he _____ away.
14. This _____ a ritual which Ulysses dreaded.
15. He _____ convinced that Aunt Helen was _____ a little touched, and indeed she _____ more eccentric over the years.
16. As a child Ulysses had _____ to prefer the wooden horse, a part of an old merry-go-round, which Aunt Helen had made into a pole lamp for her parlor.
17. Aunt Helen finally _____ convinced that Ulysses, delightful nephew though he was, lacked the spiritual resources to _____ friends with Cassandra and allowed him to _____ friends with the polelamp horse instead.
18. All this flashed through Ulysses's mind before he had _____ to grips with the problem of getting away from the office for a few days.
19. Immediately he wired the lawyer that he could _____ and _____ to make plane reservations.
20. The next morning he phoned his office, explained the situation, and promised that he would _____ back as soon as it _____ possible.
21. It never occurred to Ulysses that he would _____ into any money, so when the time _____ to board the plane, he did so sadly.
22. Aunt Helen's motto had _____ "Easy _____ , easy go," and she had _____ to gamble heavily after her trapeze days were over.
23. Although she _____ from sturdy stock, she left the trapeze at forty-seven and _____ a full-time gambler, _____ an ongoing card game in her home.
24. After arranging for the funeral in Troy, he _____ even sadder and went reluctantly to the lawyer's office, _____ with sorrow.

Chapter 3: Verbs and Verb Phrases

25. "You may _____ in," said the secretary, a young woman he'd _____ into at the funeral.
26. The lawyer _____ to the point immediately, unlike some people who _____ on and on.
27. "Your aunt left everything to you, including a sealed envelope. Ah hem, she _____ quite eccentric at the end. Her bank account doesn't _____ to anything, but the property is free and clear. The taxes _____ to more than the property's worth, however. It hasn't been _____ well in years."
28. The news _____ as no surprise to Ulysses, who asked for the letter.
29. He opened it, read, and _____ agitated. The letter _____ : "When the horse's neck is wrung, your future will be won."
30. "Don't tell me old Cassandra is still alive," he said, _____ out of his shock. "This _____ as something of a surprise. What should I do with her?"
31. "Sounds like your aunt was worried about what would _____ of the horse," said the lawyer. "Says here you're supposed to wring her neck."
32. Ulysses was mystified by his aunt's instruction. Surely one shot rather than strangled horses. She must have _____ even more unstrung in her last years when _____ the place _____ too much for her.
33. "The time has _____ to visit the property," Ulysses said firmly. "What's _____ of Cassandra since my aunt's death?"
34. "Neighbors _____ over and feed her," said the lawyer. "Evil-tempered horse they say."
35. At these words Ulysses was _____ by a flood of memories. He felt as if he had really _____ home.
36. The men drove out to the farm. "Cassandra always _____ _____ when I call her," explained Ulysses. "She takes the sugar from my hand and then tries to bite off my fingers. She _____ pretty close when I was about eleven."
37. Old Cassandra approached the two men at a stately pace; however, Ulysses noticed her eyes rolled in her head as maliciously as in her youth. She snapped ineffectually at his arm, but her performance did not _____ up to her old standards.
38. As soon as the horse _____ into sight, Ulysses knew he couldn't wring her neck.
39. "As long as we've _____ this far," the lawyer said, "we may as well _____ up to the house."
40. Although no light _____ through the blinds, Ulysses noticed that nothing much had changed. He _____ quite nostalgic.
41. "That's her old trapeze, hanging from the ceiling," he remarked, as his eyes _____ accustomed to the light. He gave it a fond push.
42. "And here's her old deck of cards," he exclaimed as he neared the card table. Tears _____ to his eyes.

Chapter 3: Verbs and Verb Phrases

43. "And this old pole lamp," he said fondly, "is my old horsie." Ulysses put an arm around its neck and gave it an affectionate hug. Off it _____ .
44. "Goodness," said Ulysses, _____ visibly upset. "I've broken it." He _____ to pick up the pieces.
45. At that moment packages of ten and twenty dollar bills wrapped in rubber bands _____ pouring out of the horse's neck.
46. "Jeepers," said Ulysses. "Where did all this _____ from?"
47. "I'll be darned," said the lawyer. "I knew your aunt was quite a card shark. In fact, the time _____ when the sheriff had to _____ out here and speak firmly to her. Some sore losers wanted to _____ her off the farm. When he _____ in, she attacked him from the trapeze. Threatened to get Cassandra on him."
48. "Good old Aunt Helen. Everyone in the family said she'd _____ to no good," said Ulysses as he _____ his hands through the money.
49. With the money _____ a note. "My time is _____ out. Don't _____ upset. My life's been a gas. Use a part of the money to take care of old Cassandra. Perhaps there's yet time for you to _____ your fear of her. Don't play cards unless you're good. Most people aren't as you can see from my winnings. Good-bye, Ulysses."
50. This moving message was taken to heart by Ulysses. "I've _____ to the good part," reflected Ulysses. "Perhaps I'll _____ a bareback rider, and Cassandra and I can stay together."

A Unique Verb: Go

Go is one of the most irregular of the irregular verbs because historically it is really two words. It might have formed as

	go	gid	gone	going
similar to	do	did	done	doing
or as	wend	went	went	wending
similar to	send	sent	sent	sending

Instead it is composed of both and is in a class by itself and its own offspring.

go	went	gone	going
forego	[no past]	foregone	foregoing
undergo	underwent	undergone	undergoing

EXERCISE 3–34

Fill in some form of the verb *go*.

A Ridiculous Story

1. I am _____ to tell you a ridiculous story about a cat who _____ mad for liver sausage.

Chapter 3: Verbs and Verb Phrases

2. I first saw the animal several nights ago when I had _____ out my back door to put out the garbage.
3. I had _____ down the steep staircase with one hand on the garbage and one hand on the bannister.
4. Having _____ this perilous route every evening for several months, I was not really afraid.
5. I might have _____ more slowly if I had anticipated any interference.
6. However, I _____ down quickly not looking where I was stepping.
7. Just as I was _____ to transfer the garbage to my left hand so I could unlock the door at the bottom of the back stairs, something _____ bump in the night.
8. My pulse rate _____ from sixty to one hundred four beats per minute within an instant.
9. I wanted to _____ back to the kitchen with the garbage, but I knew my family would hoot if I reappeared garbage-laden.
10. When the possibility of hysterical, undignified flight had _____ , I peered into the corner of the staircase.
11. "You must _____ on; you can _____ on," I admonished myself.
12. Before I could _____ any further, I heard a noise very much like the one my son Geffy makes when he wants to drive me mad.
13. When he makes the noise, his voice _____ from that of a normal six-year-old boy to that of a crazed hyena in three seconds.
14. I began to think I had _____ crazy; there simply wasn't room for a child in the dark corner.
15. Besides, minutes before I _____ out the back door, Geffy had _____ into his brother's room to torture him.
16. I _____ a step closer and threw open the door.
17. The sun had not yet _____ below the horizon, and the lingering glow of the sunset illuminated the corner.
18. A huge black cat whose eyes glowed with evil cunning not unlike Geffy's spoke before I could _____ out the back door.
19. "Have you _____ and tied that garbage up in a plastic bag again?" the cat asked.
20. Naturally I feared that I was _____ crazy and tried to get a grip on myself.
21. I _____ out with the garbage each night; obviously this night the quick descent had _____ to my head.
22. When I opened my eyes, the cat had not _____ .
23. Instead it spoke again. "_____ back upstairs and undo the plastic sack tie. I want easy access to the liver sausage wrapper."
24. Before my kids _____ to school each morning, I prepare them liver sausage sandwiches. They won't eat anything else.
25. Clearly I had _____ and run into yet a third liver sausage lover.

Chapter 3: Verbs and Verb Phrases

26. The cat _____ with me up to the landing where I discovered my best butcher knife stuck into the storage room door.
27. The boys had been _____ to play "Murder the Monster with No Nose" earlier that day when it had started raining.
28. Evidently when they had _____ in, the knife had been plunged into the door in a fit of anger.
29. Although the knife blade wasn't what it had been, at least I didn't have to _____ into the kitchen.
30. I cut open the plastic garbage bag and _____ down a few steps to where the cat waited.
31. "You must not _____ any further," the cat warned. "Just throw me the liver sausage wrapper."
32. I tossed the desired dainty at the cat, and it was _____ in two shakes.
33. Down the stairs I _____ , cautiously looking out for the cat.
34. The garbage _____ into the garbage can, and I _____ up the stairs to bed.
35. The kids still _____ off to school with liver sausage sandwiches, but the garbage now _____ down the stairs with one of the children.
36. I _____ out the back door as little as possible, and if a cat _____ into our trash at night, it reties the bags afterwards.
37. Cats have _____ to some lengths to disguise their abilities; nevertheless, a craving for liver sausage _____ a long way toward bringing some of their talents to light.

The Last Group: *Dig/Win*

There's an odd but short collection of verbs which you may be reluctant to think of as a unified group because of the variety of spellings; however, they all have the *u* sound heard in *spun* for the past and the past participle.

Present	Past	Past Participle	Present Participle
dig	dug	dug	digging
stick	stuck	stuck	sticking
strike	struck	struck (stricken)[1]	striking
spin	spun	spun	spinning
win	won	won	winning

[1] *Stricken* is used only in certain contexts such as "stricken from the record" or "stricken by disease."

EXERCISE 3–35 — write

Show that you can control any verb when you know the principal parts by writing at least twenty sentences using the above verbs and a wide variety of auxiliaries. You may do this assignment as a short, short story if you like, but the primary goal is to get you to write as many different types of verb phrases as you can, which may be difficult in a unified story.

ANALOGIZING

We've looked at nearly 130 irregular verbs thus far, but we've put them into only fifteen or sixteen groups. The few remaining irregular verbs that we haven't looked at are either old-fashioned words you probably don't use or words you won't have much occasion to you use. However, if you performed the last exercise without undue stress, then you know your helping verbs, and you know what the principal parts of verbs are all about. If you know the principal parts of *dig* are *dig, dug, dug, digging* and if you rely on your helping verbs then you should have no trouble in writing the verb correctly if it should come up. What may give you trouble, however, is trying to make a verb like *drag,* which is perfectly regular, behave like *dig.* This is called **analogizing,** and it is a process which accounts for a lot of differences in verb forms. When you come upon a word in your writing which your internal grammar tells you is irregular but which we have not studied, check the principal parts. You can be confident that the regular (*-d* or *-ed*) form is correct if no irregular form is given. The true irregulars we have left out will almost never show up in your writing; these include the following:

forbear	forebore	forborne	forbearing
shoe	shod	shod	shoeing
smite	smote	smitten	smiting
slay	slew	slain	slaying
spit	spat	spat	spitting
stave	stove	stove	staving
strive	strove	striven	striving
thrive	throve	thriven	thriving

Hardly anyone gets smitten by anything but love anymore, but you must still be on your guard against words which try to act irregular when they're not. There are a few words which are irregular in one sense and regular in another, and we've tried to put notes on them.

Next is a list of regular verbs that are often given irregular forms. Tag the ones that you use irregular forms of and practice them. If an irregular form is given in parentheses, it is also acceptable in writing.

Present	Past	Past Participle	Present Participle
alight	alighted (alit)	alighted (alit)	alighting
ask	asked	asked	asking
awaken	awakened	awakened	awaking
bet	betted (bet)	betted (bet)	betting
boil	boiled	boiled	boiling
broadcast	broadcasted (broadcast)	broadcasted (broadcast)	broadcasting

Chapter 3: Verbs and Verb Phrases

Present	Past	Past Participle	Present Participle
climb	climbed	climbed	climbing
clothe	clothed (clad)	clothed (clad)	clothing
dare	dared	dared	daring
dive	dived (dove)	dived (dove)	diving
drag	dragged	dragged	dragging
drown	drowned	drowned	drowning
flow	flowed	flowed	flowing
forecast	forecasted (forecast)	forecasted (forecast)	forecasting
help	helped	helped	helping
knit	knitted (knit)	knitted (knit)	knitting
loan[1]	loaned	loaned	loaning
mow	mowed	mowed (mown)	mowing
prove	proved	proved (proven)	proving
rid	ridded (rid)	ridded (rid)	ridding
ring[2]	ringed	ringed	ringing
sew	sewed	sewed	sewing
shave	shaved	shaved (shaven)[3]	shaving
shine[4]	shined (shone)[4]	shined (shone)	shining
suppose	supposed	supposed	supposing
use	used	used	using
weave[5]	weaved	weaved	weaving
wed	wedded	wedded	wedding
wet	wetted	wetted (wet)	wetting

[1] *Loan* has been a verb in the English language since the thirteenth century, but we must warn you that many people turn up their noses at it. They argue that *lend, lent, lent, lending* do the job, and there's no need to have extra words lying about.

[2] *Ring* meaning to draw a ring around.

[3] *Shaven* is used only in the adjective position: "he was always clean-shaven."

[4] *Shine* is a regular verb when it means to polish; it is irregular when the subject is the sun: "the sun shone brightly."

[5] *Weave* is regular when it is used in figurative senses: "he weaved in and out of traffic"; but it is irregular when the sense is literal: "they wove cloth out of the threads."

EXERCISE 3–36 — write

Write thirty sentences using the above verbs and a wide variety of auxiliaries. You may do this assignment as a short narrative if you like, but the primary goal is to get you to write as many different types of verb phrases as you can.

IRREGULAR VERB INDEX

To understand and control standard American-English verb phrases, it is necessary for you to know two things: the principal parts of a lot of verbs and which principal part is required by each auxiliary. When a verb phrase is made up of more than one helper, the one closest to the main verb controls it.

	Present	Past	Past Participle	Present Participle
Auxiliaries:	*Group 1*		*Group 2*	*Group 3*
	can could do	(NONE)	have be	be
	may might does		has am	am
	shall should did		had is	is
	will would		having are	are
	must		was	was
	ought (to)		were	were
			been	been
			being	

Remember that *be, do,* and *have* are sometimes used as main verbs also.

BE (am, is, are)	were (was)	been	being
DO (does)	did	done	doing
HAVE (has)	had	had	having

Main Verbs:

Present	Past	Past Participle	Present Participle
arise(s)	arose	arisen	arising
awake(s)	awoke	awoken	awaking
be (am, is, are)	were (was)	been	being
bear(s)	bore	born(e)	bearing
become(s)	became	become	becoming
befall(s)	befell	befallen	befalling
beget(s)	begot	begotten	begetting
begin(s)	began	begun	beginning
bend(s)	bent	bent	bending
bid(s)	bade	bidden	bidding
bind(s)	bound	bound	binding
bite(s)	bit	bitten	biting
bleed(s)	bled	bled	bleeding
blow(s)	blew	blown	blowing
break(s)	broke	broken	breaking
breed(s)	bred	bred	breeding
bring(s)	brought	brought	bringing
build(s)	built	built	building
burst(s)	burst	burst	bursting
buy(s)	bought	bought	buying
cast(s)	cast	cast	casting
catch(es)	caught	caught	catching
choose(s)	chose	chose	choosing
cling(s)	clung	clung	clinging
come(s)	came	come	coming
cost(s)	cost	cost	costing
creep(s)	crept	crept	creeping
cut(s)	cut	cut	cutting
dig(s)	dug	dug	digging
do (does)	did	done	doing
draw(s)	drew	drawn	drawing
dream(s)	dreamed or dreamt	dreamed or dreamt	dreaming
drink(s)	drank	drunk	drinking
drive(s)	drove	driven	driving

Chapter 3: Verbs and Verb Phrases

Present	Past	Past Participle	Present Participle
eat(s)	ate	eaten	eating
fall(s)	fell	fallen	falling
feed(s)	fed	fed	feeding
feel(s)	felt	felt	feeling
fight(s)	fought	fought	fighting
find(s)	found	found	finding
flee(s)	fled	fled	fleeing
fling(s)	flung	flung	flinging
fly(ies)	flew	flown	flying
forbid(s)	forbade	forbidden	forbidding
forebear(s)	forebore	foreborne	forebearing
forego(es)	(None)	foregone	foregoing
foresee(s)	foresaw	foreseen	foreseeing
foretell(s)	foretold	foretold	foretelling
forget(s)	forgot	forgotten	forgetting
forgive(s)	forgave	forgiven	forgiving
forsake(s)	forsook	forsaken	forsaking
freeze(s)	froze	frozen	freezing
get(s)	got	gotten	getting
give(s)	gave	given	giving
go (goes)	went	gone	going
grind(s)	ground	ground	grinding
grow(s)	grew	grown	growing
hang(s)	hung	hung	hanging
have (has)	had	had	having
hear(s)	heard	heard	hearing
hide(s)	hid	hid	hiding
hit(s)	hit	hit	hitting
hold(s)	held	held	holding
hurt(s)	hurt	hurt	hurting
keep(s)	kept	kept	keeping
kneel(s)	kneeled or knelt	kneeled or knelt	kneeling
know(s)	knew	known	knowing
lay(s)	laid	laid	laying
lead(s)	led	led	leading
leap(s)	leaped or leapt	leaped or leapt	leaping
leave(s)	left	left	leaving
lend(s)	lent	lent	lending
let(s)	let	let	letting
lie(s) to recline	lay	lain	lying
lie(s) to tell a lie	lied	lied	lying
lose(s)	lost	lost	losing
make(s)	made	made	making
mean(s)	meant	meant	meaning
meet(s)	met	met	meeting
misunderstand(s)	misunderstood	misunderstood	misunderstanding
outrun(s)	outran	outrun	outrunning
overcome(s)	overcame	overcome	overcoming
overrun(s)	overran	overrun	overrunning
plead(s)	pleaded or	pleaded or	pleading

Present	Past	Past Participle	Present Participle
	pled	pled	
put(s)	put	put	putting
read(s)	read	read	reading
rend(s)	rent	rent	rending
ride(s)	rode	ridden	riding
ring(s)	rang	rung	ringing
rise(s)	rose	risen	rising
run(s)	ran	run	running
say(s)	said	said	saying
see(s)	saw	seen	seeing
seek(s)	sought	sought	seeking
sell(s)	sold	sold	selling
send(s)	sent	sent	sending
set(s)	set	set	setting
shake(s)	shook	shaken	shaking
shine(s)	shined or shone	shined or shone	shining
shoe(s)	shod	shod	shoeing
shoot(s)	shot	shot	shooting
show(s)	showed	shown	showing
shrink(s)	shrunk	shrunk	shrinking
shut(s)	shut	shut	shutting
sing(s)	sang	sung	singing
sink(s)	sank	sunk	sinking
sit(s)	sat	sat	sitting
slay(s)	slew	slain	slaying
sleep(s)	slept	slept	sleeping
sling(s)	slung	slung	slinging
slink(s)	slunk	slunk	slinking
slit(s)	slit	slit	slitting
smite(s)	smote	smitten	smiting
sow(s)	sowed	sown	sowing
speak(s)	spoke	spoken	speaking
speed(s)	speeded or sped	speeded or sped	speeding
spend(s)	spent	spent	spending
spin(s)	spun	spun	spinning
split(s)	split	split	splitting
spit(s)	spit	spit	spitting
spread(s)	spread	spread	spreading
spring(s)	sprang	sprung	springing
stand(s)	stood	stood	standing
stave(s)	stove	stove	
steal(s)	stole	stolen	stealing
stick(s)	stuck	stuck	sticking
sting(s)	stung	stung	stinging
stink(s)	stank or stunk	stunk	stinking
strike(s)	struck	struck	striking
string(s)	strung	strung	stringing
strive(s)	strove	striven	striving
swear(s)	swore	sworn	swearing

Chapter 3: Verbs and Verb Phrases

Present	Past	Past Participle	Present Participle
sweep(s)	swept	swept	sweeping
swim(s)	swam	swum	swimming
swing(s)	swung	swung	swinging
take(s)	took	taken	taking
teach(es)	taught	taught	teaching
tear(s)	tore	torn	tearing
tell(s)	told	told	telling
think(s)	thought	thought	thinking
throw(s)	threw	thrown	throwing
undergo(es)	underwent	undergone	undergoing
understand(s)	understood	understood	understanding
undertake(s)	undertook	undertaken	undertaking
wear(s)	wore	worn	wearing
weave(s)	wove	woven	weaving
weep(s)	wept	wept	weeping
win(s)	won	won	winning
wind(s)	wound	wound	winding
withhold(s)	withheld	withheld	withholding
withstand(s)	withstood	withstood	withstanding
wring(s)	wrung	wrung	wringing
write(s)	wrote	written	writing

REVIEW _____ three

The sentences in this review exercise are provided to help you check your progress in this chapter and to prepare you for what you'll find in the posttest. For the answers to this exercise, check with your instructor or tutor or listen to the appropriate audio tape.

Circle the correct choice.

1. Everyone should (quit, quits, quitting) smoking.
          A   B   C

2. Last month Lynn did (plant, plants, planted, planting) a large garden, but she (don't, doesn't) water it regularly.

3. Jim phoned the dentist and calmly (ask, asks, asked, asking) for an appointment.

4. Sometime last spring Ulysses had (come, comes, came, coming) to see his Aunt Helen.

5. When the ark was finished, Noah (choose, chooses, chose, choosed, chosen, choosing) two of each animal and a six month supply of TV dinners.

6. The girl with the bleached blue jeans (have, has) (marry, marries, married, marrying) a famous race car driver.

7. Ms. Harris was investigated by the C.I.A. and (is, are, was, were) (warn, warns, warned, warning) to stop writing novels about them.

8. A robbery (is, are, be) (happen, happens, happened, happening) in this town every seven minutes.

9. Hercules should have (go, goes, went, gone, going) to the prom with Gemma.

10. Flo should have been (use, used, using) to the computer's insults.

134

chapter 4

CONTRACTIONS

PREVIEW _____ four

The sentences in the exercise below preview the skills and principles you'll learn in this chapter. For the answers to this exercise, check with your instructor or tutor or listen to the appropriate audio tape.

Circle the correct choice.

          A   B
1. Those guys (don't, do'nt) have jobs.
    A   B   C
2. It (isn't, isnt, is'nt) time to go.
   A   B   C
3. (Your, You're, You) going to pass.
   A   B   C
4. (Its, It's, It) later than you think.
    A   B   C
5. (Thats, That's, That) Carol's cousin.
     A   B   C
6. (Whose, Who's, Who) letter to the editor was printed?
   A   B   C   D
7. (Their, They're, There, They) not out in front.
                  A   B   C
8. Mandy says (his, he's, he) good for nothing.
   A   B   C   D
9. (There, They're, Their, They) are three steps in this process.
        A   B
10. Leo (know's, knows) her number.

INTRODUCTION

Many people used to disapprove of contractions in writing other than the most informal or personal communications. However, this attitude is slowly changing, and contractions will probably be acceptable to most audiences as long as they are written correctly. To write contractions incorrectly by omitting or misplacing the apostrophe will always be considered a serious error in college writing.

FORMING CONTRACTIONS

When you use contractions, what you do is replace one or more letters of a word with an apostrophe ('). *Do not* becomes *don't* because the apostrophe replaces the *o* in *not*; *you are* becomes *you're* because the apostrophe replaces the *a* in *are*.

The most common contractions include the following:

is or has = 's
am = 'm
will = 'll
are = 're
have = 've
not = n't

As you see, most contractions involve verbs, although *not* is an adverb. The following grid illustrates some possible contractions of subjects and verbs.

Subject	Verb	Sentence
I	am	I am late.
I	'm	I'm late.
There	is	There is time.
There	's	There's time.
We	have	We have decided.
We	've	We've decided.
That	is	That is right.
That	's	That's right.
They	could have	They could have decided.
They	could've	They could've decided.

EXERCISE 4-1

Work through the grid below filling in the missing sentence in the pair.

Subject	Verb	Sentence
1. He	has	He has finished.
He	's	*He's finished*

Chapter 4: Contractions

Subject	Verb	Sentence
2. It	is	It is old.
It	's	_____
3. It	has	It has worked.
It	's	_____
4. She	is	She is tall.
She	's	_____
5. She	has	She has passed.
She	's	_____
6. We	are	We are busy.
We	're	_____
7. They	are	They are successful.
They	're	_____
8. They	will	They will agree.
They	'll	_____
9. They	have	They have eaten.
They	've	_____
10. Who	is	Who is happy?
Who	's	_____
11. That	is	That is great.
That	's	_____
12. Mary	is	Mary is happy.
Mary	's	_____
13. Somebody	is	Somebody is here.
Somebody	's	_____
14. They	have	They have left.
They	've	_____
15. It	will	It will break.
It	'll	_____

Contractions Within Verb Phrases

Do not confuse the contracted form of *have* (*'ve*) with the words *of* or *a*. If you rely on pronunciation to determine spelling, you may write *could of* or *could a* instead of the correctly spelled contraction *could've*. All three sound pretty much the same, but the only correct written form is *could've*.

EXERCISE 4–2

Fill in the missing sentence in the pairs below.

Subject	Verb	Sentence
1. The blackboard	should have been	The blackboard should have been erased.

Subject	Verb	Sentence
The blackboard	should've been	*The blackboard should've been erased.*
2. He	could have gone	He could have gone home.
He	could've gone	
3. She	might have won	She might have won the race.
She	might've won	
4. The troops	must have deserted	The troops must have deserted.
The troops	must've deserted.	
5. The leaders	would have lied	The leaders would have lied about their extra funds.
The leaders	would've lied	

Contraction of *Not*

The adverb *not* often appears in contracted form. Some people mistakenly place the apostrophe between the two words being contracted instead of between the n and the t to replace the dropped letter o.

Be careful not to omit or misplace the apostrophe. *Is not* becomes *isn't*; *should not* becomes *shouldn't*; *does not* becomes *doesn't*. The contraction of *can not* is *can't*, but the only irregular contraction occurs when *will not* becomes *won't*.

EXERCISE 4–3

The following grid illustrates some possible contractions of *not*. Fill in the missing sentence in each pair.

Subject	Verb (not)	Sentence
1. He	does not	He does not care.
He	doesn't	*He doesn't care.*
2. Hillary	can not	Hillary cannot dance.
Hillary	can't	
3. You and Bill	are not	You and Bill are not funny.
You and Bill	aren't	
4. The taxi	was not	The taxi was not available.
The taxi	wasn't	
5. The players	do not	The players do not understand.
The players	don't	
6. Phil	is not	Phil is not ready.
Phil	isn't	

Chapter 4: Contractions 141

EXERCISE 4-4

In the sentences below, first cross out the letters to be omitted in the contracted form of the italicized words and then rewrite them above as contractions.

1. *Bill's*
   Bill ~~i~~s a bore.

2. Foreign reporters often *do not* understand American politics.

3. Harold *is* not married.

4. It *has* been a long day.

5. *We are* hoping for the best.

6. The train *does not* stop here any more.

7. *Who is* the new dictator?

8. *What is* the matter?

9. You *should have* let me know sooner.

10. *You are* the apple of my eye.

Homonyms of Contractions

Homonyms are words which sound the same but are spelled differently and mean different things. Because English has so many homonyms, pronunciation is often misleading when you are learning to spell. If you can analyze the meaning of contractions and their homonyms as you write and proofread, you will avoid many needless errors. The trick is to check for the contraction first.

For example, *won't* sounds like *want*. Assume you have written the sentence *I **won't?/want?** a new car*. Check to see if the sentence makes sense as the uncontracted form *will not: I will not a new car*. The sentence doesn't make sense, so *want* must be the correct form.

Try checking the sentence *I **won't?/want?** be able to go with you. I will not be able to go with you* makes sense, so the contraction *won't* is equally acceptable.

Let's, the contraction for **let us,** sounds like **less.**
We'll, the contraction for **we will,** sounds like **will.**
He's, the contraction for **he is** or **he has,** is often confused with **his.**

EXERCISE 4-5

Proofread the following sentences for contraction homonym errors. Cross out the incorrect words and write the appropriate form above.

1. I won't to go with you to the zoo, but my father won't let me.

2. Less go find some place where there is less noise.

3. John will agree to whatever will accept.

4. His the only person responsible for his repeated errors.

5. Martha want let us do what we want, so let's go home.

Contractions and Possessive Pronoun Homonyms

One of the problems which occurs regularly in student papers is the confusion between contractions and their possessive pronoun homonyms. Now that you know what a contraction is, let's look at the possessive pronouns.

Possessive	Subject	Verb	Object or Complement
Its ⟶	fur	is	soft.
Whose ⟶	hat	fell	into the pool?
Their ⟶	trip	was postponed.	
Your ⟶	mother	called.	

The possessive pronoun describes the noun which follows it in the sentence. The apostrophe in the contraction signals that one or more letters have been omitted from the verb. If possessive pronouns are tested as contractions, they will not make sense.

Possessive pronoun		Confused contraction
Its *fur was soft.*	would read	**It is** *fur was soft.*
Whose *hat fell in the pool?*	would read	**Who is** *hat fell in the pool?*
Their *trip was postponed*	would read	**They are** *trip was postponed.*
Your *mother called*	would read	**You are** *mother called.*

Now compare the grid below illustrating possessive pronouns and their contraction homonyms.

Possessive	Subject	Verb or Verb Phrase	Object, Adverb, or Complement
Its	fur	is	soft.
	It	's	soft.
Whose	hat	fell	in the pool?
	Who	's calling?	
Their	trip	was postponed.	
	They	're	at home.
Your	mother	called.	
	You	're	lucky.

It/Its/It's

It is the pronoun substitute for places, things, animals, and activities. *It* is a word which can occupy the subject position in a sentence. *It is* and *It has* can

Chapter 4: Contractions

also be contracted by replacing the *i* in *is* or the *ha* in *has* with an apostrophe ('). Do not omit the verb, contracted or not, in standard English.

We use *it* in the subject position in sentences about time and weather.

Standard English	Nonstandard English
It is late or **It's** late.	It late.
It is cold or **It's** cold.	It cold.
It is Monday or **It's** Monday.	It Monday.

We also use *it* in the subject position in sentences about distance.

Subject Position	Linking Verb	Complement
From Chicago to Tallahassee	is	1000 miles.
It	is	1000 miles from Chicago to Tallahassee.
It	's	1000 miles from Chicago to Tallahassee.

It may be used in sentences which identify persons.

Who's singing in the shower?	**It's** Marjorie.
Who is on the phone?	**It's** Clyde.
Who was the troublemaker?	**It** was Tami.

It may also be used to stand in for verbals which function as subjects.

Subject	Linking Verb	Complement
To spell long words	is	often difficult.
It	is	often difficult to spell long words.
It	's	often difficult to spell long words.

EXERCISE 4–6

It's is a contraction for *it is* and *it has*; *its* is a possessive pronoun like *his* and *their*.

Circle the correct word in the sentences below.

1. (It, (It's,) Its) too late to change your mind.
2. (It, It's, Its) the only solution.
3. The cat has lost (it, it's, its) bell.
4. At (it, it's, its) extreme, selfishness is deadly.
5. Whether (it, it's, its) enough to warrant an investigation is undecided.
6. (It, It's, Its) is the violence of professional sports that I dislike.
7. The emotional nature of the campaign is (it, it's, its) major fault.
8. You'll find that (it, it's, its) not an unambitious goal.
9. McElroy gave the computer (it, it's, its) last chance.
10. (It, It's, Its) bound to fail again.

144 Chapter 4: Contractions

11. When that happens, (it, it's, its) made (it, it's, its) last print-out.
12. This cup has lost (it, it's, its) saucer.
13. He is anxious to go, (it, it's, its) seems.
14. (It, It's, Its) ridiculous.
15. (It, It's, Its) cold.
16. (It, It's, Its) hot.
17. (It, It's, Its) tedious listening to you complain.
18. If (it, it's, its) not too late, I'll file for a refund.
19. Have you checked (it, it's, its) radiator for leaks?
20. No, I haven't raised (it, it's, its) hood.

EXERCISE 4–7

Fill in either *it, it's* or *its* in the following sentences.

1. _*It's*_ that time of year again.
2. The plane seemed to have lost _____ way.
3. _____ time to go.
4. Darrel knows _____ important to me.
5. The sandpiper was helpless because _____ wing was broken.
6. We all know that _____ impolite to offend others.
7. That truck gets _____ best mileage at 45 mph.
8. If there's one important thing, _____ is timing.
9. The problem with the restaurant was that it couldn't decide what _____ image should be.
10. _____ no secret that Paul is responsible.
11. A newborn calf needs the attention of _____ mother.
12. _____ hard for Jason to get up early.
13. _____ a choice between being late or absent.
14. _____ choice in oil cans was important to the robot.
15. _____ Jerry's impertinence that upsets Aunt Sally.
16. _____ questionable whether they're involved in the robberies.
17. _____ actually time to leave.
18. Leave the bear cub alone; _____ mother is easily upset.
19. The lost dog finally found _____ owner.
20. Would you ask that robot what _____ doing with a polka-dotted oil can?

EXERCISE 4–8

Now write five sentences of your own using *its* correctly and five using *it's* correctly.

Who's/Whose

Who's is a contraction for both *who is* and *who has*. Whose is a possessive pronoun meaning *belonging to whom?*

Who's in the shower? means the same as Who is in the shower?
Who's got the time? means the same as Who has got the time?
Whose baby cried? asks about The baby belonging to whom?

Chapter 4: Contractions

EXERCISE 4-9

Choose the correct form, *who's* or *whose,* in the sentences below.

1. (Who's) Whose) got the most beautiful car in the world?
2. (Who's, Whose) turn is it to do the dishes?
3. We never knew (who's, whose) essay was the best.
4. (Who's, Whose) got the time?
5. (Who's, Whose) seen *The Exorcist?*
6. (Who's, Whose) bothered to call his grandmother this year?
7. (Who's, Whose) telephone answers itself and takes messages?
8. Who knows (who's, whose) this is?
9. (Who's, Whose) finished?
10. (Who's, Whose) willing to babysit?
11. (Who's, Whose) that ridiculous?
12. I asked you (who's, whose) hat is in the soup.
13. Georgette never found out (who's, whose) picture was in the paper with her brother's.
14. (Who's, Whose) to know what you're doing?
15. They wanted to know (who's, whose) trumpet it was.
16. I failed to ask (who's, whose) trumpet it was.
17. The mayor shouted, "(Who's, Whose) responsible for this fiasco?"
18. (Who's, Whose) got the courage to admit such a mistake?
19. (Who's, Whose) painting, besides Maurice's, was exhibited on Talent Day?
20. He asked again, "(Who's, Whose) going to pay for this disaster?"

EXERCISE 4-10

Fill in either *who's* or *whose* below.

1. The instructor needs to know ____*who's*____ registered for this section.
2. _____ book is that?
3. _____ coming with me and _____ staying here?
4. Mona, _____ extravagance is well documented, bought a beautiful ring.
5. _____ on the phone?
6. _____ not here?
7. _____ bike was stolen?
8. If Ginny leaves, _____ going to watch the kids?
9. If good and evil are relative, _____ to say what is acceptable behavior?
10. I want to know _____ responsible for the cost of beef today.
11. A smoker _____ health is affected by the habit often cannot leave cigarettes alone.
12. _____ boots are under the dining room table?
13. _____ seen the movie at the State Theatre?
14. Thurber was an artist _____ humor appeals to us all.

15. _____ still missing a passport?
16. _____ idea was it to have that last drink?
17. _____ at the door?
18. _____ score sheet was eaten by the computer?
19. _____ idea was that?
20. _____ moving into the third floor apartment?

EXERCISE 4-11

Write five sentences of your own using *whose* correctly and five using *who's* correctly.

They're/Their/There

They're is a contraction meaning *they are*. *They are my friends* means the same as *They're my friends*.

Their is a possessive pronoun meaning *belonging to them*. *This is their house* means the same as *This is the house belonging to them*.

There is a third homonym for *they're* and *their*, and just to keep things complicated it has two different uses. It indicates *where*, as in *The book is over there*. And it anticipates the subject before forms to the verb *be*. *There is a lot of noise in here*.

EXERCISE 4-12

Circle the correct form in the sentences below.

1. This is (their, they're, there) last chance.
2. (Their, They're, There) sure to find us before noon.
3. (Their, They're, There) will never be another dog like Rover.
4. He was (their, they're, there) only son.
5. When we get (their, they're, there), offer them nothing.
6. What was (their, they're, there) name?
7. We could finish this before (their, they're, there) ready to go.
8. To be left alone was (their, they're, there) only desire.
9. If I ask you *where*, you may answer (their, they're, there).
10. I have been (their, they're, there) a number of times.
11. This year (their, they're, there) has been considerable interest in pottery.
12. Mr. Dean has (their, they're, there) unqualified endorsement.
13. (Their, They're, There) sins are many; (their, they're, there) virtues are few.
14. Put the book over (their, they're, there).
15. (Their, They're, There) always ready for adventure.
16. (Their, They're, There) adventures are not very exciting.
17. Where (their, they're, there) is adventure, (their, they're, there) sure to be found.
18. Have you ever been (their, they're, there) alone?

Chapter 4: Contractions

19. I know (their, they're, there) has to be a better explanation.
20. They will give you (their, they're, there) advice, but not (their, they're, there) assistance.

EXERCISE 4-13

Fill in either *their, they're,* or *there* in the sentences below.

1. Erica went _____ to help out.
2. _____ the last people in the world I expect to see _____.
3. Usually _____ parties are big successes.
4. _____ is no apparent reason for _____ attitude.
5. As usual _____ late.
6. _____ a credit to _____ parents.
7. I hear that _____ phone never stops ringing.
8. _____ are days when I hate to get up.
9. You can't solve all _____ problems.
10. If _____ held up at school, _____ isn't another bus until four o'clock.
11. I stood on my head because I wanted to get _____ attention.
12. Rochelle and Roger have _____ own way of doing things.
13. The credit bureau lost all _____ records in a fire.
14. If _____ troublesome, lock them in the closet.
15. If _____ needs to be an investigation, _____ the detectives to use.
16. I got _____ before he did.
17. _____ being taken to _____ rightful owner.
18. Why are _____ so many eggplants in the taxi?
19. Ken and Kathy said _____ neighbor was a real snoop.
20. _____ wasn't any place to hide.

EXERCISE 4-14

Now write five sentences of your own using *their* correctly, five using *they're* correctly, and five using *there* correctly.

You/Your/You're

Your is a possessive pronoun meaning *belonging to you* (your glove, your ideas, your apartment). *You're* is a contraction of *you are* (you're okay; you're nice; you're tall).

A third word which sometimes gets mixed up with these two is *you,* especially when the next word begins with an *r. Don't let pronunciation confuse you. Even if we do slide together the r on your or you're and the r on* the next word in speech (your ring, you're right), don't substitute you for either the possessive pronoun or the contraction.

EXERCISE 4-15

Circle the correct word in the sentences below.

1. Don't tell me any of (your, you're) lies.
2. Her dog trampled (your, you're) tomato plants.
3. (You, Your, You're) responsible for accidents which occur on (your, you're) property.
4. If this is the reason (you, your, you're) reluctant to own (your, you're) own home, (your, you're) crazy.
5. (Your, You're) unemployment check is here.
6. Bill doesn't know (your, you're) brother.
7. (Your, You're) teacher misses classes more often than mine.
8. (Your, You're) lucky.
9. (Your, You're) not explaining (your, you're) position clearly.
10. (Your, You're) offer is the best I've had.
11. A baby chimpanzee is the last thing (you, your, you're) kids need.
12. What's (your, you're) name?
13. Have you paid (you, your, you're) rent?
14. Drop (your, you're) gun. (Your, You're) surrounded.
15. (You, Your, You're) idea is a good one.
16. Are you free if you don't know (you, your, you're) options are limited?
17. (You, Your, You're) free if (you, your, you're) feel free.
18. Do (you, your, you're) really think so?
19. (You, Your, You're) lazy.
20. (You, Your, You're) rhinoceros ate my daffodils.

EXERCISE 4-16

Circle the correct word in the exercise below.

1. (Your, You're) going to be sorry when (your, you're) license is revoked.
2. (Its, It's) time (their, they're, there) told (their, they're, there) place.
3. (Whose, Who's) car is in Kurt's parking space?
4. (Whose, Who's) watching the baby?
5. (Their, They're, There) goes my last chance to bid.
6. (Their, They're, There) dog wagged (its, it's) tail.
7. (Whose, Who's) in charge here?
8. If (their, they're, there) late, don't let them take the test.
9. Did you do (your, you're) homework?
10. (Your, You're) the best judge of that.
11. (Its, It's) (your, you're) opinion of the movie that (their, they're, there) interested in.
12. The lion cub roared for (its, it's) dinner.
13. (Whose, Who's) car is blocking (their, they're, there) driveway?

Chapter 4: Contractions

14. Russ insists (its, it's) never too late to start.
15. The sergeant snarled, "(Whose, Who's) rifle is that?"
16. If (your, you're) sister takes the car, (whose, who's) going to take Jack and Julie to baseball practice?
17. (Their, They're, There) must be fifty ways to get out of this situation.
18. He wants to know if (your, you're) sure (your, you're) doctor is being candid.
19. (Whose, Who's) on time, and (whose, who's) late?
20. If (its, it's) (your, you're) turn, make (your, you're) move.
21. (Their, They're, There) the kind of people (whose, who's) yard is filled with old, rusty cars.
22. (Whose, Who's) to blame for (your, you're) unpreparedness but you?
23. The cat washed (its, it's) nose after it sniffed (your, you're) rosebush.
24. If you don't get (your, you're) act together, (its, it's) possible you'll be fired.
25. Does (your, you're) boss know (whose, who's) the most qualified?
26. (Their, They're, There) going to say (its, it's) too hot.
27. (Whose, Who's) system is most suited to (their, they're, there) specific needs?
28. (Your, You're) counting too heavily on (their, they're, there) help.
29. (Their, They're, There) are five men, but (their, they're, there) is only one woman on the board.
30. (Its, It's) hard to say (whose, who's) right.
31. The plane lost (its, it's) landing gear near Denver.
32. Put the wounded squirrel out of (its, it's) misery.
33. If (its, it's) all right with you, (their, they're, there) project should have priority.
34. (Their, They're, There) concerned about (your, you're) health.
35. If (its, it's) too much trouble to do now, (their, they're, there) prepared to wait.
36. (Whose, Who's) to say (whose, who's) the most valuable employee.
37. (Their, They're, There) computer has finished (its, it's) program.
38. I wonder (whose, who's) umbrella this is.
39. (Your, You're) not being reasonable.
40. (Their, They're, There) phone hasn't been installed yet.
41. (Whose, Who's) at the door?
42. The store is worried about (its, it's) image.
43. (Their, They're, There) new students.
44. (Its, It's) time to leave.
45. (Their, They're, There) proposal has (its, it's) merits.
46. (Whose, Who's) stapler is on (your, you're) desk?
47. The dog brought (its, it's) bone into (their, they're, there) living room.
48. (Whose, Who's) interested in (their, they're, there) boring stories?
49. (Their, They're, There) are two pigeons and a robin on the back porch.
50. The president likes (your, you're) plan better than theirs.

EXERCISE 4–17

In the sentences below fill in a correct choice from the following pairs.

your/you're
its/it's
whose/who's
their/they're

Chapter 4: Contractions

1. _____ cat scratched you?
2. Brian says _____ time to leave.
3. Mr. Hoyt wants to see _____ new dog.
4. _____ going to Brazil with Phil?
5. They guard _____ privacy very carefully.
6. The puppy ran around with _____ tail in _____ mouth.
7. _____ too careless.
8. _____ tired of waiting.
9. _____ responsibility is this?
10. Call if _____ going to be late.
11. _____ cold outside.
12. Edith corrects _____ work.
13. Mable did _____ dishes.
14. The gas station attendant says _____ crazy to drive without a spare tire.
15. I want to know _____ telling the truth.
16. _____ used to lying.
17. Give me _____ ticket.
18. Ursula doesn't like _____ new car.
19. _____ here?
20. _____ Ralph taking to lunch?
21. _____ no one's business but _____ mother's.
22. _____ boots are those?
23. _____ misinformed.
24. _____ coming.
25. _____ idea sounds good.
26. The buffalo lost _____ leash.
27. I know how much _____ new house cost.
28. _____ too hot to dance.
29. _____ coming?
30. I want _____ advice.

EXERCISE 4–18 — write

Write ten connected sentences in which you use *your, you're, its, it's, whose, who's, their, they're,* and *there* correctly as many times as you can. Underline each one. If you have trouble getting started, you may wish to begin with one of these sentences:

It's very unlikely that *their* plan will work.

or

If *they're* the ones who took my bike, *your* sister will be sorry.

Chapter 4: Contractions

EXERCISE 4-19

In the sentences below make any necessary corrections to the contractions and possessive adjectives and insert any missing forms of the verb *to be*.

Freudian Slip

1. Debby enter's the classroom one day and say's, "Theirs something I do'nt understand."

2. "Its about the homework assignment?" her teacher ask's.

3. "No, it doesnt have anything to do with the assignment. Its about psychology."

4. "Well you're psychology teacher is the person whose best qualified to answer the question, but Ill try."

5. Deborah begin's, "I cant understand what a Freudian slip is. There are'nt any examples in the book."

6. "Thats pretty easy," said her teacher. "Freud thought that all slips of the tongue or memory had meaning. There signs of what the person subconsciously want's to say or forget."

7. "For example," the teacher said, "if you were a newlywed and suddenly forgot you're husband's or wife's name, Freud would say that the slip occurred because you were'nt in love."

8. "Thats not true," Deborah objected. "Sometimes you're mind just goes blank. Its a very common thing. Its something that could of happened to anyone."

9. Suddenly John Littleton enter's the discussion. "Your right about most slips really being accidents, Deborah, but forgetting you're husband's name does have a significance of it's own."

10. June Blake spoke up. "My sister just lost her engagement ring. Thats the second time. But that doesnt mean she does'nt love her boyfriend, does it?"

11. Before the teacher could answer, Deborah spoke up. "No one in their right mind could lose two rings. Who's boyfriend would put up with it?" she said disapprovingly. "Theres no excuse."

12. "Freud has other examples, and there even funnier," said the teacher. "One time a newspaper described a famous general as a 'battle scared veteran.'" She wrote this on the blackboard.

13. "What wrong with that?" asked Darryl. "Oh, I see."

14. "Whose unsure why the general demanded a retraction?" asked the teacher. Their were a few hands raised.

15. "See, its 'scared' not 'scarred,'" said Darryl. "A description like that might of suggested he was a coward."

16. "The really funny thing," the teacher began, "was the retraction. Next day the paper printed an apology on it's front page calling the general a 'bottle scarred veteran.'"

17. The class roared. "Its like they're calling him a veteran of fights in a bar," said Darryl with satisfaction. "Thats great. I bet he was."

18. "The writer really must of had it in for him," June Blake said reflectively.

19. "Their might of been some of this in Freud's day, but Ive never said or done anything like that," said Darryl.

20. "Have'nt you ever forgotten to pay a bill?" the teacher asked. "Have'nt you ever sent a check to someone and left off you're signature so they couldn't cash it? That a Freudian slip."

21. "No, but its a good idea," said Darryl.

22. "Whose done something like this?" the teacher ask's.

23. "They're was a time when I used to call my husband by the wrong name. Maybe I wished I wasnt married to him for a while. Hes fine now."

24. "I once saw a guy on television mentioning an actress in the audience, and he said 'shes been starving recently' instead of 'starring recently.' It might of been her first big role in a long time."

25. "Is its meaning clear now, Deborah?" asked the teacher.

26. "Yes, you're explanation is clear, but I wish you hadnt explained. My father and mother both forgot there wedding anniversary last week. If that mean's there going to be divorced, Ill end up with Momma for sure, and my apartments already crowded."

TRANSFERRING YOUR SKILL TO WRITING

You've worked through a variety of exercises now: fill-ins, editing, and some short writing. In all of them the focus has been on contractions; there have been no other problems to distract you from catching contraction mistakes. You shouldn't have too much trouble passing the posttest, but then you must go on to apply this skill in your writing.

EXERCISE 4–20 *write*

Write an essay which is free from noun number, verb, and contraction mistakes. Your instructor may assign an in-class paper or may want you to write on one of the following topics:

How to make an enemy

or

The qualities of a good (woman, man, person)

REVIEW four

The sentences in this review exercise are provided to help you check your progress in this chapter and to prepare you for what you'll find in the posttest. For the answers to this exercise, check with your instructor or tutor or listen to the appropriate audio tape.

Circle the correct choice.

                  A   B   C
1. Her brother (does'nt, doesn't, doesnt) smile much.
     A   B   C
2. It (isn't, isnt, is'nt) ready to eat.
    A   B   C
3. (Your, You're, You) nearly ready.
    A B C
4. (It's, Its, It) almost time to leave.
     A   B   C
5. (Thats, That's, That) Jodie's car.
                  A   B   C
6. Do you know (whose, who's, who) phone is ringing?
    A   B   C   D
7. (Their, They're, There, They) late.
       A   B   C
8. He (should of, should've, should a) come.
   A   B   C   D
9. (Their, They're, There, They) are four quarters in a dollar.
         A   B   C
10. Edwina (want's, wants, won't) her own apartment.

chapter 5

POSSESSIVES

PREVIEW five

The sentences in the exercise below preview the skills and principles you'll learn in this chapter. For the answers to this exercise, check with your instructor or tutor or listen to the appropriate audio tape.

Circle the correct choice.

       A   B   C
1. Have you seen (Alfred, Alfreds, Alfred's) new calculator?
   A   B   C
2. (Yesterday, Yesterdays, Yesterday's) storm damaged our elm tree.
             A   B   C
3. All three (astronauts, astronaut's, astronauts') space helmets were stolen.
       A   B   C   D
4. The (women, womens, women's, womens') medical clinic will be closed the last two weeks of August.
              A B   C   A   B
5. One album was (her, hers, her's) and one was (Alisons, Alison's).
                        A   B   C
6. Elsa has learned to handle (lifes, life's, lifes') problems.
                     A   B   C   D
7. Mrs. Anagnost called Mr. (Anagnost, Anagnosts, Anagnost's, Anagnosts') office.
                         A   B   C   D
8. Please give me three (month, months, month's, months') vacation.
   A   B   C   D
9. (Everyone, Everyones, Everyone's, Everyones') interest was aroused.
       A   B   C   D
10. Two (boy, boys, boy's, boys') knocked at the door.

INTRODUCTION

If you suspect that a chapter on possession means struggling with apostrophes again, you are probably depressed already. On the other hand, if you've never encountered the problem before, we can probably teach you to use them correctly and painlessly in just a few pages. For most students the hardest problem is giving up a half-learned rule about putting the apostrophe before or after an *s*. If you haven't been able to make that traditional rule work for you, we suggest that you try looking at the problem in a slightly different way. But first, try to forget the old rule!

What Is Meant by Possession?

When we speak of possession, we are talking about ownership as a grammatical concept. In a possessive construction we have two things: an *owner* and something which is *owned*. This is fairly straightforward when we use examples like *the boy's bicycle* or *the girl's ukulele;* however, in the examples below you will notice that the *razor* does not own the *edge*, nor does *Ruth* own her *friend* in the same way that the *boy* owns the *bicycle* and the *girl* owns the *ukulele*. The more abstract the thing owned becomes, the less willing many people are to recognize it as a possessive construction. For example, *a month's pay* and *a week's vacation* are among the most frequent possessive mistakes made. Countless people leave off the *'s* in these phrases.

Possession can be shown two ways. The first is to use an *of* phrase. In this case the *owner* follows the thing *owned*.

owned   owner
The *edge* of the *razor* is dull.

Some very traditional usage authorities insist that this is the only correct way to write a "possessive" construction when the owner is not a person. Obviously, that is a rule no longer obeyed by contemporary speakers and writers.

The second way to show possession is to add *'s* to the *owner*. In this case the *owner* comes before the *owned*.

owner owned
The *razor's edge* is dull.

It is usually not enough just to put two words side by side to show ownership, especially if the owner is a person whose name begins with a capital letter.

Nonstandard   Standard
She is **Ruth friend.**   She is **Ruth's friend.**

If a sentence like *She is Ruth friend* is not a part of your natural pattern of speaking, you may wonder how anyone could make *that* mistake, until you look at a sentence like *That is a typical Hoover statement* and try to figure out how you know it's all right to leave off the *'s* on *Hoover*.

Chapter 5: Possessives

You must also use the apostrophe when another word comes between the *owner* and the *owned*.

Nonstandard	*Standard*
the truck sleepy driver	the truck's sleepy driver
	or
	the sleepy truck driver

Although describing the grammar of the language is a very complicated business, we believe that you can learn to *write* possessive constructions fairly quickly if you take the problem one step at a time.

The first step is to make sure you understand the difference between the "grammatical" owner and the thing owned. The first exercise will help you with that distinction, then you can go on to learning the rule for forming possessives.

EXERCISE 5-1

In the following sentences underline the owner and circle the thing owned.

1. Diana's husband is a mechanic.
2. I cannot remember the titles of those books.
3. The cries of the kidnapped children led the policewoman to them.
4. The women's complaints led to a change.
5. That shirt belonging to Myron matches Marvin's socks pretty well.
6. Did you rip my brother's coat?
7. The cold hand of the ghost closed over Julie's throat.
8. Did my cousin's bookie phone?
9. Russ slammed the door on the tail of the cat.
10. It will take a lot of money to solve the problems of Claudine.

How To Form a Possessive

In the chapter on contractions and their possessive pronoun homonyms you saw that possessive pronouns were put in front of the things possessed.

Possessive	Subject	Verb	Complement
Its	fur	was	soft.
Their	time	has come.	

Nouns showing possession fit into the same sentence position, but 's is added to the owner to show that they are possessives and not ordinary nouns.

Possessive	Subject	Verb	Complement
Father's	temper	is	violent.
The cat's	tail	is	short.
The children's	games	are	noisy.
The boss's	desk	is	cluttered.
A week's	pay	disappeared.	

Notice that we said, "Add *'s* to the owner." We didn't say anything about singular or plural. The rule begins like this:

*To show possession, add **'s** to the owner.*

Obviously an owner may own one thing (singular) such as a *frog* or more than one thing (plural) such as *frogs;* and more than one owner may own a singular thing together or they may hold many things in common. For example:

Owner		Thing Owned
One boy	owns	a frog.
One boy	owns	several frogs.
Two boys	own	a frog.
Two boys	own	several frogs.

Now let's finish the rule: *To show possession, add **'s** to the owner; if the owner is a plural noun that already ends in **s**, drop the **s** following the apostrophe to make the word easier to pronounce.* People who have difficulty forming possessives are usually confusing the *s* which makes a word plural with the *'s* which makes a noun possessive. To avoid confusion, do not try to make a short cut through the rule. Write the word (the owner), whether it's singular or plural will be obvious from context, then add *'s.* If the word already ends in *s,* drop the possessive *s* in order to make the word easier to pronounce but keep the apostrophe.

Owner	Owned	
One boy'S	frog	won the contest.
One boy'S	frogs	disappeared mysteriously.
Two boys'X̶	frog	smiled.
Two boys'X̶	frogs	jumped in the pond.

The importance of going through the possessive rule in two stages is even more apparent when the noun is *irregular.* Some plural nouns do not end in *s,* but the rule for possession does not change: add *'s* to the owner.

	Owner		Owned
(sng)	child'S	(sng)	toy
(pl)	children'S	(pl)	games
(sng)	woman'S	(sng)	hat
(pl)	women'S	(sng)	opinion

Handle proper names exactly like other nouns. Notice that when a *singular noun* already ends in *s* (like Williams or bus), we do not drop the *S* following the apostrophe; however, usage varies on this point. You will see both *James's hat* and *James' hat.* Be consistent whichever version you choose.

Chapter 5: Possessives

	Owner	Owned
(sng)	Mrs. Williams'S	purse
(pl)	the Joneses'~~X~~	vacations
(sng)	the bus'S	route
(pl)	the buses'~~X~~	routes
(sng)	James's	essay
	or	
	James'~~X~~	essay

EXERCISE 5-2

Paying attention to singular and plural signals, finish filling in the chart below with owners and things owned. Use your imagination.

	Owner		Owned
sng.	*Mrs. Ross's*	pl.	*parakeet*
sng.		sng.	*blouse*
pl.	*boys'*	sng.	
pl.		sng.	
sng.		pl.	
pl.		pl.	*stories*
sng.		pl.	
pl.	*those guys'*	sng.	
pl.		pl.	
sng.	*my aunt's*	sng.	
pl.		pl.	
sng.		sng.	*typewriter*

EXERCISE 5-3

Fill in owners from the nouns in the lefthand column and circle the correct verb. Remember that the verb must agree with the subject and not the possessive.

	Noun to Be Changed into Possessive Form	Possessive Form (Owner)	Noun Used As Subject	Verb	Possessive Form (Owner)	Noun Used As Direct Object
1.	Mary, John	Mary's	cat	(eat, *eats*)	John's	bird.
2.	The owner, the store		watchdog	(attack, attacks)		deliveryperson.
3.	The knife, the table		blade	(cut, cuts)		edge.
4.	The car, the boys		horn	(interrupt, interrupts)		game.
5.	The campers, the forest		lanterns	(illuminate, illuminates)		gloom.
6.	The cowboy, the horse		manner	(quiet, quiets)		fears.
7.	The fire, the Joneses		damage	(ruin, ruins)		home.
8.	Mr. Miller, veterans		wife	(collect, collects)		insurance.
9.	The neighbors, my mother		chicken	(chase, chases)		cat.
10.	Old Jim, the teacher		bear	(attack, attacks)		dog.
11.	Most ministers, the church		sermons	(inspire, inspires)		congregation.
12.	My mother, my brothers		curiosity	(change, changes)		plans.
13.	The assassin, the country		bullet	(kill, kills)		leader.
14.	The zoo, the visitors		elephants	(eat, eats)		peanuts.
15.	The surgeons, the hospital		Cadillacs	(block, blocks)		driveway.

160

EXERCISE 5-4

Fill in owners from the nouns in the lefthand column and circle the correct verb.

	Noun to Be Changed into Possessive Form	Possessive Form (Owner)	Noun Used As Subject	Verb	Possessive Form (Owner)	Noun Used As Direct Object
1.	Paul Revere, Boston	Paul Revere's	announcement	(warn, warns)	Boston's	citizens.
2.	His fans, the star		demands	(spoil, spoils)		evening.
3.	The player, a spectator		bat	(hit, hits)		head.
4.	The critic, the book		review	(anger, angers)		author.
5.	The camels, the tourists		smell	(offend, offends)		noses.
6.	Atlanta, the city		weather	(please, pleases)		visitors.
7.	The theater, Rock Hudson		patrons	(prefer, prefers)		acting.
8.	The university, the year		president	(utter, utters)		banalities.
9.	Bill, the restaurant		uncle	(like, likes)		spaghetti.
10.	The cars, the cities		exhaust systems	(pollute, pollutes)		air.
11.	The pencil, the desk		point	(scratch, scratches)		top.
12.	The jobs, the technicians		duties	(challenge, challenges)		abilities.
13.	Sonia, her coach		stories	(shake, shakes)		confidence.
14.	Joan, her mother		fiance	(break, breaks)		vase.
15.	Harold, my grandparents		ghost	(haunt, haunts)		attic.

161

EXERCISE 5-5

Decide whether you want the singular or the plural form of the noun.

1. Most battery-operated (gadget, gadgets) never have worked and never will work.
2. There are four (car, cars) in the parking lot.
3. Several (paper, papers) had no name at the top.
4. That kind of (movie, movies) brings out the violent streak in an audience.
5. One of our basic (need, needs) is that of privacy.
6. The British call an (apartment, apartments) a *flat*.
7. Their (word, words) for *curb* is *kerb*; it sounds the same but is spelled differently.
8. Four (punk, punks) mugged the old man on his way to the mail box.
9. A loose light (fixture, fixtures) crashed to the dining room table and startled the family.
10. English always has been one of my worst (subject, subjects).

Decide whether you want the plural or the possessive form of the noun.

11. His (papers, paper's) have a lot of spelling mistakes.
12. The (apartments, apartment's) location is ideal.
13. Her (lives, life's) work has been helping others.
14. All the (answers, answer's) are in the back of the book.
15. There are no (curtains, curtains') in the bathroom.
16. The bus (stations, station's) lunch counter is always crowded.
17. Sandra's (days, day's) begin at 6:00 a.m.
18. The (televisions, television's) hypnotic effect acts like a sedative.
19. Their (bosses, boss's) complaints are infuriating.
20. The (neighbors, neighbors') still hear their dog barking after midnight.

Decide whether you want the singular possessive or the plural possessive form of the noun.

21. A (cat's, cats') cries were heard in the alley.
22. Four (senator's, senators') voting records were checked by the (citizen's, citizens') organization.
23. In the distance I saw the (comet's, comets') tail.
24. All the (newspaper's, newspapers') accounts of the accident were the same.
25. That (store's, stores') prices are way out of line.
26. Most of the (commuter's, commuters') cars were parked near the station.
27. The (lady's, ladies') lounge was crowded.
28. The (bicycle's, bicycles') tire is flat.
29. The (girl's, girls') dates were late.
30. Many (grammar school's, grammar schools') windows are broken.

Chapter 5: Possessives

EXERCISE 5–6

Fill in the remaining forms of each noun on the grid.

	Singular	Plural	Singular Possessive	Plural Possessive
1.	aspirin	aspirins	*aspirin's* cost	aspirins' effects
2.		curtains	length	color
3.			book's cover	prices
4.		churches	location	congregations
5.	hairdryer		cord	noise
6.		bedspreads	pattern	sizes
7.	telephone		rings	dials
8.		sandals	heel	fit
9.	invader		spaceship	friends
10.	gate		lock	guards
11.			garden's path	owners
12.	life		surprises	purpose
13.	glass		rim	lifespan
14.			baby's chair	cradles
15.	instructor		lecture	lounge
16.			plan	robbers' success
17.	Jones		reputation	bank account
18.		apartments	size	rents
19.			novel's conclusion	popularity
20.	shirt		collar	colors
21.		televisions	picture	stations
22.		doctors	bills	attitudes
23.	woman		plight	strike
24.	day		pay	wait
25.			thief's fear	methods

When the Possessive Isn't a Person

Many students who are perfectly content to write about *Mary's hat* and *the girls' notebooks* balk at *a week's vacation*. Because the vacation does not belong to the week in the same way that Mary's hat clearly belongs to her, you may be uncertain about whether they are the same construction. Grammatically they are. To convince yourself, compare these sentence diagrams:

Possessive	Subject	Verb	Complement
Mary's	hat	is	too small.

Possessive	Subject	Verb	Complement
A week's	vacation	is	too short.

The surest test for a possessive form is to change it back into a prepositional phrase with *of*.

Subject	Prepositional Phrase	Verb	Complement
The hat	of Mary	is	too small.
A vacation	of a week	is	too short.

EXERCISE 5–7

Rewrite each of the sentences below so that the italicized prepositional phrase is turned into a possessive containing an apostrophe. Circle the thing owned or possessed.

1. The immediate (success) *of the business* pleased the investors.

2. Wednesday is the day *for ladies* at the ball park.

3. The whistle *of the teapot* alarmed the canary.

4. The illegal campaign contributions *of the companies* led to the indictment of four chairmen of the board.

5. The arrival *of my sister* has been delayed by an air strike.

6. The performance *of the dolphins* was applauded by the crowd.

7. A student has called into question the accuracy *of the tests*.

8. The handle *of the umbrella* is broken.

9. Police estimated the damage *of the fire* at $80,000.

10. The inquiry *of the government* into proposed rate increases resulted from the protests *of commuters*.

11. The brakes *of the car* have been repaired.

12. All the rims *of the glasses* were chipped.

Chapter 5: Possessives

13. Even the energy crisis can't dull the appeal *of London*.

14. The appearance *of the jazz musicians* was a well-kept secret.

15. The athletic facilities *for women* are very much inferior to those for men.

16. Clare's baby was awakened by the rattling *of the storm windows*.

17. The mayor ignored the needs *of the community*.

18. The son *of the Williamses* was arrested.

19. The end *of the story* is happy.

20. Yolanda could not understand the jealousy *of her stepsister*.

21. The plans *of Mr. Moss* were upset by the accident.

22. You must give the notice *of a month*.

23. The letter *of the secretary* was signed by the president.

24. He has the experience *of a year* in selling real estate.

25. We anticipate the delay *of a day* in filling the orders *of our customers*.

EXERCISE 5-8

Change the italicized prepositional phrase into a possessive containing an apostrophe.

1. The temper *of the dog* worsened as it grew older.
   the dog's temper

2. The lounge *of the ladies* is closed.

3. The appearance *of the room* depressed the young homemaker.

4. The bindings *of the books* were torn.

5. The projects *of Mayor Daley* were always a great success.

6. The ringing *of the phone* awakened the baby.

166   Chapter 5: Possessives

7. The bike *of Bill* was stolen.

8. The license *of the driver* was suspended.

9. The brakes *of my car* need repair.

10. The demands *of my teachers* are unreasonable.

11. The rights *of women* are much discussed.

12. The responsibility for the recovery *of Vietnam* is a shared one.

13. In the midst of the casualties *of war* the death *of the old man* seemed insignificant.

14. After nine o'clock the citizens *of all the cities* were forbidden to leave their homes.

15. The wallet *of my sister* was stolen.

16. The wages *of four days* paid the gas bill.

17. The demands *of her children* are endless.

18. The wife *of Sir Alfred Ayer* is a fine novelist.

19. The location *of the buried treasure* was a well-kept secret.

20. The cooking *of Coolidge* leaves something to be desired.

21. A child had converted the lid *of the box* into a sled.

22. Safety pins held up the hem *of the dress*.

23. The threats *of his boss* were the last straw.

24. The decision *of the judges* is final.

25. The results *of the election* are being disputed.

EXERCISE 5–9

Transform the possessives in the following sentences into prepositional phrases beginning with *of*.

Chapter 5: Possessives

1. The mayor's response was vicious.

2. The people's choice is a demagogue.

3. The women's voices will be heard.

4. The girls' screams could be heard from the street.

5. The students' wishes should be considered too.

6. The bully's taunts did not upset the young hero.

7. The teachers' salaries had not kept pace with the economy.

8. My parents' position has stood unaltered for half a century.

9. His feelings' depth surprised his father.

10. The ball hit the boys' sandcastle.

11. Asimov's mysteries usually involve a clever pun.

12. The sorceress's cauldron contained a delicious brew.

13. The queen's every wish is my command.

14. The players' costumes were wrinkled and dirty.

15. We left the baby's stroller out in the rain.

16. The corporal traced the rocket's trajectory on the overhead chart.

17. The Buick's cough sounded like a terminal disease.

18. We found a turtle's nest of eggs behind the big rocks.

19. They hid the baby's Jack-in-the-box in the laundry hamper.

20. Seismographs measured the earthquake's force.

21. One of the finalists glanced covetously at the winner's trophy.

Chapter 5: Possessives

22. In their new location the travel agents' business prospered.

23. The sun's rays lit the room.

24. Victoria's mother's aunt left her a small fortune.

25. The spectators were annoyed by the police officers' behavior.

EXERCISE 5–10

In the sentences below answer the question with a complete sentence which contains a possessive containing an apostrophe. Underline the *owner* and circle the *owned*.

1. Which airline has several women pilots?
   Several of America's (pilots) are women.

2. Whose nerves were shot?

3. Whose sister walks in her sleep?

4. Which state park system offers the nicest facilities?

5. Whose motorcycle is painted pink?

6. Which radio station has the best programming?

7. Whose dog can float on its back?

8. Which restaurant has the best fried chicken?

9. Whose younger brother swears like a trooper?

10. Whose mother plays the harp at midnight?

Absolute Possessives

Sometimes the thing possessed does not immediately follow the owner. Instead of saying *This is my book*, we say *This book is mine*. *Mine* is an absolute possessive, so named because the construction stands by itself.

Chapter 5: Possessives

The absolute possessives appear to cause no difficulty unless they end in *s*. However, nothing changes about the rules. Personal pronouns still do *not* take apostrophes; nouns do.

Ordinary Possessives	Absolute Possessives
This is **my** book.	This book is **mine**.
This is **your** cup.	This cup is **yours**.
This is **their** ranch.	This ranch is **theirs**.
This is **Jim's** duffle bag.	This duffle bag is **Jim's**.
This is the **professor's** house.	This house is the **professor's**.
This is the **senators'** private lounge.	This private lounge is the **senators'**.

EXERCISE 5–11

Change the following ordinary possessives in the following sentences into absolute possessives.

1. That is their house.
   That house is theirs.

2. This is the child's toy.

3. We need the mayor's opinion.

4. This is the sheriff's badge.

5. This is the secretaries' lament.

Now change the following absolute possessives into ordinary possessive constructions.

6. This monograph is the therapist's.

7. The vote we have called for is the committee's.

8. The most dangerous wood-burning stove is theirs.

9. Ours is largest float in the parade.

10. This house is the Watsons'.

EXERCISE 5-12

Circle the correct form.

A Narrow Escape

1. Mrs. (Poppels, Poppel's) four (cats, cat's) were locked in the bathroom.
2. The (owners, owner's) attempts to free them were futile.
3. She used a (rulers, ruler's) edge to try to force the lock.
4. She tried the (neighbors, neighbor's) suggestion of crawling along the (buildings, building's) ledge to reach the bathroom window.
5. The ledge was so narrow her (attempts, attempt's) were frightening.
6. The other (womans, woman's) obvious alarm brought her back to safety.
7. Their (cries, cries') upset the (cats, cats').
8. The four (animal's, animals') yowling upset the (ladies, ladies') even more.
9. The rescue squad they called was the fire (department's, departments).
10. The excitement and the (meows, meow's) attracted the (janitor's, janitors) attention.
11. His (efforts, effort) were directed at quieting the noise, both the (cats, cats') and (theirs, their's).
12. Several of his other (tenant, tenants) were complaining.
13. He spoke in soothing tones to the (feline, felines) in the bathroom and to the two (lady, ladies) in the next window.
14. Neither group could hear his (entreaty's, entreaties) over their own howling.
15. By now a cast of (thousand's, thousands) had gathered on the sidewalk below the two (window, windows).
16. The many interested (spectator, spectators) joined the (womans, women) in their chorus.
17. "Hush, (kitty's, kitties)," urged the frantic janitor.
18. "We'll save you, precious (ones, one's)," promised their owner.
19. "The cats would be (her's, hers)," muttered the janitor.
20. The fire (trucks, truck's) siren was heard in the distance.
21. The (woman, women) leaned out the window and waved frantically.
22. Five (members, member's) of the rescue squad flung (ladders, ladders') against the building.
23. The two agitated (womans, women) watched anxiously as their (kitties, kitties') (rescuers, rescuer's) climbed the (ladders, ladder's).
24. However, the (firefighters', firefighters) efforts were directed at removing the two (woman, women) from a fiery blaze.
25. The firefighters hadn't noticed the absence of a (fire, fires), and they completely ignored the (cats', cats) predicament.
26. The firefighters broke the window and heaved the two concerned cat (lovers, lover's) over their (shoulders, shoulder's). The new yowls were (Mrs. Poppels, Mrs. Poppel's).
27. Both the outraged (woman's, women) struggled violently, and one accidently broke the bathroom window in her struggles.
28. The four (cats, cats') were out the window in a flash.
29. Three of the (cats, cat's) fearlessly tread the ledge and re-entered the building through the window the firefighters had broken when they carried down the women.
30. The fourth (cats, cat's) courage failed him, and he wailed pitifully from the ledge.
31. The (shouts, shout's) of the crowd below frightened him.
2. The five (member, members) of the rescue squad exchanged pained glances, and one of them ascended the ladder.

Chapter 5: Possessives 171

33. He descended with the cowardly (cats', cat's) claws embedded in his flesh.
34. Once on firm ground the cat glared at the (ladies, lady's) and haughtily stalked away.
35. The (members, member's) of the crowd cheered the (firefighters, firefighters'), and the (ladders, ladders') were returned to the fire truck.
36. Now it's the (janitors, janitor's) turn to worry about who will pay for the two broken (window, windows).
37. (Its, It's) all in a (days, day's) work for all concerned.

Confusing Possessives and Contractions

Occasionally a confusion arises in distinguishing between a possessive and a contraction since both end in 's. You must look into the sentence to find the meaning.

Carol's is a possessive when ownership is involved.
_____*pos.*_____ Carol's (job) is boring.
Carol's is a contraction when it's a way of shortening *Carol is* or *Carol has*.
_____*contr.*_____ Carol's late. (Carol *is* late.)

EXERCISE 5-13

If the italicized word below is a possessive, label it "pos." and circle the thing owned. If the italicized word is a contraction, label it "contr."

1. _____ The city council approved Mayor *Carter's* proposal.
2. _____ The radio in *Jack's* car doesn't work.
3. _____ Her supervisor says that *Carmen's* late again.
4. _____ I noticed immediately that the *glass's* rim was chipped.
5. _____ The salt *shaker's* not where it should be.
6. _____ The cat was frightened by the tea *kettle's* whistle.
7. _____ My bathroom *faucet's* been leaking for two weeks.
8. _____ Wait until you've heard *John's* excuse!
9. _____ Maude was alerted by the *tuna's* smell.
10. _____ *Jerold's* keys jingled in his pocket.
11. _____ *Neal's* successful in everything he tries.
12. _____ *Rhoni's* paper was well written.
13. _____ *Yolanda's* sick and tired of all the complaining.
14. _____ Have you noticed that *Clara's* always at the front of the room?
15. _____ I heard the *alarm's* shriek before Larry.
16. _____ *Alton's* composure was badly shaken.
17. _____ *Stan's* up and around on his crutches.
18. _____ *Stan's* foot was broken in a fall from his moped.
19. _____ Guests are sometimes startled by my *sister's* jokes.
20. _____ It's clear that the *landlady's* anxious for the rent.

21. _____ The *bank's* loan officer looked like a zombie.
22. _____ *New York's* an expensive city to visit.
23. _____ *Ice cream's* his favorite dessert.
24. _____ The *minister's* description of hell shook me in my shoes.
25. _____ One *thing's* sure: I'm headed there.
26. _____ Meryl's convinced that *hell's* no fun.
27. _____ Where *there's* smoke, fire can usually be found.
28. _____ Her shower *curtain's* color reminded me of an eggplant.
29. _____ The *curtain's* caught on the door handle.
30. _____ The sign says that this parking *place's* reserved.

Indefinite Pronouns and Their Possessive Forms

There is a group of pronouns which behave like nouns. They can appear in possessive form and as contractions. These are the **indefinite** pronouns, pronouns which leave the person unspecified. When these pronouns are used in their possessive forms, the apostrophe *must* be present. And, of course, when they are used as contractions, the apostrophe must replace the missing letter (as in *is* and *has*).

Adjective	Noun or Pronoun Used as Subject	Verb or Verb Phrase	Object, Adverb, or Complement
Everyone's	Everyone → car	's (is) emits	here. pollutants.
Anybody's	Anyone → carelessness	's (is) will damage	welcome. it.

Indefinite Pronoun	Possessive Form	Contraction
one	one's mother	one's (one is or has)
another	another's problems	another's (another is or has)
anyone	anyone's help	anyone's (anyone is or has)
anybody	anybody's business	anybody's (anybody is or has)
each one	each one's choice	each one's (each one is or has)
everyone	everyone's wishes	everyone's (everyone is or has)
everybody	everybody's car	everybody's (everybody is or has)
no one	no one's report	no one's (no one is or has)
nobody	nobody's luck	nobody's (nobody is or has)
somebody	somebody's cat	somebody's (somebody is or has)
someone	someone's dog	someone's (someone is or has)

EXERCISE 5-14

In this exercise you will find indefinite pronouns used as subjects, objects, possessives, and as parts of contractions. Circle the correct form of the indefinite pronoun to complete the sentence correctly and on the line to the left indicate whether it is used as a possessive ("pos") or a contraction ("cont"). If the correct form does not need either type of apostrophe, just write "pron" or pronoun on the line.

Chapter 5: Possessives

_____ 1. (Somebody, Somebodys, Somebody's) is here.
_____ 2. (Nobody, Nobodys, Nobody's) essay was printed in the student paper.
_____ 3. Brad invited (everyone, everyones, everyone's) to his picnic.
_____ 4. Dan likes to act as if all problems were (someone elses, someone else's) concern.
_____ 5. It's (anybodys', anybody's, anybody) guess.
_____ 6. (No one, No one's, No ones) been here.
_____ 7. We heard (someone, someones, someone's) had been singing in the shower.
_____ 8. Russ noticed that (someone, someones, someone's) umbrella had been left in the hall.
_____ 9. (No one, No one's, No ones) car started this morning.
_____ 10. The blizzard upset (everybody, everybodies, everybody's) plans.
_____ 11. (Everyone, Everyones, Everyone's) doing something to help.
_____ 12. Tony should ask (somebody, somebodies, somebody's) advice.
_____ 13. (Everyone, Everyones, Everyone's) paycheck was delayed this week.
_____ 14. Hand (each one, each ones, each one's) of the students a test.
_____ 15. Can (anyone, anyones, anyone's) tell me the way to San Jose?
_____ 16. (Nobody, Nobodys, Nobody's) ever on time at this place.
_____ 17. Judith thinks that (no one, no ones, no one's) cares.
_____ 18. Donald won't use (anyone, anyones, anyone's) typewriter but his own.
_____ 19. You can't tell (anybody, anybodies, anybody's) anything.
_____ 20. Learn to respect (others, other's, others') property.
_____ 21. It's (nobody, nobodies', nobody's) business but his own.
_____ 22. (Someone, Someones, Someone's) at the door.
_____ 23. Tell (everybody, everybodies, everybody's) to leave Sam alone.
_____ 24. He'll listen to (anyone, anyones, anyone's) stories.
_____ 25. (Everyone, Everyones, Everyone's) supposed to do their own work.

TRANSFERRING YOUR SKILLS TO WRITING

The use of the apostrophe is among the most troublesome and confusing skills you will ever have to acquire, and also one of the most trivial. As you begin to transfer the skill developed in this chapter to your own writing, the error you are most likely to make is putting an apostrophe on every word that ends with the letter *s*. Don't.

If you must guess, guess that a word doesn't have an apostrophe instead of guessing that it does. The odds are much better because the letter *s* has a surprisingly large number of uses in English. We put an *s* on nouns to indicate that they're plural, and we put one on the end of verbs to indicate that in the present tense the subject is *he, she,* or *it*. The words *is* and *has* are often contracted to *'s,* and, of course, we add *'s* to nouns to indicate that they are possessive. This is doubly confusing because we *don't* add apostrophes to pronouns to indicate that they're possessive, unless they're indefinite pronouns, and then we do.

Study the following chart:

Contractions	Possessive Pronouns	Possessive Nouns
he's = he is, he has	his car	John's car
it's = it is, it has	its engine	the car's engine
you're = you are	your car	a student's car
they're = they are	their cars	the students' cars
who's = who is, who has	whose car?	someone's car[1]

[1]*Someone's,* of course, is not a noun but a pronoun. You can see why it's called an *indefinite* pronoun.

> **NOTE:** Don't forget the triple homonym, *there,* in expressions like *There is a dog, There are several cats, There must be a zoo,* and *There was a dinosaur. There* also indicates *where,* as in *here, there,* and *everywhere.*

EXERCISE 5–15 — write

Write an essay free from noun number, present tense verb, contraction, and possessive errors. Your instructor may wish you to do an in-class essay or may wish you to write on one of the following topics:

How to complain effectively

or

A realistic goal

REVIEW _____ five

The sentences in this review exercise are provided to help you check your progress in this chapter and to prepare you for what you'll find in the posttest. For the answers to this exercise, check with your instructor or tutor or listen to the appropriate audio tape.

Circle the correct choice.

                       A   B   C   D

1. Have you seen (Ginny, Ginnys, Ginny's, Ginnys') new sportscar?
    A   B   C
2. (Today, Todays, Today's) snowstorm really snarled traffic.
         A   B   C
3. All four (candidates, candidate's, candidates') armed security guards drank the beer.
      A   B   C   D
4. The (women, womens, women's, womens') investment counselor will offer a workshop on

   money management for widows on Thursday night.
                      A   B   A   B
5. The two pictures I like best are (Russells, Russell's) and (yours, your's).
                                              A   B   C   D
6. Cleet has finally decided to face (fatherhood, fatherhoods, fatherhood's, fatherhoods')

   many responsibilities.
                      A   B   C   D
7. Mrs. Prest visited Mr. (Prest, Prests, Prest's, Prests') psychiatrist.
                                       A   B   C   D
8. You should give an employer two (week, weeks, week's, weeks') notice before you leave.
    A   B   C   D   A
9. (Somebody, Somebodys, Somebody's, Somebodys') car didn't start, and (somebody,
     B   C   D

   somebodys, somebody's, somebodys') is knocking at the door.
                                                                                      A   B
10. Two of my friends have little brothers playing today: that kid is (Marshall, Marshalls,
     C   A   B   C

   Marshall's) brother, and this one is (Eric, Erics, Eric's).

chapter 6

PRONOUNS

PREVIEW six

The sentences in the exercise below preview the skills and principles you'll learn in this chapter. For the answers to this exercise, check with your instructor or tutor or listen to the appropriate audio tape.

Circle the correct word in the first nine sentences and revise the tenth to remove the ambiguity.

                                                            A B
1. Was the criticism directed at Claudine and (I, me)?

                          A B
2. My sister is taller than (he, him).

    A   B
3. (Who, Whom) is at the door?

                                             A   B   C
4. A clown is someone who can perform while (he is, he or she is, they are) crying inside.

                                                                                 A B
5. Don't plan on leaving your snake in the same room with Valentine and (we, us).

                   A   B   C   D
6. Have you seen (they, their, there, they're) new home?

                                                  A   B   C   D   E
7. As you began talking with interviewers, (one, you, they, he, she) realized it was just a game to them.

                                                                                  A   B   C   D   E
8. A lot of people have been told if they want to get ahead (one, you, they, he, she) must have a college degree.

                                                                             A   B
9. If we examined our prejudices carefully, we'd find out a lot about (ourselfs, ourselves, yourself, yourselves, themselves, himself, herself).
    C   D   E   F   G

10. My grandmother took this picture of my mother when she was living in Elkhart, Indiana.

INTRODUCTION

Our language is undergoing a constant process of change. One change we accept very readily is the addition of new words to name new inventions, concepts, and processes. The space industry provides numerous examples from *payload* to *spinoff* to *biofeedback*. We add content words—nouns, verbs, adjectives, and even adverbs—to the vocabulary of English whenever we feel the need to do so; however, we accept change in the function words—like prepositions and conjunctions—much less readily. Nevertheless, pronouns, which are usually classified as function words, are changing slowly.

As we examine the rules for the "proper" use of pronouns, it will help if you remember that we are not describing natural laws, like the law of gravity, that never change: if you stand on the surface of the planet Earth and drop a lead weight, it *will* fall. On the other hand, we are not describing matters of pure convention, such as the rule that students must sit in alphabetical order in your afternoon class. So long as the planet Earth continues in its present orbit around the sun, lead weights will continue to fall down, but it really doesn't make a bit of difference to anyone except the person who made up the rule how students distribute themselves in your afternoon class.

Language rules are more like the matters of convention than they are like laws of nature, but because we learn the particulars of our language while we are so young, the matters of convention become a part of our intuition and we *feel* as if they are as unchangeable as the laws of nature. Very conservative speakers will even refer to new vocabulary words as "barbarisms," suggesting that we already have enough words and don't need any new ones. Language, spoken or written, is *rule-governed behavior*, but the rules continue to change in spite of protests that all change is corrupting the language. One of the things that makes studying pronouns so interesting is that we can observe some profound changes in acceptable usage as they are taking place.

For example, before the sixteenth century, the English pronoun system included two forms of *you: thee* and *thou* were singular pronouns referring to one person; *you* and *ye* were plural pronouns. However, by the eighteenth century, *thee* and *thou* had disappeared from the standard language except in religious contexts. We are familiar with them now primarily because they are used in the King James version of the Christian Bible. Starting in the seventeenth century, some grammarians decided that English needed to be more logical, so they declared that *who* should be used only as the subject of a sentence or clause and that *whom* should be used only as an object. Making this careful distinction came to be regarded as one of the signs of an educated person, but *whom* has gradually slipped from common usage. In the nineteenth century, some of these gentlemen grammarians introduced the rule that *he* should be used to refer to any person who was not clearly identified as female. In 1850 the British Parliament even passed a law to enforce this change. Recently constructions like *Anyone can do it if he tries* have come under vigorous attack. The argument that *he* refers to both men and women is being rejected by linguistic scholars as well as by educated speakers of the language.

The changes illustrated here point to the four *properties* or characteristics of pronouns: **number** (meaning singular or plural); **person** (first person—*I* or *we;* second person—*you;* third—*he, she, it,* and *they);* **case** (subject, object, or possessive); and **gender** (masculine, feminine, neuter, or common). The rules of pronoun usage will all involve one or more of these characteristics.

PRONOUN CASE

A **pronoun** has traditionally been defined as a word that takes the place of a noun. The noun that the pronoun replaces or refers back to is called its **antecedent.**

Like nouns, pronouns can be used in sentences as subjects, objects, complements, and possessives. Unlike nouns, however, some pronouns have separate forms for subjects and objects. If English is your first language, you are already familiar with these distinctions, although you may not know the grammatical terms for the different forms or **cases** of the pronouns.

In the chapter on noun number, you learned to substitute subject pronouns for nouns.

$$\left\{\begin{array}{l}\text{He}\\ \text{Harold}\end{array}\right\} \text{complains a lot.}$$

$$\left\{\begin{array}{l}\text{They}\\ \text{His daughters}\end{array}\right\} \text{were working.}$$

$$\left\{\begin{array}{l}\text{It}\\ \text{Love}\end{array}\right\} \text{doesn't last.}$$

$$\left\{\begin{array}{l}\text{We}\\ \text{Peggy and I}\end{array}\right\} \text{collect stamps.}$$

In chapters 4 and 5 you worked with possessive pronouns. Notice that only the **indefinite pronouns** like *everyone, anybody,* and *no one* use apostrophes to form their possessives.

The coat **of someone** is on the bed.
Someone's coat is on the bed.
The coat **of him** is on the floor.
His coat is on the floor.
Charles dropped the coat **belonging to Charles** on the floor.
Charles dropped **his** coat on the floor.

A third kind of pronoun is the object pronoun. Object pronouns can be used to replace objects in sentences in exactly the same way that subject pronouns can be used to replace subjects.

$$\text{Leonard bought} \left\{\begin{array}{l}\text{them}\\ \text{both cars}\end{array}\right\}.$$

The sheriff shot {**her** / Martha}.

The deputy captured {**him** or **her** / the embezzler}.

The chart below summarizes the different cases of the pronouns.

Subject	Possessive	Object
I	my, mine	me
you	your, yours	you
he	his	him
she	her, hers	her
it	its	it
we	our, ours	us
they	their, theirs	them
who	whose	whom
everyone	everyone's	everyone
anyone	anyone's	anyone
someone	someone's	someone

EXERCISE 6-1

Substitute the appropriate pronoun for the subject, object, or possessive construction italicized in the sentences below.

It   1. *Inflation* destroyed my raise this year.
_____ 2. Last January *Mike and I* adopted a kitten.
_____ 3. I left the lunch *belonging to me* on the bus.
_____ 4. We plan to meet *the Harrisons* for dinner.
_____ 5. A party has been planned for Janice and *Bob*.
_____ 6. *The doctor* could not find her stethoscope.
_____ 7. Cindy dropped books *belonging to Cindy* in the snow.
_____ 8. My brother borrowed *my* car last week.
_____ 9. *Nancy and her grandmother* have gone sailing again.
_____ 10. The astronauts wore pressure suits *belonging to them* for the interview.
_____ 11. *What person* has been rifling through my desk?
_____ 12. To *what person* should the application be sent?
_____ 13. The car *of what person* is parked in my driveway?
_____ 14. Give *Lisa* the missing data.
_____ 15. Lester gave the sister *of me* a ride to work.

Compound Pronouns

Use only subject pronouns as subjects of sentences.

{**She** / Jean} left town.

Chapter 6: Pronouns

If a compound subject contains a pronoun, in polite usage the pronoun follows the noun. If the subject contains two pronouns, *I* always appears last.

The doctor and he disagreed about the diagnosis.
You and I can still be friends.
She and I drove to Jacksonville together.

A sentence like *Him and the doctor disagreed* violates two rules. *Him* is an object pronoun, not a subject pronoun, and it precedes the noun in the compound subject. It is unlikely that you would use *him* or any other object pronoun as the subject of a sentence if it were not compounded, however. *Him disagreed with the doctor* sounds wrong to any native speaker of English.

A similar rule applies to object pronouns. Object pronouns are used as objects of verbs and as objects of prepositions.

My cat eats $\begin{Bmatrix} \text{it} \\ \text{celery} \end{Bmatrix}$

Jonah gave $\begin{Bmatrix} \textbf{them} \\ \text{the cows} \end{Bmatrix}$ some hay.

Clarence borrowed money from both the bank and $\begin{Bmatrix} \textbf{her} \\ \text{Clarissa} \end{Bmatrix}$.

If the object is compound and contains both a noun and a pronoun, the pronoun follows the noun. If the object contains two pronouns, *me* always comes last.

Give the papers to **Rose and her.**
The state trooper gave **Scott and me** a warning.

Most middle-class speakers of English have been thoroughly conditioned against using object pronouns as subjects. Sentences such as *Him and me went home* are shunned in writing and also avoided in careful speech. As a consequence, many speakers take the rule too far and avoid object pronouns completely. Subject pronouns sound more ''polite'' to many people, so you frequently hear sentences such as *A registered letter came for my brother and I* from people who are otherwise very careful about their speech.

Compound objects may especially tempt you to use a subject pronoun instead of an object pronoun. You can test which form is correct in your sentence by omitting the first part of the compound. If you are a native speaker of English, you would never say *The state trooper gave I a warning;* therefore, you should never say *The state trooper gave Scott and I a warning.*

Although you may hear sentences like *A registered letter came for my brother and I* and *The state trooper gave Scott and I a warning,* and although they may sound ''correct'' or more ''polite'' to you, this change in the pronoun system is not accepted by usage authorities.

Pushing the rule too far in an attempt to sound educated or polite is called **hypercorrecting.**

Although usage authorities generally insist upon only subject pronouns in subject positions and only object pronouns in objection positions, some changes are becoming accepted. We will talk about three: subject complements, comparisons with *than,* and *who/whom.*

Avoid Double Subjects

A pronoun problem which deserves a brief comment is the adding of a subject pronoun following a noun. For example:

> My mother, **she** makes chicken soup.
> The clowns, **they** left the circus.

A speaker who hesitates after the subject often feels obliged to repeat the subject at least with its pronoun substitute before continuing the interrupted sentence. This frequent occurrence, which goes unnoticed in speech, is considered an error in writing. Omit **she** and **they** to correct.

A similar but entirely acceptable construction in polite usage is the insertion of *we* before subjects and *us* before objects in sentences like the following:

> **We students** must take a stand on the issue of tuition.
> Most of **us students** cannot afford another increase.
> The administration never asks **us students** for input.

To determine whether to use *we* or *us,* simply delete the word *students* in the above constructions. *We* is used only in subject positions; *us* is used only in object positions.

EXERCISE 6-2

In the following sentences, choose the correct subject or object pronoun. Do not hypercorrect.

1. There was a violent disagreement between Constance and (she, her).
2. Last winter Craig and (I, me) went tobagganing.
3. Can you wait for Milton and (I, me)?
4. Let (he, him) and (I, me) finish painting the kitchen.
5. The McCarthys and (we, us) went to the barn dance.
6. The Davises have asked me to shovel the snow for their parents and (they, them) this winter.
7. The Christmas bonus came as a complete surprise to Beulah and (she, her).
8. Just between you and (I, me), I think his proposal will be rejected.
9. Her mother, his sister, and (she, her) bought a restaurant and went into business together.
10. You and (I, me) got the worst assignments this week.
11. My science teacher, (he, him) spilled hydrochloric acid on my lab notes.
12. Whenever Grandpa and (we, us) grandchildren get together, we go fishing.
13. (They, Them) and (I, me) have our differences.
14. I resent the suggestion that Edie and (I, me) cannot get along.
15. (We, Us) semifinalists were the last contestants of the day.

Chapter 6: Pronouns

16. The TV star sent my brother and (he, him) an autograph.
17. No one except you and (they, them) will see the final report.
18. Thomas Jefferson Davis, (he, him) hates the name his parents gave him.
19. (Who, Whom) will be called on today for oral reports?
20. Why have they done such a thing to (we, us) innocent employees?

EXERCISE 6-3

Edit the following passage substituting polite and correct forms for hypercorrections and errors.

Last summer, my sisters and me, we decided to earn a little extra money, so we went to work on a tobacco farm in Connecticut. For three weeks Cheryl and me did nothing but walk up and down the fields tieing up small plants. Nancy, she managed to get assigned to kitchen duty. She was lucky because the field boss treated we field hands like a chain gang. He yelled at Cheryl and I at least once an hour. Me and Nancy were worried that Cheryl would do something violent to the valuable leaves or he before it was over.

On July 1, they moved the other field workers and us to the sheds to sew the leaves up for curing. Nancy and I were sewers, and Cheryl, she was our leafer. Whomever could put the most leaves on wooden lathes could make the most money. It was up to Cheryl to see that Nancy and me always had leaves at our machine. We girls used to race to make the time go faster, but the shed boss, she was worse than the field boss. If she saw a damaged leaf, she turned off the machines and yelled, "Whom is responsible for this?"

Cheryl and me sometimes hid broken leaves inside our jackets so she wouldn't see them. At the end of August, they asked Nancy if she would come back next year as a shed boss. They asked Cheryl and me if we would please look for jobs on a ranch in Arizona next summer.

Subject Complements

Most sentences in English have the subject/verb/object order.

Subject	Verb	Object
The dog	bit	the man.
The dog	bit	him.

In a subject/verb/object sentence, the subject and the object are different from each other; usually the subject *does* something *to* the object.

There is another type of sentence in which the word that follows the verb renames or describes the subject.

Subject	Verb	Subject Complement
The man	is	a dog.
The dog	is	a hound.
This	is	the man.

Because the subject and the subject complement are the same, the old grammarians insisted that they must be in the same *case*. The only time you can tell what the case is, however, is when the subject complement is a pronoun. Thus, we should say:

The dog bit {**him.** / *the man.*}

but:

This is {**he.** / *the man.*}

Much to the dismay of some grammarians, what we *should* do according to their rules and what we actually do are two different things. Pretend your name is Kenneth. The phone rings. You answer it with, "Hello." The caller says, "May I speak to Kenneth?" What do you say?

Traditionally, the only polite response to such a question was considered to be, "This is he." The natural and increasingly accepted response for most people is, "This is me."

Because *This is he* may sound pretentious to you, in very formal or academic situations, you can avoid the construction:

"May I speak to Kenneth?"

"Speaking." or "This is Kenneth."

In conversation, where the problem naturally arises, you should feel free to say, "This is me," or "This is him."

Some people have trained themselves to say, "This is he," or "This is she," when answering the phone, but almost no one is fastidious enough to say, "That is she," when pointing out a new arrival to someone. They will either say, "That's her," or, "She's the one."

Comparisons With *Than*

Another place where object pronouns are replacing subject pronouns is in comparisons using the word *than*. Consider the following sentence:

Professor Duffy gave my sister a higher grade **than she gave me.** Sentences like this can be shortened. For example:

Professor Duffy gave my sister a higher grade **than me.**

Both constructions are perfectly correct in formal and informal situations. The trouble arises, however, when the pronoun in the original construction is a subject pronoun. For example:

My brother is shorter **than I am.**

Traditional usage authorities object strongly to reducing this sentence to

*My brother is shorter **than me.*** They have insisted on *My brother is shorter **than I*** because the subject pronoun is necessary in the original sentence. Some people, however, feel that the word *than* is a preposition like *by* or *on* or *of*. As you know, following a preposition, you must use an object pronoun.

> **to me**
> **from me**
> **between Matilda and them**
> and by analogy, **"than" me**

Thus, you would expect people to say *than me* more often than they would say *than I*. But again a reverse sort of logic gets applied to these sentences. The reasoning is that *than I* sounds slightly more polite or elegant. The prejudice in favor of subject pronouns leads some people to hypercorrect, producing ambiguous sentences like:

> The waitress gave Amanda more strawberries **than I.**

Unless you mean to say that both the waitress and I gave Amanda some strawberries, but the waitress gave her more than I did, you must write:

> The waitress gave Amanda more strawberries **than she gave me.**
> or
> The waitress gave Amanda more strawberries **than me.**

You can always test these sentences when you proofread your writing by expanding the clause and checking the way the pronoun is being used in the complete sentence. In informal situations or in speech when you don't have time to test the sentence, it is probably better to say *than me,* which is always acceptable informal English, than it is to say *than I,* which may sound silly and pretentious, especially when it is a hypercorrection.

Who? or Is It *Whom?*

There is probably no point of grammar which is more puzzling to students who are native speakers of English than the distinction between *who* and *whom*. If you refer back to the list of subject, object, and possessive pronouns on page 180, you should be able to state the difference according to the traditional textbook rules very easily: *who* is used as a subject and *whom* is used only as an object of a verb or as an object of a preposition. For example:

> **Who** is on the phone?
> **To whom** was the package addressed?

The difficulty arises because sentences using *who* and *whom* are not usually as easy to analyze as the two examples given above. In the first place, the expected word order—subject/verb/object—is often inverted to ask a question. For example:

> **Whom** did you call?

In this sentence *you* is the subject; *did call* is the verb; and *whom* is the object of the verb.

This inverted order for questions confuses speakers of English because in English we expect the first noun or pronoun before the verb to be the subject of the sentence, not the object. Most of us will ask *Who did you call?* unless we have been taught that it is more polite to say *Whom.*

A second problem that arises when we are trying to analyze *who/whom* sentences is that the troublesome pronoun may appear as the subject or object of a noun clause within the sentence. For example:

I know **who** is at the door.

The usual textbook rule is that the case of the pronoun is determined by the clause in which it appears. In this case, *I* is the subject of the sentence and *know* is the verb; *who is at the door* is a noun clause being used as the direct object. The sentence is similar to *I know Chad* in which *I* is the subject, *know* is the verb, and *Chad* is the direct object. If you substituted a pronoun for *Chad*, however, you would have to choose *him: I know him.* If you substituted another pronoun for *who* in the first sentence, you would choose *he: I know he is at the door.* You can make these substitutions infallibly and unself-consciously simply because you speak English, and in English you know intuitively that the case of the pronoun is determined by the clause in which it appears.

Now you may justifiably ask why, if you know this intuitively, you can't just as infallibly choose between *who* and *whom*. There are two reasons: the first and probably the most important is that you have learned that *whom* correctly used is a sign of a good education and high social prestige; the second is that sentences using *who* and *whom* are often inverted so that you have to make a choice about the case of the pronoun long before you get to the clause in which it appears.

Whoever and *whomever* follow the same rules in traditional grammar as do *who* and *whom,* but they add one more bit of confusion. Most people remember to say *whom* following the prepositions *to* and *for;* however, if a noun clause follows the preposition, they continue to analyze the next word as the object of the preposition rather than the subject of the clause as the rulemakers say they should:

To whom should we send the bill? (*whom* is only the object of the preposition.)
Send it **to whoever signed the charge slip.** (*whoever* is the subject of *signed* and the whole clause is the object of the preposition.)

If your curiosity has been satisfied, for all practical purposes you may feel free to forget the distinctions between *who* and *whom* and *whoever* and *whomever* in favor of one simple principle: if in doubt, use *who.* It is better to sound like a confident but informal speaker or writer than it is to hypercorrect.

Who did you meet? is accepted not only by most educated speakers and writers, but also by most contemporary usage authorities. On the other hand, *Whom is singing in the shower?* is rejected by practically all authorities and,

Chapter 6: Pronouns

in addition, sounds silly and pretentious (as well as wrong) to most educated speakers and writers.

> **NOTE: If in doubt, use *who*. Avoid *whom* except after prepositions.**

EXERCISE 6-4

In the following sentences, choose the correct subject or object pronoun in contemporary informal English. Do not hypercorrect.

1. (Who, Whom) will be our next vice president?
2. Cousin Billy shoveled more snow than (I, me).
3. Would you be kind enough to deliver this envelope to Mr. Gregory and (she, her)?
4. When the final results are announced, you can just guess (who, whom) the winner will be.
5. The truck driver told Blair and (I, me) that I-35 by-passes Des Moines.
6. Schultz always makes the same number of mistakes as (I, me).
7. All semester long Dwight, Margaret, and (he, him) have been studying from the wrong book.
8. Pronouns are more troublesome for David than (she, her).
9. Creswell wants to find out (who, whom) started the rumor about Clark and (they, them).
10. Please tell me you aren't sending the dogs with Bob and (we, us).
11. (Who, Whom) did the dean appoint to replace Bitzer?
12. Just between you and (I, me), this car will never make it to Oregon.
13. Mother always favored my sister more than (I, me).
14. If you're looking for Leonard, that's (he, him) at the bar.
15. Linda and (they, them) are planning a home-coming party for Mike and (she, her).
16. (Who, Whom) are you going to the party with?
17. (Who, Whom) besides Joseph and (he, him) knows how to dive?
18. The aliens are waiting on the surface of the planet for the Captain and (we, us).
19. If I've ever seen a natural athlete, it's (she, her).
20. We saw the MacDonalds and (he, him) getting off the plane at Gate D-4.

The pronoun problems we've dealt with so far in this chapter have involved distinguishing between subject and object pronouns. The next set of problems requires you to recognize possessive pronouns and to distinguish them from subject and object pronouns.

Confusion of *Them* and *Those*

The object pronoun *them* is occasionally misused in constructions requiring the word *those*.

> INCORRECT: **Them books** should be returned to the library.
> CORRECT: **Those books** should be returned to the library.

Although this usage has been around for some time in nonstandard speech, usage authorities continue to refuse to recognize it, and it is considered illiterate by the general population. You should avoid it even in informal writing situations.

POSSESSIVE PRONOUNS

Possessive pronouns often invite two kinds of mistakes. The first mistake is to use a subject pronoun instead of a possessive pronoun:

> INCORRECT: **They** house is on fire.
> CORRECT: **Their** house is on fire.

The second mistake is to confuse a possessive pronoun with its contraction homonym:

> INCORRECT: **They're** dog is chasing my cat.
> CORRECT: **Their** dog is chasing my cat.

As we saw in the chapter on noun possessives, simply putting two nouns side by side is sometimes enough to show possession:

> the cat food = the food of the cat
> that truck driver = the driver of the truck

In most cases, however, we form possessive constructions by adding an apostrophe (') plus an *s* to the noun owner:

> Marcia's cat = the cat belonging to Marcia
> Ace Transport's new truck = the new truck belonging to Ace Transport

Both of these methods of forming noun possessives confuse student writers who try to apply them to possessive pronouns. Simply putting a subject pronoun next to the word it should modify is not accepted in written English:

> INCORRECT: **She sister** worked on the farm all summer.
> CORRECT: **Her sister** worked on the farm all summer.
> INCORRECT: **You record** has a scratch on it.
> CORRECT: **Your record** has a scratch on it.

Notice that in the last example, pronunciation could mislead you as the *r* at the end of *your* elides (or runs together) with the *r* at the beginning of *record*.

The second and most common confusion between possessive nouns and possessive pronouns is brought about by the apostrophe. Only the indefinite pronouns form their possessives with apostrophes in the same way that nouns do. (See page 172 in Chapter 5). The fact that the possessive forms of the personal pronouns do not take apostrophes is doubly confusing because, as we saw in Chapter 4, they have contraction homonyms which *do* take apostrophes.

Possessive Prounouns

This is *your* paper.
It is *yours*.
Whose bicycle is that?
It is *hers*.

My snowmobile ran into *their* fence.
Theirs was the only fence completely snow-covered.
The clerk found *his* forms but couldn't find *ours*.

Don't throw an apostrophe into a word haphazardly. Work it out. The way to check the homonyms is to try first to reformulate the sound into two words:

you're = you are	*You're* next.
who's = who is or who has	*Who's* here?
they're = they are	*They're* right.
it's = it is or it has	*It's* lost for good.
he's = he is or he has	*He's* late.

Review Chapter 4 if this distinction is not yet clear to you.

SPELLING THE REFLEXIVE PRONOUNS

Other nonstandard forms which are not gaining acceptance even among the most liberal usage authorities are among the reflexive or *-self* pronouns.

There are singular reflexives ending in *-self* and plural reflexives ending in *-selves*. Misspelling is the first of two problems with these pronouns.

Singular words ending in f or fe, like *wolf* or *knife*, form their plurals by changing the f or fe to v and adding es. Reflexive pronouns follow the same pattern.

Singular	Plural
myself	ourselves
yourself	yourselves
himself	themselves
herself	
itself	

A second problem with these pronouns illustrates that grammar is not always logical. *My, your,* and *our* are clearly possessive pronouns, and you might conclude that the way to form reflexives is to add *-self* to singular possessive pronouns and *-selves* to plural possessive pronouns. For example:

Singular	Plural
my + self = myself	our + selves = ourselves
your + self = yourself	your + selves = yourselves

The two troublesome forms are those which don't, in fact, follow this pattern. *Him* and *them* are objective pronouns, and the mistake usually made is to substitute the possessive pronouns *his* and *their* to produce, quite logically, *hisself* and *theirselves* with a variety of different spellings. Usage authorities have insisted that these forms do not exist in English, and they are even more intolerant when one of these supposedly non-existent forms is combined with a spelling error, producing something like *theirselfs*. Avoid combining *his* and *their* with *self* or any variation of it.

A third problem arises from using *themselves* to refer to a singular antecedent. For example, *Everyone wanted to see for themselves*. Here usage opinion is divided: some authorities insist that words like *everyone* are grammatically singular and must, therefore, be followed by the singular pronoun *himself*; others insist that *himself* refers only to masculine nouns, ignoring the feminine half of the world, and that, therefore, *themselves* should be tolerated. Very careful speakers and writers most often avoid the grammatical problem by pluralizing: *All of the people at the demonstration wanted to see for themselves*. This third problem will be discussed again under *Indefinite Pronouns*.

EXERCISE 6-5

Circle the correct form of the pronoun in each of the following sentences.

1. (They, Their) lost (they, their) home in a terrible fire.
2. (They, Them, Those) books belong to my brother.
3. The Carlsons would rather do the job (theirselves, themselves, themselfs).
4. (They, Their, They're) dog knows (it, its, it's) way home.
5. Do (you, your) have (you, your, you're) receipts with you?
6. The computer wrecked (itsself, itself) by trying to solve all of (it, its, it's) problems at once.
7. Calvin beat up (he, his, he's) brother.
8. (They, Their, They're) don't believe in the same things (they, their, they're, there) parents believed in.
9. Did Claude give the stegosaurus (it, its, it's) bone?
10. My sixth-grade brother should have to do his homework by (himself, hiself, hisself, himselves).
11. (Who, Whose, Who's) softballs broke (they, their, them) windows?
12. I will pick up income tax forms for Margaret and (myself, myselve, me).
13. (I, I'm) tired of (you, your, you're) stories.
14. A boy doesn't have to grow up the same way (he, his, he's) father did.
15. Did (they, they're, them) finish (they, their, them) reports?
16. (You, Your, You're) mother wants (you, you're).
17. We will have to make (them, those) decisions (ourself, ourselves, ourselves).
18. I've heard about that creek; (it, its, it's) a lot deeper than (you, your, you're) think.
19. Give the news to the McCoys and (they, their, they're, there) cousins.
20. The coaches (theyselves, themselves, theirselfs) assigned extra homework to the basketball players.

"THE TYPICAL PERSON" AND INDEFINITE PRONOUNS

In formal writing, we often refer to "the doctor," "the lawyer," "the student," or "the teacher" with a singular noun when we actually mean the *typical* doctor, lawyer, student, or teacher. This construction assumes that whatever is being said applies equally to any person who fits the category being discussed. Likewise, we have a group of pronouns, called *indefinite pronouns* that are usually grammatically singular, although they may be said to be "psychologically" plural since they refer theoretically to *anyone* or *everyone* in the world.

A few of the indefinite pronouns are clearly plural, both in form and in meaning. For example: *few, many, several,* and *others* leave no doubt that they are plural. Another group of the indefinite pronouns may be singular or plural depending on their use in a particular sentence. *All of the boxes* is plural, but *all of the salt* is singular; *some of the students* is plural, but *some of the mayonnaise* is singular. These differences are important in subject/verb agreement. They are diagrammed and discussed on page 47. You may want to review that section.

Except for those obvious exceptions, the indefinite pronouns listed below are traditionally defined as singular.

Indefinite Pronouns

anyone	anybody	anyone else
everyone	everybody	everyone else
someone	somebody	someone else
no one	nobody	no one else
one	another	one another
other	each one	each other
something	nothing	anything
either	neither	none

Consider the sentence *Everybody wants to win*. Despite the plural intention of the indefinite pronoun *everybody,* there is no disagreement among usage authorities about the verb: it is singular. There *is* disagreement about the pronoun that should follow the indefinite pronouns, however. All of the sentences below will be called "wrong"[1] by one or more grammar books published this year.

(1) **The average person** will do what **they** can to help if **they** recognize that an emergency exists.

(2) **Either** Gloria or Brian will bring the volleyball with **them.**

(3) **Everyone** was concerned about the chemistry test, but **they** all passed.

Traditional grammarians argued in the nineteenth century that if the indefinite pronoun is singular (as the present tense verb suggests it is), then it should be followed by a singular pronoun. They decreed that unless the antecedent was unmistakably or exclusively feminine, the pronoun should be masculine because *he* was being used "generically," that is, to refer to all human beings, not just men. Thus:

(1) **The average person** will do what **he** can to help if **he** recognizes that an emergency exists.

If you write this sentence, whether it is your intention or not, you perpetuate the demeaning and inaccurate assumption that in an emergency a

---

[1] As most students know, "informal" means much the same thing as "wrong" when it comes to writing.

man will rise to the occasion while a woman will either fall apart or stand by helplessly.

Another popular but misleading tradition among textbook writers has been to avoid the problem presented in our second example (2) above by making both people male or both female. For example:

(2) **Either** Gloria or Eleanor will bring the volleyball with **her.**
or
(2) **Either** Jeffrey or Brian will bring the volleyball with **him.**

If listening to grammarians argue makes you nervous, you can rewrite this type of sentence so as to avoid the problem altogether:

(2) Either Gloria will bring the volleyball or Brian will.

No sensible native speaker of English is fond enough of the traditional "rules" of grammar to go so far as to "correct" our last example like this:

(3) **Everybody** was worried about the chemistry test, but **he** passed.

Like most hypercorrections, it sounds perfectly silly. The grammar books that have bothered to mention this type of sentence at all usually tell you that the only solution is to rewrite to avoid the agreement problem. They might suggest something like this, making the subject plural:

(3) **All of the students** were worried about the chemistry test, but **they** all passed.

As a speaker and as a writer, you will encounter many occasions when using *they/their/them* following an indefinite pronoun or the typical person construction is clearly more convenient and stylistically more desirable. You have two choices: You can address the problem (choose a side in the controversy and stick with it until *they* is firmly established as an acceptable choice as it will be in a few short years) or you can avoid the problem (which is what more careful writers have been doing for years).

Strategies for Avoiding Sexism

Whether the writer intends it or not, referring to the typical person as *he* suggests that the typical person is male. One of the most useful side effects of becoming sensitive to the pronoun problems involved in these constructions is beginning to question the ease with which you refer to "the typical" anything. Here are some things you can do:

1. Write in the plural.
   All of the students passed **their** chemistry tests.
   Most people will help out if **they** recognize that an emergency exists.
2. Use *he or she*. As long as you don't overdo it, this is a perfectly acceptable solution.
   Anyone will do what **he or she** can to help out in an emergency.
3. Substitute an indefinite article (*a, an, the*) for *his* or eliminate it entirely.
   Instead of saying *A conservative is someone who can endure the suffering of others for the sake of his principles,* try one of these:

Chapter 6: Pronouns

> A conservative is someone who can endure the suffering of others for the sake **of principle....**or for the sake **of a principle.**

4. Delete the pronoun completely by revising the sentence. Instead of saying Each student turned in **his** report, try:

   A report was turned in by each student.

5. Use a synonym or repeat the word when you might otherwise use a pronoun.

   Take your broker's suggestions. { **This individual** / **This is a person who** / **A broker** } knows what the market has been up to.

The most difficult syntactic tangles occur when it is necessary to describe one-to-one interaction and it is not as neat to use the plural. Don't assume that the only thing you can do is to keep repeating *he or she,* however. Consider the next sentence:

> The typical student will not know what is expected of **him or her** unless **he or she** has had an opportunity to work through the routine with **his or her** partner and then has repeated the procedure by **himself or herself.**

After a little thought and maybe a little experimenting, you should be able to come up with a solution like the following one:

> The student will not know what is expected without an opportunity first to work through the routine with a partner and then to repeat the procedure alone.

EXERCISE 6-6

Using the strategies suggested, edit the following passages.

1. A snob is someone who thinks more highly of themselves than anyone else, so much so that they don't even bother with people who don't measure to their standards. An example that we all know of is Suzie Neat. She walks about haughtily with her books pulled to her chest and her nose in the air. She won't even acknowledge a hello unless it's from the captain of the football team.

2. A first-class phony is the person who can tell absolute lies while keeping a straight face. They can rattle on about their royal blood in Austria, their quest for an Olympic gold medal, or their studies in entomology. Why does a phony have to try to impress people with things that they aren't? Don't they realize that people will accept them more for what they are than what they wish they were?

SHIFTING PRONOUNS

In practice, instructors who are sensitive to changes taking place in society and in the profession will not penalize students who use either *he* consistently to refer to the typical person or who consistently use *they* as a singular, sex-indefinite pronoun. What they will object strenuously to is starting off a paragraph with one form and shifting to another.

If enough context is provided, readers will accept any of the personal pronouns as referring to "the typical person" or to "people in general."

> As **people** grow older, **they** grow more conservative.
> As **one** grows older, **one** grows more conservative.
> As **we** grow older, **we** grow more conservative.
> As **you** grow older, **you** grow more conservative.
> As **a woman** grows older, **she** grows more conservative.
> As **a man** grows older, **he** grows more conservative.

The term *pronoun shifting* refers to any inappropriate shift, but in practice it occurs when a writer starts talking about the typical person or people in general, refers to the typical person as *he* or *one,* and then relaxes into the more comfortable *they* or *you* forms.

In the next example, the student writer (a woman) decided to use the frequently seen device *he/she, his/her* instead of saying *he* throughout her essay to refer to the typical student. She was clearly thinking of her own situation and the decisions she had made before coming to college, but half-way through her paragraph she began to find the double pronouns very tiresome. She gave up on them by shifting to *you.*

PRONOUN SHIFT

> Although both living at home and commuting have some advantages, I feel going away to school has more. I do not think a person really becomes **his/her** own individual until given an opportunity to be on **his/her** own. Living at college provides that opportunity. There is room for real personal growth and development without **your** parents standing over **you**. The academic education **you** seek is not the only education **you** will obtain by living away at school.

The traditional advice for correcting the biggest problem in this paragraph, the pronoun shifting, would be to change all of the pronouns to *he, him,* or *his*. Female students writing from and about their own experiences are entirely justified in finding this solution particularly unsatisfactory. In revision this student chose to use *you/your* consistently since she was writing for an audience of college freshmen.

INFORMAL

> Although both living at home and commuting have some advantages, I feel going away to school has more. I do not think **you** really become your own person until **you** have the opportunity to be on **your** own. Living at college provides that opportunity. There is room for real personal growth without **your** parents standing over **you**. The academic education **you** seek is not the only education **you** will obtain while living away at school.

Readers who are themselves long past making decisions about whether to go away to school or to live at home and commute might protest that this writer's revision is "illogical." A more formal tone, appropriate for a wider audience can be obtained by pluralizing.

Chapter 6: Pronouns

FORMAL

Although both living at home and commuting have some advantages, going away to school has more. **People** do not really become **themselves** until **they** have an opportunity to be on **their** own. Living at college provides that opportunity. **They** have room for real personal growth without **their** parents standing over them. The academic education **they** seek is not the only education **they** will obtain while living away at school.

EXERCISE 6-7

Many of the following passages contain pronoun shifts or pronoun agreement errors. Edit by writing above the words that must be changed to make the passages acceptable.

1. A walk through a Douglas Fir Grove tantalizes my senses with the fresh smell of evergreen. If one is lucky, he might catch a glimpse of a porcupine or a peregrine falcon. Suddenly you step out of the dark forest into a small meadow of bear grass high above the roads.

2. If a person does not use his or her brain to its capacity, their mind will grow stale.

3. Nothing really strange or exciting has ever happened to me like seeing a UFO or getting snowed in on your vacation in a mountain cabin in Alaska.

4. One's freshman year is a trying experience. One meets many new people, develops new interests, and experiences many new things, but you are also in a totally new environment and must make the necessary adjustments.

5. Many of the girls I went to high school with, unlike their mothers, plan to attend college because she wants a different sort of life.

6. A security guard patrolled the parking lot after five o'clock, but I never spoke to them.

7. Anyone who wants to lose weight must do two things: you must eat less, and you must exercise more.

8. Everyone smiled at the bride as she walked down the aisle, and when she reached the door, she turned and waved at him.

9. A musician in a successful band makes a lot of money, but you get sick of spending half your life in a hotel room.

10. Either Pamela or Leonard will bring a radio with him.

11. Every wage earner must attach a copy of his W-2 form to his income tax return.

12. Every student in my morning English class had his heart set on making an A.

13. Taxpayers often believe that our confiscatory tax laws make earning more money not worth your effort.

14. The average person will do what they can to help if they recognize that an emergency exists.

15. What kind of person engages in continuing education? What motivates them? How is their job performance affected?

16. No one in their right mind would make fun of Bull Johnson.

17. When an unpublished author sees no way of getting his book accepted by a commercial publisher, you can go to a vanity press.

18. Tracy's softball team felt they had a good chance of raising money for new uniforms with a backyard carnival.

19. My high school teacher always said that if I proofread my papers carefully, you'd see the difference in your grades.

20. As one matures, he or she soon realizes that he/she cannot always do everything by yourself.

EXERCISE 6-8

Read through the following short essay; decide upon how you wish to refer to the typical student; then edit carefully, making any changes in wording that will make the passage read more smoothly.

Note Taking

The ability to take good notes is essential to the student who is bombarded with new information every day. Your success in school may well depend on how efficiently you can organize and learn what you read in your textbooks and what you hear in lectures. The student who lets information wash over him without capturing the important details in the form of careful notes will not remember what he has heard or read, and when it comes time to write up reports on the material or take exams over it, you have a real problem.

Some students fill notebooks full of meaningless or unrelated bits of information that are worse than useless when you try to review them. He or she finds that they waste more time trying to make sense out of cryptic messages than he does studying the material: "1874 IMPORTANT DATE!!!! Harvard." No one can possibly tell from this note why 1874 was important to Harvard or anyone else.

If your notes are to do you any good, it must be complete enough. "1874, Harvard started entrance exam in composition" gives the notetaker some reason he or she might want to remember the date. On the other hand, if the instructor reads Harvard's announcement of its upcoming entrance exams to the class, one will probably not be able to get it all down:

> Each candidate will be required to write a short English composition, correct in spelling, punctuation, grammar, and expression, the subject to be taken from such works of standard authors as shall be announced from time to time. The subject for 1874 will be taken from one of the following works: Shakespeare's *Tempest, Julius Caesar,* and *Merchant of Venice;* Goldsmith's *Vicar of Wakefield;* Scott's *Ivanhoe,* and *Lay of the Last Minstrel.*

If you try to get it all down, the student will still be writing "as shall be announced from time to time," while their instructor is summarizing the importance of the announcement.

Chapter 6: Pronouns

The most important thing to remember about good note taking is to use a standard form and to put the notes in your own words. Leave room in your left-hand margin to ask yourself questions when you review it after class.

| Why important to modern composition courses? | 1874 Harvard entrance exam
—defined comp as prerequisite skill
—required correctness in spelling, grammar, punctuation, expression
—subjects from literature |

Students who use this form can review quickly and easily the night before an exam. He or she will have a record that they can refer to and still make sense of years later, and they will be able to write clear, logical reports almost directly from one's notes. Try these suggestions, and you'll be a better student because of it.

PRONOUN REFERENCE

Vague, misleading, indefinite, or awkward pronoun reference are all terms that have been used to describe the last problem to be discussed in this chapter. A reader should always be able to clearly identify the antecedent of a pronoun (what the pronoun refers back to). Don't be satisfied with "You know what I mean" as an explanation.

Sometimes the vague reference is strictly a mechanical problem. You may know what you mean, but you haven't made the meaning entirely clear to the reader. For example:

REF? The F-15 fightercraft are more sophisticated than the older F-4s, but **they** are more reliable.

Which fightercraft are more reliable, the F-15s or the F-4s? Rewrite to make it clear:

The F-15 fightercraft are more sophisticated than the older F-4s, but the F-4s are more reliable.

In the next example, the referent for the pronoun is slightly more vague than in the previous one:

REF? When the TV picture gets snowy, Uncle Jason goes up on the roof and adjusts **it.**

What does Uncle Jason adjust while he's up on the roof? Obviously, it's the TV *antenna,* even though the antenna isn't mentioned. When he adjusts the antenna, of course, the picture also gets adjusted; this causal relationship between the two adjustments may encourage you to think the example sentence is all right as it stands. Rewrite, however, to make your meaning explicit:

When the TV picture gets snowy, Uncle Jason goes up on the roof and adjusts **the antenna.**

The overlapping meanings of possible referents for vague pronouns probably create more of these reference errors than any other cause. A good example is the vague use of *they* to refer to some unspecified group of people when a writer is not entirely sure who *they* are. For example:

REF?   In this state **they** make you take driver's education before you can apply for a license.

Whether *they* refers to the examiners at a particular location in a particular city, to the Department of Motor Vehicles, the State Legislature that passed the law, the state itself, or ultimately to the voters in the state who elected the representatives who voted for the law is not clear. Not only is the referent not clear, it probably is not important to the sentence. To correct the problem either specify who *they* are or rewrite avoiding the problem altogether.

In this state, the Department of Motor Vehicles requires that you take driver's education before you can apply for a license.

or

Before applying for a license in this state, motorists are required to take driver's education.

Pronoun reference is most clear when the pronoun refers back to a single word within the sentence:

Clark solved the problem **that had baffled the team for weeks.**

The relative pronoun *that* introduces a clause that clearly refers back to the single word *problem*.

I chopped down the lilac trees **which were trying to pollinate with me.**

The relative pronoun *which* introduces a clause that clearly refers back to the single word *trees*.

Sometimes it isn't clear from the sentence whether the adjective clause modifies the noun it follows or the whole clause that comes before it. In other words, the reference is *ambiguous*—it could be read in two ways:

Grace's father cancelled her subscription to *Field and Stream*, **which made Grace furious.**

What made Grace furious, *Field and Stream* or the fact that her father cancelled her subscription? Sometimes punctuation will help a careful reader sort out the ambiguity, but careful writers will usually rewrite to avoid any confusion. (Punctuation of this type of sentence is discussed more fully under "Nonrestrictive Modifiers" on page 241.)

Grace was furious when her father cancelled her subscription to *Field and Stream*.

or

It made Grace furious that her father had cancelled her subscription to *Field and Stream*.

or

Grace's father cancelled her subscription to *Field and Stream* because the magazine always made her furious.

Chapter 6: Pronouns 199

To avoid any possibility of confusion arising, some textbooks and teachers have made the mistake of claiming that every pronoun must refer only to a single word and never to a whole clause. But consider this perfectly acceptable sentence:

> If an accident should occur, **which I don't think is very likely,** we'll have to call for help.

What isn't very likely? Clearly, in my opinion, it isn't very likely that an accident will occur. **Which** *I don't think is very likely* refers back to the whole idea and not to a single word. The sentence is in no way ambiguous.

It is BECAUSE pronouns can refer back to a whole clause or to a complex idea that many vague reference problems arise. If you speak English—or write it, you are very familiar with the practice. Our best authors let their pronouns refer back to clauses and abstract ideas whenever they need to. Here is an example from an essay by Jacques Barzun:

> Writing comes before reading, in logic and also in the public mind. No one cares whether you read fast or slow, well or ill, but as soon as you put pen to paper, somebody may be puzzled, angry, bored, or ecstatic; and if the occasion permits, your reader is almost sure to exclaim about the schools not doing their duty. **This** is the oldest literary tradition. . . .

What is the oldest literary tradition? Or to put the question another way, how far back does the pronoun *this* have to reach for its referent? *Tradition* is beliefs or customs handed down from generation to generation; it is not the literature handed down which Barzun is talking about here but the *custom* of blaming the schools for poor writing. *This* refers back to an abstract idea and it does so clearly.

Textbook writers usually save themselves a page or two or explanation by not mentioning passages like the one above. Instead they begin by discussing sentences like the following one by a student in which it is *not* clear what the pronoun refers to:

> Why is it that guys are raised to make choices but girls **are** not? Even with increased opportunities for females in the job market, women are raised to think that the biggest choice they'll have to make is the selection of a new last name when they marry. **This** was found in a recent study of middle-class university women conducted by a California research institute.

What was found out by the research study? What, in other words, does *this* refer to? Since only women were involved in the study, it couldn't have made a comparison between men and women. The study might have found out some things that these women think, but without involving their parents, it's unlikely to have investigated what they *were raised* to think. Does the writer then mean to say that the women *reported* that the biggest choice they expected to make was what their last names would be when they married? Or is the reader expected to know that the last name choice is a metaphorical way of suggesting that the women were concerned only with finding a husband? The writer is saying, in other words, "You *know* what I mean." The fact that countless women would challenge the "shared" understanding further complicates this student's problem.

Structurally, the passage by Barzun and the passage by the student look very similar. The difference between the two is that the referent for Barzun's *this* is within the text itself. The idea is an abstract one, but it is there. He doesn't demand that the reader already share his opinion of what the oldest literary tradition is. The student, on the other hand, suggests the reader is already familiar with the phenomenon being discussed and relies on that shared understanding for the passage to make sense.

It is a vast over-simplification to suggest that all pronouns must have single-word antecedents to refer to, but whether the antecedent is in fact a single word, a clause, or an abstract idea, the referent should be clear. The surest way to make the pronoun reference clear is to include the antecedent explicitly within the passage. When one sentence follows naturally from the preceding one and all references are unmistakable, your writing will be *coherent*. When you say to the reader, "You *know* what I mean," it is not.

EXERCISE 6-9

Revise the following sentences or passages to make all pronoun references clear and unambiguous. If all references are unmistakable, write *coherent* next to the item number.

1. Carson was turning the knob and jiggling the antenna when ~~it~~ *the knob* came off in his hand.

2. As long as Barb held her hand on the TV antenna, it was clear.

3. At this school they use the Honor System to ignore cheating on exams.

4. If Sam leaves the country, which could happen at any time, the whole plan will collapse.

5. Beth was more popular than her co-star in the senior play, although she tried not to acknowledge it.

6. Marlena makes more money than her husband, but it doesn't seem to bother him.

7. Someday you may need to know how to change a tire. It usually happens when you have a limited amount of time to get where you are going.

8. You can ask my friends what I know about changing tires. I seem to have had an epidemic of them.

9. A Jesuit priest wrote the book, which is difficult to understand.

10. Benedetto Croce wrote the book *Breviary of Esthetic*, which is very difficult to read.

11. Some people live out their lives believing in superstitions. They control practically everything that happens to them, and sometimes they can prove to be fatal.

Chapter 6: Pronouns

12. Georgina made a mistake tabulating the night's receipts, and her boss covered for her. This was very foolish.
13. Steven turned in all of his workbook exercises on time but the last one, which surprised his teacher.
14. Webster defines a *hero* as a man known for his bold exploits. This definition fits the word *daredevil* better. This is why *hero* and *daredevil* are so often confused and interchanged.
15. James finally mastered his shyness, which had a great effect on his career as an actor.

TRANSFERRING YOUR SKILLS TO WRITING

In this chapter you've had an opportunity to view an area of usage where the rules are slowly changing. There are still many hard and fast rules (i.e., don't use *me* as a subject pronoun), but there are also areas where the conventions are changing (i.e., using *he* to refer to the "typical" citizen or teacher or farmer). The preview test should have helped you identify your pronoun problems (Do you hypercorrect? Do you shift pronouns?) and the exercises should have helped you solve them. The real trick, as we've said before, is transferring the skill to your writing.

We've tried to be honest with you; in doing so we've probably told you more than you ever thought there was to consider about pronoun selection. Unfortunately, pronoun usage is nowhere near as cut and dried as subject/verb agreement. That's what makes it interesting: the focus is on what you mean.

EXERCISE 6–10 — *write*

Using an example or an anecdote, write a brief description of one of the following: a snob, a phony, a physical education major, a teaching assistant, a math major, an English major. Or you may choose another typical person or stereotype to describe. Watch out for pronoun mistakes.

REVIEW _____ six

The sentences in this review exercise are provided to help you check your progress in this chapter and to prepare you for what you'll find in the posttest. For the answers to this exercise, check with your instructor or tutor or listen to the appropriate audio tape.

Circle the correct choice in the first nine sentences and correct the ambiguity in the tenth.

                                              A B

1. The arrangement must be agreed upon by you and (I, me).

                                    A B

2. No one was kinder to the newcomer than (he, him).

    A   B

3. (Who, Whom) passed you the hot sauce?

                                A B

4. The police officer was as annoyed as (I, me).

                         A B

5. The organization was left up to (we, us) women.

                                 A B   C   D

6. Have you reviewed (they, their, there, they're) papers?

                                                  A B   C D E   A   B

7. People should treat others' ideas with respect if (one, you, they, he, she) (want or wants) to be liked.

                                                            A   B   C   D

8. Many college students today are unsure of (oneself, yourself, theirself, themselfs,
       E   F   G
themselves, himself, herself).

                                                                    A   B   C   D

9. Everyone should have to meet the minimum standards set for (his, her, his or her, his/her,
  E
their) job.

10. My grandfather gave my father this book when he was thirty years old.

chapter 7

PUNCTUATION

PREVIEW seven

The sentences in the exercise below preview the skills and principles you'll learn in this chapter. For the answers to this exercise, check with your instructor or tutor or listen to the appropriate audio tape.

Supply any *necessary* punctuation or make any necessary revisions in pencil. You may have to erase later.

1. During the commercial the cat rose and left the room.
2. I faced my attorney she faced the judge.
3. She gave him careful instructions however he still lost his way.
4. I can give you my advice but you must decide for yourself.
5. The rubber plant on the other hand survived its cruel neglect.
6. After I noticed the police car I drove more slowly. Because I couldn't afford another ticket.
7. Dallas took his foot off the accelerator when he saw the police car hiding behind the viaduct. Which only partially concealed it from view.
8. On New Year's Robert made the following resolutions to eat less to study more and to visit his mother once a year.
9. Stay where you are Hilda said threateningly.
10. The sun broke through the clouds and shone brightly but it rained soon after.

INTRODUCTION

For the beginning writer, learning to punctuate skillfully should be a means to an end rather than an end in itself. The end that punctuation can help you achieve is clear, unified writing. If your sentences are well-developed and the relationships among the ideas you mean to convey are unambiguous, the misplacing or omission of a couple of commas here and there won't make too much difference to most readers. When your ideas are not clearly developed and the relationships between sentences are also unclear, paying attention to punctuation, asking yourself whether two ideas should be coordinate (on the same level) with one another or whether one ought to be subordinate to or modify another idea, can help you organize your writing so that you emphasize what needs emphasis, giving the reader clear grammatical signals to follow as your writing unfolds.

Before the invention of the printing press, most people got what information or entertainment there was to be had from books by listening to someone read to them. Punctuation was invented to let the reader take a breath. The comma was defined as "a small crooked point to help our breath a little," and a period was called "a small round point to help our breath at full." After the invention of the printing press, typesetters felt there should be a consistent set of rules for these little marks, and by the nineteenth century the primary purpose of punctuation had become marking the grammatical units in the sentence.

Many people still punctuate by putting in commas when they make a short pause and periods when they make a long pause, while most textbooks try to teach punctuation by listing the marks of punctuation and telling the student which grammatical unit each mark should follow. The rules say things like "use commas to set off nonrestrictive modifiers" and "use the semicolon between independent clauses joined by a transitional connective (conjunctive adverb)." If you know what nonrestrictive modifiers, transitional connectives, and conjunctive adverbs are, then the rules are fine; if you don't know these terms, you probably punctuate by guess and by gosh, putting in commas when you need to help your breath a little and periods when you need to help your breath at full. Often your pauses will in fact come at grammatical junctures, but too frequently they will not. Sometimes you will pause where there should be no comma, or you may not pause where one should be.

To learn how to punctuate according to the conventions of today, most people find it necessary to learn a little bit about grammatical units—better known as clauses and phrases. This chapter will not present punctuation as a bunch of marks (periods, semicolons, commas, etc.), but instead will present the different types of sentences that are possible in English, give you some practice in recognizing and in writing them AS SENTENCE TYPES, and incidentally show you how the different types of sentences are punctuated.

Look at the Punctuation Pattern Sheet on page 207. The underlying

Chapter 7: Punctuation

PUNCTUATION PATTERN SHEET

#1 [Independent clause] .

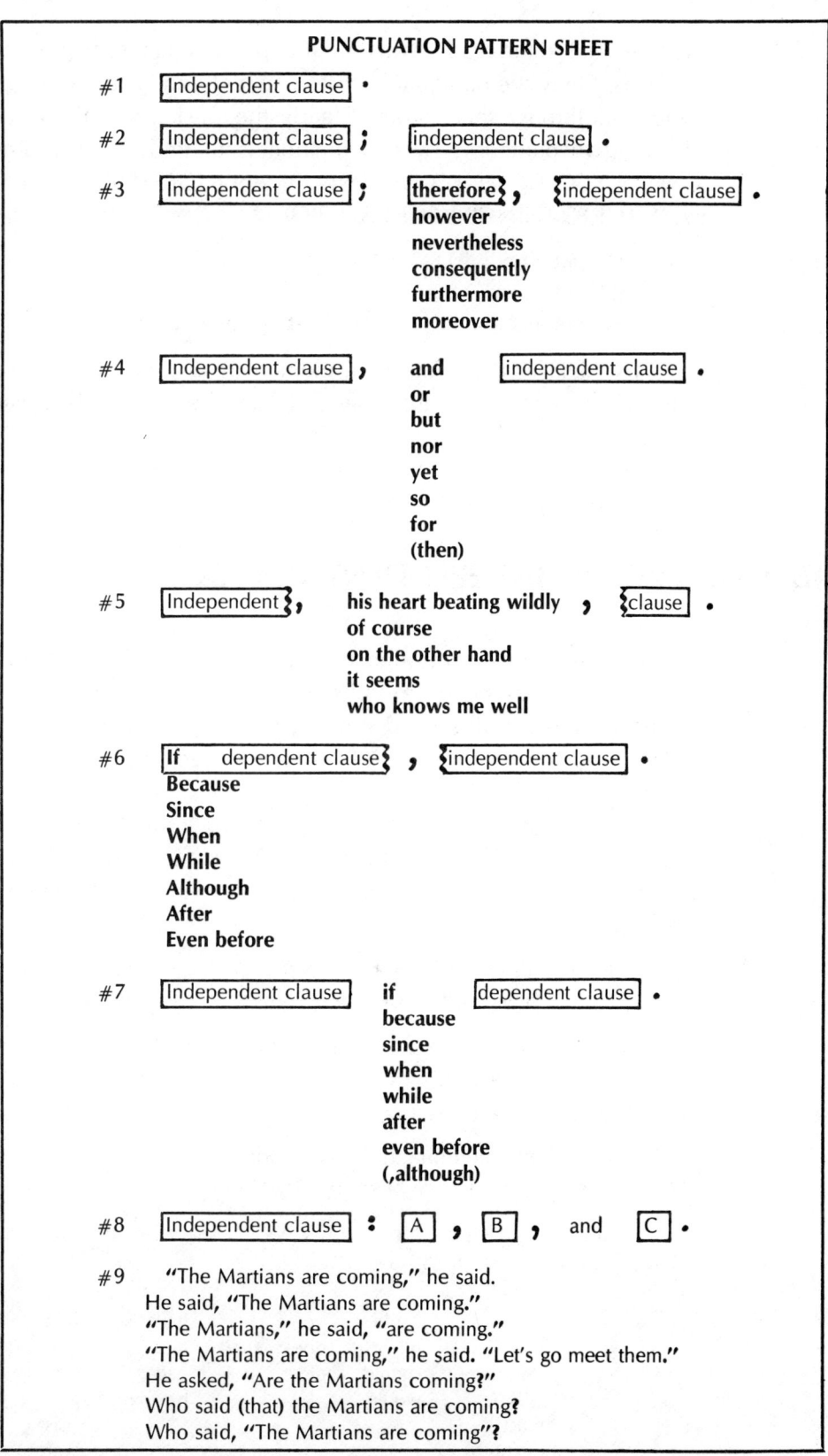

#2 [Independent clause] ; [independent clause] .

#3 [Independent clause] ; {therefore}, [independent clause] .
however
nevertheless
consequently
furthermore
moreover

#4 [Independent clause] , and [independent clause] .
or
but
nor
yet
so
for
(then)

#5 [Independent], his heart beating wildly, [clause] .
of course
on the other hand
it seems
who knows me well

#6 {If dependent clause}, [independent clause] .
Because
Since
When
While
Although
After
Even before

#7 [Independent clause] if [dependent clause] .
because
since
when
while
after
even before
(,although)

#8 [Independent clause] : [A], [B], and [C] .

#9 "The Martians are coming," he said.
He said, "The Martians are coming."
"The Martians," he said, "are coming."
"The Martians are coming," he said. "Let's go meet them."
He asked, "Are the Martians coming?"
Who said (that) the Martians are coming?
Who said, "The Martians are coming"?

assumption in the punctuation patterns is that the independent clause is the trunk or base of every formal written sentence. The purpose of punctuation is to point out to the reader when an independent clause begins, is interrupted, or ends. Study the punctuation pattern sheet and keep referring back to it as you work through this chapter. Clearly, the most crucial thing you must do in learning to punctuate by this method is to find the independent clause. WHEN YOU COME TO THE END OF AN INDEPENDENT CLAUSE, THERE ARE THREE THINGS YOU CAN DO:

(1) put a period [.]
(2) put a semicolon [;]
(3) put a comma and a coordinating conjunction [, and]

IN ADDITION, unessential elements that precede, interrupt, or follow an independent clause are separated from the independent clause by commas.

AND FINALLY, the only time punctuation does not serve to point out the independent clause is when there are items in a series.

IDENTIFYING THE INDEPENDENT CLAUSE

If you have worked through earlier chapters in this text, particularly the chapter on present tense verbs (Chapter 2), then you have already had considerable practice in identifying independent clauses. An independent clause is just a *simple sentence*. It has a subject and a verb and makes sense read by itself.

Let's begin with verbs; as you worked through the verb chapters you probably became fairly skillful at identifying them. Verbs tell what the subject *is* or *does* or *has*. In the present tense and in the simple past tense, the verb will be one word.

> June **reads** mysteries. (Present tense)
> Harold **finished** the novel. (Past tense)

The verb may also be composed of several words: one main verb and one, two, or three helping verbs (often called *auxiliaries*). We call this whole unit the *verb phrase*.

> June **should be doing** her homework.
> The page **must have been torn** by Harold.

The helping verbs are always verbs. You should know them by sight. They include the following:

can	could	do*	have*	be*
may	might	does*	has*	am*
shall	should	did*	had*	is*
will	would		having	are*
must				was*
ought to				were*
				been
				being

Chapter 7: Punctuation

The auxiliaries marked with an asterisk (*) sometimes function as main verbs and stand alone, and they sometimes function as helping verbs and accompany other verbs. The rest of the helpers will almost never be found alone. Except for short emphatic sentences like *I can!* or *You must!* they will always be part of a verb phrase. If you take the time right now to learn the auxiliaries, identifying verbs and verb phrases will be considerably easier.

Now let's take another look at subjects. The device we used in chapters 1 and 2 to help you find subjects was pronoun substitution. Every noun subject can be replaced in a sentence by a *pronoun*. The personal pronouns which can function as subjects include the following:

Singular	Plural
I	we
you	you (all)
he	they
she	
it	

Pronoun Substitute	Subject	Verb or Verb Phrase
(he)	Donald	has left.
(she)	His wife	skates.
(it)	The interrogation	was continued.
(we)	My brother and I	argued.
(they)	The flowers	are blooming.
(s/he)	Our leader	should speak.

Grammarians often divide the sentences of English into seven basic types. These types represent grammatical relationships that you, as a native speaker of the language, recognize intuitively and use daily. All of the sentence types consist of subjects and predicates. The predicate includes the verb and whatever objects, complements, or modifiers follow it. The distinction that you must make in order to learn to punctuate is the distinction between the subject and the predicate; it is not necessary that you learn the names of the different objects and complements that make up predicates if you can recognize them simply as part of the predicate of an independent clause.

Some predicates consist entirely of the verb:

Type #1: *John* **laughed.**

When the subject does something to an object, the predicate consists of the verb plus the object:

Type #2: *John* **has hit the ball.**

The indirect object in type #3 can readily be identified because it can be moved after the object by transforming it into a prepositional phrase beginning with *to* or *for* or occasionally *of*.

> Type #3: *John* **gave Mary the hammer.**
> *John* **gave the hammer to Mary.**

A fourth kind of predicate renames or describes the object:

> Type #4: *Martha* **painted her nails blue.** (*Blue* is an adjective.)
> Type #5: *His friends* **elected him monitor.** (*Monitor* is a noun.)

The object complements of sentence types #4 and #5 illustrated above rename or describe objects; subject complements rename or describe subjects.

> Type #6: *Hilda* **seems upset.** (*Upset* is an adjective.)
> Type #7: *The engineers* **are women.** (*Women* is a noun.)

EXERCISE 7-1

In the sentences below, underline the subject once and the predicate twice. On the line to the left, write the correct pronoun substitute for the subject. (Can you identify the sentence type?)

he   Shelby has finished his homework.
she   My father's aunt is ill.

1. _____ The judge reached a decision.
2. _____ The squirrel grabbed the marshmallow.
3. _____ The puppy wagged its tail.
4. _____ Your grandmother seems sleepy.
5. _____ Jack should tell Roberta the truth.
6. _____ Patience is a virtue.
7. _____ Several cottages were demolished.
8. _____ Senator Wright's arrest shocked the public.
9. _____ Ms. Bailey gave her old furniture to Cathy.
10. _____ Inflation has been this country's worst problem.

RUN-ON SENTENCES

In order to punctuate accurately, you must be able to identify an independent clause. You should know that a sentence *must contain a subject and a verb and make sense when read by itself.*

Failing to recognize when one independent clause ends and a new one begins creates one of the most serious of all student mistakes: the run-on (RO) sentence. For example:

Chapter 7: Punctuation

    RO   The students played cards during study period they failed their exams as a result.

In order to prevent this mistake all you need to do is to find the subject and the verb of both independent clauses.

Subject (Who or what does it?)	Verb (What does subject do?)
Students	played
They	failed

The most common run-ons occur in student essays when the subject of the second independent clause repeats or stands for the subject of the first independent clause. You correct run-ons of this type by inserting a period and capitalizing the first word of the second independent clause.

    The students played cards during their study period. They failed their exams as a result.

Despite the claim of some authorities that you can learn to punctuate correctly simply by listening for the pauses in your sentences, the run-on remains one of the most serious and most persistent of composition errors. Many students even signal the "pause" between the two independent clauses by putting a comma between them; this is known as a *comma splice*, a special type of run-on sentence.

Most students who write run-ons know that a sentence is "a complete thought," but they are not sure how complete a thought must really be in order to "make sense read by itself." Consider:

    RO   John opened a savings account, he wanted to save up for a new car.

They will look at these two sentences and reason this way: "I don't know who *he* refers to without the word *John*; therefore, *he wanted to save up for a new car* is not a complete thought." This fairly logical reasoning process accounts for upwards to 80% of the run-on and comma-spliced sentences produced by beginning writers. The overwhelming majority of the run-ons written by students have a subject in the second independent clause that repeats or stands for something (usually the subject) in the first independent clause. A pronoun is a word which characteristically stands for another word or idea, and the subject of most run-on sentences is a pronoun.

    RO   Run-ons are serious errors, they can ruin your grade in comp.
    RO   We're going to the football game on Saturday, that's all we ever do together.
    RO   Look back on time with kindly eyes, he doubtless did his best.

Pronoun Substitute	Subject	Predicate (Verb + Objects, Complements, Etc.)
(they)	Run-ons	*are* serious errors.
(they)	They	*can ruin* your grade in comp.

Pronoun Substitute	Subject	Predicate (Verb + Objects, Complements, Etc.)
(*we*)	We	(*a*)re going to the football game on Saturday.
(*it*)	That	(*i*)s all we ever do together.
(*you* understood)		*Look* back on time with kindly eyes.
(*he*)	He	doubtless *did* his best.

EXERCISE 7–2

Correct the run-ons in the following sentences by inserting a period and capitalizing where appropriate.

The Daring Young Typist

1. Caroline has decided to join the circus. She is bored with her typing job.
2. Her boss is appalled by her announcement, he cannot get along without her.
3. Her co-workers give her a going-away party they wish her all the best.
4. Caroline comes to the party wearing her trapeze outfit this is the proudest day of her life.
5. Everyone drinks a lot, Caroline has her share too.
6. Someone urges her to demonstrate her flying act, it seems like a good idea.
7. Caroline mounts the dining room table, she leaps for the dangling chandelier, she hangs by one arm.
8. The Assistant Manager of Sales pushes the table from beneath her the switchboard operator has another martini.
9. Caroline continues to dangle by one arm the Personnel Director hiccups expectantly, he has another martini.
10. The District Sales Manager pushes Caroline's knees to start her swinging this is not very helpful.
11. Caroline is becoming nauseous, she moans pitifully.
12. Someone from accounting calls the Fire Department Rescue Squad they arrive with wailing sirens and flashing lights.
13. They enter from the patio by breaking the sliding glass doors with their hatchets a tall firefighter in a raincoat and rubber boots drapes Caroline over his shoulder.
14. In the process of being rescued Caroline dislocates her tights and her hip this throws a wrench into her career plans.
15. Caroline's fellow typist Helen borrows the trapeze outfit it is lying idle while Caroline is in traction.
16. Helen auditions for Caroline's job she gets it and quits her job to join the circus.
17. Caroline's rescuer falls madly in love with her, he visits her in the hospital daily.
18. Caroline never gets over her first love for the trapeze she refuses to marry the handsome firefighter, she attends all of Helen's performances.
19. Neither Helen, Caroline, or the firefighter ever marry they all live happily ever after.

Sentence Complexity

If all your essays were composed of sentences consisting of one independent clause containing one subject and one verb, readers would label your writing immature. They would say sentences like the following lack variety.

The engine sputtered. The engine died.

One of the first ways speakers learn to expand upon the basic sentence types is called *coordination*. When two or more grammatically equivalent elements in a sentence are joined together, they are said to be *compound*.

The engine **sputtered** and **died**.

We could also add a third verb to this series:

The engine **sputtered, coughed,** and **died**.

When three or more equal elements within a sentence are used in a series, they should be separated from one another by commas.

SUBJECTS: **Diana, Russ,** and **Tony** went to lunch.
VERBS: The child **hopped, skipped,** and **jumped**.
ADJECTIVES: Our flag is **red, white,** and **blue**.
ADVERBS: She dealt with the problem **quickly, quietly,** and **efficiently**.
PREPOSITIONS: Clarence went **over, under, around,** and **through** the monkeybars.
DIRECT OBJECTS: Monica phoned **the plumber, Joe's 24-Hour Tow Service,** and **the babysitter**.
SUBORDINATE CLAUSES: Milly knew **what Richard wanted, what he needed,** and **what he would settle for**.

Learn the coordinating conjunctions. When one appears in a sentence, ask yourself what elements are compounded.

Coordinating Conjunctions:

and
but
or
nor
yet
so

> **NOTE:** It is only when the coordinating conjunction joins more than two items in a series or when it joins two independent clauses that it is preceded by a comma.

The owl, the pussycat, and **the turkey** had terrible headaches.
My mother cut out the jacket**, and** I put it together.

Except for items in a series, a comma plus a coordinating conjunction functions in the same manner as a period. Together they tell you that an independent clause has gone before and that another is to follow.

```
#1   [INDEPENDENT CLAUSE] .   [INDEPENDENT CLAUSE] .

#4   [INDEPENDENT CLAUSE]  , and    [INDEPENDENT CLAUSE] .
                           , but
                           , or
                           , nor
                           , for
                           , yet
                           , so
                           , (then)
```

I planted the tulips. The neighbors picked them.
I planted the tulips, but the neighbors picked them.

EXERCISE 7–3

Combine the following short sentence clusters into one good sentence by using the coordinating conjunctions listed on page 213 and punctuate them correctly.

For example: The child hopped.
                 The child skipped.

The child hopped and skipped.

1. The restaurant served steak.
   The restaurant served chicken.

2. Carol is drinking beer.
   Mona is drinking beer.
   Frannie is drinking beer.

3. Carol is watching TV.
   Mona is watching TV.
   Frannie is watching TV.

4. Combine the three sentences from #2 and the three from #3.

5. I shot the sheriff.
   I did not shoot the deputy.

6. Grace prepared her mother's income tax.
   Her mother forgot to mail the return.

7. The news article included distortions of the truth.
   The news article included exaggerations.

Chapter 7: Punctuation

The news article included outright lies.

_____

_____

8. The news article distorted the truth.
   The news article exaggerated what really happened.
   The news article lied about the people involved.

_____

_____

9. Collette shopped carefully.
   Collette's husband shopped carefully.
   Their combined salaries would not stretch to the end of the month.

_____

_____

10. He will learn to spell.
    He will probably not pass composition.

_____

_____

EXERCISE 7-4

Punctuate the following sentences according to punctuation patterns 1 and 2. Correct run-ons by inserting a period or a comma plus conjunction and capitalizing as necessary.

Ms. Hubbard and Dog

1. Old Mother Hubbard and her dog lived all alone at 1315 Mulberry Street.
2. The dog generally slept through the day and whined through the night.
3. Ms. Hubbard worked as a seamstress during the day, in the evening she came home to be with her dog.
4. Jack Horner of 1313 Mulberry Street was distressed by the dog's nightly caterwauling and decided to investigate.
5. He crept into Ms. Hubbard's back yard and up onto the porch.
6. Through the open window he could hear the dog the television and Ms. Hubbard.
7. The dog was whining scratching at the kitchen cupboard and pacing peevishly back and forth in front of a bowl of dry dog food.
8. The television and Ms. Hubbard were not visible but were clearly audible.
9. Neither Jack Horner nor any of the neighbors had ever gone beyond this strange couple's back porch.
10. Tonight Jack decided he would satisfy his curiosity or know the reason why, he felt there was no reason for this constant disturbance nor was he willing to put up with it any longer.
11. He called the police and the Society for the Prevention of Cruelty to Animals.
12. The police finally arrived with sirens wailing but the SPCA was a little slower in racing to the rescue of the helpless brute.

13. A tall and burly looking police sergeant banged on the kitchen door, the noise from the dog rose twenty decibels.
14. Jack stepped back into the shadow of the porch so he would not be seen.
15. Suddenly there was a startling silence the back door was opened a crack.
16. Ms. Hubbard peeked out over the door chain, the dog stuck its nose out past her knees.
17. Jack decided on the spot that Ms. Hubbard was a vision of loveliness and that nothing would keep them apart.
18. The sergeant explained that there had been complaints about disturbing the peace, the neighbors felt there was no excuse for such noise.
19. The yellow SPCA station wagon an ambulance and a firetruck then arrived on the scene.
20. Ms. Hubbard saw all this yet she would not open the door, she explained clearly and carefully that her dog wanted a bone but that she had only dry dog food to give it.
21. The SPCA officer pushed his way through the gathering crowd and took charge of the situation.
22. He demanded to know why she did not feed the animal properly or give it up for adoption, this was an awful moment for Jack.
23. Ms. Hubbard replied that her dog food was highly advertised that the TV dogs ate it greedily and that her dog certainly was not as elegant as a TV dog.
24. The SPCA took the dog into protective custody, the police carted off Ms. Hubbard.
25. Jack Horner the neighbors the milkman and the newspaper girl had a week's respite from the animal but Jack could not get Ms. Hubbard out of his mind.
26. Ms. Hubbard paid a $500 fine for disturbing the peace then got her dog back from the SPCA.
27. She was obliged to report to the SPCA probation officer once a month and to sign an affidavit that she had disposed of the dry dog food.
28. Jack Horner was delighted by the turn of events, he made every effort to offer his neighborly advice on the care and feeding of animals to Ms. Hubbard.
29. He brought soup bones over for the dog and a Christmas pie for the dog's lovely mistress, the dog ate the bones in a lavish display of gratitude curled up behind the stove and slept quietly through the night.
30. Ms. Hubbard gave up her job as a seamstress married Jack and was then able to take the dog for long daytime strolls in the park, they all lived happily ever after.

The Colon: Punctuation Pattern #8

Within an independent clause you've seen that elements in a series are separated from one another by commas and that any sentence element may be compounded into a series. For example:

Deidre was **cold, tired,** and **hungry.**

Do not interrupt an independent clause with a colon just because you have items in a series.

Chapter 7: Punctuation

WRONG: Their usual excuses are: **fatigue, boredom,** and **inadequate support.**

If an independent clause precedes and "sets up" a series, the independent clause is followed by a colon (:). The colon is used within a sentence to show that what follows it completes the idea of what comes before it by providing amplification, explanation, or a list.

#8 INDEPENDENT CLAUSE : A , B , and C .

Three people have influenced my life: my mother, my father, and Kermit the Frog.
Idealist ethics has centered on one thing: an ideal of individual development.

EXERCISE 7-5

Fill in the missing elements to complete the thought of the following sentences. Punctuate according to Pattern 8.

1. There are three animals I cannot stand the smell of *: skunks, polecats, and dogs.*

2. I have only one reason to give for not finishing my homework _____.

3. There are a number of special problems involved in learning to punctuate: _____.

4. My grandmother had three children _____.

5. Charles knew the reason for his consistent failure _____.

6. Isaac Asimov, Ray Bradbury, and Ursula Le Guin: _____.

7. These are the women I most admire _____.

8. I have done the following things _____.

9. The Martians want three things from Earth: _____.

10. I have invited the following people _____.

11. _____:
hard work and careful planning.

The Semicolon: Punctuation Pattern #2

Some students use the semicolon [;] when they take a deep breath; others use it when they want to add a touch of elegance to their papers. Elegance

218   Chapter 7: Punctuation

and breathing are not useful punctuation guides. Use the semicolon between independent clauses that show a comparison or opposition. A comma between two independent clauses is a comma splice (RO).

#2 [INDEPENDENT CLAUSE] ; [INDEPENDENT CLAUSE] .

Clara cleaned the kitchen; Mike cleaned the bathroom.
John bought dinner; Matilda paid for the cab.

EXERCISE 7–6

Fill in independent clauses below which make the use of the semicolon appropriate in the completed sentence.

1. Hugh loved Alice; *Alice loved Rodney.*
2. _____ ; sophomore year is tougher.
3. The child gave the babysitter a rough time; _____
4. _____ ; the dogs barked wildly.
5. My car was in for its 12,000 mile check-up; _____
6. _____ ; taking the bus is worse.
7. A coward dies a thousand deaths; _____
8. The cool, empty church filled me with peace; _____
9. _____ ; the crowd applauded wildly.
10. Fifteen inches of snow covered the city; _____

LET'S SUMMARIZE

#1 [Independent clause] .

#2 [Independent clause] ; [independent clause] .

#4 [Independent clause] , and [independent clause] .

Chapter 7: Punctuation

but
or
for
nor
yet
so
(then)

An independent clause has at least one subject and one verb and makes sense when read by itself. An independent clause may be followed by a period, a semicolon, or a comma and a conjunction. The semicolon is used only if both clauses are independent, are similar in structure and form, or show a comparison or opposition.

EXERCISE 7-7

Punctuate the following sentences according to the patterns above.

A Medical Story

1. Roger and his brother considered stage careers but finally decided in favor of medicine.
2. Roger wanted to be a surgeon his brother wanted to wear a stethoscope and head lamp.
3. The elaborate equipment appealed to his romantic nature but the years of study seemed prohibitive.
4. Roger talked for hours about saving lives and serving people.
5. Harold could see himself dressed in green surgical garb or breaking the sad news to the distraught family.
6. Roger was enthralled by the causes of disease his brother was interested in the surgical arena.
7. Roger studied until late at night for he wanted to qualify for medical school.
8. Roger's brother watched Medical Center so he could get a feel for the profession.
9. Harold studied from time to time yet he was never dedicated.
10. Roger passed his entrance exams with excellent marks his brother barely squeaked through.
11. A highly qualified female student was denied admission to medical school but was given a scholarship for nurse's training as a consolation prize.
12. The school's quota of women had already been filled but there was still room for three more males.
13. Harold and Rochelle met over a kidney patient and were married after midterms.
14. Roger felt she had married the wrong brother but he couldn't interfere.
15. He buried himself in his work to disguise his bitterness and despair.
16. Final exams approached the pressure increased.
17. Harold's self-image suffered somewhat but he relied on Rochelle to help him cram.

18. She was genuinely intrigued by the material and was an excellent tutor.
19. Rochelle wrote out elaborate notes for Harold but he could not seem to get around to reading them.
20. Exam day came Harold was not prepared.
21. He pleaded with Rochelle to sit in for him or call the instructor to say he was ill but she refused.
22. "I told you this would happen but you wouldn't listen," she said.
23. Harold knew who was responsible for his failure so he decided to ask his brother for help.
24. In desperation he called Roger he felt sure his brother would help him out Roger flatly refused to help him cheat and hung up in the middle of the conversation.
25. Harold ran away to Mexico got a job as a waiter divorced Rochelle and for the next sixty-three years pretended he was a terminally ill leukemia patient.
26. Rochelle did not marry Roger nor did she suffer from Harold's absence she signed into the exam using Harold's name and in a few years she became quite famous for her research efforts in immunology.
27. Many people were surprised to discover that Dr. Harold Jesperson was a woman but she felt it was a small price to pay.
28. Of the three only Roger lived unhappily ever after but he did it with perseverance dignity and his usual plodding care.

The Semicolon and Conjunctive Adverb: Punctuation Pattern 3

A slight variation of Pattern 2 is Pattern 3. In this pattern, the second independent clause begins with a logical word called a *conjunctive adverb* which is separated from the rest of the sentence by a comma. **However** and **therefore** are the words most frequently connected with this pattern.

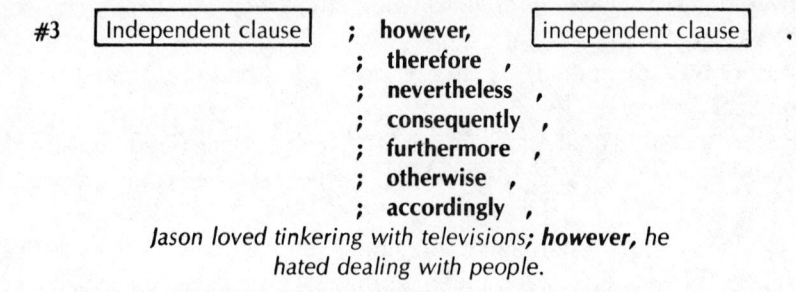

#3 | Independent clause | ; however, | independent clause | .
                              ; therefore ,
                              ; nevertheless ,
                              ; consequently ,
                              ; furthermore ,
                              ; otherwise ,
                              ; accordingly ,

*Jason loved tinkering with televisions; **however,** he hated dealing with people.*

NOTE: Independent clauses must be followed by either a period, a semicolon (as in Pattern #2), or a comma and a conjunction (as in Pattern #4). Commas around the conjunctive adverb between two independent clauses create comma splices.

  RO   *Jason loved TVs, **however,** he hated people.*

EXERCISE 7–8

Fill in independent clauses to make logical and correct sentences according to Punctuation Pattern 3.

Chapter 7: Punctuation

1. The party was a flop; consequently, *we left early*.
2. _____ ; however, I stayed home.
3. Julie started shouting; therefore, _____
   _____
4. _____ ; consequently, the police tracked him down in no time.
5. John couldn't afford a tank of gas; therefore, _____
   _____
6. _____ ; nevertheless, he failed.
7. The boss knew Randy was lying; however, _____
   _____
8. Sonia hated her boss; nevertheless, _____
   _____
9. _____ ; therefore, the game was postponed.
10. More votes were cast in the city than there were registered voters; however, _____
11. The scientist was uninterested in the problem; furthermore, _____
    _____
12. The cop knew he wasn't being told the whole story; however, _____
    _____
13. _____ ; nevertheless, hundreds of volunteers turned up to search for the missing child.
14. Power and happiness are not synonymous; however, _____
    _____
15. _____ ; however, the old man had no place else to go.

EXERCISE 7-9

Punctuate the following sentences according to the above patterns. Correct run-ons and comma splices, and capitalize as necessary.

Pigeons' Rights

1. In September of 1972 pigeons reached epic numbers in New York Chicago and Los Angeles consequently citizens deluged their Congressional representatives with letters demanding a solution to the pigeon epidemic.
2. The federal government became involved and set up a program to poison the pigeons, however, the Bird Lovers of America vigorously and successfully opposed this plan.

3. The government then decided to establish a bird sanctuary for the pigeons, an island in the Delaware River was selected as its site.
4. Unfortunately ten families lived on the island however the houses were falling apart and they were only too happy to sell their land to the federal government at vastly inflated prices.
5. Funds for the project had been frozen therefore the pigeons were not transported to the now vacant island.
6. Meanwhile apartment rents soared and more and more young people found the nine-to-five a drag.
7. It is difficult to pay high rents and to refuse to work, consequently, a band of penniless and homeless young people discovered the site selected for the bird sanctuary and claimed the people's right to live in condemned buildings.
8. Nearly one hundred fifty men women children dogs and chickens moved into the houses and worked on rehabilitating them, they were sure the president would never unfreeze the federal funds.
9. The squatters and the pigeons both went unmolested by the Feds, however the former owners of the homes were incensed that so-called hippies were living in them.
10. The owners protested to Congress consequently, the the occupants of the condemned buildings on the island received eviction notices.
11. The ex-owners continued their outcries consequently three months later shortly after midnight seventy-five federal marshals turned up with guns to evict the squatters.
12. Unfortunately they could not have chosen a more inopportune moment for one of the young women had decided to give birth and had gone into labor three hours earlier.
13. The marshals were decent people doing an unpleasant job however the squatters started calling them "pigs" so they felt obliged to live up to the stereotype.
14. The screams of the young woman in labor echoed throughout the small island nevertheless the marshals began to put their plan into action.
15. The marshals collected all the hippies' belongings and threatened to destroy them, therefore, the squatters started leaving the island slowly.
16. The hippies collected their belongings, the eviction was progressing smoothly.
17. Finally all were gone except the woman in labor and two friends attending her.
18. The women insisted frantically that the baby was about to be born, however, one of the marshals assured the others that the birth was hours off.
19. None of the marshals had ever delivered a baby and none of them wanted to furthermore they assumed the two young women were too inexperienced to do it.
20. They loaded the three women into the first coast guard launch with nine marshals and started across the river.
21. Midway across the river the baby decided to make its appearance into the world consequently one of the women rose to the occasion and delivered a beautiful little girl.
22. Mother and child did fine, however, four of the marshals went into shock and the worst case was hustled into the ambulance meant for the maternity case.

Chapter 7: Punctuation

23. Meanwhile back on the banks of the Delaware the young mother and daughter got sick of waiting for the second ambulance so they left.
24. They joined the other unhappy evicted band, without too much trouble they found a new home on an abandoned ferry boat.
25. All the federal marshals recovered however the launch drifted into a rock and sank.
26. The pigeons never heard anything about all the trouble they had caused consequently they lived happily ever after.

Interrupting or Parenthetical Expressions

Punctuation pattern 5 includes any element of a sentence that interrupts the independent clause and that is unnecessary to the meaning of the sentence.

#5   Independent   , however ,   clause   .
, of course ,
, it seems ,
, I believe ,
, for example ,
, on the other hand ,
, his heart beating wildly ,
, who knew me well ,

The commas in pattern 5 come in pairs unless, of course, the element interrupting the sentence comes at the beginning or the end of the sentence. For example:

Of course, I knew we would succeed.
I knew, **of course,** we would succeed.
I knew we would succeed, **of course.**

> **NOTE:** The purpose of punctuation is to signal the reader of the existence or position of an independent clause. Notice also that the logical words of pattern 3 are interrupting elements and may occur within as well as the beginning or end of an independent clause.

Introductory Phrases

Usage varies in the setting off of introductory phrases. Some writers set off almost every introductory phrase whatever its function or length:

Last spring, we had an unexpected blizzard.

Some authorities advise setting off only "long" introductory phrases. Some define "long" as a phrase having five or more words:

Late last spring we had a blizzard.
During the last several springs, we have had blizzards.

The most troublesome of these phrases function as adverbs (telling how, when, where, why, or under what condition something happened). Moved to the end of the sentence, they would not be set off as they would if they were truly parenthetical.

We had an unexpected blizzard **last spring.**
We have had blizzards **during the last several springs.**

EXERCISE 7-10

Punctuate the following sentences, setting off parenthetical expression with commas. Correct any run-ons or commas splices.

Spades, Spiders, and Mother

1. My mother it seems had always been afraid of spiders.
2. She of course knew they were the gardener's little helpers, she said however that she could do without their help.
3. Consequently she made a determined effort to rid her garden of them.
4. She therefore spread vast amounts of DDT along the wall behind the rose bushes, however, this did not rid her of the eight-legged little demons.
5. Furthermore they moved from the wall to her roses this I believe was the first time she had been seriously threatened by Mother Nature.
6. As a child she had I think survived a violent hurricane.
7. Hurricanes are not it seems as threatening as spiders.
8. The hurricane went away, the spiders of course stayed.
9. My mother therefore resorted to hitting the pesky little beasts with the spade, this tactic by the way was one she learned from my father.
10. My father wanted if possible for my mother to conquer the tiny invaders, on the other hand, he was really not emotionally committed to their extermination.
11. Nevertheless he contributed a little moral support for example he often handed her the spade when a spider appeared along the garden walk.
12. Perhaps he felt the continuing battle was beneficial to mother's mental health, I suppose he was right.
13. My mother seemed on the whole quite content while flailing away at the tiny creatures.
14. I would say generally speaking spades are less expensive than psychiatrists, the spiders themselves might think after all they had sacrificed themselves to a worthy cause.
15. It was my mother not the spiders who experienced the anger and fear.

Chapter 7: Punctuation

16. The spiders for their part never seemed to miss their comrades, they were all things considered quite sporting about the whole affair.

17. Several years later having moved from the house with the spider covered rose garden my mother admitted she missed the exercise but I feel certain it was the spiders and not the exercise she really remembered so fondly.

> **NOTE:** Never separate a subject from its verb with a single comma, even though the one-comma-per-pause method may seem to require it.

Introductory Verbal Phrases

The introductory verbal phrase is a very common type of structure handled by punctuation pattern 5. When an introductory phrase contains some form of a verb, it is set off from the rest of the sentence by a comma. The verbal may be an *infinitive* (*to* plus a verb), a *present participle* (verb form ending in *-ing*), and sometimes a *past participle* (regular forms end in -d or -ed; see Chapter 3 for irregular forms).

#5 | Verbal phrase | , | independent clause | .

To get to the city by train, you will need courage and a map.
Throwing a temper tantrum, Stanley refused to accept second prize.
Frightened by a noise in the alley, the police officers drew their service revolvers.

There are three common sentence structure mistakes created by the verbal constructions. The first is to create a *fragment* by punctuating the verbal phrase as if it were a sentence. For example:

Fragment   **[To get to the city by train.]** You will need courage and a map.
Fragment   **[Throwing a temper tantrum.]** Stanley refused second prize.
Fragment   **[Frightened by a noise in the alley.]** The officers drew their revolvers.

The second mistake is to separate the verbal phrase from the sentence when it is in fact an essential part of the independent clause.

Running upstairs caused the professor to wheeze loudly.
SOMETHING caused the professor to wheeze loudly.

Running upstairs is the subject of the independent clause, not an introductory phrase. Do not set it off with a comma.

To get to the city requires courage and a map.
SOMETHING requires courage and a map.

To get to the city is the subject of the independent clause, not an introductory phrase. Do not set it off with a comma.

The third error created by the use of verbals is known as the *dangling* or *misplaced modifier*. This occurs when the first word following an introductory verbal phrase is not correctly modified by the phrase. The effect is often comical:

Standing under the elm tree, lightning struck.

Paraphrased literally, this sentence says that the *lightning* was standing under the elm tree.

To get to the city on the train, maps should be distributed at the ticket counters.

This sentence suggests that *maps* want *to get to the city*.
There are two ways to correct the dangling modifier.
(1) Rearrange the sentence or insert a word in the independent clause so that the introductory phrase precedes the correct subject:

Standing under the elm tree, **we were struck by lightning.**

(2) Give the verbal construction itself a subject. When the verbal has a subject expressed, it is called an *absolute* construction and is not considered a dangling modifier.

To help inexperienced travelers to get to the city on the train, maps should be distributed at the ticket counters.

EXERCISE 7–11

Combine the following short sentences into one good sentence incorporating verbal phrases as introductory modifiers and as subject or objects of the completed sentence. Beware of dangling modifiers and punctuate correctly. Suggestions for combining are given in brackets following some of the sentences.

1. Stanley throws a temper tantrum. [-ING]
   Stanley refuses to accept second prize.
   The second prize is for the bathing suit competition.

   Throwing a temper tantrum, Stanley refuses to accept second prize in the bathing suit competition.

2. The jealous kitten spits and hisses furiously. [-ING]
   The kitten bit the Cocker Spaniel on the tail.

   _____

3. The professor wheezes loudly. [-ING]
   The professor runs upstairs.
   The professor must get to class on time. [TO]

   _____

4. The Chicago *Tribune* surprises its readers.
   The Chicago *Tribune* surprises its publisher.
   The Chicago *Tribune* prints a denunciation of the mayor. [by _____-ING]

   _____

Chapter 7: Punctuation

5. Maid Marian saves Robin Hood.   [To]
   Maid Marian tricks the Sheriff of Nottingham.
   Maid Marian dresses in Robin Hood's green suit.   [by _____-ING]
   Main Marian carries a bow and arrow.   [-ING]

   _____
   _____
   _____

6. SOMETHING upset Martha.
   Martha opens the morning mail.   [-ING]

   _____
   _____

7. SOMETHING causes the fish to leave the cove.
   The nearby chemical plant drains its waste into the water.   [_____'s _____-ING]

   _____
   _____

8. We devise a map of the Earth.
   We assume that the Earth is a sphere.   [_____-ING]
   The assumption is to simplify the problem.   [to]

   _____
   _____
   _____

9. The speaker summarizes his remarks.   [_____-ING]
   The speaker extends his arms toward the audience.
   The speaker lowers his voice.
   The speaker pleads with the audience to take action.

   _____
   _____

10. The group combats the prejudice.   [To]
    The prejudice grows in the small town.   [-ING]
    The prejudice is against settlers from Uranus.
    The groups sponsors a community fish fry.
    The group invites the townspeople.
    The group invites the settlers.

    _____
    _____
    _____

Subordinate Clauses

A *clause* is a group of words that has a subject and a verb. A sentence is an *independent clause*: it has a subject, a verb, and makes sense read by itself. It is called *independent* because it stands alone. All of the basic sentence types (see page 207) are independent clauses.

A *subordinate* or *dependent clause* has a subject and verb also, but unless it is connected in some logical way to an independent clause, it is a **fragment** of a sentence.

There are three types of subordinate clauses.

(1) The noun clause can be used in any position in a sentence where a noun can be used.

Subject (noun)	Verb	Object or Complement (noun)
WHAT YOU WANT	is	not possible.
Cynthia	knew	WHAT SHE WANTED.
WHAT HE WANTS	is	WHAT HE GETS.

(2) The adverbial clause, like most adverbs, can be placed before, after, or occasionally in the middle of an independent clause.
Although he was tired, John worked *until the job was finished.*
(3) The adjective or relative clause follows a noun or noun substitute and modifies it. You encountered this type of sentence in Chapter 2, page 48.
The barn *that burned down* **was sixty-three years old.**

Fragments from Noun Clauses

A sentence is an independent clause. It has a subject and a verb and makes sense when read by itself. A subordinate or dependent clause has a subject and a verb, but it does not make sense by itself. A noun clause is a subordinate clause: it has a subject and a verb, but the clause is used as a noun in the sentence.

The best way to determine if a group of words within a sentence is a noun clause is to try substituting a noun or pronoun for the group. A noun clause may appear in a sentence in any of the following noun positions:

SUBJECT
How you answer the question matters. (**It** matters.)
DIRECT OBJECT
The boy knew **that I would help.** (The boy knew **it.**)
    or
The boy knew **I would help.** (The boy knew **it.**)
SUBJECT COMPLEMENT
Her excuse was **that she couldn't sing.** (Her excuse was **that.**)
    or
Her excuse was **she couldn't sing.** (Her excuse was **that.**)
OBJECT OF PREPOSITION
We knew him **FOR what he was.** (We knew him **for that.**)

A *fragment* is any piece of a sentence which is punctuated as if it were a whole sentence. You create a fragment when you put a period in too soon. The longer and more complicated your sentences become, the more likely you are to create a fragment. For example, you may recognize the subject

Chapter 7: Punctuation

and verb in a noun clause and punctuate the noun clause as if it were a sentence:

Fragment **How you answer the question.** Matters greatly to the people interested in hiring you for such an important position. (**Something** matters. What is **it**?)

Because you are likely to take a breath before or after a subordinate clause, most fragments are really stranded clauses.

> **NOTE:** Many noun clauses begin with *that, whether, what, how, who, where,* and *if*. Some of these words also begin adverb and adjective clauses or function independently in a sentence and should not be relied on to identify a noun clause. The only sure way to determine whether there is a noun clause is by its use within the sentence. Although you may pause before or after the noun clause, do not set the noun clause off with a comma.

EXERCISE 7-12

In the following groups of words, put brackets around the noun clause if there is one and on the line to the left indicate whether the group of words is a sentence or a fragment by marking S or F.

_____ 1. Whatever he could get.
_____ 2. She waited for what would happen next.
_____ 3. He didn't understand the question.
_____ 4. My feeling was that he didn't understand the question.
_____ 5. What I have to say to you.
_____ 6. That the early student gets the best grade.
_____ 7. Who is responsible for this mess?
_____ 8. I asked my children who was responsible for the mess.
_____ 9. My fear was that the rent would be raised.
_____ 10. Where we sit does not matter to me.

EXERCISE 7-13

Below are some fragments and sentences. Identify the fragments by writing FRAG in the margin to the left. Combine the fragments with the sentence next to it to produce one good sentence. The word SOMEONE or SOMETHING means that a noun or a noun clause can be substituted in that position.

1. The sergeant knew SOMETHING.
   That his troops were ready for the inspection.
   The sergeant knew that his troops were ready for the inspection.

2. The gym teacher will not listen to SOMETHING.
   Anything Kim has to say.

3. Whoever wants the puppy.
   SOMEONE can have the puppy.

4. Roberta will do SOMETHING.
   Whatever you suggest.

5. Whether Valley High can win the tournament or not.
   SOMETHING depends on Friday night's game.

6. SOMETHING is SOMETHING.
   What you see.
   What you get.

7. SOMETHING is not always SOMETHING.
   What Carla needs.
   What Carla gets.

8. McLuhan is curious to know SOMETHING.
   Whether art can survive in the twentieth century.

9. SOMETHING will determine SOMETHING.
   How the President handles the present crisis.
   How well the President does in the next election.

10. Why he said SOMETHING.
    What he said.
    SOMETHING is not clear.

Subordinating Conjunctions

There are two types of conjunctions important in learning to punctuate.

Coordinating conjunctions (*and, but, or*) join together elements within a sentence which are grammatically equal to one another. For example:

Carolyn *and* Donald wrote a novel. (Compound subjects)
Joseph **could dance *but* could** not **sing**. (Compound verb phrases)
Sandra will eat **the watermelon *or* the pizza**. (Compound direct objects)
His mother was wealthy, ***but*** she was also very cranky. (Compound sentence)

Subordinating conjunctions join clauses, but when a subordinating conjunction appears, one clause is grammatically subordinate to another within the sentence. The subordinate clause is used as an adverb in the sentence. The list of subordinating conjunctions should be committed to memory.

WHEN	AS
when	as
whenever	like
before	just as
after	as if
until	as though
since	whereas
while	as long as
even before	so long as
even after	than
even when	more than
even while	less than
just before	
just after	WHERE
shortly after	where
as soon as	wherever
now that	
once	

BECAUSE

because
since
so that
in order that
provided that

IF

if
unless
in case
even if
whether (or not)

ALTHOUGH

although
though
even though

Chapter 7: Punctuation

When a subordinating conjunction introduces a clause, it is called an adverbial clause. An adverbial clause is a *subordinate* or *dependent* clause. It has a subject and a verb but does not make sense read by itself.

Fragments from Adverbial Clauses

A fragment is a piece of a sentence. The principal test for a fragment is the question *does this make sense read by itself?* The most common fragments are really subordinate clauses (noun clauses, adverbial clauses, adjective clauses) which, because of the natural pause that comes around them, get separated from the sentence to which they belong.

EXERCISE 7-14

Not all fragments are created by stranded subordinate clauses; however, an enormous number are. Label the word groups below as fragments (F) or sentences (S). If the fragment is an adverbial clause, underline the subordinating conjunction.

Frag.   1. Just <u>as</u> I started to understand.
_____ 2. When the alarm went off.
_____ 3. Because I wanted to go.
_____ 4. Our grass needs cutting.
_____ 5. Even before the results were in.
_____ 6. Although he wouldn't get paid until Friday.
_____ 7. The newspaper is in the oven.
_____ 8. After she had her say, Bess left.
_____ 9. While the audience applauded, before the Senator finished his speech.
_____ 10. Whoever answers the description.
_____ 11. So that all our questions will be answered before the next meeting takes place.
_____ 12. If she is right, I'll eat my hat.
_____ 13. It's time.
_____ 14. Even after John could recognize subordinating conjunctions, until he started checking for the independent clause.
_____ 15. Garbage is picked up only when the city employees are not on strike.
_____ 16. If we can, we will.
_____ 17. After we had turned off all the lights but before we had managed to shout "surprise" at the unwary birthday-girl.
_____ 18. Finally the class ended.
_____ 19. When the class ended.
_____ 20. The class ended when Judy fainted.

Adverbial Clauses: Punctuation Patterns #6 and #7

#6   [If dependent clause / Since]   ,   [independent clause]   .

Chapter 7: Punctuation

```
            When
            Because
            Although
    #7   [Independent clause]  { if  dependent clause } .
                                 since
                                 when
                                 because
                               , although
```

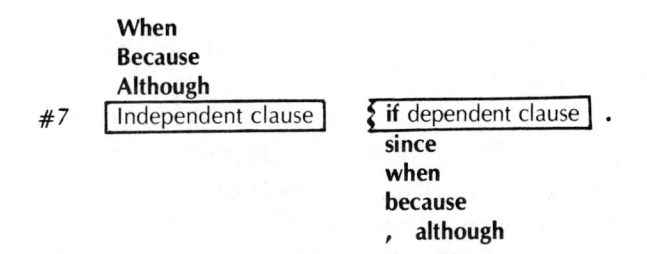

When the subordinate clause comes at the beginning of the sentence (#6), it is followed by a comma. The comma tells the reader where the independent clause begins. For example:

Although Harvey was disorganized , he was brilliant.
If I come in a taxi , I will bring an eggplant.
Because he was hungry , Raymond ate a brontosaurus burger.

However, the subordinate clause is usually *not* set off by a comma if it comes at the ends of the sentence (#8). In this position the adverbial clause is almost always considered essential to the meaning of the sentence.

I will bring an eggplant *if* **I come in a taxi.**
Raymond ate a brontosaurus burger **because** he was hungry.

There are a couple of general exceptions to pattern #7. The first and most important involves the *although* conjunctions: *although, though, even though, as though.* When a subordinate clause beginning with *although* comes at the end of the sentence, it is set off with a comma.

Rachel is brilliant, **although** she is disorganized.

The distinction that is being made by the comma here is between subordinate clauses which are essential to the meaning of the independent clause and those which are unessential. Our example sentence makes two true statements:

(1) Rachel is brilliant. (2) Rachel is disorganized.

Both clauses are true at all times. The subordinate clause does not change or *restrict* the meaning of the independent clause. Compare Rachel to James, however.

James is brilliant **when** he is disorganized.

In fact, *James is not brilliant* **unless** he is disorganized. If subjected to a good deal of housecleaning and orderliness, James loses his grasp on brilliance. James's brilliance is dependent upon clutter; Rachel is always brilliant and, incidentally, always disorganized.

The other time that this distinction arises with adverbial clauses involves the conjunction *because.* When the independent clause is a negative statement and the *because* clause gives the reason why not for the negative, it is preceded by a comma.

Harvey is not brilliant, **because** he is disorganized.

Independent clause: Harvey is *not* brilliant. Why not? Because he is disorganized.

Again the comma says that both clauses are independently true. Without the comma, the sentence would mean that Harvey is brilliant but for some other reason. Harvey is not brilliant (like James) *because* he is disorganized but because he studies hard.

> **NOTE:** In real life when you want to make it very clear that the negative is definitely negative—Let's face it; Harvey is *not* brilliant—rewrite the sentence in pattern #6. *Because he is disorganized, Harvey is not brilliant.*

EXERCISE 7–15

Using the subordinating conjunctions from page 231, combine the following independent clauses to make a single sentence in patterns 6 and 7 or a combination of the two. A subordinating conjunction has been suggested for the first few; choose any subordinating conjunction that makes sense for the last few. Omit unnecessary words as you combine and punctuate carefully.

1. The director of the agency gets a raise.
   The director of the agency will resign.   [UNLESS]
   Unless the director of the agency gets a raise, she will resign.

2. The lawyer saw the damning evidence.
   The lawyer didn't believe his client was guilty.   [UNTIL]

3. The fire trucks arrived on the scene.
   The blaze was quickly put out.   [AFTER]

4. The position was vacant.
   The former sheriff had been shot.   [SINCE/BECAUSE]
   The deputy applied for the job.

5. Thanksgiving comes.
   Jesse goes Christmas shopping.   [BEFORE/SO THAT]
   Jesse can avoid the crowds.

Chapter 7: Punctuation 235

6. School let out.
   It started to rain.   [JUST AS]
   _____
   _____

7. The day of the party came.
   Jolinda had not found a babysitter.   [EVEN WHEN]
   _____
   _____

8. Ed stops for gas.
   Ed adds a quart of oil.
   Ed's car is ten years old.
   _____
   _____

9. All the winter merchandise was on sale.
   The store was crowded.
   _____
   _____

10. Polya dropped the ball.
    Polya was combing his hair.
    The fans booed.
    _____
    _____

11. The phone rang fourteen times.
    J. R. did not answer the phone.
    J. R. was in the shower.
    _____
    _____

12. Joe's grade average dropped each term.
    Joe became more and more depressed.
    Joe dropped out of school.
    _____
    _____

13. There were more votes than there were registered voters.
    The defeated candidate demanded a recount.
    The Commissioner of Elections was sure to be offended.
    _____
    _____
    _____

14. You will get the job in six months.
    Your references are in order.
    You still want the job.
    _____
    _____

15. Carmine continued writing checks.
His checking account was overdrawn.
The bank manager called him.

Run-ons Around Adverbial Clauses

When we first introduced run-on or comma-spliced sentences, we used two independent clauses side by side as examples:

RO   John opened a savings account, he wanted to save up for a new car.

To correct the run-on, it was necessary simply to figure out where one independent clause ended and the second one began. Now consider the same two sentences with an adverbial clause comma-spliced between them.

RO   John opened a savings account, **since he now had a good job at the deli,** he wanted to save up for a new car.

When an adverbial clause comes between two independent clauses it may be more difficult for you to see the run-on, especially when the subordinate clause could be read with either sentence. For example:

John opened a savings account **since he now had a good job at the deli.**
or
Since he now had a good job at the deli, he wanted to save up for a new car.

To correct the run-on, it will be necessary to decide which independent clause the adverbial clause should go with; it cannot go with both.

RO   Run-ons are serious errors, **although they are easy enough to correct,** they can ruin your grade in composition.
Should read:
Run-ons are serious errors, although they are easy enough to correct.
or
Although they are easy enough to correct, run-ons can ruin your grade in composition.

EXERCISE 7–16

The following story consists of sentences containing adverbial clauses. The numbered segments may include more than one independent clause. Capitalize and punctuate according to meaning. This story is told entirely in patterns #6 and #7.

Chapter 7: Punctuation 237

Third Planet from the Sun

1. Marlan is a resident of the third planet of a class G star in the Milky Way Galaxy although she has never gone beyond her own world she is a patriotic citizen of the United Federation of Galaxies.
2. The Federation has been the undisputed government of the 3,517 worlds bearing intelligent life since it was established under the terms of the Covenant long ago the surprising cultural developments of Marlan's home world during the last two thousand planetary years have forced an Emergency Session of the Congress of the Federation.
3. Marlan has been elected by her people to present the problem which has developed to the Congress while this highest governing body is in session Marlan will be the sole representative of the intelligent life of her world.
4. There are many life forms in the Federation before Marlan attends the Congress she will familiarize herself with their appearances and their customs.
5. The Emergency Session will convene within three years on the second planet of Rigel because that is the only world within this corner of the universe to have established a convention hall with the necessary life support systems many Federation citizens cannot tolerate the oxygen atmosphere which is conducive to intelligent life on most planets.
6. Marlan considered herself fortunate to be an oxygen breather after she discovered the elaborate care necessary to sustain some of the other representatives to the Federation Congress with the aid of respirators and tanks of noxious gasses.
7. The reptilian-life Nantwi of Betelgeuse whenever they whiffed oxygen became nauseous if they were not administered large doses of neon gas they would soon lapse into convulsions and die.
8. Marlan was deeply distressed by this story even though she was assured all precautions would be taken for the safety of the Nantwi the Bxyrl of their host world responded in the same manner to neon gas.
9. Marlan was happy to be an oxygenating mammal in order that she would not feel deprived on the long trip to Rigel her mother arranged for a large supply of her favorite seafood to be taken along.
10. Marlan's people were not technologically oriented because they had never needed the advantages technology could provide a less adaptable life form before their present emergency the world in which they lived had seemed both large and benevolent.
11. Her race had watched the problem develop without making an adequate response for hundred of years even after the excuse of ignorance was gone their gentle nature made many hesitate to condemn the guilty.
12. Many worlds produce more than one form of intelligent life but when a second appears on a single world the weaker soon becomes extinct.
13. The third planet from the sun was unusual because two intelligent species had not only appeared but had evolved simultaneously one lived on land and one in the oceans.
14. They had both managed to survive just as if the other did not exist some Federation observers felt this situation could continue indefinitely.
15. Other socio-cultural counseling executives felt a crisis had come in the interrela-

tional stasis after their findings were recorded and disseminated throughout the Galaxies the Emergency Session of the Federation Congress was called.
16. Marlan's race had not exploited current advances in the physical sciences although their civilization was considered of a very high order they had not developed interplanetary travel.
17. Passage was arranged for Marlan since she could not get to Rigel under her own power the Federation world of the fourth planet from her own sun was honored to serve her.
18. The Martians shared a vested interest in the crisis festering in their solar system as if Marlan were their sister they prepared a special berth on their ship for her.
19. At the Congress Marlan presented their concern clearly and concisely even when she was questioned by a ten-foot bird with yellow feathers she conducted herself with grace and poise.
20. The problem after her explanation was complete was given careful scrutiny when two intelligent life forms appeared on one world the Federation would ordinarily not interfere.
21. Both Earth creatures were mammals although the dominant land form was bipedal and had an opposable thumb and the aquatic form was handless.
22. They had been essentially unaware of one another's existence until the land mammals took to the sea in frail wooden boats the oceanic mammals had always welcomed intergalactic travelers and were eager to make contact with the other life from their own world.
23. They were amazed when they discovered the great number of languages spoken by the bipeds and confounded when the bipeds seemed unable to communicate with them even telepathically.
24. The ocean creatures were sympathetic to the low level of intelligence evidenced by their unresponsive visitors even though the bipeds were not sufficiently evolved yet to be candidates for admission to the Federation the ocean dwellers watched their progress through the Federation monitoring system set up on the crowded land surfaces occupied by the bipeds and hoped for the best.
25. The problem developed when the bipeds undertook a technological course of cultural modification because the land creatures were endowed with an opposable thumb they were able to bumble into discoveries more intelligent life forms had taken centuries to perfect.
26. Their ecologically unsound technological bumbling was threatening the ocean residents' existence even before they had sent their first rocket to the planet's one moon although the Federation had observed their moronic exploitation of the planet carefully they were not inclined to interfere until the bipeds developed a successful means of leaving their home world.
27. Some action had to be taken if the bipeds were to be contained on a single planet until they had evolved a greater intelligence.
28. Marlan urged compassion to the Congress even though her own race had been hunted for candle wax and imprisoned by the bipeds they only wanted regulation not vengeance.
29. The Martians were more harsh since they had achieved interplanetary travel while Earth's bipeds were still huddled in caves they had been monitoring their activities in the name of the Federation more closely than the aquatic members of the same world.

Chapter 7: Punctuation

30. The Nantwi gently reminded the Martian representative that it had been only a scant million years since war had been abolished on Martian soil by Federation intervention the Martian tucked his small beak under his fleshy wing in humble assent.
31. It was resolved by the Congress of the Federation that the Earth creature that called itself *human* would be denied Federation citizenship for another 100,000 of its planetary years unless it stopped destroying the air and water and buried its weapons of war it would be restricted to travel back and forth to its one moon.
32. The dolphin Marlan was crushed by the severity of the resolve although she could not deny its justice she had hoped that the Federation would undertake a program of education and enlightenment for the dextrous morons who shared her world.
33. The Federation would not interfere with the process of human evolution although the Congress assured Marlan that whales or porpoises who feared for their safety or that of their families could easily be evacuated to another watery world for the safety of the universe the small biped with the opposable thumb would be restricted to its own planet for some time to come.

Punctuating the Adjective Clause

In learning to punctuate adjective clauses, you must do two things: first, learn to recognize an adjective clause when you see one; and second, learn to distinguish between the two types of adjective clauses. When you can recognize the adjective clause construction, you can easily avoid the most serious error it creates, the sentence fragment. When you begin to distinguish between *restrictive* and *nonrestrictive* adjective clauses, you will have mastered what many people consider to be the most difficult problem in punctuation.

In this text, you first encountered the adjective clause in the chapter on present tense verbs, page 26. There we presented adjective clauses that come between the subject and verb of the independent clause as a special problem in subject/verb agreement. You might want to review that section.

An adjective clause has a subject and verb, but it is subordinate to or grammatically dependent upon some noun in the sentence. Relative pronouns often introduce the adjective clause. *Who* and *whom* refer exclusively to people. *Which* refers exclusively to concrete things like tables and chairs and to abstract things like love and hate. *Whose* and *that* can be used to refer to both people and things.

Any simple adjective can be rewritten as an adjective clause:

Determiner	Adjective	Subject	Adjective Clause	Verb	Adverb Complement
The	OLD	cat		slept	all day.
The		cat	THAT WAS OLD	slept	all day.

In the same way, a prepositional phrase following a noun can be changed into an adjective clause:

Determiner	Subject	Prepositional Phrase or Adjective Clause	Verb
The	cat	on the table	meowed.
The	cat	THAT WAS ON THE TABLE	meowed.

And an adjective clause can add more detail about the noun than a single-word adjective could supply.

Determiner	Subject	Adjective Clause	Verb
The	kitten	THAT WE WANT TO ADOPT	meows a lot.

EXERCISE 7-17

Fill in the missing elements in the following sentence grid to make complete sentences containing adjective clauses.

	Determiner	Subject	Adjective Clause	Verb
1.	The	man	*who came to dinner*	left early.
2.	The		that I was wearing	ripped.
3.		book		was overdue.
4.			which fell down	
5.	Many			disappeared.
6.			Jack loved	
7.	Two		who couldn't swim	took lessons.
8.	That	student		failed out of school.
9.	Several		I have seen lately	were rated PG.
10.	The	light bulb		got broken.

Fragments from Adjective Clauses

Because of the very definite pause that comes after many adjective clauses, it is easy to create a fragment if you aren't used to identifying grammatical structures as you write. Most of the fragments created by this construction involve lopping off a noun and an adjective clause from the rest of the sentence.

Fragment   An artist **who has lived in paris.** Often suffers culture shock in the United States.

In the example above we have actually created *two* fragments: the first is the complete subject of the independent clause and the second is its predicate.

The creation of a fragment is even more predictable when the noun +

Chapter 7: Punctuation

adjective clause is a separable part of the sentence being used to modify the subject of an independent clause.

Fragment   An artist **who had lived in Paris for many years.** Thompson suffered culture shock upon returning to the United States.

The fragment does not make sense by itself and must be attached to the independent clause to which it belongs:

An artist who had lived in Paris for many years, Thompson suffered culture shock upon returning to the United States.

EXERCISE 7–18

On the line to the left, indicate whether each group of words is a fragment, a sentence, or a run-on.

Frag.   1. Someone who didn't like to take orders.
_____ 2. When the whistle blows.
_____ 3. Someone who can't take orders should get another job.
_____ 4. The man who came to dinner left early, he didn't like the food.
_____ 5. The man who came to dinner left early because he didn't like the food.
_____ 6. We gave a doggy-bag to the man who came to dinner.
_____ 7. How the team's record measures up in the Cental Division.
_____ 8. An engineer I know from Arkansas.
_____ 9. I know an engineer from Arkansas.
_____ 10. An engineer that I know from Arkansas collects meteorites.
_____ 11. An electrician I know from Chicago.
_____ 12. I know an electrician who comes from Chicago.
_____ 13. Anything the principal says.
_____ 14. Whatever the students from Detroit who are tired of analyzing sentences want to write about.
_____ 15. The fact that Amy destroyed the paper.
_____ 16. Who owes Faye nothing.
_____ 17. A sentence that didn't make sense appeared on the quiz.
_____ 18. Who got the hang of it quite rapidly.
_____ 19. After she had had her say, the woman who had been standing at the back of the room left the meeting.
_____ 20. The Baileys, who are people you can usually depend on, refused to campaign for the Senator, they had had it.

Restrictive vs Nonrestrictive Adjective Clauses

We assume that you have heard before that a *restrictive* clause restricts or limits the meaning of the noun it modifies and is, therefore, essential to the sentence; and we assume that you have also heard before that a *nonrestrictive clause* merely adds additional, non-essential information about the subject and is, therefore, set off from the rest of the sentence by commas. If you are like most students, we can also assume that you really aren't sure what any of that means.

Let's look at the problem from a slightly different direction and see if we can make some sense out of it.

When we discussed adverbial clauses on page 233, we suggested that subordinate clauses beginning with *although* were always unessential to the meaning of the independent clause; *although* acts as if it wants to be a coordinating conjunction like *but,* joining two independently true statements.

    Rachel is brilliant, **although she is disorganized.**
    (1) Rachel is brilliant.
    (2) Rachel is disorganized.

The comma setting off the *although* clause from the rest of the sentence is the sign that the first independent clause can stand alone.

Like the adverbial clause, the nonrestrictive adjective clause can comment on something in the independent clause without affecting the truth or meaning of the independent clause.

    Rachel, **who is a brilliant person,** is terribly disorganized.
    Rachel, **who is terribly disorganized,** is brilliant.

The nonrestrictive/nonessential adjective clause and the independent clause can be broken into two equally true statements:

    (1) Rachel is brilliant.   (2) Rachel is disorganized.

Now let's compare a sentence with a *restrictive* or essential adjective clause:

No chickens **that lay eggs** will be made into soup.
    (1) **Chickens lay eggs.** [It's true that *some* chickens lay eggs, but it would be false to say that *all* chickens lay eggs.]
    (2) **No chickens will be made into soup.** [Clearly false: chickens will continue to be made into soup. The only chickens who will be safe from the soup pot are those **that lay eggs.** The adjective clause restricts, limits, or *defines* the meaning of the independent clause.]

Try another, somewhat less obvious example:

Students **who are making As in the course** are exempt from the final exam.

(1) *Students are making As in the course.* [Some are; some aren't. More information is needed to determine whether the statement is true.]

(2) *Students are exempt from the final exam.* [Again, some are, but some are not.] Until the two clauses are combined we cannot judge the truth for falsity of either.

Chapter 7: Punctuation

What students are exempt from the final exam? **Students WHO ARE MAKING As IN THE COURSE.** The adjective clause *defines* those students who are exempt from the final exam; in other words, the exemption is *restricted* to **students WHO ARE MAKING As IN THE COURSE.**

Characteristics of restrictive adjective clauses

Most adjective clauses, about 80%, are restrictive, so if you remain absolutely befuddled about the difference between restrictive and nonrestrictive clauses, guess that the one you are puzzling over is restrictive and you will be right more often than wrong.

A reliable sign that an adjective clause is restrictive is the relative pronoun *that*. If the clause begins with *that* or if you can either insert or delete *that* from the clause, it is restrictive.

> Restrictive: They chose the **car that had the loudest horn.**
> Restrictive: The **car** (that) **I bought last week** has a yellow racing stripe.

It used to be said that *that* clauses were restrictive and *which* clauses were nonrestrictive, though we now know the second part of this statement is not true. However, if you can substitute *that* for either *which* or *who/whom* in an adjective clause, the clause is restrictive.

> Restrictive: The man {that / who} fixed my sink left his wrench.
>
> Restrictive: I returned all of the books {that / which} I had borrowed.

Following a proper name, an adjective clause will generally be nonrestrictive unless the clause indicates that of the many individuals going by that name, the one specified by the adjective clause is to be considered.

> Nonrestrictive: Bill, **who had sprained his ankle,** asked to be excused from P. E.
> Restrictive: The Bill **who sprained his ankle** asked to be excused; the other Bill **who is in our class** kept playing until the final bell.

EXERCISE 7-19

Combine the following short sentences into one longer sentence containing an adjective clause. Determine whether the adjective clause is restrictive or nonrestrictive and punctuate accordingly.

1. The teacher sent John to the Clinic.
    John had sprained his ankle.
    The teacher sent John, who had sprained his ankle, to the clinic.

2. Questions will be handled today.

Questions require an immediate answer.

___

3. Guests stay past midnight.
   Guests are treated rudely.

___

4. Buicks should be scrapped by drivers.
   Buicks make a lot of noise.
   Drivers don't want to get arrested.

___

5. The house was replaced by an urban renewal project.
   Jack built the house.

___

6. The bottles smell peculiar.
   Julie keeps the bottles in her lab.

___

7. It is surely no accident.
   Standardization of the spelling system began.
   Printing had established itself in England.   [Only after]

___

8. The Great Vowel Shift complicated matters.
   The Great Vowel Shift occurred around 1500.

___

9. Checks are safer than cash.
   Checks are personal bills of any denomination.
   Cash passes unquestioned from hand to hand.

___

10. The reader has the best chance to understand adjective clauses.
    The reader has written sentences.
    The sentences contain adjective clauses.

___

Nonrestrictive Modifiers

#5   Independent , however , clause .
          , it seems ,
        , who knows me well ,
       , a tall man with a beard ,
     , a habit (that) she is trying to break ,
         , her heart beating wildly ,
           , as everyone knows ,

Punctuation pattern #5 includes any element of a sentence which interrupts the independent clause and which is unessential to the truth of the independent clause. If you recognize the restrictive adjective clause and understand that it is excluded from punctuation pattern 5, you're ready for the fine tuning of your "comma sense."

Notice that one of the principal characteristics of the non-restrictive elements that appear in your sentences is their movability.

> **However,** the mayor fired the city manager.
> The mayor, **however,** fired the city manager.
> The mayor fired the city manager, **however.**

The *appositive* is a nonrestrictive modifier that occurs frequently in writing, though it is seldom used in ordinary conversation. The appositive is a noun plus its modifiers that usually follows another noun and renames it. It is very similar to the adjective clause in function, but it does not have a verb. Because the appositive is by nature nonrestrictive, it may precede the independent clause.

> **A tall man with a beard,** Jesse resembled Abraham Lincoln.
> Jesse, **a tall man with a beard,** resembled Abraham Lincoln.

The appositive, like any noun, may have an adjective clause attached to it.

> Overpunctuating, **a habit she is trying to break,** is Elly's major mechanical error.

When nonrestrictive modifiers occur at the end of a sentence, they are particularly susceptible to being lopped off as fragments.

> Fragment   Elly's major mechanical error is overpunctuating. **[A habit she is trying to break.]**

Words like *especially* and *plus* also introduce nonessential or additional information and can become fragmented from their proper sentences, especially when the addition occurs as an afterthought.

> Fragment   Regi felt he deserved all of the privileges of his middle-class childhood. **[Plus an assured future in his father's law firm.]**

Here the fragment can be corrected by changing the period to a comma; however, compare this sentence to the next one.

> Fragment   Regi felt he deserved all of the privileges of his middle-class childhood. **[Plus the fact that his grandparents were immigrants.]**

In this example, simply inserting a comma, while it will technically eliminate the fragment, produces a very unclear sentence. The relationship between his grandparents' being immigrants and Regi's deserving a privileged childhood is not at all obvious.

Unless the nonrestrictive modifier immediately follows the noun that it describes or explains, your sentence can be misinterpreted. Frequently this occurs when the relative pronoun *which* refers back to an abstract idea instead of to a concrete noun; the non-restrictive adjective clause may be misread as modifying the noun closest to it in the sentence rather than its true antecedent if the relationship is not made clear.

Subject	Verb	Object	Adjective Clause
Amy	destroyed	the paper	WHICH ANGERED ME GREATLY.

What angered me, the paper or the fact that Amy destroyed the paper? Without some other clue, you cannot tell.

Several approaches have been taken to try to clear up the confusion this type of sentence can create: The first is to deny the possibility that the clause can refer back to the whole idea that precedes it. From this point of view, the sentence would have to be rewritten if that were the meaning intended.

THE FACT THAT AMY DESTROYED THE PAPER angered me greatly.

or

AMY'S DESTROYING THE PAPER angered me greatly.

or

WHEN AMY DESTROYED THE PAPER, I was greatly angered.

or

AMY DESTROYED THE PAPER, an act that angered me greatly.

In fact, however, you can convey the same meaning by putting a comma in front of *which*, making the adjective clause nonrestrictive; then, like the adverbial clause, it can modify the whole sentence rather than a specific noun in the sentence.

Amy destroyed the paper, WHICH ANGERED ME GREATLY.

A second approach has been to insist that THAT is used for restrictive clauses and WHICH for nonrestrictive clauses. Notice that the sentence *Amy destroyed the paper THAT ANGERED ME GREATLY* is not ambiguous. Thus it is clear that it was the *paper* that angered me and not Amy's destruction of it.

Always be on guard against possible ambiguity as you use nonrestrictive modifiers. The movability of the nonrestrictive modifiers can create unexpected problems. Compare the modifiers in the following sentences.

His heart beating wildly, *the mayor fired the city manager.* Whose heart was beating wildly? The mayor's.

The mayor, **his heart beating wildly,** *fired the city manager.* Whose heart was beating wildly? The mayor's.

The mayor fired the city manager, **his heart beating wildly.** Whose heart was beating wildly? Without some other clue, we must assume it was the city manager's.

Chapter 7: Punctuation

The mayor fired the rifle, **his heart beating wildly.** Whose heart was beating wildly? Obviously, the mayor's since rifles are not known to have hearts.

> **NOTE:** Dashes are sometimes used in place of the commas in pattern 5 when the break in the independent clause is felt to be particularly strong or abrupt. This is especially true when a nonrestrictive modifier itself contains a nonrestrictive modifier or when a repetition for the purpose of emphasis is included.
>
> *He was a man—a New England man—of considerable stature in his community.*
>
> Some students become enamored of the all-purpose dash and use it to the exclusion of all other punctuation—in place of colons, between independent clauses, following subordinate clauses—driving their teachers bananas in the process. Preserve it for abrupt changes in tone lest it lose its punch by overuse.

EXERCISE 7–20

Combine the following clusters of short sentences into one complete sentence. Punctuate carefully.

1. Our belief gives way to a contrary belief.
   The shoemaker is honest.
   The shoemaker is a thief.

   Our belief that the shoemaker is honest gives way to a contrary belief that the shoemaker is a thief.

2. John Denver and the Muppets made an album.
   The album is *A Christmas Together*.
   The album combines music and humor.

3. Christopher Reeve made a movie.
   The movie is *Superman: The Movie*.
   The movie made him an overnight success.

4. It is important to distinguish between disbelief and nonbelief.
   Disbelief is believing a sentence is false.
   Nonbelief is not believing a sentence is true.

248 Chapter 7: Punctuation

_____

5. Euphemism is the substitution of pleasant term for an offensive one.
   Euphemism comes from a Greek word.
   The Greek word means "to use words of good omen."

_____

_____

6. Jargon contributes to euphemism.
   Jargon is the sublanguage peculiar to any trade.
   The terms of the trade become generally used.   [When]

_____

_____

7. Everyone should learn to recognize poison ivy.
   Poison ivy is a wild-growing, three-leaf plant.
   Poison ivy causes an itchy skin rash at the slightest touch.

_____

_____

8. Somnambulism is fairly common in children.
   Somnabulism is rarer in adults.
   Somnambulism is more significant in adults.

_____

_____

9. Somnambulism refers to sleepwalking.
   Somnambulism stems from some conflict in the mind.
   The conflict is unresolved.
   The conflict continues to stimulate a person even during sleep.

_____

_____

10. I have established a scenario.   [-ING]
    I have discovered the style and key steps.
    I then sit down at my desk.
    I work out the pattern of the dances.   [and]

_____

_____

11. People seek goals.

Chapter 7: Punctuation 249

The goals conform to the lower values.   [When]
There is usually conflict.
The objects valued are necessarily in short supply. [because]
The objects valued are money, status, power.

_____
_____
_____

12. The Incas possessed a memory-aiding device.
    The device involved knotted ropes.   [-ING]
    The device enabled them to keep statistical records.

_____
_____
_____

13. The students know SOMETHING.
    The purpose of all discussion is to solve problems.
    The purpose is not to find fault.
    The purpose is not to punish.

_____
_____
_____

14. Eugenia was instructed in "Greek philosophy and Latin eloquence."
    Eugenia was the daughter of Philip.
    Philip was the pagan ruler of Alexandria under Emperor Commodus.

_____
_____

15. In scene one a man is driving his sleigh somewhere at night.
    Scene one coincides with stanza one.
    The man is a New England man.

_____
_____
_____

16. Yes, Austria was far from the world.
    Austria was asleep.
    Our village was in the middle of that sleep.
    Our village was in the middle of Austria.   [-ING]

_____
_____

17. This is the title of a long poem.
    The poem was very popular in classical days.

The poem was by the third-century poet Apollonius of Rhodes.

_____
_____

18. There is no uneasy feeling.
    The feeling is owing to the difficulty of communication.
    The feeling is that the programer has diverged from the central interests of the study.

_____
_____

19. Failure is denied.   [-ED]
    Encysted failure can turn malignant.
    Failure spreads.   [-ING]
    Failure corrupts.   [-ING]
    Failure destroys.   [-ING]

_____
_____

20. Now writing is not an art.
    One can succeed by the production of interesting ruins.   [in which]
    The total or partial paralysis of the writer's will is a fearsome and mysterious blight.   [and since]
    Most writers come to recognize the need of a discipline.
    The discipline is a set of ritual practices.
    The practices will put the momentum of habit behind their refractory ego.   [that]
    The practices will push them over the obstacle.   [and]

_____
_____

21. At length you have shown the truth of your case.   [When]
    You have shown the falsity of your opponent's case.
    It is in the nature of things.
    You should commend yourself.   [that]
    You should censure your opponent.
    You should drive the difference home.

_____
_____

22. This book arises out of certain beliefs.
    The beliefs concern the study of argumentation.   [-ING]

Chapter 7: Punctuation

The beliefs have not as yet found recognition in the literature of the subject.
The beliefs are perhaps not wholly novel.   [though]

_____
_____

23. We have to surmise SOMETHING.   [What]
    Whately can proceed as he did.   [how]
    Whately follows and sums up the whole history of the subject.   [-ING]

_____
_____

24. The experienced writer characteristically reveals SOMETHING.
    SOMETHING is a much greater tolerance than the inexperienced writer reveals.
    The tolerance is for SOMETHING.   [what]
    Dewey called the SOMETHING "an attitude of suspended conclusion."
    The thought of the inexperienced writer seems to halt at the boundary of each sentence rather than move on.   [whose]
    The moving is by gradations of subsequent comment.
    The moving is to an elaboration of the sentence.

_____
_____
_____
_____

25. Campbell's *Philosophy of Rhetoric* was founded on the "Common Sense" school.
    Philosophy of Rhetoric was first published in 1776.
    The publication was during a period of renewed interest in oratory.
    The "Common Sense" school was that of his Scotch colleagues.
    His Scotch colleagues were Reid and Beattie.
    The faculty psychology of Reid and Beattie provided the base for the "mental and moral science."   [whose]
    The mental and moral science served orthodoxy.   [-ING]

_____
_____
_____
_____

EXERCISE 7–21

Punctuate the following sentences according to all of the patterns covered thus far.

Cinderella Retold

1. Cinderella her three stepsisters and her wicked stepmother lived together in a run-down English manor many years ago.
2. Although Cinderella wanted a handsome prince to come and take her away from all this her wishes her dreams and her prayers seemed to be in vain.
3. Cleaning the hearth washing the dishes and taking care of the chickens seemed to be her destiny.
4. Her stepsisters were mean wicked and cruel to her.
5. Her stepmother was indulgent to her own daughters intolerant of Cinderella and pitifully deluded about her own waning beauty.
6. The stepsisters were called Hazel Gretchen and Bertha.
7. Hazel was arrogant impudent and rude Gretchen was sly dishonest and evil Bertha was loud angry and insufferable.
8. On the day that the royal messenger came to deliver the invitations to the royal ball they were all sitting in the parlor eating bread and honey and singing off key.
9. Cinderella was in the parlor but she was not singing.
10. She was either scrubbing the hearth or collecting the ashes.
11. The royal messenger entered the parlor and bowed to the stepmother before he presented the royal invitations to her daughters.
12. He chanted the following names Gretchen Bertha Hazel and Cinderella.
13. The wicked stepsisters laughed and laughed but Cinderella was not amused she curtsied to the messenger and graciously accepted her scroll.
14. Gretchen squealed that there must be some mistake and attempted to snatch the soiled invitation from Cinderella's smudgy fingers therefore Cinderella whacked her stepsister with the ash-filled broom and tucked the scroll into her apron pocket.
15. At that moment the fairy godmother appeared carrying a pumpkin a cage full of mice and her magic wand but in her confusion at this unexpected change in the story she sprinkled magic fairy dust over everyone said a few magic words warned them to be back by midnight and left.
16. The messenger the wicked stepmother the three evil sisters and Cinderella found themselves transformed in a wink into gorgeously dressed mice they spent the rest of the afternoon and the entire evening until midnight scurrying about on the parlor floor hiding from the cat and bemoaning their awful fate.
17. Because the messenger didn't deliver the invitations no one came to the royal ball the prince was angry but the fairy godmother was furious.
18. At the stroke of midnight she returned to discover the terrible blunder but there was nothing she could do about what was past however with a wave of her wand she transformed Cinderella into a beautiful damsel two of the real mice into Arabian stallions the pumpkin into a carriage and the messenger into a knight who was by the way quite willing to take her away from all this.
19. Although the cat ate the stepmother before the stroke of midnight the three stepsisters lived out their natural lives being mean wicked and cruel to one another.
20. The fairy godmother offered three basic reasons for this great magical disaster Cinderella's bad temper bad timing and bad planning on her part.

QUOTATIONS

Always put the exact words of a speaker or writer you are quoting inside quotation marks. Quotations marks are pairs of marks: the first shows where the speaker begins, and the second shows where the speaker finishes talking. In dialogue (written conversations), it is customary to begin a new paragraph each time the speaker changes.

Be careful that you don't confuse a direct quotation—one showing the exact words of a speaker—with an indirect one. If you are talking about what the speaker said, or paraphrasing, you are putting another's ideas into your own words. If you introduce someone else's remarks with words like *he said that* or *she asked whether,* you are using indirect quotations not direct ones:

DIRECT (exact words): Someone said, "The Martians are coming."
INDIRECT: He said that the Martians are coming.
INDIRECT: She asked whether the Martians were coming.

Punctuation Pattern #9

a) "The Martians are coming."
b) "The Martians are coming," he said.
c) He said, "The Martians are coming."
d) "The Martians," he said, "are coming."
e) "The Martians are coming," he said. "Let's go see them."
f) John said, "The Martians are coming"; Jane said they weren't.

Periods and commas go inside the final quotation marks; semicolons and colons go outside. Notice the difference between (d) and (e). In (d) the quoted material, an independent clause, is interrupted by words identifying the speaker; therefore, the first word in the quoted material following *he said* is not capitalized. In (e) the quoted material is two separate independent clauses; therefore, the second quoted sentence must begin with a capital letter, and there is a period (.) not a comma (,) after *said*.

Questions and Quotations

g) Who said (that) the Martians are coming?
h) Who shouted, "The Martians are coming"?
i) Jane asked, "Are the Martians really coming?"
j) "Are the Martians coming?" asked Jane.

In (g) the sentence is a question and an indirect quotation. The question mark indicates that the whole sentence is a question.

In (h), the sentence asks a question, but the direct quotation is not itself a question. The question mark goes outside the quotation marks to indicate that it is the sentence and not the quotation which is a question.

In (i) the quotation itself is a question. The question mark goes inside the quotation marks to indicate that the exact words spoken by Jane formed a question. Notice in (j) that you *do not* double up punctuation following the quotation mark. Never write ?", or ?".

The Partial Quotation

When only part of a sentence is quoted directly, commas do not precede and/or follow the quotation. In dialogue, what is said acts as the direct object of *he said, she asked*, etc.; in exposition, students often use the partial quotation to complete their own sentences.

> INDIRECT: Edgar Allan Poe believed that the essence of poetry was beauty.
> DIRECT: Percy Bysshe Shelley wrote, "Poetry is the record of the best and happiest moments of the happiest and best minds."
> PARTIAL: Matthew Arnold defined poetry as "a criticism of life under conditions fixed for such criticism by the laws of poetic truth and beauty."
> PARTIAL: William Wordsworth called poetry "the imaginative expression of strong feeling."

Use single quotations for quotes within quotes.

> J. Mitchell Morse says that students are "not offended by the language of advertising, which seduces them with the subliminal appeal of such meaningless statements as 'Canada Dry tastes like love' and 'Schmidt's—the velvety soft beer, with no hard edges to get in the way of pleasure.'"

EXERCISE 7–22

Punctuate the following story according to the punctuation patterns you have learned, capitalizing as necessary.

What Brings Us to the Hospital Today?

Edward DelVecchio was a first-year medical student who was taking his first patient case histories at the hospital his instructor had told the students to begin with the question what brings us to the hospital today Ed did and he ran into trouble.

Patient One

1. What brings us to the hospital today Ed asked with as much aplomb as he could muster.
2. What the hell do you think the patient answered wearily I'm sick get lost.

Patient Two

3. Ed entered the next patient's room and asked the same question of an obviously upset woman in the bed what brings us to the hospital today.
4. I came here to pick up my mother the young woman in the bed began and a doctor and nurse dragged me in here there's nothing wrong with me.
5. Ed stared at the woman suspiciously and said I don't understand.
6. Me either. A nurse came down the hallway shouting Johnson my name is Johnson and I told her so she whipped a hypodermic grabbed my arm and gave me a shot I woke up in here.
7. I'll go see the nurse about this Ed promised.

Chapter 7: Punctuation

8. You'd better she said I think my arm was broken dragging me in here and I'm filing suit as soon as I get out.

Ed and the Nurse

9. You've got the wrong woman in there Ed said.
10. The nurse sized up the young smart-aleck med student and asked so what.
11. Ed was nonplussed he thought the nurse hadn't understood him that is not the Johnson who should be in the bed Ed explained she's not a patient she came to pick up her mother.
12. The nurse pushed by him angrily and said I haven't got time to talk to you I've got to get her ready for surgery.
13. It's the wrong woman Ed shouted.
14. What do you want me to do asked the annoyed nurse.
15. Get someone up here from admissions said Ed as he fled.

Patient Three

16. What brings us to the hospital today he tried again on his third patient.
17. I don't know why a fatuous fool like you is here bellowed the man in the bed but I'm here because I had a heart attack.
18. Medical students aren't supposed to argue with patients but Ed had had a tough morning.
19. What do you mean fatuous asked the injured Ed.
20. You question is fatuous responded the patient.
21. Ed thought about this and answered I agree the phrasing of the question is ridiculous but I don't think it's fatuous.
22. Then you don't know what the word means answered the man besides everyone knows all doctors are fatuous fools get out of my room.

Patient Four

23. Before Ed could even open his mouth the creature in the next room started complaining.
24. Why do I have to wear this ugly hospital gown I know I don't look my best.
25. Ed glanced at the patient warily and said rules are rules.
26. That's a stupid answer pouted the patient and you don't look like a stupid young man.
27. What brings us to the hospital today asked Ed forcefully.
28. I came to see you flirted the patient Ed fled as the patient started to get out of bed.

Patient Five

29. Although Ed had lost his thin veneer of poise he managed to ask his question once more.
30. Floyd and I are hiding from the FBI the patient responded.
31. I see said Ed where's Floyd.
32. He's sleeping under the bed said the man don't wake him up.
33. Ed looked under the bed and said I don't see anyone there.
34. Of course you don't said the man Floyd is a six-foot tall bunny rabbit and he's invisible.

35. You and Floyd take it easy said Ed as he left quietly.

. . . *Later at home*

36. What are you doing asked Ed's mother when she discovered him in his bedroom packing.
37. I'm going to join the circus answered Ed briefly but civilly.
38. His shocked mother asked what about medical school why did you study so hard all those months to get in.
39. I was crazy said Ed you'd have to be to get mixed up in that business everyone's crazy the doctors the nurses the patients.
40. Wait until your father gets home implored Mother DelVecchio.
41. Okay said Ed but I'll need a drink.

. . . *Still later*

42. What's this I hear son said Dr. DelVecchio when he got home.
43. Dad I'm leaving medical school said Ed everyone in medicine is crazy.
44. You know son I've suspected that for years wait until I pack and I'll go with you.
45. Father and son left home that very night and lived happily ever after.

EXERCISE 7–23

Punctuate the following sentences. Read each numbered item separately, not as a continuing narrative. Most contain quotations, but beware of indirect and partial quotations.

1. The history of composition instruction Professor Gray indicated really began in the late nineteenth century.
2. Who invented the sentence diagram asked the professor.
3. The students wanted to know whether rhetoric was ever as important as the study of grammar which so many composition students have learned to abhor.
4. Barrett Wendell the director of composition at Harvard invented the daily theme said the professor.
5. Professor Gray continued after Alexander Bain read Joseph Angus's discussion of the paragraph he announced that he had derived his own theory of the paragraph to use his exact words from original principles.
6. The professor paused for dramatic effect and then proceeded Bain also claimed credit for deriving the Forms of Discourse narration description exposition argumentation and poetry from original principles the professor concluded sneeringly slightly.
7. Although Bain did not invent the Forms of Discourse the professor added he was certainly responsible for their popularity.
8. Shuffling through some papers the professor continued let me quote Kitzhaber Alexander Bain was characteristically a dogmatic writer.
9. There were more flexible writers in composition theory during this period the professor noted however their books did not sell as well as Bain's did.
10. Fred Newton Scott was one such writer Gertrude Buck was another we'll

Chapter 7: Punctuation

continue the discussion tomorrow with the Reform Movement of the 1890s if there are no questions you're dismissed the professor concluded.

SPECIAL CASES

Throughout this chapter we have emphasized that putting a comma into a sentence whenever you pause is not the best way to punctuate. If you can identify an independent clause, which in practice means that you don't write *fragments* and *run-ons,* you can generally rely on the nine punctuation patterns as a guide.

However, there are some subtleties in punctuation that we have not mentioned. When you come across a sentence that seems troublesome to punctuate because it doesn't seem to fit one of the patterns, the first thing to ask yourself is whether what you have written makes sense. Adding a comma will almost never make a tangled sentence clear; however, commas may always be included or omitted if doing so increases clarity. If you find yourself invoking this privilege frequently, it might be best to rewrite the troublesome sentences.

1. If you have two independent clauses and one or more adverbial clauses, you may choose not to put the comma after the introductory adverbial clause.
   When the clock struck five *Mary Ellen left, but Tony stayed at his desk until six-thirty.*
2. If you have other internal punctuation in the sentence, you may choose to leave parenthetical expressions unmarked.
   Three inmates escaped from the state penitentiary, so **of course** *Mom wouldn't let us go on the camping trip.*
3. If you invert a sentence to begin with a direct object that could be mistaken for the subject, you can add a comma to clarify the meaning of the sentence.
   What you call lunch, *Lester calls a banquet.*
   That Petula is a sensitive artist, *no one will deny.*
4. If you're listing items in a series with internal punctuation, you might choose to separate them with semicolons to avoid confusion.
   Maurice invited the following people to his costume party: *Solange, who came dressed as a python; Regnal, who dressed up as the Shah of Iran; Florence, who dressed like a gypsy and, in fact, acted like one; Lolita, who was disguised as Nabokov; and ten or twelve people who never took off their masks.*
5. Parentheses ( ) can always—technically—replace the pair of commas in pattern #5. They are used to enclose explanations, qualifications, or elaborations. Inside the parentheses may be anything from a single word to a complete independent clause.
   Wolfe's bitter satire **(***which may be nothing more than accurately reporting what he sees***)** *of the pundits is not directed at the people who suffer from repression, poverty, and discrimination.*

—James Mellard

The girl (myself) is walking through Braden's, that excellent store.
—Joyce Carol Oates

Maureen, nothing if not alert for her Big Chance, for which her whole life had prepared her, accepted her mother's gift of a hundred pounds (she did not thank her, no thanks were due) and actually wrote to the school where she would be taught voice training.
—Doris Lessing

6. Brackets [ ] or *square brackets*, as they're sometimes called, are similar to parentheses but their principal use is to set off editorial comment, explanation, or elaboration in reporting what someone has said. In the next example Kenneth Burke is quoting Edgar Allen Poe's discussion of *supremeness* as a poetic goal. Burke puts his own words inside brackets.

Never losing sight of the object **supremeness,** or perfection, at all points, [and for later use in this chapter, I would also emphasize those words, "**supremeness,** or perfection"] I asked myself—"Of all melancholy topics, what according to the **universal** understanding of mankind, is the **most** melancholy?"

TRANSFERRING YOUR SKILL TO WRITING

If you follow the punctuation patterns consistently, you will always be technically correct in your punctuation. However, no real human author is or even wants to be technically correct all of the time time. Real people write comma splices and fragments occasionally for special effects, but writers who consistently work for these effects become tiresome very quickly and alienate their readers, which is never a good idea. Remember, punctuation should clarify, not obscure meaning. If you really cannot decide whether to use a comma or not, leave it out.

REVIEW ──────────── seven

The sentences in this review exercise are provided to help you check your progress in this chapter and to prepare you for what you'll find in the posttest. For the answers to this exercise, check with your instructor or tutor or listen to the appropriate audio tape.

Supply any *necessary* punctuation or make any necessary revisions in pencil. You may have to erase later.

1. During the meteor storm the electric light flickered and died in the space ship.
2. Mother writes science fiction novels father writes checks.
3. The astronauts discovered a credit card in a Martian soil sample therefore they left quietly.
4. The senior astronaut took the credit card home with him to Earth but he couldn't find an Alpha Centauri service station.
5. This considering the circumstances is not too surprising.
6. After the capsule returned to Earth the astronauts were quarantined. Because they had brought home a new flu virus.
7. Although they caught the flu they grew ten inches. Which made it difficult to get out of the space capsule.
8. Upon their return they made the following recommendations to establish a Martian colony to erect interplanetary service stations and to construct larger space ships.
9. This will be humanity's largest step said a six-foot ten-inch astronaut as she untangled herself from her ship.
10. The Martian colony was established and attracted many short colonists and the Alpha Centauri gas stations did a thriving business.

appendix A

SUBJECT/VERB RECOGNITION: A REVIEW

PREVIEW —— appendix A

The sentences in the exercise below preview the skills and principles you'll learn in this section. For the answers to this exercise, check with your instructor or tutor or listen to the appropriate audio tape.

In the sentences below first circle the verb or verb phrase (auxiliaries and main verb). Then underline the subject and write its pronoun substitute *(he, she, it, they, I, you,* or *we)* to the left.

PRONOUN
SUBSTITUTE

_____ 1. My brother-in-law wants a motorcycle.
_____ 2. The noise from the compressor practically deafened me.
_____ 3. At the sound of the fire alarm the guy in the corner rushed for the exit.
_____ 4. The ice-cream truck is blocking the intersection.
_____ 5. All of the students need to review that chapter.
_____ 6. The textbook which was on the booklist is in the bookstore.
_____ 7. The company's lawyer has not been notified of the trouble.
_____ 8. Carol and her brother have always refused to eat chicken for dinner.
_____ 9. Most buyers in this area are finally being warned by telephone.
_____ 10. There is no reason to worry.

INTRODUCTION

When you express yourself in formal, written communication, you almost always do so in sentences. You may have punctuation problems which create fragments and run-ons, but the important thing is that if what you say makes sense to other people who speak English, you do use sentences. An adequate definition of what a sentence is would lead us into a complete grammar of the language; what follows is not a grammar of the language, nor is it meant as a substitute for one. It would be more accurate to refer to it as a grammatical lexicon; it attempts to teach as efficiently as possible the names of the parts of some basic sentences of English.

Every sentence contains at least one subject and one verb or verb phrase. Traditional grammarians said that the subject was the person, place, or thing the sentence was about; another way of saying it is that the subject is the noun or noun substitute that fits into the subject position. Anyone who can already find the subject of a sentence will find those definitions quite adequate; if you are not one of those people who can already find the subject of a sentence, you will probably find that practicing finding them will help more than any set of definitions. Likewise the verb tells what the subject *is*, *does*, or *has*. Again, the definition is not very helpful unless you already have some skill in identifying verbs.

For convenience, we will divide the sentences of English into seven basic types. All of these basic sentences can be expanded by adding modifiers, substituting words, phrases, and clauses for any of the nouns in the basic sentence, and by coordinating any of the elements in the basic types. When you complete this section, you should be able to identify the basic sentence types within the most complex sentences you write.

	Subject	Verb	
Type #1	John The truck The pie Six fish	laughed. was wrecked. burned. sneezed.	

	Subject	Verb	Direct Object
Type #2	John The driver Clara This camera	has hit wrecked bought needs	the ball. the truck. a motorcycle. film.

	Subject	Linking Verb*	Subject Complement (Adjective)
Type #3	The teachers This crayon The monitor The fish	are tastes appears looks	weary. waxy. tired. cold.

Appendix A: Subject/Verb Recognition: A Review

	Subject	Linking Verb*	Subject Complement (Noun)	
Type #4	Hilda	should be	president.	
	The batter	is	a pinch hitter.	
	Gerald	will be	our monitor.	
	Love	is	a mystery.	

	Subject	Verb	Object	Object Complement (Adjective)
Type #5	Martha	painted	her nails	blue.
	The pot	called	the kettle	black.

	Subject	Verb	Object	Object Complement (Noun)
Type #6	His friends	elected	him	monitor.
	Southerners	call	a spade	a shovel.

	Subject	Verb	Indirect Object	Object
Type #7	John	gave	Mary	the ball.
	Ace Transit	sold	the driver	the truck.
	Goldilocks	sent	the bears	a pie.
	The reporter	bought	her photographers	some film.

*The linking verbs include any form of the verb *be* (am, is, are, was, were, can be, will be, etc.) plus seem, appear, look, feel, taste, smell, sound, become, grow, continue, and remain.

EXERCISE A–1

Put these basic sentences onto the following blank chart.

1. Time flies.
2. My sister hates beer.
3. Sandra gave Harold her cold.
4. Harold called Sandra a louse.
5. My sister is a bartender.
6. Harold is sick.
7. Time changes everything.
8. His brother-in-law wants a motorcycle.
9. That noise deafens me.
10. Their textbook is outdated.
11. Our textbook is *Teaching English Usage*.
12. Bertha called her grandfather a taxi.
13. Bertha called her grandfather "Pops."
14. The bomb dropped.
15. The colonel fainted.
16. The rifle jammed.
17. The Army gave Josephine a medal.
18. The medal appears rusty.
19. You are my niece.
20. Marc considered grammar impossible.

21. His country considered Raphael king.
22. The king shot the prime minister.
23. We will give the devil his due.
24. Bill became a student.
25. The grass is yellow.
26. His pain was an excuse.
27. They called him a phoney.
28. They gave him a discharge.
29. He opened a diner.
30. Money talks.

	Subject	Verb		
#1				

	Subject	Verb	Direct Object	
#2				

	Subject	Verb	Indirect Object	Direct Object
#3				

	Subject	Verb	Object	Object Complement (Adjective)
#4				

	Subject	Verb	Object	Object Complement (Noun)
#5				

	Subject	Verb	Subject Complement (Noun)
#6			

Subject	Verb	Subject Complement (Adjective)
#7		

FINDING VERBS AND VERB PHRASES

Verbs tell what the subject *is* or *does* or *has*. In the present tense and in the simple past tense, the verb will be one word.

June **reads** mysteries. (Present tense)
Harold **finished** the novel. (Past tense)

In English the verb can also be composed of up to four words: one main verb and one, two, or three helping verbs (often called *auxiliaries*). We will call this whole unit the *verb phrase*.

June **should be doing** her homework.
The page **must have been torn** by Harold.

The helping verbs are *always* verbs. You should know them by sight. They include the following:

can	could	do*	have*	be*
may	might	does*	has*	am*
shall	should	did*	had*	is*
will	would		having	are*
must				was*
ought to				were*
				been
				being

The auxiliaries marked with an asterisk (*) sometimes function as main verbs and stand alone, and they sometimes function as helping verbs and accompany other verbs. The rest of the helpers will almost never be found alone. Except for short emphatic sentences like *I can!* or *You must!* they will always be part of a verb phrase. If you take the time right now to learn the auxiliaries, identifying verbs and verb phrases in the exercise sentences which follow will be considerably easier.

EXERCISE A–2

1. Write a sentence with a two-word verb phrase.
2. Write a sentence with a three-word verb phrase.
3. Write a sentence with a four-word verb phrase.
4. Close your book and list the auxiliary verbs from memory.

PRONOUN SUBSTITUTION

Every noun subject can be replaced in a sentence by a *pronoun*. The personal pronouns which can function as subjects include the following:

Singular	Plural
I	we
you	you (all)
he	they
she	
it	

Pronoun Substitute	Subject	Verb or Verb Phrase
he	Dustin	has quit.
she	His wife	drives.
it	The meeting	was adjourned.
we	My brother and I	juggle.
they	The Martians	are coming.
s/he	Our leader	spoke.

If you have trouble with subject/verb agreement, learning automatically to substitute the correct pronoun for the subject will make applying the rule for subject/verb agreement considerably easier.

EXERCISE A–3

In the sentences below, underline the subject once and the verb twice. On the line to the left, write the correct pronoun substitute for the subject. (Can you identify the sentence type?)

    he   <u>Shelby</u> <u><u>has finished</u></u> his homework.
    she   My father's <u>aunt</u> <u><u>is</u></u> ill.

1. _____ The painter reached a decision.
2. _____ The squirrel grabbed the peanut.
3. _____ The puppy wagged its tail.
4. _____ Your baby looks sleepy.
5. _____ Jack should tell Robert the secret.
6. _____ Patience is a virtue.
7. _____ Several houses were destroyed.
8. _____ Senator Wright's arrest shocked the public.

Appendix A: Subject/Verb Recognition: A Review

9. _____ Ms. Bailey gave her new sofa to Good Will.
10. _____ Apathy has been this school's worst problem.

COORDINATION

One of the first ways speakers learn to expand upon the basic sentence types is called coordination. When two or more grammatically equivalent elements in a sentence are joined together, they are said to be *compound*. Learn the coordinating conjunctions, and when one appears in a sentence, ask yourself what elements are compounded.

Coordinating Conjunctions

and
but
or
nor
yet
so

Carolyn AND **Donald** wrote a novel. (COMPOUND NOUNS—subject)
Joseph **could dance** BUT **could** not **sing**. (COMPOUND VERBS)
Sandra will eat **the watermelon** OR **the pizza**. (COMPOUND NOUNS—direct object)
His mother was wealthy, AND **she was also very cranky**. (COMPOUND INDEPENDENT CLAUSES)

EXERCISE A-4

In the sentences below, underline the subject once and the verb twice. On the line to the left, write the correct pronoun substitute for the subject. (Can you still identify the sentence type?)

1. _____ Chickens and geese were sold at the auction.
2. _____ Father Flannagan sold his car and bought a mule.
3. _____ Linda and her twin sister tried out for the lead in the school play.
4. _____ Bobby and Sally brought home fifteen apples and artichokes.
5. _____ Pizza, potato chips, and chocolate cake destroyed my health and ruined my complexion.
6. _____ Bonnie and Clyde robbed banks and shot tellers.
7. _____ The gorillas and giraffes slept forty days and forty nights.
8. _____ The walls were painted blue and white.
9. _____ You and Mr. Royal must pay the rent, or the management will threaten and harrass you.
10. _____ Regina washed her cow, brushed its coat, and painted its hooves black, but it would not walk into the ring.

EXERCISE A-5

Combine the following short sentence clusters into one good sentence by using the coordinating conjunctions listed on page 267.

Can you analyze the new sentence according to the basic patterns?

> For example: The child hopped.
> The child skipped.

The child hopped and skipped.

1. The restaurant served steak.
   The restaurant served chicken.

2. Carol is drinking beer.
   Mona is drinking beer.
   Frannie is drinking beer.

3. Carol is watching TV.
   Mona is watching TV.
   Frannie is watching TV.

4. Combine the three sentences from #2 and the three from #3.

5. I shot the sheriff.
   I did not shoot the deputy.

PRENOMINAL MODIFIERS

Traditional grammarians called all of the modifiers which appear before nouns *adjectives*. These included all of the *determiners:*

articles: a, an, the
demonstratives: this, that, these, those
possessives: my, your, his, her, their, its, Mary's, John's
cardinals: one, two, three, four, etc.
qualifiers: another, each, either, most, some, few

Structural grammarians redefined *adjectives* as those words that modify nouns and take adjective endings (-er, -est) or are preceded by *more* or *most.*

The **old** book was read.
The **oldER** book was put on reserve.

Appendix A: Subject/Verb Recognition: A Review

The **oldEST** book was put in a glass case.
A **beautiful** cow took third place at the show.
A **more beautiful** cow took second place.
The **most beautiful** cow took first place.

Another type of prenominal construction similar to the adjective is the *noun adjunct* or compound noun. Like true adjectives, these add descriptive detail about the nouns they modify, but unlike adjectives, they do not show degrees of comparison.

The { *it* / **stone wall** } collapsed.

What collapsed? The *wall*. *Wall* is the noun subject; *stone* tells what kind of wall it was.

The { *they* / **ink bottles** } overflowed.

What overflowed? The bottles. *Bottles* is the noun subject; *ink* tells what kind of bottles they were.

Any of the six basic sentence patterns can be expanded with prenominal modifiers: determiners, adjectives, or noun adjuncts. Wherever a noun appears in the basic pattern, a prenominal modifier can be inserted to add detail about the noun.

Subject/Verb
The **old** truck was wrecked.
Subject/Verb/Direct Object
The **careless** driver wrecked the **old** truck.
Subject/Verb/Indirect Object/Direct Object
Ace Transit sold the **careless** driver his **old** truck.
Subject/Verb/Object/Object Complement
Ace Transit called the **foolish** driver a **dangerous highway** menace.
Subject/Linking Verb/Noun Complement
The **foolish** trucker was a **dangerous** driver.
Subject/Linking Verb/Adjective Complement
A **careless** driver is **dangerous.**

POSSESSIVES

When a possessive comes before the subject, it may confuse you into thinking it is the subject. We like our subjects to be people, and also the capital letter attracts attention. Again, however, you must analyze the sentence to see whether a noun is being used as a determiner or as a subject. For example:

Mary's *dog* **died** yesterday.
Who died, Mary or the dog?
The dog. Dog is the subject. Mary's is a possessive.

EXERCISE A-6

In the sentences below, underline the subject once and the verb twice. On the line to the left, write the pronoun substitute for the subject. (Can you analyze the rest of the sentence?)

1. _____ The senators' aides met for lunch.
2. _____ My father's jalopy burns a lot of oil.
3. _____ The new laboratory assistant earns eight hundred dollars a month.
4. _____ The mayor's truck rolled down the hill.
5. _____ Many members of the old gang ended up in jail.
6. _____ Quickly my sister's friend ran under the bridge.
7. _____ The faculty assistant walked into the office slowly.
8. _____ Shortages of fuel plague the nation.
9. _____ Your son's report card is hidden under the bed.
10. _____ The victim's parents were admitted to the hospital.
11. _____ Throughout the city the police searched frantically.
12. _____ Suddenly Frank's brother fell off the horse.
13. _____ One of the dishes is broken.
14. _____ Storms in this area of the country are fierce.
15. _____ The distance to the carpet's edge can be measured with a meter stick.
16. _____ The Miller's house is burning furiously.
17. _____ The queen's jewels were buried beneath the tree.
18. _____ A recital of Angela's mother's hardships is dreadful.
19. _____ On Sundays traffic on the exit to the racetrack comes to a standstill.
20. _____ All of Rachel's floors need wax.

EXERCISE A—7

Write a sentence expanded with adjectives and other prenominal modifiers to match each of the basic sentence patterns discussed. A chart is provided to make this exercise somewhat easier to do.

Determiner	Adjective	Noun Subject		VERB	

Determiner	Adjective	Noun Subject		VERB	
Both	*old*	*ducks*		*quacked*	

Determiner	Adjective	Noun Subject	VERB	Prenominal Modifier(s)[2]	Noun Direct Object

Determiner	Adjective	Noun Subject	VERB	Indirect Object	Prenominal Modifier(s)[2]	Noun Direct Object

Determiner	Adjective	Noun Subject	VERB	Prenominal Modifier[2]	Object	Object Complement (adjective)

Determiner	Adjective	Noun Subject	VERB	Prenominal Modifier[2]	Object	Prenominal modifier[2]	Object Complement (noun)

Determiner	Adjective	Noun Subject	Linking VERB	Determiner	Adjective	Noun Complement

Determiner	Adjective	Noun Subject	Linking VERB	Adjective Complement		

[2] The term prenominal modifier has been used simply to save space on the chart. The prenominal modifiers include any of the determiners plus adjectives or noun adjuncts necessary to make your sentences complete.

ADVERBS

Traditionally adverbs were said to modify verbs, adjectives, and other adverbs, though it is now recognized that they also modify phrases, clauses, and whole sentences as well. The adverb can be most readily identified in a sentence if you ask the questions *how, when, where, why,* and *under what condition*. Another clue for identifying the adverb is the *-ly* at the end of the word. Some of the most common adverbs do not end in *-ly*, however, so it will be useful to familiarize yourself with the following partial list of common adverbs.

WHEN?

now	early	yesterday
then	late	tomorrow
often	twice	a month ago
seldom	today	last Tuesday
sometimes	before	yet
already	immediately	frequently

HOW OFTEN? (when?)

never	daily	annually
always	again	occasionally
four times	regularly	usually

WHERE?

here	up	nearby
there	down	high
everywhere	out	low
nowhere	in	home

HOW?

	very	too
slowly	easily	hard really
quickly	fast	badly sure/surely
well	skillfully	(most words ending in *-ly*)

WHAT CONDITION?

yes	possibly	maybe
no	probably	perhaps
not	almost	fortunately

While most of the grammatical elements in English sentences have a fixed position, adverbs move around more freely. Adverbs usually add more information about the verb, and verb phrases are frequently interrupted by adverbs.

> JoAnna was **unanimously** elected.
> JoAnna was elected **unanimously.**
> John and I had **always** disagreed.
> John and I **always** had disagreed.
> John and I had disagreed **always.**

Appendix A: Subject/Verb Recognition: A Review　　　273

EXERCISE A-8

In the following sentences, underline the subject once and the verb twice. On the blank in each sentence, insert any adverb from the list on page 272. (Can you identify the basic sentence type? Notice that the adverb does not affect your analysis of the sentence.) For example:

Time flies _*fast*_ .

1. My sister _____ hates beer.
2. _____ Sandra gave Harold her cold.
3. Money talks _____ .
4. Mother _____ called my brother _____ .
5. Susan went _____ .
6. Sergeant Collins _____ received a medal.
7. The club has a paper drive _____ .
8. The history instructor put the maps _____ .
9. The metal appears _____ rusty.
10. The squirrel understood the cat _____ .

EXERCISE A-9

In the sentences below, underline the subject once and the verb twice. Circle the adverbs. On the line to the left write the pronoun substitute for the subject. (Can you identify the basic sentence type?)

1. _____ The bumbling plumber then dropped the heavy wrench.
2. _____ Twice the patient was subdued.
3. _____ My older sister had come home late.
4. _____ I have now done my homework.
5. _____ Rarely did she request sick leave.
6. _____ The neighbor children have seldom visited their backyard.
7. _____ Somewhere Bill will find a new Shetland Terrier.
8. _____ Bruce is going away soon.
9. _____ Too much money can cause great unhappiness.
10. _____ He will probably be arrested tomorrow.
11. _____ I saw him there occasionally.
12. _____ Too little money will often cause much misery.
13. _____ The last contestant will probably finish today.
14. _____ My ruler is never here.
15. _____ A month ago Gerald was oddly quiet, now he is almost obstreperous.

PREPOSITIONS AND THEIR OBJECTS

When only one noun precedes the verb, finding the subject is quite simple. However, sometimes a construction called a *prepositional phrase* comes between the subject and verb and adds detail about the subject. For example:

The leader **of the gang** looks sick.

Prepositional phrases can also be used as adverbs, in which case they may appear at various points within a sentence telling *how, when, where, why,* or *under what condition* something occurs. For example:

In the spring the swallows fly **to Capistrano.**

A prepositional phrase is composed of the preposition (a list of common prepositions follows) and its object (a noun or noun substitute) together with any prenominal modifiers of the object.

Above the tiny little lake
Along that lake's edge
Beside his secret lake

More than one word may also be considered "a preposition."

Out of the lake
From behind the lake
Down under the lake

SOME COMMON PREPOSITIONS

WITHOUT the lake
UP the lake
UNTIL the lake
OUTSIDE the lake
BEYOND the lake
AROUND the lake
ACROSS the lake
BETWEEN the lake and the tree
OF the lake
FOR the lake
INTO the lake
OVER the lake
UPON the lake

BEFORE the lake
ABOUT the lake
BY the lake
TO the lake
IN the lake
AGAINST the lake
AT the lake
INSIDE the lake

OUT OF the lake
DESPITE the lake
DOWN the lake
TOWARD the lake
ON the lake
THROUGH the lake
BENEATH the lake
UNDER the lake

Appendix A: Subject/Verb Recognition: A Review

PAST the lake	THROUGHOUT the lake	UNDERNEATH the lake
	AFTER the lake	WITH the lake
	BEHIND the lake	WITHIN the lake
	BELOW the lake	LIKE the lake
	DURING the lake	UNTIL the lake
	OFF the lake	
	OUT the lake	
	EXCEPT the lake	
	ABOVE the lake	
	NEAR the lake	
	BESIDE the lake	
	FROM the lake	
	ALONG the lake	

You will not confuse the subject of the sentence with the object of a preposition which modifies the subject if you remember that the object of a preposition is never the subject of a sentence.

	Subject	Prepositional Phrase	Verb
What fell?	*they* The bottles		fell.
What fell, bottles or shelf?	*they* The bottles	on the bathroom shelf	fell.
What fell?	*it* The shelf		fell.
What fell, shelf or door?	*it* The shelf	near the door	fell.
Who smiled?	*she* The girl		smiled.
Who/What smiled, girl or eyes?	*she* The girl	with green eyes	smiled.

When a noun substitute, such as a pronoun, functions as the subject of the sentence, many students are tempted to call the object of the preposition that follows it the subject. The object of the preposition seems more substantial than the pronoun. Just apply the same rule and you won't miss the subject: THE OBJECT OF A PREPOSITION IS NOT THE SUBJECT OF THE SENTENCE.

Subject	Prepositional Phrase	Verb
they Most	of the students	left.

Appendix A: Subject/Verb Recognition: A Review

Subject	Prepositional Phrase	Verb
they Many	of the plants	died.
they All	of the reporters	write.
s/he One	of the candidates	is speaking.
he None	of the boys	laughed.

When the prepositional phrase in a sentence is being used as an adverb to tell *how, when, where, why,* or *under what condition* something occurs, there is less temptation to call the object of the preposition the subject of the sentence.

	Prepositional Phrase	Subject	Verb or Verb Phrase
Who will assemble? The *protestors*. *Who* will assemble, the class or the protestors? The *protestors*.	After class	The protestors the protestors	will assemble. will assemble.
What streaked? The *mouse*. *What* streaked, the door or the mouse? The *mouse*.	Out the door	The mouse the mouse	streaked. streaked.

Even though prepositional phrases precede, *protestors* and *mouse* remain the subjects in the two sentences above because they answer the questions *who?* or *what?* before the verb.

EXERCISE A–10

In the following sentences, underline the subject once and the verb twice. On the line to the left write the pronoun substitute for the subject. Put all prepositional phrases in parentheses; above each indicate whether it is being used as an adjective or an adverb. (Can you identify the basic sentence type? Do you recognize incidental adjectives and adverbs when they occur?)

1. _____ In a minute the phone will ring.
2. _____ Down the hole the rat scurried.
3. _____ Last summer the Dambergers drove to California.
4. _____ Once a day Fred takes a pill.
5. _____ In Iran young children weave rugs from camel's hair.
6. _____ At the intersection two cars collided.
7. _____ The cowboy galloped into the intersection on his black horse.
8. _____ The flowerpot flew past the window and crashed on the sidewalk.

Appendix A: Subject/Verb Recognition: A Review

9. _____ Occasionally Bill went to the store for his sister.
10. _____ Your sock is under the bed.
11. _____ Carmen walked slowly toward the deserted parking lot.
12. _____ You are tall for your age.
13. _____ Over the river and through the woods to grandmother's house we go.
14. _____ After the fall of Rome in 412, chaos prevailed for a long time.
15. _____ Several times during the performance my brother almost laughed out loud.
16. _____ For breakfast the cat caught three mice.
17. _____ On Monday mornings the expressways into the city are jammed with cars on their way to work.
18. _____ You, above all, should know the answer to that question.
19. _____ Next Tuesday the polls in Chicago will open at 6 a.m.
20. _____ Every hour the nurse on the fourth floor visited her critically ill patient and took his pulse.

Prepositional phrases used as adjectives

Prepositional phrases used as adjectives follow the nouns they modify:

The cat becomes *the cat on the table.*

When a prepositional phrase follows a noun, it either modifies the noun or the sentence may be misread. For example:

Martha ate the last pickle **in the jar.**

As peculiar as she is, it seems unlikely that Martha climbed into the jar to eat the pickle.

However, in the next sentence, the prepositional phrase is ambiguous. It is possible that it tells **where** the bug ate.

The bug ate the last pickle **in the jar.**

A bug well-adapted to swimming in vinegar might have climbed into the jar to eat the last pickle.

EXERCISE A–11

Fill in the following grid. Use as many different prepositions as you can in the prepositional phrase slot.

Appendix A: Subject/Verb Recognition: A Review

	Determiner	Descriptive Adjective	Subject	Prepositional Phrase Used As Adjective	Verb or Verb Phrase
1.	The	aging	lady	*on the corner*	fainted.
2.	One		cat		meowed.
3.		latest			
4.				of the committee	
5.	Every				stumbled.
6.				in the backroom	groans.
7.			letters		were mailed.
8.	A		tree		died.
9.				near the firehouse	
10.	Two	beaten	players		
11.					was lost.
12.		red	lamp		
13.	Those		books		fell.
14.	The		slacks		ripped.
15.	A				crashed.
16.	The		girl		succeeded.
17.		fat			collapsed.
18.				from Texas	
19.		lonely			
20.			gym shoe		was found.
21.					phoned.
22.			postcard		arrived.
23.	An	obnoxious	tourist		swore.
24.	The	helpful			volunteered.
25.			ice cream		
26.	The			against the garage	was stolen.
27.			steak		has been eaten.
28.	A	bright	star		
29.	Most	older	students		attended.
30.	The	great			

EXERCISE A-12

Write ten connected sentences that have prepositional phrases between every subject and verb. Don't worry if it sounds ridiculous. If you have trouble getting started, you may wish to use one of the following starter sentences.

The robot **in the corner** clanked to life.
The mermaid **from the blue lagoon** capsized our boat.
One **of my relatives** robbed a bank.

THE VERBALS

Now that you have learned to disregard prepositional phrases, prenominal modifiers, and adverbs while looking for subjects and verbs, you should familiarize yourself with another distractor, the *verbal*. Verbals resemble verbs and are, in fact, formed from them, but verbals function as either nouns (which may be subjects if they come at the beginning of sentences) or adjectives (if they describe nouns within sentences).

Present participles end in *-ing*: **running, jumping, singing.**
Past participles end in *-ed* unless they're irregular: **jumped, hopped, skipped, forgotten, sung, wound.**
Infinitives are formed by *to* plus the present form of the verb: **to run, to jump, to wind, to sing.**

Because they often complicate the finding of subjects and verbs, we will look at each kind closely.

Verbals ending in -ing

The first kind of verbal we will discuss ends in *-ing*. It either names an activity or process, or it describes a noun; *-ing* words are formed from verbs and resemble them, but they function as NOUNS or ADJECTIVES in sentences. If you are trying to decide whether an *-ing* word is a verbal or part of a verb phrase, look around. If it is part of a verb phrase, one of the following helping verbs *must* be in front of it:

be, am, is, are, was, were, been
Charles **is** going.
Martha **was** waiting.
Caroline might have **been** swinging.

Remember that the sentence might have a compound verb; in this case, the helping verb may be in front of only the first present participle.

Charles *is* **going** AND **coming.**
Martha *was* **waiting** AND **watching.**
Caroline *might have been* **swinging** OR **playing** cards.

Compare the use of the present participle in the following sets of sentences:

Charles *has* **been** *diving*.	(Verb: the last helper is *been*.)
Charles likes *diving*.	(Object: he likes *it*.)
Diving relaxes Charles.	(Subject: *it* relaxes him.)
His *diving* coach is wet.	(Adjective: what kind of coach?)
I *am* cooking a chicken.	(Verb: *am* is the helper.)
Cooking takes time.	(Subject: *it* takes time.)
I hate *cooking*.	(Object: I hate *it*.)
My *cooking* teacher is hot.	(Adjective: what kind of teacher?)

Appendix A: Subject/Verb Recognition: A Review

Determiner or Adjective Used to Describe Subject	Noun, Pronoun, or Verbal Used As Subject	Verb or Verb Phrase	Noun, Pronoun, or Verbal Used As Object or Complement
	(It) *Winning*	demands	skill.
	(She) Liz	**is** *winning*	the race.
A *winning*	(it) team	makes	money.

EXERCISE A-13

In the sentences below, underline the subject once and the verb twice. Write the correct pronoun substitute for the subject on the line to the left. (Can you identify the basic sentence type?)

1. _____ Cooking requires patience.
2. _____ Driving takes time.
3. _____ A driving rain flattened the daisies.
4. _____ My typing teacher chews bubble gum.
5. _____ Kissing spreads germs.
6. _____ Spelling correctly presents many problems.
7. _____ The spelling test was cancelled.
8. _____ Inaccurate spelling ruined the essay.
9. _____ Birds hate flying and singing.
10. _____ Harold caught the laughing hyena.

Objects with -ing words

Like verbs, the *-ing* words sometimes take objects. The *-ing* word plus its object functions as a single unit within the sentence and can be replaced by the pronoun substitute *it*.

Answering phones tires Arlene.   (Subject: *it* tires Arlene.)
Arlene **is** *answering* the phones.   (Verb: **is** is the helper.)
Ringing phones annoy Arlene.   (Adjective: what kind of phones?)

Noun, Pronoun, or Verbal Used As Subject	Verb or Verb Phrase	Determiner	Noun, Pronoun or Verbal Used As Direct Object
(It) Answering phones*	tires		Arlene.

Appendix A: Subject/Verb Recognition: A Review

Noun, Pronoun, or Verbal Used As Subject	Verb or Verb Phrase	Determiner	Noun, Pronoun or Verbal Used As Direct Object
(She) Arlene	**is** answering	the	phones.
(They) Ringing phones	annoy		Arlene.

*Notice the whole -*ing* expression functions as the subject and its pronoun substitute is *it*. When *phones* is the subject, the pronoun substitute is *they*.

Phones (they) tire Arlene.

Answering phones (it) tires Arlene.

Ringing phones (they) tire Arlene.

Only meaning can determine whether the -*ing* word is a noun or whether it is an adjective describing the following noun. Keep this in mind as you work through the following exercise.

EXERCISE A-14

In the sentences below, underline the subject once and the verb twice. On the line to the left write the correct pronoun substitute for the subject. (Can you identify the basic sentence type?)

1. _____ Preparing dinner at our house takes about an hour.
2. _____ Parking the cars in front of our apartment building for a party can be a serious problem.
3. _____ Dwight is responding to letters and listening to music.
4. _____ The shooting galleries are closed.
5. _____ Cindy detests cleaning the fireplace.
6. _____ John and his brothers always liked knowing all of the answers.
7. _____ The winning candidate was named Arnetta Dooley.
8. _____ Completing the questionnaire and sitting through the interview took an hour.
9. _____ Jack dislikes repairing televisions.
10. _____ Bonnie hates planning parties.

Infinitives

In addition to the -*ing* words, there is a second group of verbals that can function as nouns or adjectives in a sentence. These are called *infinitives*. *To run*, *to dance*, and *to say* are all infinitives. They consist of the word *to* plus a verb. Although they are formed from verbs and resemble them, like -*ing* words, they usually function as nouns or adjectives in a sentence.

When you are trying to decide whether a word is functioning as a noun, an adjective, or a verb, look around. If it's an infinitive functioning as a noun or adjective, the word *to* will usually be nearby. When the infinitive is functioning as a noun, the pronoun substitute is *it*.

The Cubs **win** the game. (Verb: *to* is absent.)
He wants **to win.** (Object: he wants **it** more than anything.)
He wants **to win, place,** or **show.** (Objects: **place** and **show** are also infinitives. Compound infinitives can all rely on the same **to.**)
An urge **to tell** seized Shirley. (Adjective: what kind of urge?)
To lose hurts. (Subject: **it** hurts.)

Determiner	Noun, Pronoun, or Verbal Used As Subject	Adjective	Verb or Verb Phrase	Noun, Pronoun, or Verbal Used As Direct Object
	He		wants	to win.
The	(they) Cubs		win	the game.
An	(it) urge	to tell	seized	Shirley.
	(it) To lose		hurts.	
	He		wants	to win, place, or show.

EXERCISE A-15

In the sentences below, underline the subject once and the verb twice. Then on the line to the left write the correct pronoun substitute for the subject. (Can you identify the basic sentence type?)

1. _____ Philip wants to leave.
2. _____ To dance is to live.
3. _____ She plans to sing and dance for a living.
4. _____ He likes to complain.
5. _____ To complain causes trouble.
6. _____ To complain and cause trouble is risky in this business.
7. _____ They refuse to help.
8. _____ Tony hates to wait.
9. _____ Going to the store requires cash.
10. _____ To play or coach takes a lot of skill.

Objects of infinitives

Infinitives resemble verbs in that they sometimes take objects. The whole infinitive phrase functions as a single unit within the sentence and has as its pronoun substitute *it*.

Appendix A: Subject/Verb Recognition: A Review

To break the law means trouble. (Subject: **it** means trouble.)
The boys **break** the law. (Verb: **to** is absent.)
Kevin hates **to break the law.** (Object: Kevin hates **it**.)
An urge **to break the law** seized Kevin. (Adjective: what kind of urge?)

Lawbreakers go **to jail.** (To jail is a prepositional phrase used as an an adverb telling where lawbreakers go. This is NOT an infinitive.)

Determiner	Noun, Pronoun or Verbal Used As Subject	Adjective	Verb or Verb Phrase	Determiner	Noun, Pronoun, or Verbal Used As Direct Object
	(it) To break the law		means		trouble.
The	(they) boys		break		the law.
An	(it) urge	to break the law	seized		Kevin.
	Kevin		hates		to break the law.

EXERCISE A-16

In the sentences below, underline the subject once and the verb twice. On the line to the left, write the correct pronoun substitute for the subject. (Can you identify the basic sentence type?)

1. _____ The manager agreed to credit my account.
2. _____ To waste time annoys Patty.
3. _____ Ms. Bibson refuses to choose.
4. _____ Loretta called to cancel her appointment.
5. _____ Jack hopes to get a car next semester.
6. _____ Vivian likes to watch TV.
7. _____ To lose a game always disappoints the fans.
8. _____ We hope to find a solution.
9. _____ Ron tries to answer their questions.
10. _____ The militants decided to bomb the Embassy.

Compound Infinitives

When there is more than one infinitive in a sentence, the second *to* may be left out. This is called an *unmarked infinitive;* the word *to* is called an infinitive marker.

George wanted **to leave** home and **buy** a car. (Compound objects: George wanted two things.)
Gloria wanted **to leave** home and **join** the circus. (Compound objects: Gloria wanted two things.)

Do not mistake the compound infinitive for a compound verb.

George **left** home and **bought** a car. (Compound verbs: he did two things.)
Gloria **left** home and **joined** the circus. (Compound verbs: she did two things.)

EXERCISE A–17

In the sentences below, underline the subject once and the verb twice. On the line to the left write the correct pronoun substitute for the subject. (Can you identify the basic sentence type?)

1. _____ Leonard charged up the stairs and leapt onto the train.
2. _____ I talked to the credit manager and convinced her to correct the billing error.
3. _____ The angry parent called to obtain his child's report card and make an appointment with the principal.
4. _____ The photographers refused to pick up their equipment or move from the mayor's office.
5. _____ My grandfather used to wear a handlebar moustache and sing in a barbershop quartet.
6. _____ The Martians plan to enter a pale green candidate in the Miss Universe Pageant.
7. _____ To attend school and to get an education may be two different things.
8. _____ The mechanics expect to replace the carburetor, inspect the brakes, and rotate the tires before 5:00.
9. _____ Ronald wants to overthrow the government and become King of the United States.
10. _____ Astrologers claim to explain the past and predict the future.

Past participles (Verbals ending in -ed and -en)

Usually an *-ed* ending is the signal for a simple past tense verb.

He **disappointed** the child. (Verb: past tense)

Often the word which ends in *-ed* will be part of a verb phrase. If it is a part of a verb phrase, one of the following helping verbs must be in front of it:

have	be	was
has	am	were
had	is	been
having	are	being

Appendix A: Subject/Verb Recognition: A Review

The child *was* **disappointed.** (Verb phrase: helper is WAS)
He *had* **disappointed** the child. (Verb phrase: helper is HAD)

Irregular past participles may end in *-en, unk, a/ought, t,* or they may have the same form as the infinitive—*to put, put; to cut, cut,* etc. Check the verb index on page 130 or a good dictionary when you are not sure of the correct past participle form.

Whether they are regular or irregular, the past participles of most verbs can function as nouns or adjectives within sentences. The most common use of the past participle as a verbal is the adjective:

Although these verbals resemble verbs, they can function as adjectives and nouns within the sentence. The most common use of the *-ed* verbal is as an adjective.

The **disappointed child** cried. (Adjective: what kind of child?)

A **disappointed candidate** wept. (Adjective: what kind of candidate?)

The **forgotten movie star** made an appearance on stage.
(Adjective: what kind of movie star?)

The **bent jail bars** were evidence enough that Superman had made his escape.
(Adjective: what kind of jail bars?)

Very infrequently the past participle will be used as a noun.

The **disappointed** were very noisy. (Noun: **They** were noisy.)
The **forgotten** have returned. (Noun: **They** have returned.)
The **undefeated** were quite happy. (Noun: **They** were happy.)
The **accused** took the stand. (Noun: **S/He** took the stand.)

EXERCISE A-18

In the sentences below, underline the subject once and the verb twice. On the line to the left write the correct pronoun substitute for the subject. (Can you identify the basic sentence type?)

1. _____ The beginning disc jockey forgot his lines.
2. _____ A watched pot never boils.
3. _____ Latecomers missed the beginning of the show.
4. _____ A shocked bystander offered a helping hand.
5. _____ Susan forgets to mail letters.
6. _____ Nina has been painting garages.
7. _____ A disgusted parent left the room.
8. _____ The newspaper is printing the angry letter.
9. _____ Martha has omitted mentioning her paper.
10. _____ The displaced homemaker returned to college.

286 **Appendix A: Subject/Verb Recognition: A Review**

11. _____ My tired and disgruntled father watches TV for hours.
12. _____ The police discovered the wrecked car.
13. _____ Preparing big meals and being nice to thirty in-laws ruined Hilda's vacation.
14. _____ The experienced seldom brag.
15. _____ The outraged patient hit his dentist.
16. _____ The bored and the lazy will not respond in class.
17. _____ Kenneth loves forbidden fruit.
18. _____ My uncle is a most understanding relative.
19. _____ Marvin cannot stand for unopened mail to stay on the table.
20. _____ The dancing teacher wears purple tights.

SUBORDINATE CLAUSES

A *clause* is a group of words that has a subject and a verb. A sentence is, among other things, an *independent clause:* it has a subject and a verb and it makes sense by itself. It is independent because it stands alone. All of the basic sentence types are independent clauses. A *subordinate* or *dependent clause* has a subject and verb also, but unless it is connected in some logical way to an independent clause, it is a fragment of a sentence.

There are three types of subordinate clause:

1) The adjective or relative clause follows a noun or noun substitute and modifies it.
   The barn **that burned down** was sixty-three years old.
2) The adverbial clause, like most adverbs, can be placed before, after, or in the middle of an independent clause.
   Although he was tired, John worked **until the job was finished.**
3) The noun clause can be used in any position in a sentence where a noun can be used.

Subject	Verb	Object or Complement
WHAT YOU WANT	is	not possible.
Cynthia	knew	WHAT SHE WANTED.
WHAT HE WANTS	is	WHAT HE GETS.

A sentence that has one or more subordinate clauses attached to the independent clause is called a *complex sentence.*

The Adjective Clause

You have learned to recognize prepositional phrases that come between the subject and verb in an independent clause. An even more distracting construction coming between the subject and verb in an independent clause is the adjective or relative clause.

Appendix A: Subject/Verb Recognition: A Review

Any simple adjective can also be written as a clause without changing the basic sentence. They are often introduced by the *relative pronouns*—*who, whom, whose, that,* and *which,* and unless the clause follows the noun it modifies, the sentence can be misinterpreted.

The **tall** man coughed.
The man **who was tall** coughed.

In both of the example sentences, the subject of the independent clause is *man* and the verb is *coughed*.

The cat **on the table** meowed.
The cat **that was on the table** meowed.

In both of these example sentences, the subject of the independent clause is *cat* and the verb is *meowed*.

EXERCISE A-19

Fill in the missing elements in the following sentence grid.

	Determiner	Pronoun Substitute and Subject	Adjective Clause	Verb or Verb Phrase
1.	The	man	*who came to dinner*	left.
2.	A		that I was wearing	ripped.
3.		book		
4.			which fell down	
5.	Many			disappeared.
6.			Jack loved	
7.	Two			
8.				screamed.
9.	Several			
10.			who couldn't swim	

> **NOTE:** The purpose of punctuation is to point out for the reader where the independent clause is within a sentence.

Some adjective clauses create a problem in punctuation because they limit or restrict the meaning of the nouns they modify; these clauses are essential to the meaning of the sentence. **If the element is essential to the meaning of the sentence, it should not be set off from it by commas.** For example (a sentence with an essential clause):

No chickens **which lay eggs** will be made into soup.

If the italicized clause were taken out of the sentence with commas, the independent clause would be a false statement. For example:

No chickens will be made into soup.

The adjective clause is necessary to understand the true meaning of the independent clause. Chickens will continue to be made into soup; however, those *which lay eggs* will **not** be made into soup. Notice that the essential clause refers to *some* chickens, *not* all.

Taken out of context, most clauses of this type may be either set off or not. Meaning must be the final test; however, it will be useful to you to know that most clauses which come in the adjective position following a noun *are* essential to the meaning of the independent clause and should not be set off from it. If you are dubious about a particular sentence, therefore, it would be prudent to leave out the commas.

EXERCISE A-20

In the sentences below, first put all adjective clauses in parentheses. Underline the subject of the independent clause once and the verb twice. On the line to the left write the pronoun substitute for the subject of the independent clause. Set off non-essential clauses with commas.

1. _____ Questions that require an immediate answer will be handled today.
2. _____ The teacher excused the boy who had sprained his ankle.
3. _____ Songs that cannot be sung make poor national anthems.
4. _____ Parrots who actually talk are expensive.
5. _____ Chez Charles is looking for a waiter who can sing, dance, and tell jokes.
6. _____ Guests who stay past midnight are treated rudely.
7. _____ Buicks that make a lot of noise should be scrapped by drivers who don't want to get arrested.
8. _____ Cocker Spaniels who make marvelous pets are always popular.
9. _____ Cowboys who are generally considered bold are often afraid of city streets.
10. _____ My teachers who have always seemed to prefer neatness to insight have never recognized my true talents.
11. _____ The house that Jack built was replaced by an urban renewal project.
12. _____ The strange character who rang my doorbell was collecting money for the starving vultures in California.
13. _____ Cinderella who had three wicked stepsisters always had dirty fingernails.
14. _____ Fluffy who was the only dog I ever loved died of diabetes.
15. _____ My cousin who drives a Model T is a first-rate mechanic.

Appendix A: Subject/Verb Recognition: A Review 289

16. _____ My father who drives a Model T is a first-rate mechanic.
17. _____ Students who can type will have a better chance to succeed in college.
18. _____ The reasons we have given do not completely explain our position.
19. _____ The difficulties we enountered nearly stopped the project.
20. _____ The bottles Jackson keeps in the lab smell peculiar.

The Noun Clause

A *noun clause* has a subject (often a relative pronoun) and a verb, but it is a subordinate clause because it functions as piece of a complete sentence. In the basic sentence types, any slot that can be filled with a noun can also be filled with a noun clause.

SUBJECT
How you answer the question matters. (**It** matters.)
DIRECT OBJECT
The boy knew **that I would help.**
       or   (The boy knew **it**.)
The boy knew **I would help.**
SUBJECT COMPLEMENT
His excuse was **that he couldn't sing.**
His excuse was **he couldn't sing.**   (His excuse was **that**.)

EXERCISE A-21

In the sentences below, first put all noun clauses in brackets. Underline the subject of the independent clause once and the verb twice. On the line to the left write the pronoun substitute for the subject of the independent clause. (Can you determine the basic sentence type?)

Example: ____*it*____ [Where we sit] does not matter to me.
1. _____ He took whatever he could get.
2. _____ She waited for what would happen next.
3. _____ My feeling was that he didn't understand the question.
4. _____ What I have to say to you cannot be printed.
5. _____ Who is responsible for this mess?
6. _____ I asked my children who was responsible for the mess.
7. _____ Whatever you say can and will be held against you.
8. _____ Harry's wife knew he wasn't guilty.
9. _____ My aunt from Dallas predicted Harry would come to no good.
10. _____ What you see is what you get.
11. _____ That such a thing could happen to Marlene was hard to believe.
12. _____ Whoever wants the puppy can have it.
13. _____ I know who wants the puppy.

14. _____ I know someone who wants the puppy.
15. _____ Why he confessed is not known.
16. _____ Harry confessed that he had robbed the bank.
17. _____ His wife thought he was lying to get some attention.
18. _____ I don't understand what the question is.
19. _____ Anyone who can put up with Ronald is a saint.
20. _____ Who can put up with Ronald without wanting to call in a professional babysitter?

THE ADVERBIAL CLAUSE

An adverbial clause is a subordinate clause used as an adverb in a sentence. It is always grammatically dependent upon an independent clause. Like an independent clause, the adverbial clause has a subject and a verb, but unlike an independent clause, the adverbial clause does not make sense by itself.

The first step in recognizing adverbial clauses is to learn the subordinating conjunctions that introduce them and indicate the relationship of the subordinate clause to the independent clause.

When

before
after
until
since
when
whenever
while
even before
even after
even when
even while
just before
just after
shortly after
as soon as
now that
once

Because

because
since
so that
in order that
provided that

If

if
unless
in case
even if
whether (or not)

Although

although
even though
though
even if

As

as
just as
as if
as though
whereas
as long as
so long as
more than
less than
than

Where

where
wherever

Appendix A: Subject/Verb Recognition: A Review

When the subordinate clause comes at the beginning of the sentence, it is followed by a comma. The commas tells the reader where the independent clause begins. For example:

Although **Harvey was disorganized,** he was brilliant.
If **I come in a taxi,** I will bring an eggplant.
Because **I was hungry,** I ate a brontosaurus burger.

If the subordinate clause comes in the middle of the independent clause, it is set off, as if it were an interrupting expression, by commas. For example:

Harvey, *although* **he was disorganized,** was brilliant.
I will, *if* **I come in a taxi,** bring an eggplant.
Raymong, *because* **he was hungry,** ate a brontosaurus burger.

However, the subordinate adverbial clause is usually not set off by commas if it comes at the end of the sentence. Clauses that begin with the subordinating conjunction *although* are an exception to that general rule. For example:

Harvey was brilliant, *although* **he was disorganized.**
I will bring an eggplant *if* **I come in a taxi.**
Raymond ate a brontosaurus burger *because* **he was hungry.**

EXERCISE A-22

Punctuate the following sentences. Circle the subordinating conjunctions introducing adverbial clauses. Underline the subject of the independent clause once and put its pronoun substitute on the line to the left; underline the verb in the independent clause twice.

_____ 1. Although there is no good reason to believe in ghosts many people do.
_____ 2. If you thought there were one in your house you might begin to believe in them too.
_____ 3. Never having seen one I certainly did not take them seriously before I moved into my apartment on Jones Street.
_____ 4. I had moved in unpacked and set up housekeeping there without seeing the ghost either.
_____ 5. Since it was an old building I was not surprised to hear some creaking of floor boards and squeaking of hinges.
_____ 6. While I had never heard a chain dragged across a floor I recognized the sound immediately.
_____ 7. If there were a burglar I could handle him I thought.
_____ 8. As I did not believe in the supernatural I looked for a rational explanation.
_____ 9. The first night I spent in the new apartment was not frightening but annoying.

Appendix A: Subject/Verb Recognition: A Review

_____ 10. When I heard the chain dragging I got out of bed armed myself with an andiron and pursued the noise.

_____ 11. Even though I did not find a burglar or a chain I did find an open window and a banging shutter.

_____ 12. My heart beating wildly I crouched behind a packing crate and surveyed the scene.

_____ 13. Since nothing moved I crept across the floor fastened the shutter and closed the window.

_____ 14. The next day after cleaning the new apartment I was ready to forget the previous night's experience.

_____ 15. Before I quit for the night I secured all the shutters and locked the windows.

_____ 16. I knew of course that I could not lock out a ghost.

_____ 17. Because I was not a person to be easily spooked this did not seem like a serious problem.

_____ 18. I ordered a pizza from down the street started the water running in the tub and tried to relax.

_____ 19. When the doorbell rang so soon I was amazed at their quick delivery service and turned off the water.

_____ 20. Answering the door in my bathrobe I expected to find a teenage boy with acne and a pepperoni pizza.

_____ 21. I found nothing even though I stuck my head out and craned my neck around the corner.

_____ 22. Puzzling over this mystery I returned to my apartment feeling somewhat cautious.

_____ 23. As I closed the door behind me and fastened the chain the unmistakable sound of running water filled the apartment.

_____ 24. Knowing full well that I had turned off the faucet before going downstairs I picked up the andiron clutched my robe tightly around me and made bravely for the bathroom.

_____ 25. The water stopped as suddenly as it had started.

_____ 26. I threw open the door holding the andiron ready to strike and saw an empty bathroom with a half-full tub.

_____ 27. Hearing the doorbell ring again I raced to answer it as if I *had* seen a ghost.

_____ 28. When there was still no one there I began to get angry.

_____ 29. After I had turned on all the lights in my lovely new apartment I took my bath.

_____ 30. The doorbell rang of course while I was in the tub.

_____ 31. Knowing there would be no one there I wrapped a towel around myself and stalked angrily to open the door.

_____ 32. A teenage boy with acne handed me the pepperoni pizza shaking his head in disbelief.

Appendix A: Subject/Verb Recognition: A Review

_____33. I told him to keep the change as I did not have a hand free to receive it.
_____34. When he had gone I took my hard-won supper into the kitchen and returned to my bath.
_____35. If I had known what would follow I would have eaten it then.
_____36. When I was putting on my pajamas the sound of clattering chains seemed to reverberate back and forth through the apartment.
_____37. Having made a fool of myself once that evening I decided not to call the police.
_____38. If it were a ghost who was haunting my apartment I assured myself it could have no effect on the physical world.
_____39. I thought that until I opened the door and found the apartment as dark as a tomb.
_____40. Because I was certain I had turned on every light I owned I knew this must be no ordinary ghost.
_____41. Taking up my bulky weapon again I stealthily edged around some boxes and turned on the kitchen light.
_____42. The pizza box was open with one slice missing.
_____43. This hungry, noisy ghost was getting on my nerves even though I still had not seen it.
_____44. Munching on a slice of the pizza I went through the apartment again turning on all the lights.
_____45. When I returned to the kitchen the pizza was more than half gone.
_____46. To feed an expensive ghost was not part of my lease.
_____47. If this kept up I couldn't afford the apartment.
_____48. Since I had never heard of a pizza eating ghost I finally called the police.
_____49. They arrived skeptically heard my story searched the building and left although they had not found the ghost.
_____50. By the time they had gone so had the pizza.
_____51. Although I managed to get through the night hungry hearing the floor squeak and the shutters bang the next day I went apartment hunting again.

WORD ORDER IN SENTENCES

In trying to find the subject of the sentence, you've been helped by the fact that most sentences in English follow a pattern:

Subject/Verb/Object or Complement

There are, however, three exceptions to regular order which you should learn to recognize before you take a posttest in this chapter:

1. The question
2. The command
3. "There (Here) is" and "There (Here) are"

Exceptions to regular order

One time the usual *Subject/Verb/Direct Object or Complement* order is changed is in a question. In questions the helping verb moves to the front of the sentence.

Inverted Order

Part of Verb Phrase	Noun Subject	Part of Verb Phrase	Noun Direct Object
Did	Frankie	kill	Johnnie?
Has	the dog	been chasing	the cat?

Regular Order

Noun Subject	Verb Phrase	Noun Direct Object
Frankie	did kill	Johnnie.
The dog	has been chasing	the cat?

Another time the subject fails to appear before the verb is in a command or request. In this case the subject *you* is not expressed but is *understood*. *You* is the only subject which can be *understood*.

Subject Omitted

Verb	Noun Direct Object
Consider	the alternatives.

Subject Present

Pronoun Subject	Verb Phrase	Noun Direct Object
You	should consider	the alternatives.

Another time the word order is altered is when the words *there* or *here* begin the sentences. These words are *adverbs,* not subjects. The subject in such a sentence comes after the verb *be (am, is, are, was, were).*

Inverted Order

Adverb	Linking Verb	Noun Subject	Prepositional Phrase
There	was	a mouse	in the bathroom.

Appendix A: Subject/Verb Recognition: A Review

	Regular Order	
Subject	Verb	Prepositional Phrase
A mouse	was	in the bathroom.

EXERCISE A-23

In the sentences below, underline the subject once and the verb twice. On the line to the left write the correct pronoun substitute for the subject.

1. There is an escaped killer at large.
2. Did his mother hold a job?
3. Ralph lacked his brother's patience.
4. Jean is eating the banana cream pie.
5. Did the demonstration upset the embassy employees?
6. Was there a telephone in the room?
7. Get a new slave.
8. A loser always has the same excuses.
9. Here is someone you should meet.
10. Please drop your gun!
11. A cocky young messenger entered the university office.
12. Regular mail service makes business possible.
13. The new secretary discovered some terrible mistakes.
14. Does the library have good books?
15. Did the phone call wake the sleeping boa constrictor?
16. Always check your answers.
17. That new dictionary contains most spelling rules also.
18. One small gold earring pierced his left ear.
19. There will be some changes after the next election.
20. Your cigarette smoke has ruined her meal.
21. Those new black shoes hurt my feet.
22. Has the radio mentioned the tornado alert?
23. A small, green Martian charmed both young children.
24. Do the dishes.
25. What resolutions did Lochinvar make?

PUTTING IT ALL TOGETHER

Starting with seven basic sentence types, you have learned to expand sentences by adding modifiers, substituting verbal phrases and clauses in noun positions, and by subordinating clauses to a base sentence. You will be able to analyze the most complicated sentences if you can go through the following steps:

1. Identify the independent clause.
2. Identify the subject and verb within the independent clause:
   a. eliminate distracting constructions;
   b. determine what elements are being joined by coordinating conjunctions.
3. Decide how subordinate elements are being used in the sentence.

The usual test of students' ability to do basic sentence analysis is to present them with a very complicated sentence using as many of the basic constructions as the tester can come up with.

Here is the sentence used by Paul Diederich in *Measuring Growth in English*:

> I have a little shadow that goes in and out with me, but what can be the use of him is more than I can see.

Here is the sentence used by J. N. Hook and Michael Crowell in their *Modern English Grammar for Teachers*.

> While a gay carborundum slithered recklessly in the wanton breeze, a doleful flibbertigibbet dressed in spangles that scarcely reached her ankles recounted to whoever would listen her experiences and hardships in the ink bottle.

Can you find the subject and verb of the independent clause?

REVIEW — appendix A

The sentences in this review exercise are provided to help you check your progress in this section and to prepare you for what you'll find in the posttest. For the answers to this exercise, check with your instructor or tutor or listen to the appropriate audio tape.

In the sentences below first circle the verb or verb phrase (auxiliaries plus main verb). Then underline the subject and write its pronoun substitute to the left.

(Pronoun Substitute)

_____ 1. Several teachers demanded a raise.
_____ 2. The notes from my daughter's principal really bother me.
_____ 3. At the end of the movie the people in the theater walked up the aisle.
_____ 4. A vacuum cleaner salesman is selling Mama a four-hundred-dollar machine.
_____ 5. All of the boys want to join the Navy after high school.
_____ 6. The price which Ronald paid for the car was not fair.
_____ 7. One child's parents have not been informed of the accident.
_____ 8. James, Tami, and Carlos always sat and smoked on the porch in the evening.
_____ 9. Brush fires in this part of the country are usually started by careless campers.
_____ 10. There are many books in the bookstore.

appendix B

SPELLING AND HOMONYMS

PREVIEW ———— appendix B

The sentences in the exercise below preview the skills and principles you'll learn in this section. This is a dictation exercise. For the dictation and the answers to this exercise, check with your instructor or tutor or listen to the appropriate audio tape.

1. The three _____ bought new black _____ .
2. The disgruntled _____ opened their own auto repair _____ .
3. A tornado _____ at the _____ of spring.
4. As the students were _____ into the classroom, the teacher was _____ on the board.
5. I _____ I should _____ a medal.
6. The people downstairs have _____ orangutan _____ two children.
7. _____ question three didn't make any _____ , Mario didn't answer it.
8. _____ Joann _____ to lunch, Bruce went through her files.
9. Natalie can't _____ criticism from anyone _____ her sister.
10. Sherman took a large _____ of Vitamin C, but it _____ seem to have helped.

INTRODUCTION

If you've been kidding yourself that spelling isn't important for you to learn because you'll eventually have a secretary, please stop. First of all, it's despicable to think that a menial task unworthy of oneself may appropriately be passed on to another human being. And if poor spelling is a mark of self-conscious pride with you, we owe it to you to tell you that no one else will be amused. This section won't turn you into a spelling champion overnight, but it can help you clear up your most appalling errors. The rules we have chosen to illustrate are those which will turn up over and over again. They are necessary for forming plurals, making subjects and verbs agree, and for forming the past tense and verb phrases.

The first thing to do is start a list of the words you misspell and make sure you know what every word means. Then follow these steps:

1. **Copy the word carefully.** Make a habit of opening the dictionary, and while you're there, make sure you know what the word means. If there's more than one spelling, pick the one that obeys the rule you've learned.
2. **Check what you've copied letter by letter.** It's harder to unlearn than to learn, and you'll pay in time and frustration for careless copying.
3. **Cover the word and write it from memory.**
4. **Check your spelling letter by letter.**
5. **Repeat this procedure five times for each word.** Some authorities say three times; you may find ten is right for you.
6. **If you make a mistake at any point, start over.**
7. **Use the word.** If you are aware that you are spelling it correctly as you use it in a sentence, you have learned the word.

ADDING ENDINGS TO WORDS

If you have gone through Chapters 1 and 2, you already know at least two of the most useful spelling rules.

Rule 1. When a word ends in *ch, sh, s, z,* or *x* (notice that all of these sounds hiss), ad *es* to form the plural of the noun or the third person singular form of the verb.

Noun	Verb
patCH / patchES	patCH / patchES
The patCHES were worn ragged.	She patCHES her blue jeans.

EXERCISE B-1

List ten words that obey this rule.

1. _____   2. _____   3. _____
4. _____   5. _____   6. _____

Appendix B: Spelling and Homonyms

7. _____ 8. _____ 9. _____
10. _____

Rule 2. When there is a consonant in front of *y,* change the *y* to *i* before adding *es* to make a noun plural or to form the third person singular of the verb.

Noun	Verb
tRy / trIES	tRy / trIES
Three trIES and you're out.	He trIES too hard.

Rule 2 applies to all endings except those beginning with the letter *I.*

beauTy / beautIful		stuDy / studyIng
hapPy / happIness	*but not*	tRy / tryIng
likeLy / likelIhood		carRy / carryIng

Notice that when you pronounce the words in the second column that you hear both the *y* and the *i*.

Special problems you can banish with this rule include:

Busy / business	copy / copying
early / earlier	apply / applying
lonely / loneliness	

EXERCISE B–2

List ten words that obey this rule.

1. _____ 2. _____ 3. _____
4. _____ 5. _____ 6. _____
7. _____ 8. _____ 9. _____
10. _____

EXERCISE B–3   write

Write a short narrative including at least one example of words covered by rules 1 and 2 in each sentence. Underline and list all your target words and try to include those which are personally troublesome to you.

If you have trouble getting started, you may wish to begin with the following sentence:

I'm sitting there minding my own *business* when a short little lady with pointed ears *flies* through the window, *perches* on the radiator, and says, "OK, cutey, you've got three *wishes.* What are they?"

Reviewing Endings

In Chapter 3 before adding -ed or -ing to a verb, you often had to drop a vowel or double a consonant. The frequency with which you must do this makes this an important problem.

Rule 3. In one syllable words which end in a consonant with a single vowel in front of it, double the final consonant before adding an ending which begins with a vowel (-ed, -ing, -age, -ish, -er, -ar, and -y).

zIp / ziPPed   mAn / maNNish
swIm / swiMMing   bAt / baTTery
bAg / baGGage   bEg / beGGar
mOb / moBBed   fUr / fuRRy

This rule also applies to words of more than one syllable where the accent is on the final syllable.

permIt/permiTTed
begIn/begiNNing

Let's consider this rule. The reason we double the consonant is to keep the vowel short. Consider the verb *to win,* a one syllable word ending in a consonant preceded by a vowel.

Root word   They **win** at cards.
Root word and ending   They were **winning** the game.

If you had neglected to double the consonant, the sound of the word would change. The vowel would become long and say its own name. *Wining* sounds like *signing* and means something completely different from *winning.*

The contractor was **wining** and **dining** the politician so that he could win the contract.

Consider (hop) *hopping* and (hope) *hoping.* The *o* in *hopping* is short because of the double consonant (*p*). The *o* in *hoping* is long (says its own name, *o*) because the consonant isn't doubled.

Special spelling problems that can be solved with this rule include:

(be-gin) beginning   (ex-cel) excellent
(oc-cur) occurred   (plan) planning
(o-mit) omitted   (ad-mit) admitted

EXERCISE B–4

List ten words that obey Rule 3.

1. _____   2. _____   3. _____
4. _____   5. _____   6. _____

Appendix B: Spelling and Homonyms

7. _____   8. _____   9. _____
10. _____

Rule 4.   In words which end with a silent e, drop the e before adding an ending which starts with a vowel (a, e, i, o, u).

givE* / givING   imaginE / imaginABLE
smokE / smokING   curvE / curvATURE
takE / takING   creatE / creatOR
savE / savING   hopE / hopING
communicatE / communicatING

Special spelling problems which you can manage with this rule include:

comE* / comING
losE* / losing
writE / writING
makE / makING
havE* / havING

* *Give, come, have,* and *lose* are peculiar because the *i* and *o* are short rather than long, but since the vowel sound is already established in the root form, it is not necessary to double the consonant. Except for these, you will notice that Rule 4 is really the reverse of Rule 3. Rule 3 keeps the vowel short, and Rule 4 keeps it long.

EXERCISE B–5

List ten words that obey Rule 4.

1. _____   2. _____   3. _____
4. _____   5. _____   6. _____
7. _____   8. _____   9. _____
10. _____

Rule 5.   Put *i* before *e* except after *c* or when sounded like *ay* as in *neighbor* and *weigh*.

frIEnd   deCEIve   vEIl
achIEve ...but... perCEIve ...and...   EIght
relIEve

Two of the most frequent spelling errors made by students can be avoided with this familiar rule:

belIEve   and   reCEIve

(Notice that *receiving* also follows Rule 4 about words ending in silent *e*.)

EXERCISE B–6

List ten words that obey Rule 5.

1. _____ 2. _____ 3. _____
4. _____ 5. _____ 6. _____
7. _____ 8. _____ 9. _____
10. _____

EXERCISE B–7 *write*

Make a list of twenty words that obey Rules 4 and 5 and then use them in a short, short story.

HOMONYMS

Because differences between words sometimes disappear in spoken English, becoming a good speller will be difficult if you depend solely on your ears. In speech final *d*s and *t*s are often not pronounced. Think about it. When is the last time you heard anyone pronounce the *d* on *used* in a sentence like "I used to take the bus to work"?

Another time when your ears won't help you is when the word you use has a *homonym*, a word which sounds the same but has a different meaning and is spelled differently. *Accept* and *except* are homonyms. They sound the same, but the words mean different things.

Homonym mistakes in your writing can turn serious statements into ridiculous ones. Do you think "human *beans* deserve respect"? Would you rent an apartment with "built-in *shudders*"?

If you have a homonym problem, the first thing you must do is to identify the words which give you trouble and work on them. The glossary we've attached to the end of this chapter lists some of the homonyms which turn up time after time in student writing. When you look through this list, you may have trouble believing that anyone could confuse some of these words. However, other of the words may be your own special problems. Make a note of these words.

In order to solve a homonym problem, it is important that you work on both words, not just the one you happened to misuse at a particular time. First make sure you can explain the different meanings of the two words. Then write your own sentences using each word. For most students, writing five sentences with a word is enough to fix the meaning firmly in their minds, but if it takes you ten or fifteen sentences, write as many as it takes. As you write each sentence, carefully check the word. Is it spelled right? Finally, always carefully proofread everything you write.

EXERCISE B–8

Choose the correct form of the homonyms from the following frequently confused pairs. Consult a dictionary if you aren't sure of the difference between the words.

Appendix B: Spelling and Homonyms

1. Tooth decay is one (affect, effect) of high fevers in childhood.
2. High fevers in childhood can (affect, effect) the rate of tooth decay.
3. Roseanne doesn't have the (sense, since) God gave a goose.
4. The job offer presented (an, and) opportunity for advancement.
5. Regi will (pass, passed, past) the ball to Hank.
6. Sharing an apartment with your sister may not be an (idea, ideal) arrangement.
7. When Joan (pass, passed, past) trigonometry, she felt a real (sense, since) of accomplishment.
8. April's winter (close, clothes) are full of (wholes, holes).
9. Michelle didn't (by, buy) anything at the Going-Out-of-Business (Sell, Sale, Sail).
10. The lawyer was (sighted, sided, cited) for contempt.
11. You should (break, brake) in the (breaks, brakes) of your new car slowly.
12. No one (accept, except) Chekov could have handled the secret mission.
13. There is one (thing, think) you should understand.
14. Janice (knew, new) she couldn't afford a (knew, new) car.
15. Is salary always more important (than, then) fringe benefits?
16. The criminal had (loss, lost) all respect for the law.
17. There's (know, no) smoking at Penney's house if you (know, no) what's good for you.
18. By the time they (were, where) ready to move, they had accumulated so much junk it seemed as if they had (to, too, two) of everything (accept, except) the things they really needed.
19. My father (sighted, sided, cited) with my brother in the argument as usual.
20. We are (quiet, quite) tired of your complaints and would really appreciate it if you would just be (quiet, quite).
21. Do you care (weather, whether) Parnell comes (alone, along) with us?

EXERCISE B-9

Each of the following sentences contains at least one common homonym error. Find the error and correct it.

1. I loss my watch on the beach.

2. Mom doesn't let my younger brother see violence TV shows.

3. Jack's car much have broken down.

4. The police knew than there would be trouble.

5. Those who do not study the pass are doomed to relive it.

6. The poor looser insisted that the judge was prejudice.

7. The committee doesn't intent to release its decision today.

8. Richard can't fine his glasses an it's getting late.

9. Peter had too must ice cream for dessert.

10. She was certain than the charges were groundless.

11. Doug things his phone has been tap for two months.

12. Dallas is steal one of Tony's favorite cities.

13. Does this music brother you as much as it does me?
14. Griff's uncalled for remark bought about the fight.
15. Have you every seen anything to beat that?
16. Frank is the principle character is the school play.
17. The mechanic when out to lunch.
18. This calculator dose not work.
19. The man form Mars applied for a bank credit card.
20. I'll need a description in one from or another of your future plans.
21. There must be away to finish the project.
22. Have you two all ready met.
23. This day has been all together too much for me.
24. Less get a way from this place or soon it maybe to late.
25. Doesn't your conscious ever bother you, Herb?

GLOSSARY OF HOMONYMS

ACCEPT (verb): to take when offered, to believe, to agree to
EXCEPT (preposition): to exclude or leave out

> All of the parties to the contract decided to **accept** the terms in the third paragraph **except** Carol Baldwin.

AFFECT (verb): to act upon, to influence
EFFECT (noun or verb): a result; to cause or bring about a result

> High inflation will certainly **affect** election rhetoric. Whether it will have an **effect** on on tax cut legislation is not yet known.

ALONE (adjective or adverb): solitary or unique
ALONG (preposition or adverb): by the side of, onward

> I can get **along** with the boss if I'm left **alone.**

ALREADY (adverb): prior to this time
ALL READY (pronoun plus adjective): prepared, everybody prepared

> We were **all ready** to leave at eight o'clock, but Milt had **already** left.

ALTHOUGH (subordinating conjunction): in spite of the fact that
ALL, THOUGH (pronoun plus subordinating conjunction): **though** is an abbreviated form of **although**

> **Although** I voted for Dover, Hastings won the election. Ms. Hastings thanked us **all, though** she made special mention of Pat Conway's efforts.

Appendix B: Spelling and Homonyms

AND (coordinating conjunction): plus, in addition to
AN (noun determiner before words beginning with vowel): an apple, a single apple
IN (preposition): inside, towards, through

> **In** the early seventies **an** energy crisis developed **and** persists to this day.

AWAY (adverb): in another place or direction
A WAY (noun determiner plus noun): direction, route

> When Maria earned enough money to go **away** to college, her mother remarked, "Where there's a will, there's **a way**."

BOTHER (verb or noun): to pester or annoy; a nuisance
BROTHER (noun): a male who has the same parents as another

> Don't **bother** Marita's **brother.**

BOUGHT (verb): to purchase
BROUGHT (verb): to carry or lead

> Letitia's mother **brought** over a cake she had **bought** at the French bakery.

BRAKE (noun or verb): a device for slowing or stopping; to slow or stop
BREAK (noun or verb): a separation; to separate, rupture, or violate

> The assassin tried to **break** the connection between the steering column and the **brake.**

BUY (verb or noun): to purchase, to accept, or believe (slang); a purchase at an advantageous price
BY (preposition or adverb): near, around, or close at hand

> The Sandbergs will **buy** a new car **by** Memorial Day.

CLOSE (verb, adjective, or adverb): to shut, end, or finish (pronounced kloz); intimate, strict, or accurate (pronounced klos); near
CLOTHES (noun): clothing, wearing apparel
CLOTHS (noun): pieces of fabric

> Before I could **close** the door, the pastor made me promise to provide two table **cloths** and a box of old **clothes** for the church bazaar.

CONSCIENCE (noun): a sense of right and wrong
CONSCIOUS (adjective): aware, reflective

> When I didn't call my mother on Mother's Day, I was all too **conscious** that my **conscience** would bother me later.

DOES (verb): a form of the verb **do**; its contraction is **doesn't**
DOSE (noun or verb): a portion of medicine; to give a portion of medicine

> Give him a **dose** of his own medicine if he **does** that again: just smile wisely and refuse to answer.

EVER (adverb): always or at any time, in any way

EVERY (adjective): without exception, complete, entire

>Have you **ever** heard the memory device, "**Every** good boy does fine"?

FIND (verb or noun): to discover; a remarkable discovery
FINE (adjective, verb, or noun): of excellent quality or delicacy; to punish with a penalty; a penalty

>Augusta and Melody are **fine** people; they never **find** fault with anyone.

FORM (noun or verb): the shape or structure of something; to give form or shape to, to develop or acquire
FROM (preposition): a starting point, cause, agent, or basis

>Fill in the **form from** top to bottom.

HOLE (noun): an opening in or through a thing
WHOLE (adjective): entire, total, or all

>The **whole** crew stared into the black **hole**.

IDEA (noun): a thought, concept, or plan
IDEAL (adjective or noun): something which exists only in the imagination because it is so perfect; a standard or model or excellence or beauty

>My **idea** of the **ideal** vacation is a sunny, unpopulated beach.

INTEND (verb): to plan, to have in mind as a purpose
INTENT (noun or adjective): the purpose, meaning, significance, or state of mind with which an act is done; with strained, eager, or concentrated attention

>Her **intent** was to kill, not wound him; I **intend** to let a court decide what her punishment should be.

KNOW (verb): to be acquainted with or to be certain of as objectively true
NO (adjective or adverb): not any or not one; not so
NOW (adverb): at the present time

>I **know** that **no** harm will come to you **now**.

LESS: (adjective): a smaller quantity
LET'S (contraction): **Let us**

>**Let's** order **less** chicken next time.

LOSE (verb): to misplace, to suffer defeat
LOSS (noun): a failure to win or keep
LOST (verb or adjective): to part with unintentionally; not recovered, missed, wanted
LOOSE (adjective): unattached, not tight

>I had some **loose** change in my pocket, but I must have **lost** it when I turned the cartwheel. Although I hate to **lose** money, the **loss** was not serious.

MUCH (adjective, adverb, or pronoun): in great quantity, amount, extent, or degree

Appendix B: Spelling and Homonyms

MUST (verb): bound to, urged to, or commanded to do something

> You **must** learn not to expect too **much** creativity from Kelly.

NEW (adjective): recently come into existence, lately discovered, changed in essence
KNEW (verb): to be acquainted with or to be certain of as objectively true

> I **knew** that all the car needed was a **new** battery.

PASS (verb or noun): to move, to go by, over, around, through, beyond; a way or opening, permission for a soldier to be absent, or a grade
PASSED (verb): to move, to go by, to elapse
PAST (noun, adjective, or preposition): time gone by; belonging to time gone by; beyond in time and place

> Just as I was worrying about how to **pass** calculus, a police car **passed** me on the right and roared **past** the used car lot.

PRINCIPAL (adjective or noun): head or chief; the head of a school; amount of a debt aside from the interest
PRINCIPLE (noun): a general truth, a standard

> The **principal** concern of the lending officer, a former high school **principal** and a woman of strong **principle**, was how soon the **principal** and interest of the loan would be paid back.

QUIET (adjective or noun): absence of noise and uproar; tranquility or silence
QUITE (adverb): completely, wholly, or positively

> Although Julie is **quiet**, she's **quite** smart.

SAIL (noun or verb): fabric which gathers the wind which propels a boat; to travel on water in a boat
SALE (noun): the act of selling
SELL (verb): to give something to another for money or other valuable consideration

> I bought the **sail** on **sale** when Land's End decided to **sell** out their stock.

SIDED (verb or adjective): to agree or support; having sides of a specific number or kind
SIGHTED (verb): to view in the distance, to see
CITED (verb): to refer to, to quote

> My near-**sighted** father **cited** my numerous shortcomings as a driver, but my mother **sided** with me and said I should be permitted to drive to game downstate.

SINCE (preposition or subordinating conjunction): how much time has elapsed; something happened because of something else
SENSE (noun): sound judgment; meaning; way we receive impressions from the world

Since he was involved in the auto accident, Bruce's **sense** of balance has been disturbed.

STEAL (verb or noun): to take the property of another; a bargain (slang)
STILL (adverb or adjective): without motion or the continuance of an action or condition; calm, tranquil, or peaceful

The crowd was very **still** and even my little brother sat **still**, waiting for Marcie to **steal** second base.

THAN (conjunction or preposition): compared with
THAT (pronoun or noun determiner): refers to the person, thing, or idea indicated
THEN (adverb): at that time or after that time

The aliens read our minds easily; **then** we knew **that** they were not only more intelligent but more compassionate **than** we had suspected.

THING (noun): an object
THINK (verb): to exercise the mind actively in any way

I don't **think** a **thing** like that would scare Cavan.

TWO (adjective): a number telling us how many
TOO (adverb): also, more than sufficiently
TO (part of an infinitive or preposition): toward

The front staircase is **too** narrow for him **to** carry up the **two** suitcases at once.

WERE (verb): past tense of the verb **be**
WHERE (adverb): at or from what place

Where were you at the time of the crime?

WHEN (adverb or subordinating conjunction): at what time
WENT (verb): past tense of the verb **go**

When the commercial came on, Bill **went** to the kitchen.

WHETHER (subordinating conjunction): if
WEATHER (noun or verb): climate; to endure through difficulties

The captain wasn't sure **whether** the boat could **weather** such a storm, so she set a course for better **weather**.

WON'T (contraction): **will not**
WANT (verb): to desire, to wish for

Won't you believe that I sincerely **want** to help?

REVIEW ———— appendix B

The sentences in this review exercise are provided to help you check your progress in this section and to prepare you for what you'll find in the posttest. For the dictation and the answers to this exercise, check with your instructor or tutor or listen to the appropriate audio tape.

1. These _____ are filled with _____ .
2. Ronkowski _____ to find _____ by dieting.
3. Ronkowski is _____ _____ foods from his diet.
4. _____ weight is _____ him very happy.
5. When he has _____ his _____ pound goal, he will _____ two hundred and ninety pounds.
6. You _____ your business, and I'll _____ _____ .
7. I _____ don't know whether Ronkowski will _____ my recipe for shortcake.
8. _____ _____ you _____ he _____ through my secret recipe files?
9. Ronkowski is _____ heavy _____ eat _____ desserts.
10. You have said _____ enough; now please be _____ .

311

ANSWER SECTION

CHAPTER 1

When an answer is given in parentheses, a word of your choice may be substituted if it has the necessary characteristics.

Recognizing Nouns (Definition and Characteristic Endings)

Any proper or common noun naming a person (Jim, girl)
Any animal (horse)
Any activity (eating); all of these words will end in -ing

(motherhood, neighborhood)
(driver, waiter)
(country, bigotry)
(Catholicism, extremism)
(astrology, apology)

Recognizing Nouns (Noun (Determiners)

S = singular; P = plural; c = must begin with consonant; v = must begin with vowel

a (peanut) S/c	the (witnesses) S or P	those (carrots) P
every (man) S	several (threats) P	some (time, kids) S or P
his (headache) S or P	this (hat) S	two (pints) P
one (turnip) S	most (money, cats) S or P	my (sister) S or P
your (decision) S or P	few (radios) P	both (lamps) P
a group of (pigeons) P	their (troubles) S or P	that (gun) S
another (story) S	all (students) P	our (heads) S or P

Recognizing Nouns (Function and Position)

(Carol) Make sure this is not a pronoun.
(woman)
(Biloxi)
(record)
(Sally) Make sure this is not a pronoun.
(secretary)

Exercise 1–1

1. he
3. it
5. it
7. s/he
9. she
11. it
13. they
15. they
17. they
19. it

Exercise 1–2

1. Answer must begin with a consonant (dog)
3. (money, time, etc.)
5. Answer must begin with a vowel (apple)
7. Answer must begin with a vowel sound (hour)
9. Answer must begin with a consonant (rabbit)

Exercise 1–3

All plural nouns; misspelled words are wrong.
1. A group of (hecklers)
3. Both (proposals)
5. Many (threats)
7. Several (frogs)
9. Those (lunches)

Exercise 1-4

1. pl (cats)
3. sng (insult)
5. pl because of the verb (hubcaps)
7. sng (ice cream)
9. sng or pl (war or wars)

Exercise 1-5

1. pl (desks)
3. pl (guests)
5. pl (wasps)
7. pl (artists)
9. pl (guests)
11. pl (witnesses)
13. sng (witness)
15. pl (drivers)
17. pl (marchers)
19. sng (bug)

Exercise 1-6

1. Honesty
3. Working
5. Onions
7. Worms
9. Laughter

Exercise 1-7

1. trucks, truck
3. Oak, Oaks
5. graduates, graduate
7. foot, feet
9. newspaper, newspapers
11. examinations, examination
13. pillows, pillow
15. dogs, dog

Exercise 1-8

1. sng (foot)
3. sng (salt)
5. pl (blocks)
7. sng, mass noun (money) or pl (bill collectors)
9. sng, must begin with a consonant (haircut)
11. pl (latches)
13. sng (parachute)
15. pl because of the verb *are* (steaks) sng (cent)
17. sng mass noun (whiskey) or pl (pretzels)
19. sng (advantage)

Exercise 1-9

Single noun,	pronoun	Plural noun,	pronoun
1. (noun)	it	(nouns)	they
3. (apple)	it	(apples)	they
5. (book)	it	(books)	they
7. (depression)	it	(depressions)	they
9. (telephone)	it	(telephones)	they
11. (riot)	it	(riots)	they
13. (horse)	it	(horses)	they
15. tourist)	s/he	(tourists)	they

Exercise 1-10

1. (kings) they
3. (friends) they
5. (laborers) they

Exercise 1–10 (cont.)

7. (balloon) it
9. (losers) they
11. (hyenas) they
13. (visitors) they
15. (dish) it

Exercise 1–11

1. tutors, students
3. office, test
5. problem, terms
7. desks, students
9. tests, blizzard
11. microscopes
13. plane
15. feet, pounds

Exercise 1–12

1. (train) it
3. (play) it
5. (train) it
7. (door) it
9. (athlete) s/he
11. (baby) s/he
13. (person) s/he
15. (wheat) it

Exercise 1–13

1. (bells) they
3. (supervisors) they
5. (Indians) they
7. (spectators) they
9. (mothers) they
11. (dishes) they
13. (ankles) they
15. (civilizations) they

Exercise 1–14

1. dishes
3. catches
5. TAs (or TA's)
7. flies
9. wharves
11. thieves
13. Smiths
15. Johnsons
17. deer
19. mice, dice
21. fathers-in-law, sons-in-law
23. teeth
25. nuclei

Exercise 1–15

1. boxes
3. punch
5. families
7. Cs (or C's)
9. ourselves
11. lives
13. Walshes
15. halves
17. textbooks
19. series
21. bases
23. controversies
25. raspberries

Exercise 1–16

1. kids, contests, stations
3. giveaways
5. Tylers
7. subscribers, calls, call-in

Answer: Exercises: 1–16 to 2–5

Exercise 1–16 (cont.)

9. messages, callers
11. cries
13. times, ladies, guests
15. departures, card
17. lives
19. lessons
21. phones, dials, digits, contest
23. key, Tylers
25. ones
27. rings, gentleman
29. seconds
31. suitcases, tickets
33. mysteries, contests
35. jobs, weeks

Exercise 1–17

Student Writing

CHAPTER 2

Exercise 2–1

1. knows
3. believes
5. try
7. drive
9. writes
11. seems
13. frown
15. buy
17. talk
19. empties

Exercise 2–2

1. movies (they)/make
3. day (it) ruins
5. teacher (she)/praises
7. Nobody (s/he)/knows
9. Men (they)/buy
11. spaghetti (it)/tastes
13. Swimming (it)/takes
15. Sonia (she)/fixes
17. dictionary (it)/contains
19. subject, verb (they)/agree
21. bathrobe (it)/dissolves
23. apartment (it)/floods
25. butterflies (they)/wander
27. Creativity (it)/is
29. Olives (they)/improve
31. disposition (it)/drives
33. Ken Kramer (he)/refuses
35. Richard, I (we)/buy
37. Technicians (they)/earn
39. mother-in-law (she)/drinks
41. Affirmative Action Program (it)/helps
43. assembler (s/he) finds
45. Mary (she)/smiles
47. vet (s/he)/cares
49. qualifications (they)/impress

Exercise 2–3

1. (She)/is
3. (it)/is
5. (it)/is
7. (they)/are
9. (they)/are
11. (he)/is
13. (she)/is
15. (she)/is
17. (it)/is
19. (they)/are

Exercise 2–4

1. (he)/was
3. (they)/were
5. (they)/were
7. (it)/was
9. (they)/were
11. (they)/were
13. (they)/were
15. (they)/were
17. (they)/were
19. (it)/was

Exercise 2–5

1. are or were
3. is or was

Exercise 2-5 (cont.)

5. is or was
7. Is or was that your car?
9. speaks/are, spoke/were
11. is or was
13. is or was
15. hits/will be, or is, hit/was

Exercise 2-6

1. (he)/isn't
3. (they)/aren't
5. (it)/isn't
7. (they)/aren't
9. (it)/isn't
11. (they)/aren't
13. (they)/aren't
15. (they)/aren't
17. (it)/isn't
19. (it)/isn't)

Exercise 2-7

1. (s/he)/wasn't
3. (it)/wasn't
5. (they/weren't
7. (they)/weren't
9. (they)/weren't
11. (it)/wasn't
13. (You)/weren't
15. (it)/wasn't
17. (they)/weren't
19. (it)/wasn't)

Exercise 2-8

1. (he)/is, isn't
3. (they)/are, aren't
5. (s/he)/is, isn't
7. (they)/were, weren't
9. (it)/was, wasn't
11. (it)/was, wasn't
13. (they)/are, aren't
15. (they)/were, weren't
17. (they)/were, weren't
19. (s/he)/is, isn't

Exercise 2-9

1. hospitals (they) are/were
3. something (it) is/was
5. excuse (it) was/is
7. notebooks (they) are/were
9. student (s/he) is/was
11. motive (it) is/was
13. books (they) are/were
15. problems (they) are/were
17. witness (s/he) is/was
19. firefighter, police officer (they) are/were

Exercise 2-10

1. P/sleep
3. P/curse
5. P/dream
7. P/joke
9. S/trips
11. P/succeed
13. S/dies
15. S/scolds
17. P/sigh
19. S/smokes

Exercise 2-11

1. (they)/do
3. (they)/do
5. (they)/do
7. (it)/does
9. do
11. (they)/do
13. (s/he)/does
15. (they)/do

Exercise 2-12

1. (s/he)/doesn't
3. doesn't
5. (they)/don't
7. (they)/don't

Answer: Exercises: 2–12 to 2–18

Exercise 2–12 (cont.)

9. (it)/doesn't
11. (it)/doesn't
13. (it)/doesn't
15. s/he (doesn't)
17. (it)/doesn't
19. (they)/don't

Exercise 2–13

1. (he) has
3. (they) have
5. (it) has
7. (they) have
9. (it) has
11. (he/she) hasn't
13. (it) hasn't
15. (it) hasn't

Exercise 2–14

The following are possible answers only. Finish the sentences any way you like, as long as you use a present tense verb.

1. are sisters.
3. love sailing.
5. can keep each other company.
7. scared my poodle.
9. are very different in size.
11. are fun to play in.
13. go together.
15. move fast
17. want their dinner.
19. learns many tribal custom.

Exercise 2–15

1. problem (it)/exists
3. John (he)/asks
5. questions (they)/persist
7. victims (they)/grasp
9. salesclerks (they)/enlist
11. God, Nietzsche (they)/exist
13. Jeff (he)/asks
15. you/desist

Exercise 2–16

1. (they)/P; (in my closet)
3. (they)/P; (on my record)
5. (it)/S; (between us)
7. (they)/P; (on the shelf)
9. (it)/S; (under the sink)
11. (they)/P; (of salmon)
13. (it)/S
15. (it)/S; (of the clocks)
17. (s/he)/S; (for the defense)
19. (it)/S; (near the hydrant)

Exercise 2–17

1. reasons (they)/command—*for silence*
3. brakes (they)/stick—*on Harlon's car*
5. rats (they)/sneak—*under the garage*
7. star (he)/lives—*of the Chicago Black Hawks*
9. winds (they)/cool—*off the lake*
11. plants (they)/appear—*in the window*
13. lady (she)/exists—*in the apartment above me*
15. Canvassers (they)/pass—*for the Democratic candidate*

Exercise 2–18

1. all (they)/bore—*of the stories of their vacation*
3. someone (s/he)/is—*in this class*
5. Several (they)/need—*of the buildings near the lake*

Exercise 2-18 (cont.)

7. Some (it)/belongs—*of the land beyond the prairie*
9. Everything (it)/depresses—*in the newspapers*
11. Each (it)/is—*of the cars*
13. Much (it)/consists—*of his speech*
15. Something (it)/looks—*in these sentences*

Exercise 2-19

Student writing

Exercise 2-20

1. which/eat; parakeets/are
3. who/curses; man/is
5. which/discuss; papers/bore
7. which/threatens; Obesity/amuses
9. that/haunts; music/refuses
11. who/tracks; Dora/deserves
13. which/is; Discipline/becomes
15. who/hate; executives/drink

Exercise 2-21

1. John/wants; are
3. challenges/are; is
5. she/types; bore
7. models/fear; amuses
9. composer/imagines; refuses
11. time/means; deserves
13. mother/hesitates; becomes
15. money/is; drink
17. divers/find; contain
19. he/gives; sound

Exercise 2-22

1. car (it)/costs; (that I want)
3. bracelet (it)/needs; (that he holds in his hands)
5. girl (she)/wins; (to whom you refer)
7. bank (it)/sits; (to which I refer)
9. carpets (they)/seem; (that I loved yesterday)
11. calls (they)/drive; (that interrupt meals)
13. The Great Gatsby (it)/deserves; (which was recently filmed)
15. fan belt (it)/slips; (which really belongs on a larger car)
17. books (they)/annoy; (which have many misprints in them)
19. grounds (they)/attract; (which I put in a pile near the garage)
21. rings (they)/are; (I buy)
23. shoes (they)/are; (the department stores offer)
25. words (they)/are; (George learns to spell)

Exercise 2-23

Student Writing

Exercise 2-24

1. landlord (he)/likes
3. two (they)/are
5. they/work; they/have
7. he/smokes; smoking (it)/is
9. this (it)/gives; what's
11. lumber, tools (they)/litter
13. friends (they)/arrive
15. music (it)/flows
17. it/chews, soils
19. they/concern
21. waiting (it)/gives
23. I/listen
25. explanation (it)/is
27. landlord (he)/betrays
29. life (it)/exacts

Exercise 2-25

1. Red Riding Hood (she)/lives
3. parents (they)/sigh; they/remember
5. works (they)/make
7. She/wants

Answer: Exercises: 2–25 to 3–3

Exercise 2–25 (cont.)

9. lectures (they)/annoy they/amuse
11. Billy Watkins (he)/has, doesn't
13. Red Riding Hood (she)/agrees; mother (she) fills
15. She/puts, kisses, skips
17. They/shake, hope; someone (s/he)/knocks
19. creatures (they)/listen
21. person (s/he) croaks
23. you/look; Red Riding Hood (she)/says

25. Red Riding Hood (she)/notices
27. Red Riding Hood (she)/volunteers
29. Little Red Riding Hood (she)/exclaims; you/are
31. growls (they)/alert; she/doesn't
33. pamphlets (they)/choke; it/falls
35. cries (they)/attract; officer (s/he)/enters, stops
37. department (it)/releases; they/let

Exercise 2–26

Student writing

CHAPTER 3

Exercise 3–1

1. park/parked
3. tires/tired
5. want/wanted
7. minds/minded; works/worked
9. ask/asked; receive/received
11. explodes/exploded; burns/burned
13. need/needed
15. unite/united
17. helps/helped
19. results/resulted

21. interest/interested
23. warps/warped
25. stops/stopped
27. settles/settled; look/looked
29. air/aired; hopes/hoped
31. believe/believed; exists/existed
33. play/played; place/placed
35. states/stated; suffers/suffered
37. wants/wanted
39. brags/bragged; ignore/ignored

Exercise 3–2

1. lived, called
3. studied, turned, asked
5. asked, learned, was
7. wondered, was
9. seemed
11. carried, used
13. computed, was
15. figured
17. was
19. focused

21. computed, flashed, clicked
23. looked
25. bundled
27. computed, consumed
29. combined
31. chirped, strolled
33. reasoned, was
35. agreed
37. nodded, agreed
39. toddled

41. replaced, turned
43. clutched, eased
45. murmured
47. raced
49. whirred
51. glowed, churned
53. eased, punched
55. answered
57. responded
59. groaned, hummed
61. hummed

The writer decides whether to use past or present depending upon the effect wanted.

Do not change words in quotations because they are there to indicate that these were the exact words of the speaker. Quotation marks are used to indicate an exact and unchanged reflection of what was actually said.

Exercise 3–3

1. Last April/marched
3. rainS/calls
5. Two possible answers; *cooks* suggesting someone is still cooking for them; *cooked* is also correct and suggests that no one cooks for them anymore. The absence of a time determiner leads to this ambiguity

7. is/doesn't
9. floodED/stepped
11. lieS/cheats, steals
13. smilED/asked
15. came/said
17. last night's/answered, handled
19. find/study

Exercise 3-4

1. fashions (they)/fight
3. show (it)/ends; Mike (he)/leaves
5. blocks (they)/separate; lights (they)/illuminate
7. Mike (he)/hears, quickens
9. Mike (he)/prays
11. savior (s/he)/appears
13. cats (they) yowl; he/passes
15. patience (it)/matches
17. he/streaks, crashes
19. Mike (he)/loses; he/comes
21. correct
23. offer (it)/amuses; they/agree
25. Mike (he)/pulls, delivers
27. assailant (he)/approaches
29. he/curses; mugger (he)/pulls
31. Mike (he)/trips, ties
33. correct
35. they/have

Exercise 3-5

Student writing

Exercise 3-6

Self-generated

Exercise 3-7

can	could	do
may	might	does
shall	should	did
will	would	
must		
ought (to)		

Exercise 3-8

The following are suggested answers only.
1. never, quit
3. do, unnecessarily
5. should
7. will
9. will
11. fly
13. wreck
15. write

Exercise 3-9

Student writing

Exercise 3-10

1. don't
3. don't, don't
5. does, doesn't
7. does
9. done
11. doing
13. do, done
15. didn't
17. done
19. does, does or did, did
21. didn't, did
23. don't
25. do, don't
27. doing, didn't
29. did, done
31. didn't
33. done, do
35. do, done
37. did, did, doing or do
39. done
41. Doing
43. didn't
45. didn't, do
47. done
49. do
51. didn't, do
53. done, do
55. done
57. doing
59. don't, doing
61. do, do, does

Exercise 3-11

Student writing. All sentences should have three-word verb phrases in the following pattern: present auxiliary

Exercise 3–11 (cont.)

+ *have* + past participle. All of the past participles you use should either end in *-ed* or should come from the third column of the Irregular Verb Index.

Exercise 3–12

1. was
3. was
5. be
7. is (was)
9. were
11. be
13. be
15. is (was)
17. be
19. are (were)
21. are (were)
23. are (were)
25. be
27. is (was)
29. was
31. be
33. are (were)
35. is (was)
37. are (were)
39. is (was)
41. am (was)
43. is (was)
45. are (were)
47. is (was)
49. be

Exercise 3–13

1. has (had)
3. has (had)
5. has (had)
7. has (had)
9. has (had)
11. has (had)
13. have (had)
15. has (had)
17. has (had)
19. having, have, had

Exercise 3–14

1. having
3. caring
5. studying
7. asked
9. tortured
11. growing or grown
13. getting
15. ripped
17. dried, pressed
19. reprimanded

Exercise 3–15

1. yelling
3. consist
5. dunked
7. fried or frying
9. leaning
11. searching
13. veered or veers
15. asked
17. renewed
19. combing
21. reached
23. figured
25. strolling

Exercise 3–16

1. lived
3. stalked
5. bored
7. cleaned, used, stroll
9. surprised
11. walked
13. notice, stopped
15. distressed
17. locked, obstructed
19. domesticated, consider
21. warmed, seemed
23. paralyzed
25. encircled, gathered
27. rushed, pleading
29. refuse
31. awakened
33. stepped
35. trust, risk
37. recognized, wanted, continue
39. waiting
41. fired
43. ignored, padded

Exercise 3–16 (cont.)

45. raised, aimed
47. crumpled
49. yawned, stretched
51. confused, excited, related

Exercise 3–17

1. used, wants
3. started, supposed
5. used
7. learned (or learns)
9. used, include
11. asked (or asks), considered.
13. jumped
15. insisted, closed

Exercise 3–18

1. met, built, dwelled
3. spoiled, dreamed (or dreamt)
5. spelled, called
7. spilled, burned
9. learned, knelt, wept
11. dispatched, sped
13. done
15. kept, spoiled
17. blended, presented
19. lost, snarled
21. cackled, left
23. left, stepped, pleaded (or pled)
25. ordered, survived
27. met, begged
29. pricked, dreamed (or dreamt)
31. dwelled, knelt, wept
33. built, left

Exercise 3–19

The following are suggested answers only. Finish the sentences any way you like just as long as you use the correct form of one of the verbs in the group being studied.

1. (bent the bars to escape.)
3. (bending over my machine.)
5. (spent your money wisely?)
7. (rent in two by the news.) *Rend* is an old-fashioned word which you won't have much use for.
9. (lend Maisie a dime.)

Exercise 3–20

1. set
3. shut, spread
5. shut, hurt, set
7. split, putting
9. cut, slitting
11. put, set (Definitely not *setting*)
13. set, put, cost
15. casting
17. spread
19. casting, put
21. hurt, cut
23. put, hurt
25. let
27. setting
29. spread
31. cut, set

Exercise 3–21

1. read
3. fed
5. speeding
7. fled or sped (speeded)
9. bleed, led
11. led
13. fed, led
15. read
17. bleeding
19. led, fed
21. led, lead
23. sped (speeded), read
25. bred
27. fed
29. breed

Answer: Exercises: 3-22 to 3-26

Exercise 3-22

1. say	21. sell	41. stand
3. said	23. foretelling	43. withstand or stand
5. say	25. selling	45. withstand
7. said	27. selling	47. stand
9. said	29. sell	49. misunderstood
11. hear	31. hold	51. binding
13. hearing	33. holding	53. wound
15. heard	35. held	55. found
17. heard	37. held	57. bound
19. heard or hears	39. held	59. ground

Exercise 3-23

This story will work best if told entirely in the past tense.

1. brought (Don't assume the confusion between *brought* and *bought* is a careless slip of the pen. These words are homonyms for some students who seem to favor *brought* and exclude *bought* altogether.)
3. caught
5. fought
7. caught
9. taught, catch, thought
11. buy
13. teach
15. fought, brought
17. buying, thought
19. thought, teach
21. thinks, brought, thought
23. thinks, buys
25. bought, sought
27. fought, taught, sought, catch, bought

Exercise 3-24

More than one verb may be possible in some sentences. Check for the correct verb form in the answers: long *o* sound in the past tense and *n* or *en* on the past participle.

1. frozen
3. awoken (arisen)
5. driven
7. spoken
9. broken
11. spoken
13. written
15. begotten
17. risen, broken
19. woven
21. worn
23. awoken (awakened)
25. driven, broken
27. worn
29. frozen

Exercise 3-25

1. Choose
3. choose, chooses
5. chosen
7. chosen
9. chose
11. chosen
13. chose or possibly chooses
15. Choose
17. chose or choose
19. choosing
21. choose, choose
23. chosen
25. chosen

Exercise 3-26

1. arisen, driven
3. forgotten
5. given
7. chosen
9. stole
11. written
13. spoken
15. shaken
17. spoken
19. fallen
21. gotten, eaten
23. given
25. stolen
27. spoken, forgotten, forgiven
29. taken, forbidden

Exercise 3-27

1. building
3. purchased, prejudiced
5. burned, finished
7. hurt
9. spread
11. miffed, invited
13. meant
15. sweeping, mopping, watching
17. eating (to eat)
19. got (or gotten)
21. unhurt
23. saturated
25. lifted, depressed
27. upset
29. puzzling, buying, destroyed

Exercise 3-28

1. fly
3. grown
5. blown
7. blown
9. grew or grows
11. flying
13. flown
15. grown
17. known
19. growing

Exercise 3-29

Student writing

Exercise 3-30

1. drank, sink
3. ringing
5. stank
7. drunk
9. drinking, singing
11. spring
13. sunk
15. stinks
17. drink (sink)
19. sinking
21. spring
23. stunk, stink
25. drunk
27. sprung
29. sank
31. drink
33. stink
35. drinking, singing

Exercise 3-31

1. fling
3. slung, swung
5. clung
7. strung, flung
9. wringing
11. spring, hanging (hung)
13. wrung
15. stringing
17. hanging, cling
19. hung
21. springing
23. wrung
25. fling
27. sprung
29. flung
31. string
33. wrung, swung
35. sprang
37. wringing
39. wringing, swung
41. wringing
43. wringing, flung
45. string, swing

Exercise 3-32

1. ate, made, ran
3. swam, sat
5. swam, ran
7. made, sitting, came, laid
9. eating
11. began, sat
13. begun, laid
15. Swimming, made
17. lying, making
19. begun, give, sat, saw
21. seen, eating, made, sitting
23. ran
25. laid, gave
27. saw, make
29. laid
31. sitting, lay, seen
33. came
35. began, lie
37. ate, come
39. beginning, make, ran
41. gave, made, see
43. came, giving, make

Answer: Exercises: 3–33 to 4–3

Exercise 3–33

1. came, come
3. came, overcome, run
5. overcome, come
7. coming, become
9. came, run
11. come
13. come, ran
15. became, becoming, became
17. became, become, become
19. come, ran
21. come, came
23. came, became, running
25. come, run
27. became, come, come, run, overrun
29. became, ran
31. become
33. come, become
35. overcome, come
37. come
39. come, run
41. became
43. came
45. came
47. came, come, run, came
49. came, run, become, overcome

Exercise 3–34

1. going, went
3. gone
5. gone
7. going, went
9. go
11. go, go
13. goes
15. went, gone
17. gone
19. gone
21. go, gone
23. Go
25. gone
27. going
29. go
31. go
33. went
35. go, goes
37. gone, went (or possibly goes)

Exercise 3–35

Student writing

Exercise 3–36

Student writing

CHAPTER 4

Exercise 4–1

1. He's finished.
3. It's worked.
5. She's passed.
7. They're successful.
9. They've eaten.
11. That's great.
13. Somebody's here.
15. It'll break.

Exercise 4–2

1. The blackboard should've been erased.
3. She might've won the race.
5. The leaders would've lied about their extra funds

Exercise 4–3

1. He doesn't care.
3. You and Bill aren't funny.
5. The players don't understand.

Exercise 4-4

1. Bill i̸s; Bill's
3. is no̸t; isn't
5. We a̸re; We're
7. Who i̸s; Who's
9. should ha̸ve; should've

Exercise 4-5

1. I want
3. we'll accept
5. Martha won't

Exercise 4-6

1. It's
3. its bell
5. it's
7. its major fault
9. its last chance
11. it's, its last printout
13. it
15. It's
17. It's
19. its radiator

Exercise 4-7

1. It's
3. It's
5. its wing
7. its best mileage
9. its image
11. its mother
13. It's
15. It's
17. It's
19. its owner

Exercise 4-8

Student writing

Exercise 4-9

1. Who's
3. Whose/essay
5. Who's
7. Whose/telephone
9. Who's
11. Who's
13. whose/picture
15. whose/trumpet
17. Who's
19. Whose/painting

Exercise 4-10

1. who's
3. Who's, who's
5. Who's
7. Whose/bike
9. who's
11. whose/health
13. Who's
15. Who's
17. Who's
19. Whose/idea

Exercise 4-11

Student writing

Exercise 4-12

1. their/chance
3. There
5. there
7. they're
9. there
11. there
13. Their/sins—their/virtues
15. They're
17. there, they're
19. there

Answer: Exercises: 4-13 to 4-19 329

Exercise 4-13

1. there
3. their/parties
5. they're
7. their/phone
9. their/problem
11. their/attention
13. their/records
15. there, they're
17. They're—their/owner
19. their/neighbor

Exercise 4-14

Student writing

Exercise 4-15

1. your/lies
3. you're, your/property
5. your/check
7. your/teacher
9. you're, your/position
11. you're, your/kids or you kids
13. your/rent
15. your/idea
17. you're, you
19. you're

Exercise 4-16

1. You're; your license
3. Whose car
5. There
7. Who's
9. your homework
11. It's; your opinion; they're
13. Whose car; their driveway
15. Whose rifle
17. There
19. Who's; who's
21. They're; whose yard
23. its nose; your rosebush
25. your boss; who's
27. Whose system; their needs
29. There; there
31. its landing gear
33. it's; their project
35. it's; they're
37. Their computer; its program
39. You're
41. Who's
43. They're
45. Their proposal; its merits
47. its bone; their living room
49. There

Exercise 4-17

1. Whose cat
3. your or their
5. their privacy
7. You're or They're
9. Whose responsibility
11. It's or you're or they're
13. your or their dishes
15. who's
17. your or their ticket
19. Who's
21. It's; your or their mother's
23. You're or They're
25. Your or Their
27. your or their house
29. Who's

Exercise 4-18

Student writing

Exercise 4-19

1. 4 mistakes: enters, says, There's, don't
3. 2 mistakes: doesn't, It's
5. 3 mistakes: begins, can't, aren't
7. 2 mistakes: your, weren't
9. 4 mistakes: enters, you're, your, its
11. 3 mistakes: their, Whose, There's
13. 1 mistake: What's
15. 2 mistakes: it's, might have
17. 2 mistakes: It's, That's (See note below.)
19. 3 mistakes: There, might have, I've
21. 1 mistake: it's
23. 3 mistakes: There, wasn't, He's
25. No mistakes

Exercise 4-19 (cont.)

(Note: Did you change *I bet* to *I'll bet*? I bet you didn't unless you were checking extremely carefully. This is an example of a contracted form which has almost completely disappeared in *standard* usage. If you omitted the correction, you were using exactly the same process as the student who reduces *Darryl will be mad if you don't come* to *Darryl be mad*. Anything which can be contracted is liable to be omitted by students operating in some nonstandard dialects.)

Exercise 4-20

Student writing.

CHAPTER 5

Exercise 5-1

Owner/Owned

1. Diana's/husband
3. children/cries
5. Myron/shirt; Marvin's/socks
7. ghost/hand; Julie's/throat
9. cat/tail

Exercise 5-2

Self-generating

Exercise 5-3

1. Mary's/eats/John's
3. knife's/cuts/table's
5. campers'/illuminate/forest's
7. fire's/ruins/Joneses'
9. neighbors'/chases/mother's
11. ministers'/inspire/church's
13. assassin's/kills/country's
15. surgeons'/block/hospital's

Exercise 5-4

1. Paul Revere's/warns/Boston's
3. player's/hits/spectator's
5. camels'/offends/tourists'
7. theater's/prefer/Rock Hudson's
9. Bill's/likes/restaurant's
11. pencil's/scratches/desk's
13. Sonia's/shake/coach's
15. Harold's/haunts/grandparents'

Exercise 5-5

1. gadgets
3. papers
5. needs
7. word
9. fixture
11. papers
13. life's
15. curtains
17. days
19. boss's
21. cat's
23. comet's
25. store's
27. ladies'
29. girls'

Exercise 5-6

1. aspirin's
3. book/books/books'
5. hairdryers/hairdryer's/hairdryers'
7. telephones/telephone's/telephones'
9. invaders/invader's/invaders'
11. garden/gardens/gardens'
13. glasses/glass's/glasses'
15. instructors/instructor's/instructors'
17. the Joneses/Jones's or Jones'/Joneses'
19. novel/novels/novels'
21. television/television's/televisions'
23. women/woman's/women's
25. thief/thieves/thieves'

Exercise 5-7

1. business's success
3. teapot's whistle
5. sister's arrival
7. tests' accuracy
9. fire's damage
11. car's brakes
13. London's appeal
15. women's facilities
17. community's needs
19. story's end
21. Mr. Moss's plans
23. secretary's letter
25. a day's delay; our customers' orders

Exercise 5-8

1. dog's temper
3. room's appearance
5. Mayor Daley's projects
7. Bill's bike
9. car's brakes
11. women's rights
13. war's casualties; old man's death
15. sister's wallet
17. children's demands
19. buried treasure's location
21. box's lid
23. his boss's threats
25. election results or election's results

Exercise 5-9

1. The response of the Mayor
3. The voices of women
5. The wishes of the students
7. The salaries of the teachers
9. The depth of his feelings
11. The mysteries of Asimov
13. The every wish of the queen
15. the stroller of the baby
17. The cough of the Buick
19. the Jack-in-the box of the baby
21. at the trophy of the winner.
23. The rays of the sun
25. the behavior of the police officers

Exercise 5-10

1. American Airlines has several women pilots. (no apostrophe)
3. John's sister walks in her sleep.
5. Chris's motorcycle is painted pink.
7. Gregg's dog can float on its back.
9. Linda's younger brother swears like a trooper.

Exercise 5-11

1. That house is theirs.
3. The opinion we need is the mayor's.
5. This lament is the secretaries'.
7. We have called for the committee's vote.
9. Our float is the largest in the parade.

Exercise 5-12

1. Poppel's/cats
3. ruler's
5. attempts
7. cries/cats
9. department's
11. efforts, cats'/theirs

Exercise 5-12 (cont.)

13. felines, ladies
15. thousands, windows
17. kitties
19. hers
21. woman or women
23. women/kitties'/rescuers/ladders
25. fire/cats'
27. women
29. cats
31. shouts
33. cat's
35. members/firefighters/ladders
37. It's/day's

Exercise 5-13

1. pos/proposal
3. contr
5. contr
7. contr
9. pos/smell
11. contra
13. contr
15. pos/shriek
17. contr
19. pos/jokes
21. pos/loan officer
23. contr
25. contr
27. contr
29. contr

Exercise 5-14

1. Somebody-pron
3. everyone-pron
5. anybody's-pos
7. someone-pron
9. No one's-pos
11. Everyone's-contr
13. Everyone's-pos
15. anyone-pron
17. no one-pron
19. anybody-pron
21. nobody's-pos
23. everybody-pron
25. Everyone's-contr

Exercise 5-15

Student writing

CHAPTER 6

Exercise 6-1

1. it
3. my lunch
5. him (object of preposition *for*)
7. her books
9. They
11. who
13. Whose car
15. my sister

Exercise 6-2

1. her (object of preposition *between*)
3. me (object of preposition *for*)
5. we (subject)
7. her (object of preposition *to*)
9. she (subject)
11. neither *he* nor *him* Avoid double subjects; the sentence should read "My science teacher spilled hydrochloric acid on my notes."
13. They, I (subjects)
15. We (subject)
17. either *they* or *them* is acceptable here. *They* is required because it is the subject of the clause *they will see the report*; *them* is required because it is the object of the preposition *except*. Choose whichever sounds better to you.
19. Who (subject)

Answer: Exercises: 6–3 to 6–7

Exercise 6–3

Last summer, my sisters and *I* decided to earn a little extra money, so went to work on a tobacco farm in Connecticut. For three weeks Cheryl and *I* did nothing but walk up and down the fields tieing up small plants. *Nancy managed* to get assigned to kitchen duty. She was lucky because the field boss treated *us* field hands like a chain gang. He yelled at Cheryl and me at least once an hour. *Nancy and I* were worried that Cheryl would do something violent to the valuable leaves or him before it was over.

On July 1, they moved the other field workers and us to the sheds to sew the leaves up for curing. Nancy and I were sewers, and *Cheryl was* our leafer. *Whoever* could put the most leaves on wooden lathes could make the most money. It was up to Cheryl to see that Nancy and *I* always had leaves at our machine. We girls used to race to make the time go faster, but the shed *boss was* worse than the field boss. If she saw a damaged leaf, she turned off the machines and yelled, "*Who* is responsible for this?"

Cheryl and *I* sometimes hid broken leaves inside our jackets so she wouldn't see them.

At the end of August, they asked Nancy if she would come back next year as a shed boss. They asked Cheryl and me if we would please look for jobs on a ranch in Arizona next summer.

Exercise 6–4

1. Who (subject)
3. her (object of preposition *to*)
5. me
7. he
9. who (subject of *started*); them (object of preposition *about*)
11. whom (object of *did appoint*), but *who* is perfectly acceptable
13. me (if you mean ". . . more than she favored me.") I (if you mean "Mother always favored my sister more than I favored her.")
15. they (subject), her (object of preposition *for*)
17. Who (subject of *knows*), him (object of preposition *besides*)
19. she or her (Following a form of *be*, *she* is the traditional answer, but *her* is perfectly acceptable in contemporary speech and writing.)

Exercise 6–5

1. *They* lost *their* home . . .
3. themselves
5. you/your receipts
7. his
9. its bone
11. Whose softballs/their windows
13. I'm/your stories
15. they/their reports
17. those decisions/ourselves
19. their cousins

Exercise 6–6

Snobs are people who think more highly of themselves than anyone else, so much so that they don't even bother with people who don't measure up to their standards. . . .

First-class phonies are people who can tell absolute lies while keeping straight faces. . . . Why do phonies have to try to impress people with things that they aren't?

Exercise 6–7

1. As it appears on page 195 or your senses; you are lucky; you might catch; you step out
3. to me—or getting snowed in on vacation
5. many of the girls—because they want
7. anyone who wants—two things: eat less and exercise more. If you want to lose weight, you must do two things: you must eat less and you must exercise more.
9. If you are a musician in a successful band you make a lot of money, but you get sick of spending half your life in a hotel room.
   Musicians in successful bands make a lot of money, but they get sick of spending half their lives in hotel rooms.
11. every wage earner—the W-2 form—the tax return
    wage earners—their W-2 forms—their tax returns
13. taxpayers—their effort
15. people—them—their job performance
    person—What is the motivation?—How is job performance affected?
17. unpublished authors—their books, commercial publishers—they can
19. I proofread my papers—I'd see—in my grades

Exercise 6-8

The ability to take good notes is essential to *students* who are bombarded with new information every day. *Their* success in school may well depend on how efficiently *they* can organize and learn what they read in *their* textbooks and what *they* hear in lectures. *Students who let* information wash over *them* without capturing the important details in the form of careful notes will not remember what *they* have heard or read, and when it comes time to write up reports on the material or take exams over it, *they* have a real problem.

Some students fill notebooks full of meaningless or unrelated bits of information that are worse than useless when *they* they try to review them. They find that *they* waste more time trying to make make sense out of cryptic messages than *they do* studying the material: "1874 IMPORTANT DATE!!! Harvard." They could not possibly tell from this note why 1874 was important to Harvard or anyone else.

If notes are to do any good, they must be complete enough. "1874, Harvard started entrance exam in composition" gives the notetaker some reason to remember the date. On the other hand, if the instructor reads Harvard's announcement of its upcoming entrance exams to the class, it will probably not be possible to get it all down:

Each candidate will be required to write a short English composition, correct in spelling, punctuation, grammar, and expression, the subject to be taken from such works of standard authors as shall be announced from time to time. The subject for 1874 will be taken from one of the following works: Shakespeare's *Tempest, Julius Caesar,* and *Merchant of Venice;* Goldsmith's *Vicar of Wakefield;* Scott's *Ivanhoe,* and *Lay of the Last Minstrel.*

Students who try to get it all down will still be writing "as shall be announced from time to time," while their instructor is summarizing the importance of the announcement.

The most important thing *for students* to remember about good note taking is to use a standard form and to put the notes in *their* own words. *They* should leave room in the left-hand margin to ask *themselves* questions when *they* review *them* (the notes) after class.

Why important to modern composition courses?	1874 Harvard entrance exam —defined comp as prerequisite skill —required correctness in spelling, grammar, punctuation, expression —subjects from literature

Students who use this form can review quickly and easily the night before an exam. *They* will have a record that they can refer to and still make sense of years later, and they will be able to write clear, logical reports almost directly from *their* notes. *Those who follow these suggestions* will be better students because of it.

Exercise 6-9

1. ... the knob came off in his hand.
3. The Honor System is used to ignore cheating on exams. (Note: this is a truncated sentence, a sentence in which the subject is omitted to avoid assigning responsibility. The second revision does assign responsibility: At this school the administration uses the Honor System so teachers can ignore cheating on exams.
5. Beth, who was more popular than her co-star in the senior play, tried not to acknowledge it.
   Beth was more popular than her co-star in the senior play, although her co-star tried not to acknowledge it.
7. Someday you may need to know how to change a tire. Getting the flat usually happens when you have a limited amount of time to get where you are going.
   The problem here is that *it* does not refer back to *changing a tire,* the subject of the first sentence, but to *getting a flat.*
9. A Jesuit priest wrote the difficult-to-understand book.
   It is difficult to understand why (or how) a Jesuit priest wrote such a book.
11. Some people live out their lives believing in superstitions. They control practically everything that happens to these people, and sometimes they can prove to be fatal.
13. The fact that Steven turned in all of his workbook exercises on time except the last one surprised his teacher.
15. Mastering his shyness had a great effect on James's career as an actor.

Answer: Exercises: 6–10 to 7–6   335

Exercise 6–10

Student writing

CHAPTER 7

Exercise 7–1

1. s/he   The judge <u>reached a decision</u>. Type #2
3. it   The puppy <u>wagged its tail</u>. Type #2
5. he   Jack <u>could tell Roberta the truth</u>. Type #3
7. they   Several cottages <u>were demolished</u>. Type #1
9. she   Ms. Bailey <u>gave her old furniture to Cathy</u>. Type #3

Exercise 7–2

1. Caroline ... circus. She ... job.
3. Her ... party. They ... best.
5. Everyone ... lot. Caroline ... too.
7. Caroline ... table. She ... chandelier. She ... arm.
9. Caroline ... arm. The ... expectantly. He ... martini.
11. Caroline ... nauseous. She ... pitifully.
13. They ... hatchets. A ... shoulder.
15. Helen ... outfit. It ... traction.
17. Caroline's ... her. He ... daily.
19. Neither ... marry. They ... after.

Exercise 7–3

1. The restaurant served steak and chicken.
3. Carol, Mona, and Frannie are watching TV.
5. I shot the sheriff, but I did not shoot the deputy.
7. The news article included distortions of the truth, exaggerations, and outright lies.
9. Collette and her husband shopped carefully, but their combined salaries would not stretch to the end of the month.

Exercise 7–4

NP means no punctuation is needed.
1. NP
3. day, and
5. NP
7. whining, scratching at the kitchen cupboard, and
9. NP
11. NP
13. door. The noise
15. silence, then
17. NP
19. wagon, an ambulance, and
21. NP
23. advertised, that ... greedily, and
25. Horner, the neighbors, the milkman, and ... animal, but
27. NP
29. mistress. The ... gratitude, ... stove, and

Exercise 7–5

The following are suggested answers only.
1. smell of: skunks, polecats, and dogs.
3. punctuate: finding subjects and verbs, identifying independent clauses, and avoiding fragments.
5. failure: sabotage by his enemies.
7. admire: Margaret Thatcher, Mother Teresa of India, and Margaret Mead.
9. Earth: a volume of Shakespeare's sonnets, six gray cats, and a case of Champagne.
11. She owes her success to two things: hard work and careful planning.

Exercise 7–6

The following are suggested answers only. Make sure you have an independent clause on either side of the semicolon.

Exercise 7-6 (cont.)

1. Alice; Alice loved Rodney.
3. time; the babysitter raised his rates.
5. check-up; I took a lot of taxis.
7. deaths; a brave person dies but once.
9. The conductor turned toward the audience; the . . . .

Exercise 7-7

1. NP
3. nature, but
5. NP
7. night, for
9. time, yet
11. NP
13. NP
15. NP
17. somewhat, but
19. Harold, but
21. ill, but
23. failure, so
25. Mexico, got . . . waiter, divorced Rochelle, and
27. woman, but

Exercise 7-8

1. flop; consequently, we left early.
3. therefore, Ken shouted back.
5. therefore, he walked.
7. lying; however, she couldn't prove it.
9. Torrential rain turned the outfield into a swamp; consequently, the
11. problem; furthermore, federal funding was discontinued.
13. The radio warned that a blizzard was coming; nevertheless,
15. The shed was damp and unheated; however, the

Exercise 7-9

1. New York, Chicago and Los Angeles; consequently, citizens
3. pigeons; an
5. frozen; therefore, the
7. work; consequently, a
9. Feds; however, the
11. outcries; consequently, three
13. job; however, the . . . "pigs," so
15. them; therefore, the
17. NP
19. baby, and . . . to; furthermore, they
21. born; consequently, one
23. ambulance, so
25. recovered; however, the

Exercise 7-10

1. mother, it seems, had
3. Consequently, she
5. Furthermore, they . . . roses. This, I believe, was
7. not, it seems, as
9. mother, therefore, resorted . . . spade. This tactic, by the way, was
11. Nevertheless, he . . . support. For example, he
13. seemed, on the whole, quite
15. mother, not the spiders, who
17. later, having moved from the house with the spider covered rose garden, my . . . exercise, but . . . spiders, and not the exercise, she

Exercise 7-11

1. Throwing a temper tantrum, Stanley refuses to accept second prize in the bathing suit competition.
3. Wheezing loudly, the professor runs upstairs to get to class on time.
5. To save Robin Hood Maid Marian tricks the Sheriff of Nottingham by dressing in Robin Hood's green suit and by carrying a bow and arrow.
7. The nearby chemical plant's draining its waste into the water causes the fish to leave the cove.

Exercise 7–11 (cont.)

9. Summarizing his remarks, the speaker extends his arms toward the audience and lowers his voice, pleading with them to take action.

Exercise 7–12

1. F
3. S
5. F
7. S
9. S (that the rent would be raised)

Exercise 7–13

1. The sergeant knew that his troops were ready for the inspection.
3. Whoever wants the puppy can have it.
5. Whether Valley High can win the tournament or not depends on Friday night's game.
7. What Carla needs is not always what Carla gets
9. How the President handles the present crisis will determine how well he does in the next election.

Exercise 7–14

1. F/just as
3. F/because
5. F/even before
7. S
9. F/while, before*
11. F/so that
13. S
15. S
17. F/after, before
19. F/when

*Note: Fragments are not a question of length. In these two sentences two subordinate clauses are strung together.

Exercise 7–15

1. Unless the director of the agency gets a raise, she will resign.
3. After the fire trucks arrived on the scene, the blaze was quickly put out.
5. Before Thanksgiving comes, Jesse goes Christmas shopping so that he can avoid the crowds.
7. Even when the day of the party came, Jolinda had not found a babysitter.
9. Since all the winter merchandise was on sale, the store was crowded.
11. Even though the phone rang fourteen times, J.R. did not answer it because he was in the shower.
13. Since there were more votes than there were registered voters, the defeated candidate demanded a recount even though the Commissioner of Elections was sure to be offended.
15. When Carmine continued writing checks even though his checking account was overdrawn, the bank manager called him.

Exercise 7–16

1. Galaxy. Although . . . world, she
3. session. Marlan
5. systems. Many
7. Betelgeuse, whenever . . . oxygen, became nauseous. If . . . gas, they
9. mammal. In . . . Rigel, her mother
11. years. Even . . . gone, their
13. simultaneously. One . . . land, and (*had appeared* and *had evolved* are compound verbs)
15. stasis. After . . . Galaxies, the
17. Marlan. Since . . . power, the
19. concisely. Even . . . feathers, she
21. mammals, although . . . thumb, and
23. NP
25. modification. Because . . . thumb, they
27. NP
29. harsh. Since . . . caves, they
31. years. Unless . . . war, it
33. evolution, although . . . world. For

Exercise 7–17

1. (who came to dinner)
3. (That) (which had fallen under the bed)
5. (boats which entered the Bermuda triangle)

Exercise 7-17 (cont.)

7. (fathers)
9. (movies)

Exercise 7-18

1. F	**9.** S	**15.** F
3. S	**11.** F	**17.** S
5. S	**13.** F	**19.** S
7. F		

Exercise 7-19

1. The teacher sent John, who had sprained his ankle, to the clinic.
3. Guests who stay past midnight are treated rudely.
5. The house Jack built was replaced by an urban renewal project.
7. It is surely no accident that standardization of the spelling system began only after printing had established itself in England.
9. Checks, which are personal bills of any denominations, are safer than cash, which passes unquestioned from hand to hand.

Exercise 7-20

1. Our belief that the shoemaker is honest gives way to a contrary belief that the shoemaker is a thief.
3. Christopher Reeve made a movie called *Superman: The Movie* which made him an overnight success.
5. Euphemism, which comes from a Greek word meaning "to use words of good omen," is the substitution of pleasant term for an offensive one.
7. Everyone should learn to recognize poison ivy, a wild-growing, three-leaf plant which causes an itchy skin rash at the slightest touch.
9. Somnambulism, or sleepwalking, stems from some unresolved conflict in the mind which continues to stimulate a person even during sleep.
11. When the goals people seek conform to the lower values, there is usually conflict because the objects valued—money, status, power—are necessarily in short supply.
(Elizabeth Drews)
13. The students know that the purpose of all discussion is to solve problems, not to find fault or to punish.
(William Glasser)
15. In scene one, which coincides with stanza one, a man—a New England man—is driving his sleigh somewhere at night.
(John Ciardi)
17. This is the title of a long poem, very popular in classical days, by the third-century poet Apollonius of Rhodes.
(Edith Hamilton)
19. Denied, encysted failure can turn malignant, and spread, corrupting, destroying.
(Jo Coudert)
21. When at length you have shown the truth of your case and the falsity of your opponent's, it is in the nature of things that you would commend yourself, censure you opponent, and drive the difference home.
(Aristotle)
23. What we have to surmise is how Whately, following and summing up the whole subject, can proceed as he did.
(I. A. Richards)
25. Campbell's Philosophy of Rhetoric, first published in 1776 during a period of renewed interest in oratory, was founded on the "Common Sense" school of his Scotch colleagues, Reid and Beattie, whose faculty psychology provided the base for the "mental and moral science" serving orthodoxy. (Virginia Burke)

Exercise 7-21

1. Cinderella, her three stepsisters,
3. hearth, . . . dishes,
5. daughters, . . . Cinderella,
7. arrogant, impudent, and rude; . . . sly, dishonest, and evil; . . . loud, angry,

Answer: Exercises: 7–21 to A–3   339

Exercise 7–21 (cont.)
9. parlor,
11. N.P.
13. laughed, but . . . amused; she or laughed, but . . . amused. She
15. pumpkin, . . . mice, . . . wand, . . . everyone, . . . words,   midnight,
17. invitations, . . . ball; . . . angry,
19. midnight, . . . mean, wicked,

Exercise 7–22

Introduction: hospital. His . . . question "What brings us to the hospital today?" Ed did, and

1. "What . . . today?" Ed
3. bed. "What . . . today?"
5. said, "I . . . understand."
7. "I'll . . . this," Ed
9. "You've . . . there," Ed
11. nonplussed. He . . . him. "That . . . bed, ". . . explained. "She's . . . patient. She . . . mother."
13. "It's . . . woman," Ed
15. "Get . . . admissions," said
17. "I . . . here," bellowed . . . bed, "but . . . attack."
19. "What . . . mean 'fatuous'?" asked
21. answered, "I . . . ridiculous, but . . . fatuous."
23. mouth, the
25. said, "Rules . . . rules."
27. "What . . . today?"
29. poise, he
31. "I see," said Ed. "Where's Floyd?"
33. said, "I . . . there."
35. "You . . . easy," said
37. "I'm . . . circus," answered
39. "I . . . crazy," said Ed. "You'd . . . business. Everyone's crazy: the doctors, the nurses, the patients."
41. "Okay," said Ed, "but . . . drink."
43. "Dad, I'm . . . school," said Ed. "Everyone . . . crazy."
45. NP

Exercise 7–23

1. "The . . . instruction," Professor Gray indicated, "really . . . century."
3. grammar, which
5. continued, "After . . . paragraph, he . . . from, to use his exact words, 'original principles.' "
7. "Although . . . Discourse, "the . . . added, "he . . . popularity."
9. "There . . . period," the . . . noted. "However, their . . . did."

APPENDIX A

Exercise A–1

1. #1	11. #6	21. #5
3. #3	13. #5	23. #3
5. #6	15. #1	25. #6
7. #2	17. #3	27. #5
9. #2	19. #6	29. #2

Exercise A–2

Typical answers might be:
1. He *is going* home.
3. He *might have been going* home.

Exercise A–3

(pronoun substitute) subject/verb #sentence type

1. (s/he) judge/reached #2
3. (it) puppy/wagged #2

Exercise A-3 (cont.)

5. (he) Jack/should tell #3
7. (they) cottages/were demolished #1
9. (she) Mrs. Bailey/gave #3 (*to Goodwill* is the indirect object)

Exercise A-4

1. (they) chickens and geese/were sold #1
3. (they) Linda and her sister/tried out #1
5. (they) pizza, potato chips, and chocolate cake/destroyed and ruined #2
7. (they) gorillas and giraffes/slept #1
9. (you all) You and Mr. Royal/must pay #2
   (it) management/will threaten and harrass #2

Exercise A-5

1. The restaurant served steak and chicken. #2
3. Carol, Mona, and Frannie are watching TV. #2
5. I shot the sheriff, but I did not shoot the deputy. #2, #2
   OR: I shot the sheriff, but not the deputy. #2

Exercise A-6

1. (they) aides/met #1 senators'—possessive; for lunch—adverbial
3. (s/he) assistant/earns #2 DO—dollars; laboratory—noun adjunct; eight hundred—noun adjunct; *a month*, adverb.
5. (they) members/ended up [verb + participle] #1 in jail—p.p. used as adverb; Many—qualifier [one of the determiners]; of the old gang—p.p. used as adjective modifying *members*
7. (s/he) assistant/walked #1; faculty—noun adjunct; into the office—p.p. used as adverb; slowly—adverb
9. (it) card/is hidden #1; your—possessive pronoun, son's—possessive; report—noun adjunct; under the bed—p.p. used as adverb
11. (they) police/searched #1; throughout the city—p.p. used as adverb; frantically—adverb.
13. (it) one/is broken #1; of the dishes—p.p. used as adjective modifying *one*
15. (it) distance/can be measured #1; to the carpet's (possessive) edge—p.p. used as adjective; with a meter (noun adjunct) stick—p.p. used as adverb telling *how*
17. (they) jewels/were buried #1; queen's—possessive; beneath the tree—p.p. used as adverb
19. (it) traffic/comes #1; On Sundays—p.p. used as adverb; on the exit—p.p. used as adjective modifying *traffic*; to the racetrack—p.p. used as adjective modifying *exit*; to a standstill—p.p. used as adverb

Exercise A-7

See chart on pp. 262-63.

Exercise A-8

(suggested answers)

1. really—#2
3. objectively #1
5. home—#1
7. annually—#2
9. slightly—#7

Exercise A-9

1. (s/he) plumber/dropped; adverbs: then #2
3. (she) sister/had come; adverbs; home, late #1
5. she/did request; adverbs: rarely #2
7. (he) Bill/will find; adverbs: somewhere #2
9. (it) money/can cause; adverb: too #2
11. I/saw; adverbs: there, occasionally #2
13. (s/he) contestant/will finish; adverbs: probably, today #1

Exercise A-9 (cont.)

15. (he) Gerald/was; adverbs: a month ago, oddly #7
    he/is; adverbs: now, almost #7

Exercise A-10

1. (it) phone/will ring; *in a minute*—adv #1
3. (they) Dambergs/drove; *to California*—adv #1
5. (they) children/weave; *In Iran*—adv, *from camel's hair*—adv #2
7. (he) cowboy/galloped; *into the intersection*—adv, *on his black horse*—adv #1
9. (he) Bill/went; *to the store*—adv, *for his sister*—adv #1
11. (s/he) Carmen/walked; *toward the deserted parking lot*—adv #1
13. we/go; *over the river*—adv, *through the woods*—adv, *to grandmother's house*—adv #1
15. (he) brother/laughed; *during the performance*—adv modifies *times*, *out loud*—adv #1
17. (they) expressways/are jammed; *on Monday mornings*—adv, *into the city*—adj, *with cars*—adv, *on their way*—adj, *to work*—adj #1
19. (they) polls/will open; *in Chicago*—adj, *at 6 a.m.*—adv #1

Exercise A-11

Student generated

Exercise A-12

Student writing

Exercise A-13

1. (it) cooking/requires #2
3. (it) rain/flattened #2
5. (it) kissing/spreads #2
7. (it) test/was cancelled #1
9. (they) birds/hate #2

Exercise A-14

1. (it) preparing dinner/takes #1
3. (he) Dwight/is responding, listening #1
5. (she) Cindy/detests #2
7. (she) candidate/was named #2
9. (he) Jack/dislikes #2

Exercise A-15

1. (he) Philip/wants #2
3. she/plans #2
5. (it) to complain/causes #2
7. they/refuse #2
9. (it) going to the store/requires #2

Exercise A-16

1. (s/he) manager/agreed #2
3. (she) Ms. Bibson/refuses #2
5. (he) Jack/hopes #2
7. (it) to lose a game/disappoints #2
9. (he) Ron/tires #2

Exercise A-17

1. (he) Leonard/charged and leapt #1
3. (he) parent/called #2
5. (he) grandfather/wanted #2

Exercise A-17 (cont.)

7. (they) to attend school and to get an education/may be #6
9. (he) Ronald/wants #2

Exercise A-18

1. (he) disc jockey/forgot #2
3. (they) latecomers/missed #2
5. (she) Susan/forgets #2
7. (s/he) parent/left #2
9. (she) Martha/has omitted #2
11. (he) father/watches #2
13. (they) preparing big meals and being nice to thirty in-laws/ruined #2
15. (he) patient/hit #2
17. (he) Kenneth/loves #2
19. (he) Marvin/can stand #2

Exercise A-19

Student generated

Exercise A-20

1. (they) questions/will be handled; *that require an immediate answer*; no punctuation or NP
3. (they) songs/make; *that cannot be sung*; NP
5. (it) Chez Charles/is looking for; *who can sing, dance, and tell jokes:* NP
7. (they) Buicks/should be scrapped; *that make a lot of noise, who don't want to get arrested*; NP
9. (they) cowboys/are; *,who are generally considered bold,*
11. (it) house/was replaced; *that Jack built*; NP
13. (she) Cinderella/had; *, who had three wicked stepsisters,*
15. (s/he) cousin/is; *who drives a Model T*; no punctuation to distinguish this cousin from other cousins
17. (they) students/will have; *who can type*; NP
19. (they) difficulties/stopped; *we encountered*; NP

Exercise A-21

1. he/took; *whatever he could get* #2
3. (it) feeling/was; *that he didn't understand the question* #6
5. (s/he) who/is #7
7. (it) *whatever you say*/can and will be held #1
9. (she) aunt/predicted; *Harry would come to no good* #2
11. (it) *that such a thing could happen to Marlene*/was #7
13. I/know; *who wants the puppy* #2
15. (it) *why he confessed*/is known #1
17. (she) wife/thought; *he was lying to get some attention* #2
19. (s/he) anyone/is; *who can put up with Ronald* #6

Exercise A-22

1. (they) people/do; ALTHOUGH; ghosts, many
3. I/did take; BEFORE; one, I
5. I/was surprised; SINCE; building, I
7. I/could handle; IF; burglar, I . . . him, I
9. (it) night/was
11. I/did find; EVEN THOUGH; chain, I
13. I crept, fastened, and closed; SINCE; moved, I
15. I/secured and locked; BEFORE; night, I
17. (it) this/did seem; BECAUSE; spooked, this
19. I/was amazed and turned; WHEN: soon, I
21. I/found; EVEN THOUGH; optional comma after *nothing*
23. (it) sound/filled; AS; chain, the
25. (it) water/stopped; AS SUDDENLY AS
27. I/raced; AS IF; again, I
29. I/took; AFTER; apartment, I
31. I/wrapped and stalked; there, I
33. I/told; AS; NP
35. I/would have eaten; IF; follow, I
37. I/decided; evening, I
39. I/thought; UNTIL; NP
41. I/edged and turned; again, I
43. (it) ghost/was getting; EVEN THOUGH: NP
45. (it) pizza/was; WHEN: kitchen, the
47. I/could afford; IF; up, I
49. they/arrived, heard, searched, and left; ALTHOUGH; optional comma between *left* and *although*
51. I/went; ALTHOUGH; bang, the

Exercise A-23

1. (s/he) killer is
3. (he) Ralph/lacked
5. (it) demonstration/did upset
7. you is understood/get
9. (s/he) someone/is
11. (s/he) messenger/entered
13. (s/he) secretary/discovered
15. (it) call/did wake
17. (it) dictionary/contains
19. (they) changes/will be
21. (they) shoes/hurt
23. (s/he) Martian/charmed
25. (he) Lochinvar/did make

APPENDIX B

Exercise B-1

churches, clutches, slashes, brushes, kisses, misses, whizzes, boxes, fishes, matches, benches, geniuses, foxes, hoaxes

Exercise B-2

neighborly/neighborliness;
army/armies
lady/ladies
library/libraries
sky/skies

duty/dutiful
mercy/merciful
bounty/bountiful
bury/burying
hurry/hurrying

Exercise B-3

Student writing

Exercise B-4

clan/clannish
control/controlled
get/getting
grab/grabbing
plan/planned

run/running
wit/witty
rebel/rebelled
sad/saddening
wed/wedding

Exercise B-5

argue/arguing
desire/desirable
dine/dining
guide/guidance
love/loving

plume/plumage
purple/purplish
true/truer
type/typing
mistake/mistakable

Exercise B-6

After letters other than c

achieve	brief	friend	relieve
apiece	chief	grief	shield
belief	field	niece	siege
believe	fierce	perceive	yield

After c

| ceiling | conceive | | perceive |
| conceited | deceive | | receive |

After the a sound

| freight | neighbor | rein | veil |
| heinous | reign | their | weigh |

Exercise B-7

Student writing

Exercise B-8

1. effect
3. sense
5. pass
7. passed, sense
9. buy, Sale
11. break, brakes
13. thing
15. than
17. no, know
19. sided
21. whether, along

Exercise B-9

1. lost
3. must
5. past
7. intend
9. much
11. thinks, tapped
13. bother
15. ever
17. went
19. from
21. a way
23. altogether
25. conscience

INDEX

a, an, 9
Absolute possessive, 188
Abstract noun, 12
accept,except, confusion between, 306
Adjective (*See also* Noun determiner.)
   articles, 268
   cardinals, 268
   comparative form of, 268–69
   confusion with noun, 12
   defined, 268
   demonstratives, 268
   descriptive (*See* Noun adjunct.)
   possessive, 268, 269
   position of, 268
   qualifiers, 268
Adjective clauses
   as they affect agreement of subject and verb, 48–49
   defined, 48, 239, 286–87
   position of, 48, 287
   punctuation of, 239–40, 287–88
   restrictive and nonrestrictive, 241–43, 287–88
Adverb
   conjunctive, 220
   defined, 73, 272
   inverted sentences with *there,* 38–39
   list of, 272
   not contracted, 36, 140
   position of, 73, 272
Adverbial clauses
   defined, 231–32, 286, 290–91
   punctuation of (*See* Punctuation patterns #6 and #7.)
affect,effect, confusion between, 306
Agreement of pronoun and antecedent, 190–93
Agreement of subject and verb, 26–56
   not a visual decision, 32
   with compound subject, 42–43
   within relative clause, 49
   when adjective clause intervenes, 48–49
   when prepositional phrase intervenes, 44–45
   when sentence is inverted, 38–39
   when subject is an indefinite pronoun, 47
   when subject is a personal pronoun, 29–30
   when verb is contracted with *not,* 36, 41–42
   (*See also* Substituting a pronoun for the subject; Pronunciation as it affects agreement of subject and verb.)
alone,along, confusion between, 306
already,all ready, confusion between, 306
although, all though, confusion between, 306
Ambiguous reference of pronouns, 197–200
an, a, 9

an,and,in, confusion among, 307
Analogizing verb forms, 128
Antecedent
   agreement with pronoun, 190–93
   defined, 179
   unclear reference, 197–200
Apostrophe
   in contractions, 138–40
   misuse of, 141–52, 174, 188–89
   to form plural of letters and numbers, 20
   to form possessives, 157–59
Appositive
   defined, 245
   punctuation of, 245–47
   (*See also* Punctuation pattern #5.)
Article adjectives, 268
   (*See also* Noun Determiner.)
Auxiliary verb, 71–90, 208–9, 265
   chart and explanation, 71–73
   be, 81–85
   do, 75–76
   followed by past participle, 84
   followed by present participle, 84
   get, 110–11
   have, 79–80
   longest verb phrase, 86
   present auxiliaries, 72, 80
   past participle *been,* 83
   in questions, 71
away,a way, confusion between, 307

bother,brother, confusion between, 307
bought,brought, confusion between, 307
Brackets
brake,break, confusion between, 307
buy,by, confusion between, 307

Cardinals, 268
Case, 179
cited,sided,sighted, confusion among, 309
Clauses
   adjective, 48–49, 228, 239, 286
   adverbial, 228, 231–32, 286, 290–91
   defined, 227, 286
   dependent, 228, 286
   independent, 208, 219, 227, 286
   noun, 228, 286, 289
   relative, 48–49, 286
   subordinate, 228, 286–93
clothes,cloths,close, confusion among, 307
Colon
   before summary 216–17
   misuse of, 216–17

345

Colon, *continued*
  (*See also* Punctuation pattern #8.)
Comma
  after conjunctive adverb (*See* Punctuation pattern #3.)
  after introductory clauses and phrases (*See* Punctuation patterns #5 and #6.)
  history of, 206
  misuse of, 206
  position with quotations, 253
  to prevent misreading, 257
  to separate items in a series (*See* Punctuation patterns #1 #4 and #8.)
  to set off nonrestrictive (nonessential) elements, 225–26, 233–34, 241–42, 245–47
  (*See also* Punctuation patterns #1, #4, #5, #6, #7, #8, and #9; Conjunctions; Comma splice; Essential clause; Nonessential clause; Fragment; Items in a series.)
Comma splice, 211
  (*See also* Run-on sentence.)
Complement
  object, 7, 210, 263
  subject, 6, 110–11, 183–84, 210, 263, 289
Compound noun, 269
Conjunction
  coordinating, 213
  subordinating, 231, 290
  (*See also* Punctuation patterns #4, #6, #7, and #8.)
Conjunctive adverb, 220
conscience,conscious, confusion between, 307
Contraction, 136–53
  how to form, 138–40
  confused with homonyms:
    have and *of* or *a,* 139
    possessive pronoun homonyms, 142–52
    want and *won't, let's* and *less, we'll* and *will, he's* and *his,* 141
  contraction of *not,* 36, 41–42, 140
Coordinating conjunctions
  list of, 213, 267
  to join items in a series, 213, 267
  to join independent clauses, 213, 267
  (*See also* Punctuation patterns #1, #4, and #8.)
could of, could a, 139

Dangling modifier, 225–26
Dash, 247
data, 20
Demonstrative, 268
Dialect, 4, 35, 81, 116
Direct objects, 7, 210, 262
  objects of verbals, 280–82
Direct quotations, 253–54
  (*See also* Punctuation pattern #9.)
does,dose, confusion between, 307

don't,doesn't, 41
Double subject, 182

effect,affect, confusion between, 306
Essential clauses, 233–34, 241–43, 287–88
ever,every, confusion between, 307–8
except,accept, confusion between, 306

fine,find, confusion between, 308
form,from, confusion between, 308
Fragment
  defined, 228, 232
  from adjective clause, 240–41
  from adverbial clause, 232
  from noun clause 228–29
  from verbal phrase, 225–26
Function words, 178
Future time, 71

Gender, 179
"Generic" use of *he,* 192–93
  (*See also* Sexism.)
Gerund
  defined, 279–80
  with object, 280–81
Get,got as pseudo-auxiliaries, 110–11
Glossary of Common Homonyms, 306–10

he's,his, 141
Helping verbs (*See* Auxiliary verb.)
hole,whole, confusion between, 308
Homonym
  contraction/possessive pronoun pairs, 142–52, 188–89
  defined, 304
  (*See also* Glossary of Common Homonyms.)
however as conjunctive adverb, 220
  (*See also* Punctuation pattern #3.)
Hypercorrection, 12, 181

idea,ideal, confusion between, 308
Imperative sentence (*See* Understood subject.)
in,an,and, confusion among, 307
Indefinite pronoun
  agreement with antecedent, 190–93
  agreement with verb, 47
  forming the possessive of, 172, 179
Independent clause
  defined, 206, 209, 227
  (*See also* Punctuation patterns #1–#9.)
Index of irregular verbs, 64–65, 129–33
Indirect objects, 7, 210, 262
Indirect questions, 253
  (*See also* Punctuation pattern #9.)
Indirect quotation
  defined, 253
  (*See also* Punctuation pattern #9.)

Index

Infinitives
   defined, 279, 281
   introductory, punctuation of, 225–26
   unmarked, 283–84
   with objects, 282
intend,intent, confusion between, 308
Interrupting expressions (*See* Parenthetical expressions.)
Introductory verbal phrase, 225–226
Invariant *be* (*See* Periodic or habitual action.)
Inverted sentence
   there is/there are, 38–39, 294–95
   three exceptions to regular order, 294–95
Irregular noun plurals, 18–20
Irregular or troublesome verb groups, 90–133
   alight/ask, regular verbs often analogized to irregular forms, 128
   arise/awake, internal vowel change plus *en,* 105
   be, present forms, 33, 35, past forms, 34, 81
   befall/draw, internal vowel change plus *n,* 107–8
   begin/run, past tense *a,* 119
   bid (in cards)/*burst,* no change, 96
   big (farewell), 107–8
   bleed/breed, regular with internal vowel change in spoken and written forms, 98–99
   blend/build, regular *d* or *t* endings, 91–92, 95
   blow/throw, past tense *ew* with *n* past participle, 112
   bring/buy, internal vowel change with difficult spelling, 103
   cling/fling, internal vowel change, 115–16
   come/run, high frequency word, 122
   dig/win, u sound in past and past participle, 127
   do, 40–41, 75–76
   dream/kneel, regular with internal vowel change in spoken forms, 92
   drink/ring, internal vowel change with verbs ending in *k* and *g,* 114
   forebear/smite, low frequency irregular verbs, 128
   go, a unique verb, 125
   get/got, used as auxiliary, 110–11
   have, 42, 79–80
   keep/leave, internal vowel change with final *t,* 92
   say/hear, internal vowel change with final *d,* 100–101
   used to/supposed to, when pronunciation confuses, 90
Irregular verbs, indexed, 129–33
Items in a series, punctuation of, 213
   (*See also* Punctuation patterns #1 and #8.)
its,it's, confusion between, 142–44

know,no,now, confusion among, 308

let's,less, confusion between, 141, 308
Linking verb, 110, 263

loose,lose,loss,lost, confusion among, 308

Main verb, 72, 208, 265
might of,might a
much,must, confusion between, 308–9
must of, must a, 139

Names, spelling their plurals, 19
new,knew, confusion between, 309
no,now,know, confusion among, 308
Nonessential clauses and phrases, 225–26, 233–34, 241–43, 245–47
Nonstandard English, 4, 35, 81, 189, 187
Noun
   abstract, 12
   confusion with adjective, 12
   defined, 4
   irregular, 13
   mass, 9
   possessive form, 154–75
   pronoun substitution as test for, 7–8
   recognizing nouns, 4–8
   regular, 13, 18
   singular/plural decision, 8–12
   special pronunciation problems, 11
   spelling noun plurals, 18–20
   (*See also* Complements; Fragments from noun clauses; Noun determiners; Pluralizing nouns; Subject of a sentence; Verbals; Objects.)
Noun adjunct (*See* Compound noun.)
Noun clauses, 228, 286, 289
   (*See also* Fragments from noun clauses.)
Noun determiner, 6, 8–12, 268
   no number, 10
   plural, 10–11
   singular, 9
   (*See also* Agreement of subject and verb.)
Noun number 2–25
   special problems in:
      absence of determiner, 12
      pronunciation difficulties, 11
      overcorrecting, 12
      verb as signal of noun number, 17

Object
   (*See* Direct object; Gerund with object; Indirect object; Infinitive with object; Prepositional phrase.)
Objective case
   after *than* and *as,* 184–85
   of personal pronouns, 179–80
Object complement, 7, 210
Object of a preposition, 7, 44–45, 274–77
Overcorrection (*See* Hypercorrection.)

Parenthetical expressions
   punctuation of, 245–47, 291

Parenthetical expressions, *continued*
   (*See* Punctuation patterns #3, #5, #6, and #7.)
Parts of speech (*See* Adjective, Adverb, Noun.)
pass,passed,past, confusion among, 309
Past participle
   Index of Irregular Past Participles, 129–33
   irregular, 83, 279
   regular, 84, 279
   verbal, 284–85
Past tense, 60
   difference between time and tense, 30–31, 60, 71–73
   irregular endings (*See* Irregular and troublesome verb groups.)
   regular endings, 60
Period at end of independent clause, 206, 213
   (*See also* Punctuation patterns #1–#9.)
Periodic or habitual action, expressed by present tense form of verb, 35, 81
Person, 179
Personal pronouns
   case of, 179–80
   list of, 180
   misuse of apostrophe with, 174
   pronoun substitution for subject, 29–30
Possessive, 154–75
   formation of, 157–59
   of indefinite pronouns, 172
   pronouns, 142–52, 188–89, 268
Predicate (*See* Sentence Types.)
Prenominal modifiers, list of, 268
Prepositions, list of common, 45, 274–75
Prepositional phrase, 7
   as they affect subject/verb agreement, 44–45, 275–76
   of phrase as sign of possessive, 156, 164
   used as adjective, 274, 277
   used as adverb, 274
Present participle, 84, 279
   (*See also* Index of irregular verbs.)
Present tense verbs (*See* Agreement of Subject and Verb; Periodic or habitual action.)
principal,principle, confusion between, 309
Principal parts of verbs 31–32, 64–65
   (*See also* Index of Irregular Verbs.)
Pronoun
   agreement with antecedent, 179
   as subject 29–30
   compound, 180–81
   homonyms with contractions, 142–52
   indefinite, 47, 172
   personal (*See* Personal Pronoun.)
   possessive, 142–52, 188–89, 268
   reflexive, 189
   relative pronouns introducing adjective clauses, 49, 239
   reference of, 197–200
   run-ons caused by pronouns, 211
   substitution of pronoun for noun subject, 29–30, 179
   substitution of pronoun for verbal, 281–82
Pronoun substitution
   As test for noun, 7–8
   for subject, 29–30, 179, 211, 266
Pronunciation
   as it affects agreement of subject and verb in present tense, 43–44
   as it affects spelling past tense verb endings, 60, 85, 90
   difficult to pronounce consonant clusters like *SPS, STS,* and *SKS,* 11, 44
   homonyms, 142–52, 188, 304–10
   regional variation in, 60
Punctuation
   history of, 206 (*See also* Punctuation patterns #1–#9.)
Punctuation pattern #1, 213–14
Punctuation pattern #2, 217, 219 (*See also* Semicolon.)
Punctuation pattern #3, 220 (*See also* Semicolon; Conjunctive adverb.)
Punctuation pattern #4, 213–14 (*See also* Coordinating Conjunction.)
Punctuation pattern #5, 225–26, 245–47 (*See also* Parenthetical expression.)
Punctuation pattern #6, 232–34 (*See also* Fragments from adverbial clauses.)
Punctuation pattern #7, 232–34 (*See also* Fragments from adverbial clauses.)
Punctuation pattern #8, 216–17 (*See also* Colon.)
Punctuation pattern #9, 253–54 (*See also* Quotation marks; Indirect question; Indirect quotation.)

Qualifier, 268
Question mark
   misuse after indirect question, 253
   position within quotation marks, 253
quiet,quite, confusion between, 309
Quotation marks
   for direct quotations, 253
   misuse of for indirect quotations, 253
   position in relation to other punctuation, 253
   single, for quote within a quote, 254
   (*See also* Punctuation pattern #9.)

Reference of pronouns, 197–200
   and agreement with antecedent, 190
   ambiguous, 197–200
   indefinite *it, they, you,* 197
Reflexive pronoun, spelling problems with, 189
Regular noun 13, 18
Regular verb, 60
Relative clause, 48–49

Index

Relative clause, 48–49, *continued*
   (*See also* Adjective clause and Essential and nonessential clauses.)
Relative pronoun, 49
Restrictive clause, 233–34, 241–43, 287–88
   (*See* Essential clause.)
Run-on sentence
   defined, 210
   how to correct, 210–12, 236
   (*See also* Comma splice.)

sail,sale,sell, confusion among, 309
Semicolon
   position outside quotation marks, 253
   to separate main clauses (*See* Punctuation patterns #2 and #3.)
   with conjunctive adverb (*See* Punctuation pattern #3.)
Sentence
   agreement in (*See* Agreement of subject and verb.)
   comma splice in, 211
   common sentence types, 209–10, 262–63
   defined, 29, 208, 262
   fragments in, 225–26, 228–29, 232, 240–41
   punctuation of (*See* Punctuation patterns #1–#9.)
   run-ons, 210–12
   subordination in (*See* Punctuation patterns #6 and #7.)
   variety in, 213
Sentence types, list of seven, 209–10, 262–63
Series, punctuation of items in a, 213
Sexism
   how to avoid sexist pronoun usage, 192–93
Shifts
   in pronouns, 193–95
   in verb tense, 67–68
should of, should a, 139
sided,sighted,cited, confusion among, 309
since,sense, confusion between, 309
Spelling, how to practice, 300
   (*See also* Glossary of Common Homonyms.)
Spelling rules
   changing *f* to *v*, 19, 189
   changing *y* to *i*, 19, 301
   compound nouns, 19
   doubling final consonant, 302
   i before *e*, 303
   Latin plurals, 20
   letters and figures, 20
   names, 19
   no change from singular to plural, 19
   plurals formed by internal vowel change, 19
   regular nouns, 13, 18
   words ending in *ch, sh, s, x*, and *z*, 18, 300
   words ending in silent *e*, 303

Spoken English, 4, 28, 35–36, 60, 85, 184–88
Standard English, 4, 28, 35–36, 60, 187, 189
steal,still, confusion between, 310
Subject complement, 6, 110, 183–84
Subject of sentence, 6, 29, 182, 209–10, 262–63
   (*See also* Pronoun substitution for subject; Understood subject.)
Subject/Verb agreement (*See* Agreement of subject and verb.)
Subordinate clause
   defined, 228, 286–93
   punctuation of (*See* Punctuation patterns #6 and #7.)
   used as adjective, 228, 286–88
   used as adverb, 228, 290–91
   used as noun, 228, 289
   (*See also* Dependent clause.)
Subordinating conjunctions, list of, 231, 290
Substituting pronoun for noun/subject, 7–8, 29–30, 179, 211, 266
   for verbal
supposed to, 90

Tense
   consistency in, 67–68
   difference between tense and time, 30–31, 60, 71–73
   sequence of, 72
   (*See also* Present tense and Past tense.)
than and *as*, case of pronoun after, 184–85
than,then,that, confusion among, 310
that
   as relative pronoun, 49, 198–200, 239
   punctuating clauses beginning with *that*, 228–29
   (*See also* Noun clause.)
thing,think, confusion between, 310
there,their,they're, confusion among, 146, 174
therefore, as conjunctive adverb, 220
they, indefinite use of, 197
Time, 30
   future, 31
   general truths, timeless, 31
   habitual action, 31, 35
   relation to tense, 30–31, 60, 71–73
   time determiners, 68
two,too,to, confusion among, 310

Understood subject of a sentence, 29, 82, 294
Usage
   formal and informal, 194–95
   spoken and written, 35–36, 184–88
   standard and nonstandard, 35–36, 187, 189
used to, 90

Verb (*See* Agreement of subject and verb; Auxiliary verb; Contraction; Irregular verb; Linking verb; Past participle; Past tense; Periodic or habitual

Verb, *continued*
 action; Present participle; Present tense verbs; Regular verb; Tense; Time; Index of irregular verbs.)
Verbals, 279–86 (*See also* Gerunds, Infinitives, Past participles.)
Verb phrases, 58–134, 265
 defined, 208, 265
 sequence of verbs in, 58–134

want,won't, confusion between, 141
were,where, confusion between, 310
went,when, confusion between, 310

whether,weather, confusion between, 310
which
 as relative pronoun, 49, 198–200, 239
 punctuating clauses beginning with *which*, 239–40, 287–88
who,whom, 185–87, 239
who's,whose, confusion between, 144–46
whole,hole, confusion between, 308
won't,want, confusion between, 141, 310
would of, would a, 139

you, indefinite use of, 197
your,you're, confusion between, 147–49